D1047121

DATE DUE

Rodale's Book of

Shortcuts

Rodale's Book of

Shortcuts

*Advice, Tips & Techniques on
Health, Fitness, Food, Self-Improvement,
Parenting, Home Management,
Maintenance & Repair, Gardening,
Landscaping, Retirement & Travel*

Edited by Cheryl Winters Tetreau and Carol Hupping
Illustrations by Jean Gardner

 Rodale Press, Emmaus, Pennsylvania

Printed in the United States of America on recycled paper containing a high percentage of de-inked fiber.

Library of Congress Cataloging-in-Publication Data

Rodale's book of shortcuts : advice, tips & techniques on health, fitness, food,
  self-improvement, parenting, home management, maintenance & repair, gardening,
  landscaping, retirement & travel / edited by Cheryl Winters Tetreau and Carol
  Hupping ; illustrations by Jean Gardner.
      p.   cm.
   Includes index.
   ISBN 0-87857-720-3
   1. Life skills—United States. 2. Self-help techniques. I. Tetreau, Cheryl
Winters. II. Hupping, Carol. III. Title: Book of shortcuts. IV. Title: Shortcuts.
HQ2039.U6R64 1988
640—dc19   87-32128
                                                                          CIP

2   4   6   8   10   9   7   5   3   1   hardcover

Contents

Introduction

With the hectic schedules that so many of us have, it's a wonder we manage to get through the day! When we have a chore or project to complete, how nice it would be to have a book that would tell us the quickest, the best and the most efficient ways to get through our daily tasks. Although there are many books on various topics that offer help, who has the time to track them all down? It may be easier just to ask someone else to do the job for us, to do the job poorly or to not do it at all. But we all know the sense of satisfaction we get when we take charge and do things ourselves.

Here at Rodale, we know how pressed for time many of you are because many of *us* have to juggle hectic schedules, too. So we searched high and low for a book that would pull it all together and tell us what we needed to know to help make our home and work lives run more smoothly—a book that would show us the best, the most useful and the most effective ways to get things done. But we couldn't find one. That's when we realized we had the opportunity to create such a book. So we dug in our heels and got to work compiling a book of the best shortcuts around to help all of us make the most of each day.

We've based our book on solid research by calling upon experts in health and nutrition, gardening, home maintenance, psychology, child care and a host of other topics to share their knowledge. *Rodale's Book of Shortcuts* will not only save you time, but also effort, because it gives you the *best* way to get a job done or to achieve a goal; you won't waste your energy on less efficient methods.

We've compiled all kinds of timesaving tidbits, such as:

→ preparing quick meals
→ cleaning an oven quickly
→ saving time in the grocery store
→ timesaving gardening techniques

But we're not just interested in saving time; we also want to bring you the *best* available information, so you can get right to the heart of the task at hand. You'll discover:

→ how to make the most of your medical visit
→ ways to make your diet healthier
→ how to silence squeaky floors
→ the best way to patch a wall
→ how to get results when you've got a complaint

Now when you're faced with a task, you'll know where to turn. Nothing beats the satisfaction you get from taking charge and doing the job yourself, and with this book to guide you, there's no need to put off getting the job done.

We hope you find our shortcuts to be just the time- and effort-savers you were looking for, and that they'll help you accomplish your daily tasks quickly and efficiently.

A note about our contributors: No book of this scope could ever be written by just one person. Our contributors come from all fields and gladly share their expertise with us. Their assistance in helping develop this book was invaluable. Carole Piszczek is assistant research chief for *Prevention* magazine; Tawna Clelan is an information analyst in Rodale's library; Anita Hirsch, M.S., is a nutritionist for the Rodale Food Center; Mario Alonso, Ph.D., and Arthur Katz, M.A., are cofounders and codirectors of Metropolitan Consultation Associates (MCA) and are practicing psychologists; James Margolis, Ph.D., formerly with MCA, specializes in family and adolescent therapy and is associated with Valley Psychological Associates; Meredith Margolis, Ph.D., formerly with MCA, is a psychologist with Valley Psychological Associates; Brooke C. Stoddard is a writer based in Washington, D.C.; Carol Munson is a home economist and an editor at Rodale Press; Marguerite Smolen is the life-styles editor of *New Jersey Monthly* magazine; Kim Wilson is an editor for *Rodale's Organic Gardening* magazine; Cheryl Winters Tetreau is an editor in the Book Division of Rodale Press; and Cheri Steffeck is a writer based in Washington, D.C.

CHERYL WINTERS TETREAU

Shortcuts to

Better Health

Taking care of your health runs the gamut from knowing how to handle the common cold to controlling your risk of getting some of our most deadly diseases: cancer, diabetes and heart disease. It also means paying attention to the simple things, such as good dental hygiene and a healthy diet. It's never too late to learn the best and easiest ways to care for yourself, and in this chapter, we show you how.

Cancer

The best cure for cancer is prevention. You can lower your risk for getting many kinds of cancer by altering your diet. And to prevent skin cancer, it's simply a matter of monitoring your exposure to the sun. Read on for a number of ways to keep cancer at bay.

LOWERING YOUR CANCER RISK

The American Cancer Society recommends the following 10 steps to help lower the risk of cancer.

Eat more high-fiber foods. Fiber hastens the passage of carcinogens through the colon before they have a chance to take root in the colon wall.

Add lots of foods high in vitamin A to your diet. Spinach, carrots, sweet potatoes and apricots are all high in this special cancer-fighting nutrient.

1

Vitamin A is thought to be effective in protecting the lungs, esophagus and larynx from cancer.

Eat plenty of vitamin C-rich foods. Fruits and vegetables—especially citrus fruits, tomatoes, potatoes and broccoli—are good sources of this warrior against cancers of the stomach and esophagus.

Eat more cruciferous vegetables. These vegetables are members of the cabbage family. They seem to be beneficial when it comes to battling cancer-causing chemicals that attack the gastrointestinal and respiratory tracts.

Cut back on fat. Fat is now thought to be a prime ingredient in the development of certain cancers, particularly those of the breast, colon and prostate. This includes all types of fats—saturates and polyunsaturates, animal and vegetable—when eaten to excess. It's recommended that calories from fat should not exceed 30 percent of the total daily caloric intake. To determine the percentage of fat in your diet, see the box "What Percentage of Your Diet Is Fat?" below.

Watch your weight. A definite correlation exists between obesity and the development of cancers of the uterus, gallbladder, breast, colon, kidneys and stomach.

Avoid cured meats and sausages. This includes luncheon meats, hams, hot dogs, bacon and salt-cured and smoke-cured fish that have been treated with sodium nitrates. Cancers of the esophagus and stomach can be substantially avoided by eliminating these foods from your diet.

WHAT PERCENTAGE OF YOUR DIET IS FAT?

It's really not hard to figure out the percentage of fat in your diet. One gram of fat is roughly equal to 9 calories (it varies from food to food). If the label on a package of food says each serving contains 9 grams of fat, that means that 81 calories (9 times 9) of that food come from fat. If the total amount of calories per serving of that particular food is 100, then 81 percent (81 divided by 100) of the calories in the food come from fat. A typical lean three-ounce hamburger that contains a total of 186 calories provides you with 87 calories from fat—9.67 grams or 46.77 percent fat!

Don't smoke. Approximately 30 percent of all cancer is clearly linked to cigarette smoking. Not only do you put yourself at risk, you needlessly expose those around you to the hazards of passive smoking.

Drink alcohol in moderation. This is especially important if you smoke. The risks of developing oral cancer and throat cancer increase dramatically when cigarette smoking and drinking are combined.

Use a sunscreen. Try to avoid the sun completely when it's at its zenith, between 10:00 A.M. and 2:00 P.M. (11:00 A.M. and 3:00 P.M. daylight saving time). Avoid tanning booths and sunlamps—they're harmful, too. (See "Preventing Skin Cancer" later in this chapter.)

PREVENTING CANCER WITH VITAMINS AND MINERALS

While you may know that healthy diets help prevent cancer, you may wonder why some vitamins and minerals are recommended for the prevention of this disease while others aren't. Like each of us, each nutrient is better at performing certain tasks than others. Here are the roles vitamins and minerals play in the prevention of cancer:

→ Some act as antioxidants, diffusing the effects of free radicals (molecules in the body that can cause cell-damaging chemical changes).

→ Some enhance the immune system, strengthening the body's defense against the onslaught of foreign invaders.

→ Some act directly to reduce precancer stages that may lead to cancer later on, and some affect cancer cells directly.

→ Some have antiviral effects, and some are able to neutralize toxic metals that can cause cancer.

→ Some have simply been linked to low cancer rates. That means that under similar conditions, people who exhibited no cancer were found to have more of some nutrients in their bodies than those people who did develop cancer.

So which vitamins and minerals are the cancer fighters? According to cancer specialist Charles B. Simone, M.D., the following are thought to work in specific ways to help keep cancer at bay.

Vitamin A is associated with low cancer rates. Vitamin A reverses precancer stages and directly affects cancer cells. Good food sources of vitamin A are beef liver, cantaloupe, carrots, spinach and sweet potatoes.

Thiamine (B$_1$) enhances the immune system. This vitamin can be found in brewer's yeast, kidney and navy beans, soybeans and sunflower seeds.

Riboflavin (B₂) enhances the immune system. Riboflavin is plentiful in beef kidney, beef liver, brewer's yeast, chicken liver and whole milk.

Vitamin B₆ enhances the immune system. This vitamin is found in beef and chicken liver, salmon, sunflower seeds and white chicken meat.

Vitamin C is an antioxidant. Vitamin C enhances the immune system and is associated with low cancer rates. It appears to directly affect cancer cells and has an antiviral effect. Foods high in vitamin C include cantaloupe, green peppers, orange juice, raw broccoli and tomatoes.

Vitamin E is an antioxidant. Vitamin E reduces precancer stages and directly affects cancer cells. Foods high in vitamin E include almonds, peanut butter, safflower oil, sunflower seeds and wheat germ.

Carotene (pro-vitamin A) is an antioxidant. Carotene enhances the immune system and is associated with low cancer rates. Good food sources for carotene are apricots, carrots, dark leafy greens and sweet potatoes.

Selenium is an antioxidant. Selenium is associated with low cancer rates and it neutralizes toxic metals. Selenium is found in organ meats, seafood, some dietary yeast supplements and whole grains and whole-grain breads.

Zinc is an antioxidant, and it enhances the immune system. The best food sources of zinc include dark turkey meat, lamb, lean ground beef, organ meats and sunflower seeds.

PREVENTING SKIN CANCER

Skin cancer is probably the easiest type of cancer to prevent, the easiest to self-diagnose and, therefore, the easiest to get early treatment for. It pays to take these simple steps to protect yourself.

Use a sunscreen. Look for a sunscreen that has an adequate sun protection factor (SPF) for your skin type and reapply it frequently. (Look for the SPF number and its corresponding skin type on the package.)

Avoid the sun at its peak. Stay indoors or in the shade between 10:00 A.M. and 2:00 P.M., when sunlight is most direct.

Wear a hat and tightly woven clothing. Contrary to popular belief, you *can* burn through clothes.

Learn to recognize what's normal for your skin. Check your skin from head to toe. Don't overlook your scalp, genitals and between the buttocks and toes. You may even want to plot the location of moles and other spots on a "map" of your body. See your doctor immediately if you notice any changes in the color, size, texture or shape of any of your body's "landmarks."

Don't panic if you do notice some skin changes. But do see your doctor right away. This can serve two purposes. First, she or he will be able to reassure you that the changes you noticed aren't significant (although your doctor will want to watch that particular spot in the future). Second, should you need further medical treatment, you'll be able to congratulate yourself for stopping a dreadful disease in its tracks. Studies show that early detection and treatment of skin cancers guarantee a cure rate of 90 percent.

Get a full-body skin examination once a year. This is recommended by the Skin Cancer Foundation. You'll probably have to tell your physician exactly what you want because this type of skin examination isn't usually part of an annual physical.

Colds and Flu

It's not always possible to avoid colds and flu, but there are several steps you can take to prevent catching them, and additional steps you can follow to make them shorter-lived and more tolerable once they've taken up residence in your body.

PREVENTING COLDS AND FLU

When everyone around you is falling prey to a cold or the flu, you don't have to resign yourself to being the next victim. Here are some steps you can take to stay healthy.

Keep out of germs' way. Your best protection may be lots of hand washing. Forgo the handshakes and hugs from wheezy friends, and wash your hands frequently. Try not to rub your eyes or put your hands near your nose or mouth. Handle as few objects as possible that have been handled by flu and cold sufferers. Studies show that cold and flu viruses can remain virulent for as long as five days on such things as doorknobs and drinking glasses.

Increase your consumption of vitamins C and A and zinc. A strong immune system is essential in warding off colds and flu. Many researchers believe that both vitamins C and A boost the germ-fighting powers of the immune system. Citrus juices and fruits are excellent sources of vitamin C, and vitamin A is present in generous quantities in beef liver and dark green and yellow vegetables. In addition, zinc, found in meats, seeds and some dried beans, is thought to inhibit the reproductive capacity of cold-causing viruses as well as strengthen the immune system.

Keep the humidity up. If your home is heated with a hot-air system, it may be unnaturally dry indoors during winter. Raise the humidity by raising greenery. Some plants, especially those that have broad, flat leaves, can help keep the relative humidity of the average home hovering at a comfortable 40 to 60 percent. When the humidity in the home falls to 30 percent or less, the delicate mucous membranes that line your lungs and nasal passages become dry, making them vulnerable to irritation and invasion by cold and flu viruses. If you lack a green thumb, consider buying a humidifier; this is especially important for your bedroom, where you spend a large, uninterrupted block of time each day.

Exercise. Regular exercise can help ward off colds and flu by energizing your immune system through increased production of germ-fighting white blood cells.

TREATING YOUR COLD OR FLU

If, despite all your best efforts, you fall victim to a cold or the flu, don't despair. Here are some ways to ease your discomfort.

Keep to yourself. Wash your hands frequently and use disposable tissues, not handkerchiefs, to catch your sneezes. If you can, flush away used tissues rather than just tossing them into a waste basket. Keep your kisses to yourself for a few days. Begin these precautions as soon as you feel the first symptoms—your friends and family will appreciate it.

Increase liquids. Drink lots of hot liquids to restore fluids lost through extra sweating and fever. (Try herbal teas laced with throat-soothing honey.) Warm drinks help mucus drain and calm achy, sore throats by increasing the blood flow to affected areas. And don't forget the chicken soup! It promises all the benefits of teas but adds the psychological bonus of love and caring that warm soup frequently evokes. Fruit juices should be drunk with care. Some juices, if undiluted, can cause or add to the flu sufferer's diarrhea, and the acid in citrus juices can cause even further stomach upset. Try diluting juices half-and-half with water, then sip them slowly if your stomach is queasy. If your stomach is really upset, you may prefer to suck on ice chips made from diluted juice.

Let your appetite be your guide. If you're puzzled by the "feed a cold, starve a fever" adage, forget it and let your appetite be your guide. If you retain your desire for food, eat small, infrequent snacks. Maintaining nutritional levels at this time is important, because metabolism is stepped-up while your body strives to fight off the infection. But don't feel too concerned if your appetite takes a dive; the normal adult has ample stores of proteins and other necessary nutrients that are needed to maintain an ailing body for several days.

When you do resume eating, start out with bland, starchy foods such as dry toast, bananas, boiled rice and cooked cereals. If your appetite remains depressed for more than five days, or if you've lost 5 percent or more of your normal body weight, it's a good idea to see your physician.

Avoid antibiotics. Colds and flu that are caused by viruses will *not* respond to antibiotics designed to fight bacterial infections. Don't insist that your doctor prescribe one for you unless both of you know that your illness was caused by a bacterial infection. The only positive way to know this is by having your doctor take a culture.

Go easy on antihistamines. They can reduce some of the sneezing and sniffling brought about by a runny nose, but antihistamines can have side effects—read all cautions on the over-the-counter medications you purchase and *take them seriously.*

Go easy on nose drops and decongestants. These can have temporary beneficial effects, but should also be used with care. These medications work by decreasing the size of the blood vessels inside the nose, thus reducing swelling, but the effect can soon wear off, causing the vessels to swell even more. This is what's known as the rebound effect, in which you will want to use more medication but will get less and less desirable results. For this reason, it is recommended that you not use nasal decongestants for longer than three days.

Go easy on cough drops and syrups. Lozenges can help to relieve sore, scratchy throats because most contain local anesthetics. Be wary of many over-the-counter cough drops and cough preparations, especially for children. Although youngsters take them willingly, the high sugar content in many of these products can harm developing teeth. In addition, many cough syrups have a high alcohol content—some contain up to 68 percent alcohol. The effects of alcohol on children range from flushing and accelerated heartbeat to slowed breathing and convulsions. Read the label. If the product contains more than 5 percent alcohol (an amount determined by the American Academy of Pediatrics as safe for children), choose another brand.

Take a break from exercise. Grueling workouts can fatigue an already compromised body and, therefore, can actually make you sicker. So forgo the gym for a few days and, instead, get more sleep than usual.

Dental Care

There's more to a healthy mouth than just brushing. Here are some specific teeth-cleaning techniques and a list of healthy snacks that won't compromise your dental health.

MAINTAINING HEALTHY TEETH AND GUMS

Good dental care doesn't take a lot of time or effort. Just follow these suggestions for the best possible teeth and gums.

Brush and floss regularly to remove plaque from your teeth. (Plaque is the sticky white film that is home to bacteria and food debris in your mouth.) It's best to brush after every meal and snack, but if you can't brush after eating, at least rinse your mouth thoroughly with water as soon as possible. Bacteria interacts with food debris to produce enamel-destroying acids in as little as 15 minutes after your meal! If you can brush only once a day, do so at bedtime, because while you sleep, saliva production slows down and its tooth-washing benefits are temporarily suspended.

Use a fluoride toothpaste and follow with a fluoride mouthwash. Fluoride not only strengthens tooth enamel, which is important to the developing teeth of infants and children, it also kills bacteria in the adult mouth.

Visit your dentist regularly. Every six months is sufficient for most people. However, some people build up calculus (plaque hardened with calcium) more quickly than others and need to have it removed by their dentists more than twice a year.

Cut back on snacking. Try to eliminate as many sugary treats as possible from your diet. Bacteria love sugar and will wildly produce enamel-digesting acids when any traces of sugar are left in the mouth.

Watch for signs of periodontal disease. Your teeth may look great and be cavity-free, but if the support system—bone and gum—is weak, tooth loss is inevitable. Periodontal disease, an infection of bone and gum, is a major cause of tooth loss, especially in people over 40. Early signs of periodontal disease are gums that bleed when you brush or floss or gums that appear red and swollen and may be sore. Your dentist is part of your frontline defense against periodontal disease — be sure to have checkups regularly. She or he may recommend professional cleaning around gums every two to four months.

When you brush, use a soft-bristled brush. Be sure to clean gently just below the gum line. It is there that calculus first begins to accumulate, irritating the gums and creating pockets where infection can begin. These pockets then trap food debris and bacteria, and the process snowballs.

Use a salt-and-baking-soda rinse. This kills bacteria in the mouth and helps to protect against plaque buildup. But because they can make gums look pink and healthy, homemade rinses such as this can hide infection that is occurring below the gum line. If you want to use this type of mouth preparation, be sure to discuss it with your dentist first.

Massage your gums frequently. Massage stimulates blood flow to the gums. You can massage your gums with a soft-bristled toothbrush, with the soft rubber point at the end of some brushes or even with a clean finger. Massage also helps eject plaque that has worked its way beneath the gum line.

CLEANING YOUR TEETH

Before you ever put brush to tooth there is one important step to make — choosing your toothbrush. Many dentists agree that a soft, round-bristled brush is best. This type of brush slides neatly between teeth and below the gum line to wash out plaque and food debris without injuring tender tissues. Brushes with harder bristles can actually scratch tooth enamel. With toothbrush in hand, here's the best way to clean your teeth.

Hold your brush at a 45° angle to the teeth. Begin brushing where the teeth meet the gums, working in a circular motion, intruding slightly under the gum line. Scrub *all* tooth surfaces: front, back and sides. Pay special attention to the inside of lower front teeth where calculus has a tendency to build up quickly. Brush the surface of the tongue — bacteria grow here as well. Be gentle but thorough. When you think you've brushed long enough, go back and repeat the process. (Most people have a tendency to hurry through brushing.) Then rinse, and rinse again.

Get out the dental floss. Break off a piece about 18 inches long and wrap the ends around your middle fingers. Guide the floss between your teeth with a gentle sawing motion, being careful not to damage soft interdental tissues. Scrape each tooth gently, applying pressure with each movement *away* from the gum.

Make spot checks with the aid of disclosing tablets. Your dentist should be able to supply you with these tablets or will know where you can buy them. Either chewed or dissolved in water and used as a rinse, disclosing tablets will help guide you in your oral-care program by showing you where your tooth brushing is missing plaque colonies. The missed areas will stain red and then can be brushed away. Don't be alarmed if numerous spots show up in what you thought was an immaculate mouth—just pay more attention to those areas the next time you brush.

SNACKING FOR A HEALTHY MOUTH

When it comes to food in your diet, snacks wreak the most havoc on your teeth. Although you may be in the habit of brushing after meals, brushing after snacking is sometimes difficult. The table "Snacks," below, lists foods frequently chosen for snacks. Those in the first column are the foods that bacteria thrive on. These foods allow bacteria to produce

Snacks

Snacks to Avoid	Snacks to Eat in Moderation	Snacks to Enjoy
Candy	Apple cider	Almonds
Cookies	Apples	Broccoli
Crackers	Grapes	Carrots
Dates	Orange juice	Cauliflower
Dried apples	Peaches	Celery
Dried apricots	Pears	Cheeses, most kinds
Dried pears	Soft drinks	
Milk chocolate		Filberts
Potato chips		Green peppers
		Peanuts
		Pecans
		Popcorn
		Walnuts

enamel-dissolving acids, which in turn create an environment favorable for the growth of additional bacteria. These foods should be avoided or eaten only at the end of meals, followed by brushing. The foods in the second column don't provide quite the same optimal mouth environment for bacteria as those in the first column, but they should still be eaten in moderation. The third column of snacks receives the green light—these foods can actually create an environment that *discourages* the growth of bacteria.

Doctors

It's always a good idea to be familiar with a doctor *before* a medical emergency strikes. But what's the best way to choose a doctor? And how do you make sure you're getting the best care and information from that practitioner? Here's a rundown of what you should know in your search for a doctor and how to keep the lines of communication open once you've found one.

FINDING THE DOCTOR WHO'S RIGHT FOR YOU

Don't wait until you have a medical emergency to choose a doctor or you may end up with less than satisfactory service. Start your search ahead of time by following these guidelines.

Ask friends and relatives for their recommendations. If you're new to an area, try contacting local hospitals, medical schools or the county medical society for the names of doctors who practice in your area. If you're looking for a specialist, ask other doctors who they recommend.

Think carefully about what you want in a doctor. Do you feel more comfortable with a woman doctor, do you want a family practitioner or an internist, is the doctor's age important to you, do you prefer an osteopath or an M.D.? Is charisma and bedside manner important to you or do you prefer a brisk, matter-of-fact approach? While these intangibles may not directly affect the outcome of your medical care, they will affect your *sense* of being cared for and your eventual satisfaction with the doctor.

Consider the location of the doctor's office and the office hours. If you can't get to her or him when you need to or if you have to take time off from work for regular health care, visiting the doctor may become an inconvenience for you.

Find out if the doctor practices with a group or works alone. If the doctor is part of a group, ask if that means you may not always see the same doctor. How important is this to you?

Schedule a get-acquainted consultation. You may want to have a physical examination at this time in order to give you the opportunity to observe the doctor. Does she or he:

→ take the time to check your entire body, your reflexes, lungs, eyes, ears, nose and throat?

→ ask you about drugs or treatments you currently use or have used in the past?

→ obtain from you a complete medical history and ask for permission to have your medical records forwarded from your previous physician?

→ listen to you and let you finish speaking before making additional comments?

→ speak clearly and answer your questions to your satisfaction without resorting to obscure medical terms?

→ advocate preventive medicine? In other words, does she or he stress the importance of good nutrition, exercise, healthy habits and other measures you can take to lower your risks of getting sick, in general, or of aggravating a condition you might already have?

Take a list of questions with you. It's quite easy to forget some of the things you want or need to know. Be prepared.

Check out the staff as well as the doctor. They can make it easy or difficult to reach the doctor when you need to. Garrulous secretaries and inconsiderate or inept nurses are frequently reflections of the doctor who hired them.

Check out the waiting room and surroundings. Is there helpful literature available that explains medical problems and guides you in taking preventive measures? How soon are you seen by the doctor? If you must wait, are you given any explanation as to why? When you get to see the doctor, does she or he rush you through or do you get her or his undivided attention?

Don't be afraid to speak up. A good doctor is willing to discuss her or his approach to health care. She or he will also have no problem discussing fees or medical insurance, or how phone calls, second opinions and canceled appointments are handled. Don't be afraid to speak up. You have a right to know!

ASKING YOUR DOCTOR ABOUT DRUGS

Don't be afraid to ask your physician about the drugs she or he prescribes for you. Sometimes your doctor may be distracted by a very busy practice or may simply skip over some information that can make the difference between your becoming a responsible, well-informed patient or merely someone who follows orders. Here are some questions you may want to ask about your medications:

→ Is this drug going to cure what's wrong (curative), or just help me live with the condition (symptomatic)?

→ How long do I have to take this? Many times, doctors want you to continue with the medication until it runs out, even if the symptoms have gone away.

→ What will this mean to me since I'm already taking _____? You'll want to tell the doctor all of the medications that you take, including birth control pills, other prescribed and over-the-counter drugs such as aspirin or antacids, as well as vitamin and mineral supplements. Take a list of these drugs when you visit the doctor. It's easy to forget exact dosages and names of drugs when you're sitting in the doctor's office or when you aren't feeling very well. As you'll read below, drugs can interact with each other—often in dangerous ways. (See "Understanding Drug Interactions" later in this chapter.)

→ Do I need to supplement my diet while I'm taking this drug or should I avoid any specific nutritional supplements now? Usually a good diet is enough to carry you through, but some drugs do deplete certain nutrients, which can then cause other nutritional losses. On the other side of the coin, some nutritional supplements can interfere with the effectiveness of certain drugs.

→ What side effects might I have when taking this drug? Find out if it will be safe for you to drive a car or work while you're using this drug.

→ May I drink any alcoholic beverages while on this medication? Most medications carry warnings against drinking alcohol while taking the drug. Even if you don't see a warning, ask.

→ What should I do if I think I'm having a reaction to the drug—is it safe for me to stop taking it immediately or should I continue to use it, but see you as soon as possible?

→ Exactly how should I take this drug? Find out if you should take it before or after eating, with food or without, with water or some other fluid.

→ What if I forget a dose or take an extra dose by accident? Find out if you should get up in the night to take the medication on schedule, and find out what steps you should take if you overdose.

→ Is this drug available in a generic form, and will it cost less to buy it generically? Sometimes the generic form is equally as effective as the brand the doctor has prescribed, and sometimes it isn't. Ask your doctor what the differences are, if any.

UNDERSTANDING DRUG INTERACTIONS

Some medications, when taken together, will interact with one another and thus alter the effect these drugs have on your body. What follows is a description of common drug interactions. There are others, maybe not so common, but just as potentially dangerous. To play it safe, let your doctor know about any and all drugs you use. This means over-the-counter drugs as well as prescription drugs, drugs prescribed to you by another health care practitioner and even vitamins and minerals that you take on a regular basis.

Tetracyclines and penicillin derivatives can cause birth control pills to be less effective and lead to an unplanned or unwanted pregnancy. If you are a woman on birth control pills, be sure to tell your physician so she or he can prescribe treatment that is less likely to interfere with your birth control medication. You may have to use another form of birth control while you're taking the antibacterial medication.

Antacids can decrease the effectiveness of drugs such as tetracycline that are prescribed to fight infection. They can also interfere with the action of high blood pressure medicines such as digoxin.

Aspirin has been shown to interfere with the effectiveness of drugs prescribed to control the discomforts of arthritis and of other pain medications. In both instances, the risk of developing stomach ulcers is increased. Aspirin can drastically lower the blood sugar levels of those who rely on diabetes medication, and it can increase the effectiveness of drugs used to control angina enough to require dosage adjustment by your physician.

Diuretics can decrease the effectiveness of some antidiabetic and gout medications. They can also reduce the effectiveness of potassium supplements, cause a dangerous decline in blood pressure when taken with certain drugs used to control angina and increase the effectiveness of certain blood pressure medications, resulting in very low blood pressure.

Allergy medications can increase the effectiveness of drugs that depress the central nervous system, such as antidepressants and sleeping pills, especially if the allergy medicine contains antihistamines. These same antihistamines can be made less effective when taken in combination with blood pressure and glaucoma medications.

First Aid

Splinters, scraped knees, colds, fevers—it's impossible to know just what injuries or ills life may hand you at any time, especially when you've got children in the house. The best protection is to be prepared for a wide assortment of possibilities by understanding some common childhood illnesses and by having the basic first-aid necessities on hand.

A BRIEF GUIDE TO SIMPLE AILMENTS

Childhood illnesses invariably crop up and it's best to be prepared for them. The following are common childhood medical problems and how best to deal with them. (You can also follow this advice for colds and flu in adults.)

Fever

Remember that fever is not the illness itself, but part of the body's way of fighting the illness. Up to about 103°F, fever may be helpful. Beyond that, it can lead to its own complications, such as convulsions.

Control high fevers with the aspirin substitute called acetaminophen. It is available as both a generic product under that name and as brand name products like Tylenol. (Giving aspirin itself to children may be dangerous—it has been tentatively linked to childhood Reye's syndrome, a brain and liver disorder.) With or without the use of acetaminophen, you can lower a child's fever using the following techniques:

→ Keep the room cool, about 67°F.
→ Dress the child lightly and don't use heavy blankets when she or he sleeps.

→ Sponge the child with lukewarm water and leave the skin wet, give her or him an alcohol rub, or cool with a fan.

→ Remain calm yourself—fever may make your child jumpy and she or he will only worsen by picking up nervousness from you.

Colds

Keep the air in the child's room humid. Use a vaporizer. The moisture soothes an inflamed nose and eases a dry cough.

Keep your child comfortable and warm—a chill can make the cold worse. For this reason, avoid the temptation of thinking your child will recover more quickly if she or he plays outdoors in the sunshine—the notion is not proven, and your child may become chilled.

Try to teach your child to blow her or his nose. This way, your child can clear her or his own nostrils without constantly coming to you. A nursing baby's plight is eased if you draw out mucus with a nasal syringe before putting the baby to the breast. Do not give nose drops, except on the recommendation of a doctor.

Be skeptical of cough medicines. They are not cures and only soothe a tickle in the throat. Moreover, you do not want to suppress a cough that is bringing up mucus, which is meant to be expelled from the air passages.

Realize that you cannot cure a cold virus. But you can fight bacteria, which are more likely to invade when a body is weakened by a virus. Therefore, watch for signs of complications caused by bacteria. These can be a fever beginning after the second day of a cold, a thick cough, a sore throat, an earache or lethargy. Troubles that cause these symptoms may be treatable with antibiotics prescribed by a doctor.

Earaches

Earaches usually occur two to three days after the onset of a cold. They most often strike children 3 to 4 years old. If your child develops an earache, call the doctor that day; she or he may be able to prescribe antibiotics to fight it. In the meantime, do not put anything into the ear.

Try a hot-water bottle or heating pad. Placed against the affected ear, it may ease the pain.

Try a vaporizer or a steam bath. This may help unclog congestion that's causing the ear discomfort. You may give acetaminophen (aspirin substitute) to reduce fever and fight pain.

Swallowed Object

If a child is coughing, let her or him do so. The object may be coughed up.

If the child cannot cough up the object, take immediate action. Stand behind her or him and bend her or him over your arm (or put an infant on your lap with the head lower than the feet) and give her or him four sharp slaps on the back between the shoulder blades. A better technique is the Heimlich maneuver, or abdominal thrust, where you stand behind the child and with your fist, thrust upward under her or his rib cage to extract the stuck object. For more information on the Heimlich maneuver, contact your local chapter of the American Red Cross.

Do not use your fingers to try to extract an object from the child's throat. You may push it farther down the throat or into the windpipe.

If the child begins to turn blue, rush her or him to the nearest hospital or doctor's office. Do not take time to call in advance, but let someone else alert the people there.

Don't panic if you think a child has swallowed a sharp object such as a needle or razor blade. Check her or his hand, clothes and mouth first; it is very hard for a child to swallow something sharp. If you still think she or he has swallowed it, take the child to a hospital.

If you think a child has swallowed something smooth, there is not much cause for worry. If it was small enough to swallow, it is small enough to pass all the way through. Do not give a laxative or a vomit-producing medicine. Call your doctor if the object was one that contained toxic material, such as a battery or pen cartridge.

Poison

Empty the child's mouth of any pills, capsules, plant parts, and so forth. If you do not know exactly what they are or their precise potency, save them for medical people to examine.

Call your local poison information center. You should keep the number by your telephone. Describe the toxic substance your child has taken. Personnel at the poison center will tell you what to do.

Emergency treatments for poisonings fall into two categories. The poison information center will probably give you the following advice:

→ Toxic substances such as acids, alkalines and petroleum products may cause as much harm to the throat and mouth coming up as going down. Therefore, the patient should be given milk or water to dilute the substance and should not be induced to vomit. Then take the child to the hospital.

→ Other substances are best treated by induced vomiting. This is done by giving one tablespoon of ipecac, a nonprescription syrup that should be kept in every home that has a child. Follow the ipecac with water, and ask the child to walk around—both water and walking make the ipecac work faster.

→ Take the child to a hospital on the advice of the poison information center.

→ Do not induce vomiting in any child who is unconscious or having a convulsion.

STOCKING A FIRST-AID KIT

Keep the following items together and always store them in the same place so you can find them easily if, and when, you need them. Try to replace items as you use them. Be sure to go through your first-aid kit once a year and replace outdated medications and worn-out or used-up items. These suggestions come from *Body Bulletin* newsletter (May 1986). Your basic first-aid items include:

absorbent sterile cotton
activated charcoal (for poisonings)
adhesive-strip bandages
adhesive tape
cotton-tipped swabs
hot/cold pack
household ammonia (to help revive a fainting victim)
meat tenderizer (for bee stings)
penknife
penlight with fresh batteries
petroleum jelly
rubbing alcohol
safety pins
scissors
sewing needles and tweezers (for removing splinters)
sterile gauze bandages

In addition to the above items, here are some over-the-counter medicines that you should include in your kit:

antacid (for indigestion)
antiemetic (for controlling vomiting)

aspirin substitute (acetaminophen) or aspirin (for general aches,
   headaches or fever)
cough syrup/lozenges
diarrhea medication
emetic (for inducing vomiting in case of poisoning)
general antiseptic
hydrocortisone ointment (for itchy skin)
nose drops (for nasal congestion and stuffy sinuses)

Good Nutrition

Eating well is one of the most important things you can do for your
health. A healthy diet can reduce stress, lower your risk of heart disease,
help you lose or maintain your weight and, overall, make you feel your
best. Here's some good advice on good nutrition.

BEATING STRESS

Stress often shows on your face, in the way you hold your body, in your
voice—all outward signals to the world. Less obvious signs, include
hypertension and gastric distress. Even less apparent is what stress can
do to your nutritional levels. When you're feeling especially stressed,
make sure these vitamins and minerals are part of your diet. They could
mean the difference between merely coping and coming through with
flying colors.

Vitamin A: Chronic stress causes the adrenal glands to enlarge and sometimes even to bleed. Vitamin A can counteract that reaction and, ultimately,
help your body's immune system stave off illness frequently brought on
by stress.

Good Sources of Vitamin A

Food	Serving Size	Vitamin A*
Beef liver	3 oz	45,390 IU
Sweet potato	1 medium	11,940 IU
Carrots	½ cup	8,140 IU
Spinach	½ cup	7,290 IU
Cantaloupe	¼ medium	4,620 IU

*Adult U.S.RDA 5,000 IU

Good Sources of B Vitamins

Food	Serving Size	B_6*	B_{12}†	Folic Acid‡
Beef liver	3 oz	0.5	49.0	123
Brewer's yeast	1 tbsp	0.2	none	313
Chicken liver	3 oz	0.5	16.5	654
Milk, whole	8 oz	0.1	0.9	12
Swiss cheese	2 oz	0.1	1.0	4

*Adult U.S.RDA 2 mg   §Adult U.S.RDA 20 mg
†Adult U.S.RDA 6 mcg   '' Adult U.S.RDA 1.7 mg
‡Adult U.S.RDA 400 mcg   #Adult U.S.RDA 1.5 mg

B vitamins: B_6, B_{12}, folic acid, niacin, riboflavin, thiamine—all are needed to guarantee the supply of glucose to the brain. Glucose, the brain's primary source of energy, helps fight feelings of fatigue and depression often brought on by stress. In addition, B vitamins are important in the production of neurotransmitters that deliver messages from nerve to nerve, including those in the brain.

Vitamin C: Environmental stress caused by factors such as smoggy city air and industrial toxins lowers levels of this vitamin. Emotional strain that causes stress drains vitamin C from the adrenal glands. The result is a weakening of the immune system.

Vitamin E: Environmental pollution and emotional stress aren't as overwhelming when your body's stores of this vitamin are adequate. Vitamin E helps protect your body from the ravages of environmental pollutants by destroying the toxins before they have a chance to damage delicate lung and blood cells. Your endurance increases and you stay strong.

Magnesium: People exposed to constant, high levels of traffic noise experience decreased body levels of this mineral. Magnesium is critical to the normal functioning of the heart.

EATING FOR YOUR HEART

Heart disease kills 550,000 Americans each year—one person every minute of the day! But studies show that the risk of heart disease could be reduced by half if people altered their eating habits, took advantage of available cholesterol-reducing drugs, exercised adequately, were careful about their weight and took care to reduce some of the stress in their lives. A big order, you say? Sure, but how much effort is your life worth?

The following diet guidelines can help put you on the right track to a healthier heart.

Niacin[§]	Riboflavin[ǁ]	Thiamine[#]
14.0	3.6	0.2
3.0	0.3	1.3
3.8	1.5	0.1
0.2	0.4	0.1
0.1	0.2	none

Good Sources of Vitamin C

Food	Serving Size	Vitamin C*
Orange juice, fresh	1 cup	124
Green pepper, raw	½ cup, chopped	96
Grapefruit juice, fresh	1 cup	94
Brussels sprouts	4 medium sprouts	73
Broccoli, raw	½ cup, chopped	70

*Adult U.S.RDA 60 mg

Good Sources of Vitamin E

Food	Serving Size	Vitamin E*
Sunflower seeds	¼ cup	26.8
Wheat germ, raw	½ cup	12.8
Almonds	¼ cup	12.7
Safflower oil	1 tbsp	7.9
Peanuts	¼ cup	4.9

*Adult U.S.RDA 30 IU

Good Sources of Magnesium

Food	Serving Size	Magnesium*
Soybeans, dried	¼ cup	138
Almonds, whole	¼ cup	98
Kidney beans, dried	¼ cup, cooked	82
Shredded wheat	1 cup	67
Banana	1 medium	58

*Adult U.S.RDA 400 mg

Cut Back on Cholesterol Intake

Limit consumption of red meat to three or fewer times a week. Trim away all visible fat *before* cooking and don't add fat when preparing meats. (See "Cutting Fat in Meats and Fish" in chapter 3.)

Eat organ meats sparingly. Although organ meats such as kidney and liver are excellent sources for some nutrients, they are loaded with cholesterol. Cut out luncheon meats, sausages and bacon altogether.

Eat red meat alternatives several times a week. Poultry without fat or skin, all types of fish and shellfish, dried legumes and tofu (a kind of cheese made from soybeans) are all excellent sources of lean, low-cholesterol or cholesterol-free, high-quality protein. Substitute them for red meat.

Be selective about cheeses. Hard cheeses such as cheddar and Swiss are the worst offenders; cream cheese follows close behind. Low-fat cheeses or those made with part-skim milk, such as mozzarella, ricotta and feta, offer lots of flavor and are better for you.

Make the dairy products in your diet the low-fat kind. Low-fat yogurt, skim milk and ice milk are all good examples. (See "Cutting Fat in Dairy Foods" in chapter 3.)

Use corn, safflower, cottonseed or soybean oil instead of lard or butter. Although they are still fats, these vegetable oils are high in the polyunsaturated fats that your body can safely handle. Avoid artificial creamers that contain coconut or palm oil, both of which are saturated fats. (See "Cutting Fat in Fried and Baked Foods" in chapter 3.)

Eat plenty of fruits and vegetables. They are cholesterol-free, most contain no fat at all and they are great sources of valuable fiber. Eat them freely. (See "Cutting Fat in Vegetables" in chapter 3.)

Cut Back on Salt and Sugar

Stay away from the saltshaker. Or better yet, get rid of it altogether. Many foods have salt in them naturally, and there's no need to add more. Try eating your food without salt. You may discover some new flavors.

Try herb seasonings in place of salt. If your taste buds have grown accustomed to salty foods, wean them on herb seasonings. Oregano, basil and thyme are just three of the many herbs that will add a dash of flavor to your food.

Eat fresh fruits and vegetables. Their high potassium levels have been shown to depress sodium levels, resulting in the lowering of blood pressure.

Stay away from processed foods. Whether canned or frozen, processed foods contain a lot more sodium than their freshly prepared counterparts. Read labels carefully before buying these foods. (See "Interpreting Food Labels for Less Salt" in chapter 3.)

Put away the sugar bowl. There's no need to fill up on empty calories. Try your favorite cereal without sweetener or with some fresh fruit, such as bananas or strawberries, instead.

Avoid sweet snacks. Instead of reaching for a doughnut, try a whole wheat muffin or a bagel. They're just as filling, but don't contain as much sugar or as many calories. Better still, snack on fresh fruits and vegetables. (See "Cutting Out the Sugar in Your Diet" in chapter 3.)

RECOGNIZING THE GOOD FATS

Believe it or not, there are some "good" fats you should add to your diet. By eating the foods that contain these fats, you will be lowering your risk of heart disease.

Polyunsaturated and monounsaturated fats: These are not only good for you on their own, they can actually undo some of the damage done by saturated fats (which are found in red meats, eggs and full-fat dairy products). Polyunsaturated and monounsaturated fats displace and neutralize the artery-clogging effects of saturated fats. These good fats are found primarily in vegetable oils.

Fish oils and omega-3 fatty acids: These are the superstars of the fat world. They are beneficial to our hearts and circulatory systems because they can help prevent clots from forming by thinning the blood, and they also lower blood cholesterol levels. They may even help lower blood pressure.

Read the table "Your Omega-3 Catch of the Day" on the next page and consider adding the bounty of the rivers and sea to your diet.

PREVENTING DISEASE WITH FIBER

The beneficial aspects of fiber have been implicated not only in the prevention of heart disease, but the prevention of colorectal cancer, hemorrhoids, diabetes and diverticulosis, as well. But the increased consumption of processed food and meats has resulted in a sharp decrease

---

Your Omega-3 Catch of the Day

Common Name	Omega-3 Fatty Acids (grams per 3½ oz)	Total Fat (grams per 3½ oz)
Chinook salmon, canned	3.04	16.0
Atlantic mackerel	2.18	9.8
Pink salmon	1.87	5.2
Albacore tuna, canned, light	1.69	6.8
Sablefish	1.39	13.1
Atlantic herring	1.09	6.2
Rainbow trout, U.S.	1.08	4.5
Pacific oysters	0.84	2.3
Striped bass	0.64	2.1
Channel catfish	0.61	3.6
Alaskan king crab	0.57	1.6
Ocean perch	0.51	2.5
Blue crab, cooked and canned	0.46	1.6
Pacific halibut	0.45	2.0
Shrimp, different species	0.39	1.2
Yellowtail flounder	0.30	1.2
Haddock	0.16	0.66

SOURCE: *Journal of the American Dietetic Association*, vols. 69 and 71, 1976 and 1977.

---

in the fiber in our diets. So how do we put the fiber back into our diets? Because fiber is derived from plants (not meat or dairy products) it can be found in fruits, vegetables, whole grains and dried legumes. Here's a rundown of the diseases a good daily dose of fiber can help prevent.

Colon cancer: Fiber could be one of the most important deterrents to the formation of this cancer. Carcinogens can enter the body through the food we eat or can be produced in the bowel itself through the process of digestion. Fiber scrubs out potential carcinogens before they can be absorbed into the colon wall.

Diabetes: Many diabetics also have weight problems. Fiber helps satisfy hunger while a person actually eats less. It is not only filling, but it's also found in foods rich in complex carbohydrates, which take longer to break down in the stomach. A high-fiber, ultra-low-fat diet also seems to help reduce the need for insulin in some diabetics. It is thought that fiber slows down the release of sugar into the bloodstream, thereby preventing the massive demand for insulin necessary to carry sugar molecules to the body's cells for use as energy.

Diverticulosis: Little pouches that protrude through the bowel wall (usually caused by constipation), diverticula can become inflamed and painful enough to require surgery. A diet high in fiber can alleviate the pain and strain that accompanies constipation and resultant diverticulosis. In some cases, surgery can be avoided completely.

Heart disease: Fiber, especially the pectin found in apples and citrus fruits, can protect the arteries and heart from the ravages of cholesterol. Researchers think it either helps flush excess cholesterol from the body or it selectively raises the level of high-density lipoprotein (HDL) cholesterol— found in the good fats—that is related to a healthy heart. (See "Recognizing the Good Fats" earlier in this chapter.)

Hemorrhoids: Hemorrhoids often are caused by eating a lot of foods that are overprocessed or are the result of diets high in protein and/or diets that rely heavily on dairy products. The result is small, hard stools that require straining on the toilet. Since fiber can't be digested by the human body, it passes through the bowels relatively unscathed, carrying with it the waste products of more digestible food elements. And certain fibers, such as wheat bran, are capable of absorbing water, which aids the emptying of the bowel and helps prevent hemorrhoids by reducing the need to strain.

MAINTAINING GOOD NUTRITION WHILE YOU DIET

Diets designed to help you lose weight can also drain your body of valuable nutrients, causing your resistance to infections and viruses to drop right along with the lost pounds. Although most weight-loss plans often allow no more than 1,200 calories per day, it is generally agreed among physicians who specialize in nutrition that diets lower than 1,800 to 2,000 calories a day simply cannot provide the dieter with ample nutrition. Whether you're just beginning a weight-loss program or if you've been dieting "forever," try to remember the following points.

Avoid diets that are based almost exclusively on high-protein foods. These types of diets can bring on a condition known as acidosis. Acidosis can cause weakness, malaise, headaches and heart arrhythmias. Three ounces of carbohydrates daily, as in one serving of whole wheat pasta, can prevent acidosis.

Avoid diets that rely heavily on one food. Few foods are so nutritionally complete that they fill your daily vitamin and mineral needs. Single-food diets rely on your growing so tired of that particular food that you lose your appetite and eat less. Unfortunately, you'll lose a lot more than appetite and weight.

Take calcium and iron supplements when you're dieting, especially if you're female. Women need more of these two minerals than men do, yet many women's diets are notoriously low in calcium and iron. Because calcium plays a critical role in the smooth functioning of nerve tissue, deficiencies may first show up as unexplained edginess. Prolonged calcium deficiencies can lead to osteoporosis, heart problems and muscles that cramp. Insufficient iron levels can eventually lead to anemia. Long before true anemia sets in, however, anemialike symptoms such as weariness and lack of energy can occur.

Eat your vegetables raw or cook them just enough to retain their crispness. Overcooking leaches the water-soluble B and C vitamins. The B vitamin folic acid, in particular, is needed to build red blood cells. If there's not enough folic acid present in the diet, anemia can soon develop. A shortage of vitamin C compromises the immune system and weakens the body's ability to fight off infections.

Add a well-balanced nutritional supplement to your diet. A multivitamin supplement that contains B_6, folic acid and zinc should help you through the nutritional wasteland of any diet.

Think about how you're getting your allotted number of daily calories. Choose foods that are not only low in calories, but high in nutrients as well. Lettuce, a traditional dieter's food, is low in calories, but it's also painfully low in essential nutrients. Instead of filling up on lettuce, try broccoli or carrots, which are packed with nutrition and are still low in calories.

Choose a wide variety of foods from the four basic food groups. Your chances of establishing a nutritionally balanced diet will be better. In addition, knowing that you have options when eating will fight boredom and help you to adhere to your diet.

Eat more! Add 300 extra calories to your basic 1,200-calorie-a-day diet and then burn those bonus calories through exercise. Sound wacky? Not at all. Research shows that exercise speeds up metabolism not just while you're exercising, but 24 hours a day. At the same time, it suppresses your appetite. The result is quicker weight loss, less hassle controlling your appetite, a nutritional boost and a shapelier, firmer body.

CHOOSING THE RIGHT VITAMIN SUPPLEMENT

Whether you're dieting and are concerned about meeting your nutritional needs, or your doctor recommends that you begin taking a multivitamin supplement, how do you select the multivitamin product that's best for you?

Decide what you want the product to do for you. If you are dieting and just want to be certain that you're meeting all of your daily nutritional needs, your best choice may be a multivitamin/mineral formula that is balanced, providing you with a percentage of each nutrient. However, if you know that your diet is sadly lacking in fresh citrus fruits, for example, you may want to look for a single-vitamin product that offers the United States Recommended Daily Allowance (U.S.RDA) of vitamin C or a multivitamin that has an especially high vitamin C content.

Compare products. Become familiar with the U.S.RDAs for each nutrient. Carry a list into the pharmacy or grocery store with you. A "complete" product will list all of the nutrients on its label, telling you what portion of the U.S.RDA it provides. Optimal amounts have not been established for all of the nutrients considered to be essential, but safe ranges have been determined.

Look for a balanced product. The formula on the label will tell you what percentage of the U.S.RDA for each nutrient is provided in the supplement. Those that provide 50 to 150 percent of the U.S.RDAs for all of the nutrients are generally recommended. Be on the lookout for products that concentrate on high amounts of specific nutrients while cutting back on others; this can throw the formula off balance and give you a product that may not meet your needs.

Exercise caution. If the manufacturer claims that the product will protect you from specific ailments or conditions, beware. Supplements are not designed to "fight" diseases or medical conditions. If you have a special medical problem, consult your doctor. She or he may then recommend a specific supplement along with a health-care program designed to aid you.

Look for the expiration date. Don't buy the supplement if it is past the expiration date. The vitamins are usually quite safe to take for some time past the expiration date, but oil-based nutrients such as vitamins A and E tend to lose potency with the passage of time. For best keeping, store tightly closed vitamin bottles in a cupboard or closet, not in the refrigerator or freezer.

WHAT TO LOOK FOR IN
A MULTIVITAMIN/MINERAL SUPPLEMENT

Here are the United States Recommended Daily Allowances (U.S. RDAs) for adults and children 4 or more years of age.

U.S.RDA

Vitamin A	5,000 IU	Vitamin D	400 IU
Thiamine	1.5 mg	Vitamin E	30 IU
Riboflavin	1.7 mg	Calcium	1,000 mg
Niacin	20 mg	Copper	2 mg
Vitamin B_6	2 mg	Iodine	150 mcg
Folic acid	0.4 mg	Iron	18 mg
Vitamin B_{12}	6 mcg	Magnesium	400 mg
Biotin	300 mcg	Phosphorus	1 g
Pantothenic acid	10 mg	Zinc	15 mg
Vitamin C	60 mg		

Suggested Ranges*

Selenium	50–200 mcg[†]
Chromium	50–200 mcg

*These nutrients are considered essential, but they have no U.S.RDA. Instead, they have ranges considered safe and adequate.

[†]Supplements of selenium should not exceed 100 mcg because the average diet supplies about 100 mcg.

Women's Health Problems

Because of women's hormonal makeup, they have their own set of health problems, such as premenstrual syndrome (PMS), as well as a higher incidence of breast cancer, anemia and osteoporosis than men.

PMS

PMS has been linked to bizarre, sometimes violent behavior in women during the intervals between their menstrual periods. Mood swings, irritability, depression, lethargy and a host of other psychological complaints frequently go hand in hand with physical symptoms such as edema, tender breasts and headaches. Much research still needs to be done on this puzzling condition that affects many thousands of women.

In the meantime, simple steps can be taken to help alleviate some PMS symptoms for some women.

Make sure there's vitamin B₆ in your diet. Vitamin B_6 occurs naturally in beef liver, salmon, sunflower seeds and white chicken meat, and has been linked with the alleviation of some of the physical and psychological symptoms of PMS. The U.S.RDA for vitamin B_6 is a mere 2.0 mg, easily available in a well-rounded diet. If you consider taking supplements of this vitamin, consult with your doctor.

Cut back on salt. This should help ease some of the bloating that can cause physical discomfort and the psychological feeling of "fatness" that many women experience premenstrually. Rethink your eating patterns — most of the sodium we need is available to us without the deliberate addition of salt, and many prepared foods contain far too much.

Eat small, frequent meals. This may be of help to women who experience difficulties with fluctuating glucose levels, suffering ups and downs in energy and mood as a result. Six small meals will help maintain a steady, even flow of glucose into the bloodstream much better than two or three sizable meals.

Exercise. Regular, sustained exercise that increases the heart rate, allowing the release of endorphins into the bloodstream, works wonders for some women. Because exercise is a key to overall health, incorporating it into your life-style is one of the best things you can do for happiness of mind and body.

Relax. Stress increases the intensity of PMS symptoms. One of the best ways to battle stress and, ultimately, PMS, is through deep-relaxation exercises that allow you to step back from daily pressures and get in touch with yourself. Yoga (see "Yoga" in chapter 2) and transcendental meditation (TM) are two relaxation exercises you may want to try.

BREAST CANCER

Although nothing can *guarantee* that you will never get breast cancer, there are some things you can do to help lower your chances of getting the disease or increase the likelihood of a cure through early detection.

Perform regular breast exams. They're simple and easy to do, they take a few minutes once a month and they can often pick up on a potential trouble spot long before it poses any threat to a woman's life. Self-examinations, coupled with an annual visit to your gynecologist for an

(continued on page 32)

A COMPLETE BREAST SELF-EXAM

Eating well, exercising and seeing your gynecologist regularly go a long way in protecting you from breast cancer. But you can take protection one step further by examining your breasts once each month. Use our guide here to get started. Then, the next time you see your gynecologist or physician, ask her or him for additional guidance. The most important things to remember are:

→ Apply enough finger pressure while doing the examination so that you can really feel the deep tissues, especially if your breasts are large.

→ Although breast self-examination doesn't take long, devote enough time to it to do a thorough job.

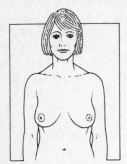

Step 1. Look at your breasts. Stand in front of a mirror and familiarize yourself with the shape and outline of your breasts.

Check for any dimpled or puckered areas, discharge from the nipples, scaly skin or unexplained swelling.

Step 2. Lift your arms overhead. Clasp your hands behind your head, tightening your chest muscles.

Check breast contours for irregularities, swellings or bumps.

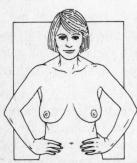

Step 3. Lower your arms to rest hands on hips. Then bend forward slightly, again flexing chest muscles slightly.

Check the contours of your breasts. This is an especially good position in which to check for dimpling.

- → It doesn't—and shouldn't—hurt! If your breasts are continuously tender, talk with your physician.
- → A breast self-exam should be done regularly, usually once a month. It's especially important for you to become familiar with what is normal for you. This is the basis against which all ensuing exams will be compared.
- → Don't be alarmed if you discover that your breasts don't match each other perfectly. It's quite common for one breast to be larger than the other or to have a slightly different shape.
- → If you are menstruating, wait until several days after your period stops to do an exam, when your breasts are in their most normal state.

Step 4. Raise one arm overhead. Using three or four fingers of the opposite hand, gently use the flat part of your fingers and work in small, overlapping circles from the outer edge toward the nipple; gradually examine one entire breast this way. (You may want to do this step in the shower or tub where soapy water makes it easier for your fingers to slide over the skin.) Repeat on the other breast.

Check for any lumps, bumps, thickened areas or hard knots.

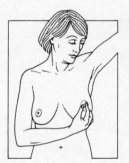

Step 5. Gently squeeze each nipple between thumb and forefinger of the opposite hand.

Check for any discharge—if a discharge is present, see your doctor.

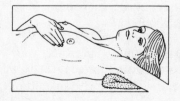

Step 6. Lie flat on your back. With a pillow or folded towel under one shoulder, raise that arm over your head. With the other hand, examine your breast using the same method described in Step 4. Repeat on the other breast.

Check for any lumps, bumps, thickened areas or hard knots.

even more thorough examination, can greatly eliminate the threat of breast cancer from your life.

This process can be fine-tuned even further by undergoing a mammography. A mammography is a low-radiation X-ray exam of the breast tissue that will detect the tiniest lumps frequently missed even by the highly trained hands of a gynecologist. It is suggested that women between the ages of 35 and 40 have a mammography exam in order to establish what is normal for them. Then, between ages 40 and 49, they should have one every two years. After age 50, when menopause usually removes the protective benefits of some hormones and makes women more vulnerable to breast cancer, annual exams are suggested.

Exercise. Another warrior in the battle against breast cancer is exercise. One study done at Harvard University found that nonathletic women had more than twice the risk of developing breast cancer than did those women who were former athletes. These findings also indicate that exercise, and not just organized athletics, begun early in life has tremendous long-range benefits that are only just now being recognized. Even if you aren't exactly young, don't think that all is lost when it comes to exercise. For each year that you do exercise and watch your weight, starting right now, you are giving yourself an additional year of protection.

Trim your body fat. Body fat seems to figure into breast cancer risk as well. Fit women generally carry around much less body fat than do their inactive sisters. Although there's no real decisive evidence that watching your weight will guarantee cancer-free breasts, leaner women do seem to exhibit fewer cases of breast cancer. It's thought to be linked to the amount and potency of estrogen that lean versus overweight women produce.

Eat more fish. In laboratory tests, fish oils actually inhibited the growth of chemically induced tumors in animals. Researchers think that fish oil may interfere with the absorption of enzymes that allow cancer to form. Salmon and mackerel are two excellent sources of dietary fish oil. (See "Recognizing the Good Fats" earlier in this chapter.)

Watch your nutrients. Don't overlook nutrients that may also protect your breasts. The Linus Pauling Institute says that vitamin C seems to have a protective influence against breast cancer. And vitamin E and selenium, both antioxidants, could help knock out the free radicals that attack healthy cells. (See "Preventing Cancer with Vitamins and Minerals" earlier in this chapter.)

ANEMIA

Women are more apt to fall victim to anemia than men are. Menstruation regularly depletes the body of iron stores necessary to maintain high energy levels. Women who jog a lot are additionally at risk because they excrete undetectable amounts of blood through their urine due to the physical trauma of jogging. Teenage girls who frequently diet and simply don't eat the foods that are high in iron are also at risk of anemia. Pregnant and lactating women may become anemic because they pass their own body stores of iron to the fetus and nursing infant. Here are the best ways to add iron to your diet.

Eat foods high in iron. Iron supplements are all right, but the best way to boost the amount of iron in your diet is by selecting foods high in the mineral. In addition to the old standby, liver, there are other foods that contain substantial amounts of iron, such as:

> almonds
> broccoli
> dried apricots
> lean ground beef
> molasses
> raisins
> roast beef
> sunflower seeds
> white turkey meat

Accompany iron-rich foods with foods high in vitamin C. Eating foods high in vitamin C, such as oranges or grapefruit, or drinking their juices assures you that the iron you get from the foods you eat will be absorbed properly.

OSTEOPOROSIS

Osteoporosis—brittle bones—can take inches off your stature as well as years off your life and can leach enjoyment out of your later years. Begin to follow these tips right now to ensure a brighter future.

End constant dieting. Many dieters steer clear of calcium-laden, high-fat dairy products. If you feel that you must diet, be sure to include skim milk and low-fat cheeses in your menu.

Eat less red meat. A high-protein diet causes the body to excrete calcium stores.

Make sure you get plenty of exercise. Activities that put stress on your body's skeleton strengthen those bones by allowing the body to lay down more bone tissue. Brisk walking is especially beneficial and can be done by most people at any age.

Expose yourself to sunshine. Vitamin D, produced by the body in response to sunshine, is essential for the body's absorption of calcium. A simple 10- to 20-minute walk each day during daylight hours should be enough to supply your body with lots of crucial vitamin D. (Don't forget to apply a sunscreen.)

Stop smoking. Smoking lowers estrogen levels, which, in turn, can decrease bone mass.

Take it easy on antacids that contain aluminum. These, along with diuretics and drugs that contain prednisone or cortisone, can cause calcium stores to be leached away.

Look at the older women in your family. If your grandmother and mother developed osteoporosis, your risk of developing weakened bones in the future is definitely greater than average. Although there's little you can do about your genetic makeup, you can follow the other tips here to lessen your chances of getting the disease.

Look to the future. Begin protecting your daughters' lifetime bone strength by being sure they get lots of calcium in their diets now. Studies show that older women whose calcium needs were adequately met early in life enjoy greater bone strength later in life.

2

Shortcuts to

A Fitter You

To stay fit, you need to exercise. But that doesn't mean you have to be a superathlete—you just have to learn how to make the most of the exercises you do. The best exercises are those that are aerobic because aerobic exercise is the easiest and fastest way to total fitness. In this chapter you'll learn how to find your target heart rate and how to get started with exercise, and you'll learn about the aerobic exercises that will give you the best workouts: aerobic dancing, bicycling, running, swimming and walking. In addition, we'll take a look at some aerobic alternatives, such as jarming. We'll also cover the essentials about injuries and how to prevent them. If you've been making excuses about not exercising, you'll find plenty of activities here that provide almost effortless ways to achieve fitness.

Aerobics

Aerobic exercise offers the best way to achieve fitness. And just what is aerobic exercise? Anything that gets your heart going at its target rate and sustains that rate for a period of time. To get started on your road to fitness, you must first have an understanding of target heart rate and how this applies to your exercise.

UNDERSTANDING MAXIMUM AND TARGET HEART RATES

Maximum heart rate is the fastest you should allow your pulse to become while you are exercising. Target heart rate is the pulse you are aiming for

EASING INTO EXERCISE

Exercise can be for everyone, regardless of age. Elderly patients who regularly exercise say they have more energy, sleep more soundly, enjoy eating more and report fewer aches. Adult exercisers of any age smoke less, drink less and handle stress better. Beginning and sticking to an exercise program will lower body fat stores and increase muscle strength and flexibility. The added stress supplied by most exercises can help ward off osteoporosis, a bane many women over the age of 45 want to avoid. If you haven't worked out in a while, follow the suggestions below to ease into exercise.

See your doctor. For beginners over the age of 30 (men) or 35 (women), the first step in any exercise program should include a physical exam. A pre-exercise exam should include a complete medical, dietary and drug history. During the physical exam the physician should look for hearing, vision and musculoskeletal problems. Some physicians may want to run a stress test, including an electrocardiogram (EKG). Individuals who smoke, people who know they have high blood pressure or high cholesterol levels and those who have chest discomfort, shortness of breath, diabetes or a family history of heart disease should check with their physician regardless of age.

Begin slowly and gradually work up to strenuous activities. Everett L. Smith, Ph.D., director of the Biogerontology Laboratory of the University of Wisconsin, suggests exercising three days a week for at least 30 minutes. Target heart rate should be 70 to 80 percent of maximum heart rate. This is a goal, not a starting point. If you have not exercised recently, training 5 to 10 minutes, twice a day, might be a reasonable start.

Strive for a fitness program that combines aerobic activities with exercises for strength and flexibility. Although water exercises are excellent activities that are less likely to cause injuries than other sports, they may not provide enough stress to maintain bone strength. Be sure to include some weight-bearing exercises (such as walking, jogging, jumping rope or weight lifting) in your exercise routine if swimming is your thing.

(continued)

If you choose a group physical fitness program, look for one directed specifically toward your age and fitness level. A trained, enthusiastic instructor and a few excited participants make good motivators. Indoor group activities are great if you don't want to have to deal with the weather, but if you rarely venture from your house, you may find that outdoor activities suit you best.

Listen to your body. Stop exercising and contact your physician if you experience chest pain or pressure, or if you feel faint. Decrease the amount of exercise you do if you're so out of breath that you can't carry on a conversation, if you have a rapid pulse or if you experience a pounding of the heart that lasts for more than 10 minutes after you stop exercising. You should also cut back on exercise if you have joint pain that lasts more than two hours after exercise or that is more intense the next morning.

Take steps to prevent dehydration. Beginning exercisers often don't realize how important it is to drink water before, during and after exercise, especially on warm days. When the weather is hot, try to exercise in the early morning or evening and increase your fluid intake.

in order to gain aerobic benefits. Your target heart rate is considered to be about 70 to 80 percent of your maximum heart rate. Here's how to figure out your maximum and target heart rates:

→ Subtract your age from 220. This will give you your maximum heart rate. Many fitness experts feel that you need to increase your heart rate to 70 to 80 percent of this maximum rate for at least 20 minutes, three times a week, to improve cardiovascular fitness.

→ Once you've determined your maximum heart rate, multiply this number by 0.70 to calculate your target heart rate. Here's an example: If you're 40 years old, your maximum heart rate is 180 (220 - 40). Your target heart rate is 126 (180 × 0.70). What this means is that to get the most out of your aerobic activity, your exercise should raise your heart rate to at least 126 beats per minute, but not exceed 180 beats per minute.

→ To find out how fast your heart is beating, take your pulse at your neck or wrist for 15 seconds, then multiply that number by four.

This will give you your heartbeat per minute. This method is fairly accurate, though your heart rate will probably turn out to be a bit lower if you take your pulse for the full minute.

→ Now that you know what your maximum and target heart rates are, you're ready to get the most out of your exercise program.

Aerobic Dancing

You don't need to be a dancer to enjoy aerobic dancing. It's a great way to get in shape while enjoying music and meeting friends. Here are a few pointers to help you find a good aerobic instructor and make the most of your aerobic dance class.

SIZING UP AN AEROBIC INSTRUCTOR

Shopping for an aerobic dance instructor can be as difficult as shopping for a new car—the body is flawless and the engine looks clean, but how does it perform? With the demand for classes in aerobic dance, jazz exercise, slimnastics and aerobic calisthenics, there's been a surge of instructor training programs, but not all training programs are alike. Programs range from university-level training to weekend seminars to mail-order certificates. So how do you determine who the qualified instructors are?

In her book *Sheila Cluff's Aerobic Body Contouring* (Rodale Press, 1987), the author strongly suggests that you seek out instructors who have been certified through one of four nationally recognized organizations:

The Aerobics & Fitness Association of America (AFAA) in Los Angeles, California

The American College of Sports Medicine (ACSM) in Indianapolis, Indiana

Dr. Kenneth Cooper's Aerobics Center in Dallas, Texas

The International Dance Exercise Association (IDEA) in San Diego, California

Sheila Cluff also has these recommendations about choosing your aerobics instructor:

→ Before you sign up for class, ask your instructor if she or he has been certified.
→ If your instructor has been certified, find out which organization issued the certificate.

→ If your instructor hasn't been certified, ask if she or he has training in emergency first aid, a valid cardiopulmonary resuscitation (CPR) certificate and a solid background in physical education or experience as a qualified dance instructor. Also ask if she or he regularly attends workshops offered by aerobic-dance professionals.

MAKING THE MOST OF YOUR AEROBICS CLASS

Once you've found an aerobics instructor and class that's right for you, don't sabotage your exercise efforts by going to your class unprepared. Here's how to get the most from your class.

Wear comfortable clothes and the right shoes. Don't wear anything that's too constricting—you want to be able to move your arms and legs freely. Also keep in mind that your temperature will rise as you exercise, so you may want to dress in layers that you can peel off as you become warmer. The proper athletic shoe is important as well. You'll need a shoe that gives you plenty of support and also cushions your feet from impact. (See "Shopping for Athletic Shoes" later in this chapter.)

Begin at a level that suits your current physical condition. Start slowly and don't worry about how fast you're progressing. Progress will be made with time and practice.

Stick to your program. Benefits of regular exercise can be quickly lost if you exercise only sporadically.

Don't neglect to warm up. It gets the body going and prevents injuries. (See "Warming Up Before a Workout" later in this chapter.)

Know what your target heart rate should be. All good aerobics instructors will break several times during the class for you to take your pulse. Make sure you keep between your target and maximum heart rate to get the most out of your exercise. (See "Understanding Maximum and Target Heart Rates" earlier in this chapter.)

Always cool down after a workout. Don't finish your exercise and then jump into your car and go home. You're more likely to suffer from leg cramps or sore muscles if you don't cool down first. Most organized aerobics classes include a cool-down period at the end. If yours doesn't, talk to your instructor about it, and then do your own cool-down exercises. A good cool-down period would include walking, either in place or around the room a few times; long, slow stretches; sitting or standing and stretching your neck from side to side and deep breathing for relaxation.

Bicycling

Riding a bike is a great form of aerobic activity that rivals running. Bicycling will give your heart a workout without stressing your leg joints the way running can. You can bicycle at your own pace, with family or friends, and you get to see the sights.

BICYCLING SAFELY

Breezing along a country road on a sunny afternoon can perk up your body and your mind. But if you haven't been out bicycling in a while, it's best not to just hop on a bike and go. Here are some pointers for safe and enjoyable cycling.

Start by making sure you have an easy-to-ride, safe and durable bike. This may mean replacing your old sentimental favorite with a safer, more comfortable bike. (See "Buying a Bicycle" later in this chapter.) If you decide you want to hang on to your old bike, be sure to have it thoroughly cleaned, lubricated and checked out by a pro at a bicycle repair shop before you hit the road.

Buy a helmet. Next to your bike, it's the most important piece of bicycling equipment you can buy. Many injuries can be prevented by wearing a helmet—helmets are not just for kids.

Consider buying sportswear designed for bicycling. Although many people wear running shoes when they're riding, cycling shoes slide in and out of toe clips (if your bike has these) more easily, which is important if you have to pull your foot out quickly to get off your bike. In addition, the soles are strong enough to hold up under constant foot pressure, which means your feet won't get sore if you go out for a long ride. Choose clothing that is lightweight and streamlined so it doesn't flap in the wind or get in your way. Shorts should be snug so they move with your legs as you pedal. Skin-hugging bicycling shorts decrease wind resistance and chafing. Sunglasses should be worn on any long daytime ride, even if the sun isn't all that strong. The glasses protect your eyes from flying objects and protect your retinas from getting "washed-out" during the day, which results in poorer vision at night.

Dress properly for bad weather. Wear warm clothing that breathes. Start with cotton against your skin, then layer on polypropylene or Gore-Tex to transfer moisture away from your body and top it all off with wool on the outside, for added warmth. A snug, wool cap under your helmet and polypropylene runner's gloves will keep heat from escaping from your head and hands. Since you don't want to impair circulation in your feet, one extra-heavy pair of socks should do the trick. A little petroleum jelly on your face is good protection against the wind.

Bring along a tool kit. Your kit should contain a few items for simple repairs and flat tires, such as screwdrivers, wrenches, a pump and tire gauge. Being able to perform a quick repair and be off riding again can mean the difference between getting where you want to go and having to hike for miles.

BUYING A BICYCLE

Even if you never plan to do much touring with your bicycle, you should still take the time to shop wisely. Here's some good advice to follow both *before* you set foot inside a shop and once you're there.

Before You Shop

Select a few reliable bicycle shops in your area. Don't shop in a department store or an auto parts store—a bicycle shop will provide you with the ongoing advice of an expert. Besides, price markups on bicycles are not very high, so a super bargain in the department store could end up becoming a super lemon later on.

Decide what type of riding you'll be doing and look for the appropriate bicycle. For instance, will you be commuting a few miles to work, touring a few miles on the weekends or getting into some fast and furious racing at the local track? Your answer will determine what type of bicycle and accessories you should buy.

Pick a price range. Take into account what kind of equipment you will need for the type of riding you will be doing and what you can afford. Think about accessories—what is necessary and what they will cost. A good helmet is a must.

When You Shop

Decide how many speeds you need. One-speed bicycles won't supply the ease of riding that most recreational bikers are looking for. Three-speeds are great for commuting on level ground or in city traffic. Their upright position of riding and wide saddle are comfortable for stop-and-go traveling, and a three-speed makes for easy shifting and low maintenance. A ten-speed, however, is the best choice for the majority of bikers. These bicycles travel a little faster with a little less work, are usually lighter and the components are normally of a better quality than those of one- and three-speed bicycles.

Be sure the bicycle fits you. A good way to check for size is to stand flat-footed and straddle the horizontal bar of the bike. The bar should be one-half to one inch below your crotch. The dealer can adjust seat height and handlebar position for optimum comfort.

Make sure the salesperson understands what your riding plans are. That way, she or he can help you make the best equipment choice. For example, a touring frame is a little longer than a racing frame. This will supply more stable steering, but at the cost of greater weight. If you're not going to be doing much touring, you will want to look at other types of bicycles.

Choose your wheels carefully. They must fit both the bicycle and your needs. Aluminum rims are recommended because of their great strength, low weight and resistance to dents as compared to steel rims. Tire width can range from 1 to 1¼ inches. A wide tire is better for touring; narrower tires are best for racing or fast recreational riding.

Opt for dropped handlebars. Dropped handlebars (the kind that turn down) offer the advantage of allowing riders to shift weight from their seats to the handlebars by leaning forward. When compared to upright handlebars, dropped handlebars offer less wind resistance, more efficient pedaling and easier breathing.

Choose a narrow seat over a wide one. Wide seats are okay if you plan to sit upright while riding. However, the type of riding most recreational riders do on a ten-speed requires a narrow seat. This type of seat is also essential with dropped handlebars because leaning forward in a wide seat would chafe the inside of your legs. Leather seats offer an advantage over plastic seats because they eventually mold to your derriere.

Don't buy toe clips if you're a beginner. Toe clips on the pedals can increase pedaling efficiency, but may be cumbersome for beginning cyclists. It might be best to go without them for a while, until you definitely have the hang of mounting and dismounting under various conditions. Then start with miniclips, which keep your foot from sliding forward, but don't have the bothersome straps.

BICYCLING IN BAD WEATHER

Unless you own an all-terrain bike (also called a mountain bike), you probably won't intentionally go riding in the rain or snow. But what if you pick a sunny winter day to start a ride, only to be surprised by bad weather several miles down the road? Here are some do's and don'ts.

Don't panic. Unless you're caught in a torrential downpour or a true blizzard, you'll get home almost as quickly as you would on a fine day if you stay calm. If you *do* get caught in really bad weather, pull over in a sheltered area and wait it out, keeping in mind that you may have to walk somewhere to phone for a ride home.

Slow down. As soon as the road gets a bit wet, slow down your pace. You're not going to get home faster if you ride faster—on slick roads you're just courting disaster. Pay particular attention to turns, and be on the lookout for icy patches. Also be aware of the traffic around you. Many automobile drivers get panicky when the weather turns bad, so you've got to be alert for potential danger.

Brake slowly. Caliper brakes lose up to 95 percent of their effectiveness when they're wet. That means you're going to need plenty of distance for stopping. If you must stop short, use this technique:

→ Apply the rear brake lightly as you apply the front brake forcefully.
→ Slide back on the seat to increase weight on the rear wheel.
→ When the rear wheel begins to skid, reduce pressure on the front brake.

Running

Did you ever wonder why so many people enjoy running? For starters, it's a great way to get into terrific shape—running reduces body fat while it increases lean body tissue. Running also improves lung capacity and strengthens leg muscles and bones. For some people, however, running is a painful experience, but it doesn't have to be. Follow the guidelines below for running success.

GETTING STARTED

Running can be a great way to improve both your physical and mental health, but getting started is always the tough part. Here are a few key rules.

Buy a good pair of running shoes. Don't run in any old pair of sneakers or your first day out could end with aching feet and knees, blisters or shin splints. (See "Shopping for Athletic Shoes" later in this chapter.)

Start slowly. Jog for a set period of time (20 minutes is a good start) every other day at a pace you feel comfortable with. Take a break on the days in between, or try walking on those days to establish the "exercise habit." Walking is also a good way to ease into a running program. (See "Walking" later in this chapter.)

Jog with a friend. A buddy provides extra motivation. It is also safer to hit the road in pairs, especially if you are female or plan to run in the city or at night. Be sure to find somebody who runs at your speed and distance.

If you can't find a human partner, perhaps a dog is the running companion for you. Start your pet off just as you started—slow and easy—and always keep a tight rein on your four-legged friend anywhere near traffic. Once a dog gets used to regular exercise, it will happily hound you when it's time to run.

RUNNING UP AGAINST AGGRESSIVE DOGS

Although the family canine makes a great exercise partner, many runners have found that someone else's pet can be a dangerous adversary. If a dog threatens you, here's what you should do.

Stop and face the dog. This ends the chase, and possibly the entire encounter.

Stay calm. Even if the dog turns out to be a bold beast, you shouldn't show your fear. Dogs like to take advantage of fearful prey.

Firmly order the dog home. Surprisingly, many will turn and leave. Don't shout or wave a stick at the animal; that may put it on the defensive.

Steadily back away without taking your eyes off your pursuer. Once out of the dog's territory or far enough away to discourage the chase, you can turn and continue your run.

Carry a legal deterrent spray. These can be found in pet stores, and may discourage an advancing animal without causing it serious injury.

Contact an animal control officer if you frequently find yourself facing the same dog. Most communities have laws against allowing dogs to roam.

RUNNING SAFELY AT NIGHT

Running in the dark can be a risky business. Drivers can't see you, but muggers can. Care and common sense will make running a safe ritual, regardless of how early the sun sets or how late the office closes.

EXERCISING AWAY YOUR FATIGUE

When you're tired, the last thing you may want to do is exercise. But doing just that is really what you need. Here's why:

→ Exercise will pump oxygen into your blood and brain. Your circulatory system and organs will benefit.
→ Exercise can help keep adrenal hormones in balance. You'll be able to deal with stress more easily if those hormones are not swinging wildly.
→ Exercise will help normalize blood sugar so your body has a steady supply of energy from which to draw. Fatigue and listlessness can result from drops in blood sugar.
→ Exercise can help emotional stress. A workout provides a healthy outlet for venting frustrations, and as your physical condition improves, self-confidence for a job well done should follow.
→ Exercise releases the body's natural painkillers. These chemicals, called endorphins, can create feelings of well-being and happiness—a big perk for a fatigued mind.

Reflective clothing is a must. Many brands of running clothes have the familiar reflective single or double stripe across the torso and down the legs. These clothes make you visible to drivers at night. To be extra safe, go one step further and wear a reflective hat or reflective bands on your wrists and ankles. And if you carry two small flashlights, they can give you visibility as well as make you visible.

Choose a safe and well-known route. Make an effort to avoid traffic, overly isolated areas and roads you aren't very familiar with.

Run defensively. Moving against traffic offers you the opportunity to spot and get out of the way of threatening drivers.

Be alert. Use your ears to pick up movements that can't be seen—that means leaving the portable radio or cassette player at home. Don't slip too deeply into a runner's meditation—spacing out could be dangerous.

Run with a partner. Everyone can benefit from safety in numbers.

Swimming

Swimming is a super sport that helps tone up muscles and increase cardiovascular fitness. Because of the nearly weightless condition, you can do all sorts of activities that would be impossible to do on land. Less stress is placed on the body as you move, and less stress means fewer injuries—which gives swimming a distinct advantage over other sports. This section takes a look at the benefits of swimming, and what you can do to make the most of your time in the pool.

GETTING STARTED WITH SWIMAEROBICS

Lack of swimming ability is no longer a good excuse for shying away from the water. Swimaerobic exercises done in the shallow end of the pool can give you a great workout. Swimaerobics is also excellent for easing back into exercise after an injury. The combination of buoyancy and water resistance offers your body the chance to gently exercise strained muscles in a nearly stress-free environment. Try the exercises illustrated below.

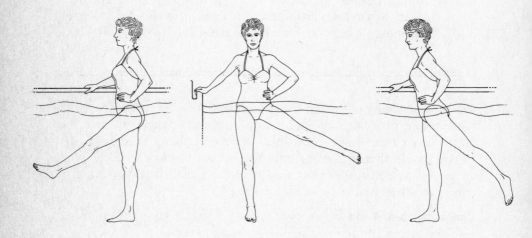

Leg lifts. Stand in water about waist high (you may want to hold on to the poolside) and slowly raise your left leg straight out in front of you. Now bring it back in. Slowly raise it straight out to the side and back in. Then extend your leg straight back behind you. Repeat for the right leg. You'll really feel the water resistance with these lifts.

Water jogging. This is just what it sounds like—jogging in the water. Even if you don't have much room in your pool, you can still jog in small circles. The idea is to get a good workout by taking advantage of the water's resistance to your movement.

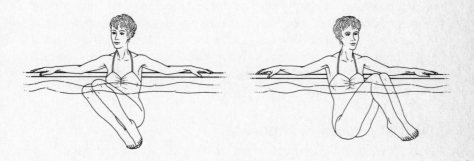

Leg tucks. While holding on to the side of the pool, raise your knees to your chest. To get in some extra toning, you can twist from side to side while doing your tucks. If you're floating, simply bring your knees to your chest and hold for a few seconds, then lower your legs. Leg tucks help tighten abdominal muscles.

SWIMMING FOR YOUR HEART

Once you have become comfortable with what your body will do in the water, you can try increasing water resistance (and increase the amount of energy expended) by changing position in the water, by changing the direction of movement or by using special equipment. Hand paddles, fins or floatation devices can give you a good workout while adding some fun. While you tone up your body, you'll also be giving your heart a good workout.

Aerobic benefits from swimming are similar to those from running. But if you keep track of your heart rate, don't be surprised to find that your heart beats a little slower in the water. Maximum heart rate is about 15 beats per minute slower in the water than it is on land. The supine position in swimming allows the heart to pump more blood with each beat. The rhythmic breathing necessary for swimming may also help slow the pulse.

The crawl stroke seems to be the best stroke for aerobic benefits. However, backstroke, breaststroke and sidestroke are also useful. Remember, gliding is really relaxing, so aerobic benefits decrease if you skim through the water doing a leisurely sidestroke. Try mixing up strokes to work out all your muscles and break up the monotony.

Walking

Walking is perfect for people who are just getting started with an exercise program and for those exercise dropouts who have given up on other programs due to lack of time or space, or the expense of joining a gym or club. There is no need for expensive or elaborate equipment— aerobic benefits can be achieved with a brisk walk that requires only a good pair of shoes and a little motivation.

STARTING A WALKING PROGRAM

Although it doesn't take much to get started with walking, it does take a bit more planning than simply marching out the door and down the street. Follow these pointers to make the most of your walks.

Find a course suitable for safe, stress-free walking. Initially, a mile of flat terrain on a track, through a park or around the neighborhood will do.

Walk the course at a comfortable pace. Time your effort. Walk at least three times a week.

When you can walk a mile in 15 minutes, increase your mileage. Try working up to two miles in 30 minutes. Always stop if you feel short of breath or are in pain.

Keep a walking diary. It will help you establish goals and record progress. Record the date, distance and time it took to complete the course. Try writing down an "observation-of-the-day" such as what the weather is like or about the people you meet along the way—it can add fun to your routine.

Consider finding a walking companion. Though certainly not an essential ingredient for a successful program, a friend can supply extra motivation for those low-energy days.

MAKING YOUR WALK MORE PRODUCTIVE

Once you've started your walking program, you can make it more productive by following these guidelines.

Be aware of your posture. Proper posture will raise your center of gravity and make striding easier. Hold your head high, straighten your back, stand tall and don't lean forward. Toes should point in the direction you are moving. Relax. Good body alignment can prevent backaches and headaches—problems that can plague the lazy walker.

Take full strides, with knees straight rather than bent, and let your arms swing naturally from the shoulders. This will help you cover the most ground with the minimum amount of effort. A steady, rhythmic cadence puts momentum on your side and adds grace to your gait.

Breathe deeply and rhythmically. This draws oxygen through your lungs and into your bloodstream, supplying working muscles with the oxygen they need. You'll be able to walk farther without tiring by deeply inhaling over a five- to six-step period, holding your breath for a similar period, then slowly exhaling.

Try wearing wrist and ankle weights. They can increase the number of calories you burn and help enhance aerobic fitness. Wearing light weights won't improve your strength, but a few extra pounds will help increase your energy expenditure without your having to increase your distance or speed.

WALKING THROUGH ALL KINDS OF WEATHER

Once you begin your walking program, don't let the weather slow you down. Here are some things you should know about summer and winter walking as well as an alternative for foul-weather trekking.

Summertime walking can be tough on your toes. Sweaty feet provide a warm, moist haven for fungal diseases. Keep feet cool and dry by applying a good foot powder and wearing absorbent socks. Never wear damp sneakers.

Wintertime walking presents its own hazards. Ice and snow can add unwanted surprises to a daily walking routine. Looking ahead will enable you to scout out dangerous spots before they are underfoot. A moderate pace combined with slightly shorter and flat-footed steps will make traveling safer on potentially slippery terrain. And footwear with extra traction will help you keep a grip on things.

Mall walking is an alternative to outdoor trekking. So if an unsafe neighborhood, excessively hilly terrain, heat, cold or wind are still stopping you from pounding the pavement, mall walking could be just the ticket. Shopping malls across the country are offering participants safe, flat, climate-controlled conditions. Contact your local mall, hospital or chapter of the American Heart Association to find out how to start or join a mall-walking group in your area.

Aerobic Alternatives

Dancing, bicycling, running, swimming, walking—what else can you do to stay aerobically fit? If you'd rather exercise in the privacy of your own home, try one or more of the following equally aerobic activities.

JARMING

Jogging has its antithesis—"jarming." Jarming is not new; it's as ancient as music and manual labor. Jarming is probably the reason that orchestra conductors, virtuoso violinists, concert pianists and window washers live so long. What is this incredible key to longevity? Jarming is, quite simply, jogging with the arms. While standing or sitting in place, simply pump your arms. The action can be more exaggerated than it would be for running. It's a great tune-up for those bound to the house or nursing home, those sitting in a wheelchair and those individuals who are unable, or perhaps unwilling, to pound the pavement, pedal furiously, swim laps endlessly or be caught racing up and down the apartment building stairs. Although jarming has not been specifically studied, the movements, and benefits, are similar to those experienced by rowers (and competitive rowers are some of the most aerobically fit athletes around).

Jarming eliminates the hazards of road and weather and is relatively injury-free. But if you are really looking for a super route to fitness, try utilizing both legs *and* arms during exercise, with some vigorous walking that incorporates hand weights and jarming arms.

JUMPING

Skipping rope is not the exclusive right of school children. Adults can gain aerobic benefits, as well as develop coordination, using the simple jump rope. Once proficiency is acquired, jumping at a rate of 120 skips per minute for 10 minutes is as aerobically beneficial as running an 8.5-minute mile.

To master the mechanical aspects of skipping rope and to begin enjoying aerobic benefits, start jumping in 30-second bouts — 30 seconds of jumping and 30 seconds of rest — for 10 bouts. Gradually increase the length of the bouts, working up to 60 seconds of jumping and 60 seconds of rest. Eventually, you will want to jump rope long enough to keep your pulse at its target rate for 20 minutes. (See "Understanding Maximum and Target Heart Rates" earlier in this chapter.) Researchers at the Institute for Aerobic Research in Dallas, Texas, found that alternating one minute of jumping with one minute of rest will keep your heart pumping at the target rate, even during those rest periods. As with any aerobic exercise, remember to warm up before serious rope jumping and try jumping on soft surfaces such as grass, dirt or carpeting to cushion the impact.

ROWING

Working out on a rowing machine strengthens your heart, lungs, knees, ankles, calves and lower back, and the movements associated with pulling the oars will also increase your upper body strength. With a rowing machine at home, you don't have to worry about foul weather ruining a day's workout. If you need a distraction to help while away the rowing time, tune in to your favorite radio program, or play some energetic music as you row.

SKIPPING

Skipping is no longer relegated to the elementary-school crowd. Even Olympic athletes are adding this exercise to their training programs. Unlike jogging, with its unrelenting pounding, skipping gives a prolonged time when both feet are off the ground. This allows muscles to take a break from the continuous pounding. There is also a period when both feet are on the ground, spreading out shock absorption. Skipping also has an edge on jogging when it comes to improving flexibility, range of motion and circulation. Besides, as Irving Dardik, physician and founding chairman of the U.S. Olympic Sports Medicine Council told *New Age*

Journal (May 1986), "I think of it as a physical form of laughing." So go ahead, laugh a little.

STAIR STEPPING

If you live or work in a building with several floors you can easily fit exercise into your daily routine—just use the stairs instead of the elevator. Stair climbing will strengthen your heart while slimming down your legs. The only equipment required is a pair of sneakers or a good pair of walking shoes—don't try ascending those steps in heels! Paul S. Fardy, Ph.D., of Physician Health Rehabilitation Services, Inc. in Merrillville, Indiana, says an effective stair workout schedule requires climbing 85 to 100 steps per flight. Do at least five flights at a time and remember, it's the *ascent*, not the descent, that counts.

Yoga

Exercise doesn't have to be all hard work. On days when you're not doing a grueling aerobic workout, you may want to try yoga, the exercise for stretching and relaxation.

UNDERSTANDING THE BENEFITS OF YOGA

Yoga postures require flexibility, and the breathing techniques promote relaxation—a combination that many exercisers find to be just the thing for their "slow" days. There are many reasons why you can benefit from yoga—here are four of the best.

High-stress professionals need only 15 minutes of yoga once or twice a day to make their day easier. Properly done postures can relieve mental stress as well as high blood pressure, backaches and neck pain. Manual laborers can use yoga to realign muscles and bones that have been pulled and kinked throughout the day.

Arthritis sufferers can find relief with yoga. Yoga can speed internal healing by carefully moving joints. As strength improves, joint vulnerability decreases. Yoga postures that put weight on specific areas can improve bone health. The Iyengar tradition of yoga teaches proper joint alignment. Proper alignment will not only aid the healing of arthritic joints, but will also strengthen other joints and muscles that have had to compensate for the painful movements experienced by those with arthritis.

Those recovering from a heart attack will find yoga to be a great healing exercise. In addition to the improved strength and flexibility experienced by all who practice yoga, the relaxation generated from slow, gentle exercise, with controlled breathing, can have a calming effect for those recuperating from a recent heart attack. Yoga diverts the mind from worries and focuses mental energy on specific points on the body.

Asthmatics may be able to breathe easier after taking up yoga. Researchers studying the effects of yoga's physical postures, breathing techniques and meditation on asthma patients found that those who regularly practiced yoga decreased the number of asthma attacks they suffered. In addition, patients practicing yoga required less medication to control their disease.

Injury Prevention

No one embarks on an exercise program expecting to be injured, but injuries do occur. There are definitely some things you can do to help prevent them, though, such as warming up, wearing the proper athletic shoes, recognizing the effect weather can have on your body's performance and knowing the best way to recover from an injury so you don't continue to harm yourself.

WARMING UP BEFORE A WORKOUT

There are several good reasons for taking the time to warm up before jumping into a workout. Here are five of them:

→ Gently exercising before a workout reduces your chances of injury, especially in cold weather.

→ Pre-exercise stretching improves flexibility, and that can improve performance.

→ A slow rehearsal of the physical movements involved in a particular sport, be it swimming, running, bicycling, or any other activity, can psychologically prepare you for the actual workout, and even get you "psyched up" to exercise on those days when you're not really in the mood.

→ Warm-up exercise warms up your heart, too. Abnormal electrocardiograms (EKGs) have been observed in subjects who have engaged in vigorous activities without easing into exercise.

→ Easy workouts before exercising at full capacity can help migraine-prone individuals avoid a painful post-exercise headache.

HOW WARM-UPS WORK

The goal of a warm-up is to raise body temperature, thereby decreasing your chances of injuring cold, stiff muscles. Here are three warm-up methods and how they work.

A passive warm-up raises body temperature by external means. A warm shower, heating pad or steam bath will do the trick. Although this method isn't always practical, it does have the advantage of minimum physical effort, thereby sparing the body's energy for more serious activity.

A general warm-up increases overall body temperature by nonspecific body movements. Calisthenics, jogging or riding a stationary bicycle can effectively elevate deep muscle temperature.

A specific warm-up is a rehearsal of the actual athletic event. For instance, a runner might perform light running before the race or a tennis player would volley before beginning a match. This type of warm-up offers the physical advantage of warming the specific muscles that will be used, as well as the psychological advantage of focusing on the event.

CHOOSING THE RIGHT ATHLETIC SHOES

Shoes that fit your feet are necessary for safe, comfortable exercising. But it's also important to buy a shoe that's made for your sport. Don't let a fast-talking salesperson pressure you into buying a shoe that fits, but may not "work" for what you want to do. You need the proper shoe to help prevent leg and foot injuries. Here's a rundown of which shoes do what.

Aerobic dance shoes are constructed for stability. The side-to-side movements practiced in aerobic dance require a stiff heel, a stable midsole and a molded insole to hold your foot in place. Shoes should have good shock absorption. Research shows that dancers who wear aerobic shoes for aerobic dancing, rather than running or tennis shoes, suffer fewer injuries.

Running shoes are designed for movement in one direction—forward. They should be lightweight, yet padded. The heel needs to be elevated with a wide heel-base for stability and shock absorption.

Tennis shoes should not have a lot of traction because sliding a bit on macadam can help prevent jammed toes. But for those who play on indoor wooden courts, shoes with a special tread are required. Tennis players can wear aerobic shoes because both tennis and aerobics have lateral movements that require extra side support, but aerobic dancers should not wear tennis shoes.

Walking shoes must support the same unilateral movement involved in running. With the slower pace of walking, though, your heel doesn't need to spring from the road surface; it strikes more slowly and softly. Shoes that put your heel lower to the ground and give a little extra cushioning in the front for a springy push-off are made for walking. A good tread pattern will provide needed traction on varied terrain.

SHOPPING FOR ATHLETIC SHOES

Whether you're buying shoes for aerobics, running, racquet sports or walking, start your search for the right shoes by looking for a store that has knowledgeable athletes selling shoes. Then follow the suggestions below for choosing shoes:

- → Buy shoes in the afternoon when your feet have expanded to their maximum size.
- → Take along a pair of socks that you exercise in, as well as inserts if you use them.
- → If your old shoes are worn unevenly, take them along, too. Let the salesperson take a look at where you've worn them down. The salesperson may be able to point out shoes with special features that minimize wear in certain places.
- → When trying on shoes, be sure the heel fits snugly and there's plenty of toe room.
- → While standing on a level surface, check for symmetry such as matching position in the arch support and identical heel-counter heights. (The heel-counter is the molded part of the shoe surrounding the heel.) The shoes should not wobble.
- → Try flexing your foot, then extending it forward. Then, with your foot flat on the floor, rock it from side to side. Do you feel flexibility and support in the appropriate places for your sport?
- → Jump or run in place or walk around the room. Your toes should not get squeezed and your foot should not slide.
- → Check inside seams to make sure there aren't any blister-causing bumps.

TIED TO FIT

Once you've found the right shoe, it's important to make sure it stays firmly on your foot. Simply lacing your shoes with a little added flair can help keep those sneaks on your heel. Lace low-top shoes (this technique won't work on high-tops) as you normally would until you come to the next-to-last hole. Loop the shoestring through the last hole on the same side, then thread the opposite string through the loop. Tying will now pull the shoes snugly against your foot.

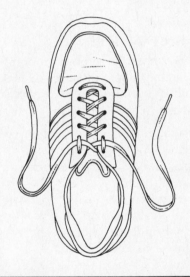

PREVENTING HEAT INJURY

Many exercisers don't realize that the sun that's shining down and making it a perfect day to be outdoors can also cause some serious heat injuries. Take these steps to ensure that you don't become a victim.

Begin acclimating to the weather several weeks before you start exercising outdoors. This is particularly important if you live in a hot, humid climate or are just beginning an exercise program in hot weather. Acclimatization involves gradually increasing the amount of time you spend exercising outdoors. Your body will be able to regulate heat better and you will perform better once you get used to working out in hot weather.

Older exercisers will require more time to acclimate than younger ones. If you know that you have circulation problems or other diseases that may impair the body's thermoregulation, avoid exercising in heat altogether.

Be sure your body fat is at a minimum. The more body mass you have, the more effort it requires to cool down, thus increasing your risk of overheating. Obese exercisers will definitely want to avoid working out in the heat.

Never exercise in the heat if you have a fever. Give your body a rest until the fever is gone.

If you're on medication, check with your physician for exercise guidelines. (This applies to exercise at *any* time of the year—some medications will make you drowsy or dizzy regardless of the weather.) Drugs such as diuretics and antihistamines can increase the risk of heat injury.

Don't drink and exercise. Alcohol can impair your thermoregulatory system.

Avoid working out during the day's hottest hours (10:00 A.M. to 2:00 P.M.). Morning and later afternoon sessions are safer.

Keep track of fluid loss. Daily weigh-ins and weigh-outs will help you keep track of how much fluid you're losing. Weight loss during exercise should not exceed 5 percent of your normal body weight; if you're losing more, you should be carefully monitored for signs of heat injury and you should take extra care to replenish fluids during exercise.

Be aware of the daily temperature and humidity and adjust your clothing accordingly. Loose, water-absorbent, light-colored clothing is best. Fishnet jerseys, cutoff T-shirts and short socks are comfortable, but should be changed when they become saturated with sweat.

Drink water before, during and after your workout. And make sure you're drinking *water*, not just any liquid. Water leaves the stomach and enters the bloodstream quicker than any other liquid. In addition, studies have shown that carbonated beverages can cause stomach cramps during and after exercise. And the high sugar content of other sweetened, but noncarbonated, drinks increases the time needed to empty the stomach, making fluid unavailable to your body when you need it most.

Cut down on fats. Dietary fat produces almost twice as much body heat as carbohydrates or proteins, so cut down on your fat intake in warm weather.

Consider adding some salt to your diet. The average American consumes 10 times the necessary sodium. But if you have a good, well-balanced diet that is normally low in sodium, a dash of salt at the table may help maintain your electrolyte balance during hot days.

RECOGNIZING AND TREATING COMMON HEAT INJURIES

Even if you've followed all of the advice for working out in hot weather, you may find yourself experiencing some symptoms of a heat injury. Here are descriptions of the common heat injuries and how to treat them.

Heat rash: Skin in constant contact with heat and humidity may develop an irritation sometimes called prickly heat. This itching, prickling rash can later be aggravated by heat exposure. Rubber workout suits, exercise belts or heavy clothing that doesn't "breathe" can create the necessary environment for a heat rash. Although it is not health-threatening, heat rash is certainly unpleasant. Loose, cool clothing and a little talcum powder or corn starch can relieve the itching.

Heat cramps: Loss of body fluids and electrolytes (such as sodium and potassium) from excessive sweating can result in muscle twitching or painful cramping, usually beginning in the legs and moving up to the abdominal muscles. Although body temperature may rise as high as 103°F, the condition is usually not life-threatening if treated immediately. Resting in a cool, shaded place and drinking fluids will bring rapid relief. Massaging muscles probably won't help the cramping, though it may force blood containing toxic metabolic products, such as lactic acid, away from your extremities.

Heat syncope: Fainting (syncope) can occur when you stand up quickly after exercising vigorously in the heat while lying down, or it may occur after spending too much time in a hot tub or sauna. In hot weather, your blood is routed toward the skin for cooling, reducing flow to the heart, brain and other organs. Fatigue, blurred vision, light-headedness or chills are warning signs that may precede a fainting episode. Fortunately, a person experiencing heat syncope gains consciousness almost immediately. Resting in a reclining position and drinking fluids will assist recovery.

Heat exhaustion: Heavy sweating over a long period of time could result in a condition termed heat exhaustion. Headache, fatigue, irritability, dizziness and cramping signal heat exhaustion. The victim will appear pale and shaky and feel cool and clammy to the touch. If you have these symptoms, immediately cease activity and rest in a cool place. Drink water or a weak saline solution—this is extremely important. If rectal temperatures are high (between 101° and 104°F) sponge your body with cold water to help lower the temperature. It is prudent to see a physician because heat exhaustion has the potential to develop into the more serious heatstroke.

Heatstroke: Heatstroke is a life-threatening illness that must be treated immediately. Body temperature will rise above 104°F—high enough to damage sensitive internal tissues. The body's heat regulatory system will shut down at these high temperatures; the result is that sweating will greatly decrease or stop. The skin becomes red, dry and warm. The victim may become dizzy and nauseated. Irrational, even psychotic behavior, is not uncommon. If the body is not cooled within an hour, seizures and coma will follow. Medical help is essential for survival, but the sooner a victim is cooled via a cold-water bath or ice packs, the better her or his chances for recovery. Dehydration may not be as severe as in heat exhaustion, so fluid replacement should proceed at a moderate rate. Once hospitalized, the victim will probably receive intravenous fluids.

PREVENTING SUMMER SKIN DAMAGE
The effect of sun exposure on your skin is cumulative. Midday runs in skimpy jogging togs can add up to leathery, wrinkled, prematurely aged skin. Worse yet, regular intense sun exposure and a history of sunburns can lead to skin cancer. How can you protect that outer layer?

Always wear a sunscreen. The higher the sun protection factor (SPF), the better. Remember to coat lips as well as areas that might catch reflected rays. The chin, tips of ears and back of legs are frequently neglected areas.

Cover your back. A T-shirt will do, but you may want to consider something light and long-sleeved if you are fair-skinned, light-haired or have a family history of skin cancer. Everyone normally wears shorts for summer exercising, but susceptible individuals might want to try long cotton pants or sweatpants.

Be aware that certain drugs and cosmetics can increase the sun's ravages on skin. If you notice a sensitivity to the sun, check your cosmetics, deodorants, deodorant soaps, detergents and perfumes. Antibiotics (tetracycline in particular), diuretics, tranquilizers, oral contraceptives and retinoic acid may also cause sun sensitivity.

Wear a waterproof sunscreen if you're engaging in water sports. Water sports add to the sun's dangers—lots of skin is showing, and reflected rays from water, sand or concrete increase exposure. Contrary to common belief, ultraviolet rays do pass through water, so being submerged is no protection at all. A waterproof sunscreen, liberally and frequently applied, is a must.

Protect yourself on cloudy days. Cloud cover doesn't offer much protection. Because clouds are composed of water, ultraviolet rays will pass right through them, reflect off land and water and be absorbed by your skin. Protect yourself with clothing and sunscreen.

PREVENTING WINTER SKIN DAMAGE

Winter can give your skin a rough time. Wind, cold, low humidity and sun can cause "winter itch." Dry, itchy skin can usually be avoided with a little foresight before hitting the slopes or ice.

Use a sunscreen. Fresh snow can reflect up to 85 percent of the ultraviolet light that hits it. That means you need a good sunscreen to protect your face, especially on mountain ski slopes, where less atmosphere lets through even more damaging ultraviolet light. Liberally apply sunscreen with an SPF of 8 or more. Be sure to cover vulnerable spots—chin, ears and the back of the neck.

Use a moisturizer. Wind and low humidity literally suck moisture from exposed skin. Moisturizers under sunscreen or makeup help retain your skin's moisture. Find a product containing a humectant, such as urea or lactic acid. These ingredients will draw moisture from the atmosphere. Don't forget to coat your hands as well as your face.

Wear protective clothing. It's the best shield for skin and eyes. Ski masks over the face are a must in extreme temperatures. Goggles will shield eyes from sun, wind and biting cold.

Use a lip balm. Frequently applied lip balm and a moisturizing sunscreen will help prevent chapped, cracked lips.

Once inside, take a warm shower. Don't try to warm up with a steaming hot shower. Hot water and harsh soaps can strip the skin of its natural oils. A warm shower and superfatted, pH-balanced soaps are the kindest things for your skin. Gently pat yourself dry and apply a moisturizer before completely drying to help keep moisture on winter-ravaged skin.

Consider buying a humidifier. A cool-air humidifier in your home will supply moisture that the cold, clear winter air has robbed from your skin. Drinking seven or eight glasses of water a day will also help maintain skin moisture.

RECOVERING QUICKLY FROM INJURIES

Unless you've been told by your doctor not to attempt any exercise at all, these tips will help you ease back into your fitness routine after an injury.

Water can do wonders. Many professional athletes hit the pool when injured; by water jogging, they can maintain aerobic fitness without stressing injured tissues. (See "Getting Started with Swimaerobics" earlier in this chapter.) Warm whirlpools are also a great place to stretch muscles and tendons before a workout. After a workout, a soak in the warm jets of water will ease muscle stiffness and soreness.

External analgesics can make exercising and recovery easier. Products containing methyl salicylate (oil of wintergreen) or menthol will warm up the skin, easing the stiffness that follows a tough workout. These over-the-counter products are also great shortcuts for warming up cold or tender muscles *before* a workout.

Family Fitness

We're all familiar with the old saw: The family that plays together stays together. The same is true of exercising. There's no need for you to feel guilty about leaving the kids behind as you run off to the gym or exercise class. You should encourage your children to participate in school sports, and involve the whole family in fitness activities. It's a great way to get or stay in shape while having some family fun.

GETTING YOUR KIDS TO EXERCISE, TOO

There was probably a day when kids got all of the exercise they needed just by playing outside with sisters, brothers and neighbors and by doing small chores. Those kids seem far different from the present television-viewing generation. Today, many children have few siblings to chase around, and they and their young neighbors may not be allowed to leave the safety of their homes. But that's no excuse. It may take a bit more effort these days, but your kids can still stay fit—with your help.

Set a good exercise example. If you're into keeping fit, your kids will be interested, too. Running, playing ball or tennis, swimming, hiking— these are all activities that can be enjoyed by the whole family. (See "Keeping Your Family Fit" later in this chapter.)

Encourage your school-age child to participate in school sports. Then back up your encouragement by your attendance. Although it's unlikely that you'll be able to attend every game or meet, make an attempt to be your child's cheerleader at as many events as possible.

KEEPING YOUR FAMILY FIT

Your children's ages will probably dictate the types of activities in which you can participate as a group. But be imaginative, and let the kids occasionally take the lead. Here are a few suggestions to keep your family fit.

Group activities can be enjoyed by two, three or ten people. That means the whole family, plus neighbors and friends, can participate. Skiing, sledding, bike riding, swimming or basketball can be enjoyed by just a few, or the whole gang can get involved. This is a great way for busy families to get involved in some neighborhood activities—try organizing a softball game with players from your neighborhood competing against a team from another part of town.

Playing at the playground is always an excellent source of exercise for the preschooler (and exhaustion for the parent). Spend an hour swinging, seesawing, running, jumping, climbing and sliding—you'll want to come home and soak in a warm bath after a romp like that!

Racquet sports are a challenging family activity. Racquetball and singles tennis can keep two people busy while the others take a rest. Or doubles play can drag the entire family onto the courts. You will be providing your children with the skills for an exciting lifelong activity by introducing them to racquet sports at an early age.

Running can be a great family sport. Even a 5-year-old can run a mile with some training. After you've gotten in some practice, you can participate in competitive and fun runs. With different distances and age categories, these runs provide good exercise for the whole family. You can arrive together, yet each family member competes at her or his own level. Although competitive running provides extra motivation, it's not a good idea to take it too seriously, especially with very young children, who may be discouraged if they're always coming in last.

Walking is an easy and inexpensive group activity. A brisk morning walk will get everyone "up and at 'em," while a leisurely nighttime stroll is a good way to wind down after a busy day. Infants can be carried in front carriers until about 6 months old, then in a framed backpack until Mom or Dad can't handle it any longer. Or use a stroller to roll along at a pleasant clip. Carrying a toddler, though, will give you a super workout. If the kids are too old to be carried, but too slow to give you an intense workout, try letting them ride a bike while you walk. That makes you the one who must keep up.

Exercising with Preschoolers

Starting the exercise habit early might be the kindest thing you could do for your child. Gymboree, a play and movement program designed for children 3 months to 4 years old, is cropping up all over the country. They have three programs to get your baby or toddler boogying.

Baby Gym (3 Months to 1 Year)

→ This age group needs a little help, so Gymboree instructors lead parents and babies in exercises called boogies. Baby's arms and legs are gently moved. Pull-ups, where baby is carefully pulled into a standing position, are also practiced.

→ Babies can be gently rolled on bright balls or left to squirm on cheerfully colored mats.

→ Although babies don't really play together, they can always enjoy the stimulating presence of other smiling babies in the room.

Gymboree (1 to 2½ Years)

→ This age group is practically uncontrollable, so lots of supervised free-play is in order.

→ Equipment might include a hollow ball that the little ones can roll around inside of or fabric tunnels that they can climb through.

→ This age group is encouraged to "do their own thing" with equipment that allows them to crawl, climb, push, pull and prod.

Gymgrad (2½ to 4 Years)

→ Children are ready for some structure and socializing at this age so play might include obstacle courses with a theme, follow-the-leader or tumbling.

→ "Gymborcises," or simple exercises, are also a lot of fun with this age group.

→ In addition to the more structured exercise activities, these children are also encouraged to play and explore on their own.

To find out more about Gymboree, and if there is a program in your area, contact Karen Anderson at the Gymboree national office: 872 Hickley Road, Burlingame, CA 94010 (415-692-8080).

KEEPING WINTER SPORTS SAFE FOR KIDS

Children love winter sports, often much more than adults do because they somehow remain oblivious to chilling temperatures and biting winds. That means extra caution should be taken to dress youngsters properly. Bundle them from head to toe and include waterproof boots, knitted face mask, sunglasses or goggles and sunscreen and moisturizer on the face and lips. It is equally important to keep the rigorous sports inspired by ice and snow safe and fun.

Ice hockey: Protect your budding athlete with a helmet, face mask and padding on vulnerable joints. Fighting is fashionable in this sport, so adult supervision is needed to prevent all sorts of injuries. Sportsmanship should be taught early. Hockey isn't a good sport for kids until the age of 8 or 9.

Ice skating: Skates should fit snugly, from ankle to heel to toe. Skating can be stressful on young muscle and skeletal systems, so make sure children take periodic rests. A 5- or 6-year-old child can safely begin skating.

Skiing: Winter injuries can be avoided with proper equipment. The selection of equipment should take into consideration the child's age, ability, weight and strength. Release settings on bindings should be regularly checked. With careful supervision, many 5-year-olds are ready to hit the slopes.

Sledding: Sledding is fun for everyone. Make sure the equipment is in good working order and the area is cleared of sharp objects, fences and unavoidable obstacles (such as a tree line right at the base of a giant hill).

3

Shortcuts to

Good Eating and Quick Cooking

When it comes to the food in our diets, most of us would probably do well to make some changes in our eating and cooking habits. There are many things you can do to eat healthier, but to make the greatest impact on your diet, you should follow these five rules for good eating: avoid eating too much fat, saturated fat and cholesterol; eat foods with adequate fiber; avoid eating too much salt; avoid eating a lot of sugar and eat a variety of foods. In addition, there are certain cooking techniques that will not only save you time in the kitchen, but will also result in healthier meals. In this chapter we'll show you how to make the most of the foods you eat and cook.

Fats

The average American's diet includes a lot more fat than is considered necessary. The American Heart Association recommends that no more than 30 percent of daily calories come from fats, but one meal at a fast-food restaurant can set you over the limit! Here are some general guidelines to help you cut down on the fats in your diet:

→ Choose lean meat, fish, poultry and dry beans and peas as protein sources.
→ Use skim or low-fat milk and milk products.
→ Moderate your use of egg yolks and organ meats.

→ Limit your intake of fats and oils, especially saturated fats such as butter, cream, lard and heavily hydrogenated fats. (Hydrogenated fats include many shortenings and foods containing palm and coconut oils. Palm and coconut oils, because they are less expensive than other oils, are the ones most often used in crackers and other commercial foods.)

→ Trim fat off meats and broil, bake or boil rather than fry them.

→ Moderate your use of foods that contain fat, such as breaded and deep-fried foods.

→ Read labels carefully to determine both the amount and type of fat present in the foods you buy (see "Shopping for Healthier Meat" later in this chapter).

CUTTING FAT IN MEATS AND FISH

Eating sensibly doesn't mean you have to *eliminate* fatty meats and fish from your diet. Follow the guidelines below to cut the fat out of these foods so you can continue to enjoy them.

Cut away the visible fat from all meat, roasts, steaks and chops. Remove the skin and fat from chicken and other poultry before cooking. This can cut the fat content by up to one-half.

When roasting, take the extra time to trim the meat well before putting it in the oven. Also remember to set the roast on a rack so the fat can run off, not around, the meat.

Spit-roast meats. This is an excellent cooking method because the slow cooking allows the meat to expel much of its fat. Don't coat the meat with high-calorie bottled sauces (a high calorie content often signifies a lot of fat). Rather, baste the meat with its own juices.

Stew or braise meats. Like spit-roasting, stewing allows the meat to give off its fat, which can then be skimmed off.

Cook roasts, chops, steaks, meatballs, hamburgers and other meat patties on a raised broiler pan. The excess fat will drip away into the lower pan.

Sauté meat, poultry and fish in a little seasoned stock or other liquid instead of in oil or butter. Stock can be frozen in ice-cube trays for use on an as-needed basis. Or, sauté chicken and fish in flavored vinegars or leftover cooking liquid from steamed vegetables.

Poach firm-fleshed fish and boned chicken. It's an ideal, tasty cooking method and it's quick. A good poaching liquid for fish or vegetables is a mixture of three parts water and one part lemon juice. A blend of four parts water and one part soy sauce is nice for chicken, vegetables and red meat. You can season the poaching liquid with vegetables and herbs.

Use stock, herbal tea or fruit juice instead of oil in marinades. If you're baking, cover the pan to keep the food moist. This is an ideal method for fish, vegetable casseroles and meat loaf.

When you're reheating meat, keep it moist and flavorful without adding fat. First, place a lettuce leaf in the bottom of a casserole or pie plate, then put the meat on the lettuce and cover it with another lettuce leaf. Add a little water to the bottom of the pan and heat at 350°F until the meat is warmed through.

Save the meat renderings in the bottom of the broiler pan to make a natural gravy without added fat or starch. To degrease the renderings quickly, place them in a heat-proof measuring cup, then submerge the cup in ice water so that it comes three-quarters of the way up, being careful not to get water inside the cup. The fat will rise to the top and begin to thicken so you can skim it off easily. If you have more time, you can alternatively place the cup of renderings in the freezer or refrigerator to cool. Reheat the remaining juices and season them with bouillon or herbs and spices to taste.

Thicken meat gravy without adding fat. First skim off excess fat from the pan drippings. Put 2 tablespoons of flour and 1 cup of water, stock or skim milk in a blender and give it a quick whirl, or shake it in a screw-top jar. Add the flour mixture to the pan drippings and stir constantly over medium heat until thickened.

Read canned fish labels carefully. Always choose tuna and other canned fish that are packed in water rather than oil.

SHOPPING FOR HEALTHIER MEAT

Reading the labels at the meat counter can be confusing. Although a label may tell you what *type* of meat you're buying, how do you know what's in it? And there are so many terms used to describe meat — *extra lean, super trim, prime, good* — how do you know what the differences are? Here's a rundown on what you should know about the meats you buy.

Read the labels. In over 3,000 stores you'll find that fresh meats now have nutrition labels, provided through the new meat Nutri-Facts program. If you don't see nutrition labels on the meats in your grocery store, ask the meat manager about it. The labels provide information about:

calories
cholesterol
iron
protein
sodium
thiamine, niacin and vitamin B_{12}
total fat (including a breakdown of saturated, monounsaturated and
    polyunsaturated fatty acids)
zinc

Know the terminology. The words *extra lean, gourmet lean* and *super trim* are not standard terms. They can mean one thing to one butcher and something else to another butcher. The words *prime, choice* and *good* are the only words on meat that are standard. These terms are initiated at the slaughterhouse to follow United States Department of Agriculture (USDA) standards. But not all meats are labeled with these terms because grading is voluntary. Those labeled *prime* are the most tender, but they also contain the most fat, cut per cut. Beef that is labeled *good* is the leanest. It will not be as juicy and tender, but it is still flavorful—and it is healthier for you. (On the other hand, pork that is highly marbled will be rated lower because marbling in pork results in a greasier cooked meat.)

Know your ground beef. The government labeling rule for ground beef is that the beef must not contain more then 30 percent fat. The beef industry has voluntarily established a "lean" standard, under which lean beef contains less than 24 percent fat and "extra lean" beef contains 15 percent or less fat. But because the action is voluntary, not all ground meat you see will be so labeled. If you are purchasing ground meat to make broiled hamburgers, don't buy the more expensive lean ground beef. Instead, buy ground chuck or meat just labeled "ground beef." Extra fat is not an issue because it will run off the burger as it is broiled. If you plan to use the ground beef in a dish where you *can't* pour off the fat, then buy the lean ground beef.

CUTTING FAT IN VEGETABLES

It's true that vegetables are naturally low in fat, but what we add to them while we're preparing them can start to tip the scales. Here are ways to prepare tasty vegetables without loading up on fats.

Instead of frying chopped onions in butter or oil, steam them. You'll find the flavor surprisingly sweet and the cooking less messy.

Sauté sliced vegetables with mushrooms. The mushrooms automatically give off lots of liquid, meaning you can use less oil to prevent your vegetables from sticking to the pan.

Steam, rather than fry, fat-absorbing vegetables such as eggplant. You can also lightly baste eggplant slices with a little vegetable oil and broil or bake them in the oven.

If you must use oil or butter to sauté, figure not more than ½ to 1 teaspoon per serving. Use the same rule when following recipes, even if the directions call for more.

Try Oriental sesame oil, extra virgin olive oil or walnut oil. They are excellent choices in recipes where a little oil is absolutely indispensable as a seasoning agent. These oils have highly concentrated flavors, so you need only a few drops of one of these to add taste to any dish—soups, salads, vegetables, sauces. It's a waste to fry with sesame or walnut oil because they are expensive. Instead, stir a few drops into the dish just before serving to add flavor.

Make a baked potato flavorful with a few drops of soy or Worcestershire sauce or an herb-and-spice blend. Or mash tofu with a little low-fat (imitation) mayonnaise. Add curry and herb seasoning to taste.

Use aromatic foods to add flavor to sauces instead of butter, cream or cheese. Some good choices include tomatoes (fresh or pureed), onions, garlic, mushrooms, peppers, leeks, fresh parsley, basil and thyme. Small amounts of such flavor concentrates are all you need.

Use pureed vegetables as the thickening base of a sauce. Tomatoes, carrots, mushrooms, spinach, broccoli, onions, leeks and watercress, for example, make excellent flavoring and good body for a sauce. Then, if you like, all you have to do is add a little cheese or low-fat milk (figure 1 tablespoon of either per serving) to enrich the sauce.

When you're making soup, you don't have to sauté vegetables in butter or oil first. Instead, either steam the vegetables using a little of the soup liquid in the covered pot, or simply omit this step and allow the vegetables to cook along with everything else in the soup. You can always add herbs or other fat-free seasonings for flavor, if necessary, as the soup cooks.

Defat soups, stocks and stews before reheating. The best way to do so is to refrigerate them for a few hours, then skim off all the congealed fat that forms on the top. Just reheat the dish to serve.

HOW ONE RECIPE LOST WEIGHT

Food scientists at the Rodale Food Center started with a luscious sour-cream coffee cake and, a bit regretfully, began to cut out the fat. After several tries, they came up with a revised recipe—still a little decadent for every day but a treat for a special occasion. The new version kept a rich taste but has less than half the fat of the original.

Low-Fat Coffee Cake

1 cup skim milk
1 cup low-fat yogurt

1 teaspoon baking soda
2 teaspoons baking powder
2½ cups whole wheat pastry flour
¼ ~~½~~ pound butter, softened
¾ cup honey
1 ~~2~~ eggs

~~½ pint sour cream~~
1 teaspoon vanilla
½ teaspoon lemon juice
3 cups peeled and sliced apples
¼ cup raisins
2 teaspoons cinnamon
¼ ~~1~~ cup chopped nuts

Preheat the oven to 375°F.

Combine baking soda, baking powder and flour. In a large bowl, cream together the butter and ½ cup of the honey until light and fluffy. Add the egg and beat well. Combine the milk, yogurt, vanilla and lemon juice.

Alternately add dry and wet ingredients to creamed mixture and blend thoroughly.

Coat an 8 × 10-inch pan or tube pan with nonstick spray. Pour in half the batter.

Mix half the apples with the raisins and 1 teaspoon of the cinnamon. Spread over batter. Drip half the remaining honey over the cinnamon mixture. Add the remaining batter and cover with the rest of the apples. Combine nuts and remaining cinnamon, and sprinkle on top of the apples. Drizzle the rest of the honey on top.

Bake at 375°F about 45 minutes.

Yields one 8 × 10-inch cake

CUTTING FAT IN FRIED AND BAKED FOODS

Although it's wise to avoid deep-fried foods such as fried chicken or french fries, there's no need to give up other fried foods such as pancakes and eggs. Here's how to cut fat in fried foods, as well as a tip on avoiding fat in baked goods.

Use nonstick pans or a nonstick vegetable spray whenever you fry. You can also use a well-seasoned pan for frying eggs, pancakes, crepes and similar foods. Use the spray in baking dishes, too.

Instead of frying corn tortillas for Mexican dishes, bake them in the oven. Wrap the tortillas securely in foil and bake just until hot and pliable, about 10 minutes at 375°F.

Crackers are often thought to be low in fat, but don't be fooled. Some crackers contain large amounts of shortening. When buying crackers or similar baked products, always check the ingredients list on the package. Avoid the product if oil or fat appears among the first three ingredients. In fact, avoid *any* packaged or processed food where oil and fat are listed in the top three ingredients.

CUTTING FAT IN DAIRY FOODS

Dairy foods are notoriously high in fat, but you *can* have your cheese and eat it, too. Just follow this fat-cutting advice.

You can reduce the fat content of sauces that call for cream, yet still retain the velvety, creamy texture. Substitute reconstituted nonfat dry milk made extra strength. Use ½ cup of milk powder to make 1 cup of milk.

Low-Fat "Sour Cream"

The fat content of this imitation is less than one-quarter that of sour cream.

1 cup part-skim ricotta cheese
1 cup plain low-fat yogurt

Process the ricotta cheese in a blender or food processor until smooth, then stir in the yogurt. Chill.
Yields 2 cups

When preparing dishes with milk, yogurt or cheese, always use nonfat, low-fat or skimmed dairy products. These include low-fat yogurt and cottage cheese, nonfat milk and part-skim mozzarella and Swiss cheese.

In recipes that call for ricotta cheese, substitute 1 percent low-fat or dry-curd cottage cheese. By doing so, you can reduce the calories by as much as 50 percent. If you want a smoother texture, cream the cottage cheese in a blender or food processor first.

To cut even more dairy calories in recipes, substitute mashed tofu for ricotta and cottage cheese. Since tofu is milder in flavor than the dairy cheese, you may want to add a little more seasoning to the recipe. Taste and see.

Substitute Neufchâtel, a soft dairy cheese, in place of cream cheese. It can cut up to 25 percent of your recipe's fat content.

Go easy on the hard cheese in recipes. When adding cheese to a recipe for flavor, calculate not more than 1 tablespoon of shredded hard cheese per serving.

Substitute farmer cheese for mozzarella. Heat the low-fat farmer cheese until the liquid separates. You'll be left with a mass of soft strings of cheese. Strain and use in place of mozzarella.

Substitute buttermilk and plain low-fat yogurt for milk and light cream in sauces and soups, cold or hot. To avoid curdling when you heat the sauce

---

Creamy, Low-Fat Dessert Topping

This is good on fresh fruit or cooked fruit desserts such as poached fruit, pies or cobblers.

1½ cups plain low-fat yogurt
　¼ cup nonfat dry milk
　2 tablespoons light honey
　　grated rind of one lemon

¼ teaspoon freshly grated nutmeg
dash ground ginger

　Combine all the ingredients and beat well.
　Yields 1½ cups

or soup, first mix 1 teaspoon cornstarch into 1 cup of the buttermilk or yogurt. You can also remove the pan from the heat and stir in the yogurt or buttermilk just before serving.

You can reduce the fat in salad dressings without losing flavor. Replace at least two-thirds of the oil in a basic vinaigrette dressing with pureed cucumber or plain low-fat yogurt.

Fiber

Lack of fiber in the diet has been linked to a host of ailments, from constipation to heart disease. (See "Preventing Disease with Fiber" in chapter 1.) Processed foods are the culprits—they contain far less fiber than their fresh counterparts. But some thoughtful menu changes can put the fiber back in your diet.

ADDING FIBER TO YOUR DIET

Throw away the white bread and the canned vegetables! Their fiber content is extremely low. Here are healthier eating alternatives:

Start your day off with a high-fiber breakfast. A bowl of oatmeal with berries and raisins, accompanied by a bran muffin, provides six times as much fiber as the typical breakfast of bacon and eggs with buttered toast.

Choose whole-grain breads and cereals. There are many whole-grain breads on the market. Two good choices are whole wheat and oatmeal bran. As for cereals, it's easy to be fooled by catchy boxes with the words "all natural" bannered across them. Be picky. Some good cereal choices include bran, shredded wheat, oatmeal, puffed rice and wheat and *unsweetened* whole-grain granola. Try a tablespoon of wheat germ sprinkled over your cereal for an extra fiber boost.

Eat plenty of raw vegetables and fruit. A cooked vegetable is a vegetable that's lost a lot of its fiber, not to mention a host of other nutrients. But if you're tired of munching on carrot and celery sticks, learn to enjoy the crisp taste of raw asparagus, broccoli and cauliflower. The next time you want a sweet snack, reach for a piece of fresh fruit. Low in calories and high in fiber, it's a lot better for you than cookies and cake.

Substitute starchy foods for those that have large amounts of fats and sugars. You'll not only be getting a good dose of fiber, but you'll also get that "full" feeling that many fatty foods give you. For example, eat whole-grain bread or cereal instead of pastries or doughnuts for breakfast, eat a whole baked potato instead of french fries, choose a brown rice pudding instead of ice cream for dessert.

Nibble on nuts and seeds. Forgo the potato chips, pretzels and other junky snacks. Peanuts, pistachios, pumpkin seeds and sunflower seeds contain plenty of fiber. Just be sure to avoid the high-fat, roasted and salted varieties—look for dry-roasted or raw.

Salt

The average American consumes 3,900 to 4,700 milligrams of sodium daily. But because our bodies conserve sodium, we really only need about 400 milligrams per day. The result—an epidemic of Americans with high blood pressure. You know salt isn't good for you, but maybe you're hooked on salty foods. Here's how to cut down.

REDUCING YOUR SODIUM INTAKE

It's not easy to give up the saltshaker, especially since most of us have been dining on salty foods since we were infants. Try some of these suggestions to help you kick the habit.

Cook without salt or with only small amounts of added salt. Start by not salting the water you cook your pasta in. Chances are, your family won't even notice. From there, cook vegetables in unsalted water, and don't salt your poultry before you roast it.

Take the saltshaker off the table. Try flavoring foods with herbs, spices and lemon juice instead. There are several brands of spice mixes on the market that are especially made as salt substitutes.

Limit your intake of salty foods. Potato chips, pretzels, salted nuts and popcorn, condiments (soy sauce, steak sauce, garlic salt), pickled foods, cured meats, some cheeses, some canned vegetables and soups and some salad dressings are loaded with salt. If you can't give up some of your snacks, at least buy the low-salt or unsalted varieties.

Read food labels carefully to determine the amount of sodium in the product. (See "Interpreting Food Labels for Less Salt" later in this chapter.) You'd be surprised at how many seemingly unsalted products contain a fair amount of the ingredient. For example, most breads, cakes, rolls, muffins, cookies and crackers are baked with salt.

SEASONING WITHOUT SALT

Keep a sturdy pepper mill near your stovetop and fill it with your favorite combination of the spices mentioned below. Add as much to the recipe as you normally would salt.

Use mustard seed and peppercorns as the bulk of your mixture. Add the other spices in small proportions according to taste. Measure with your eye. Fill the pepper mill three-quarters full with whole spices, then shake to blend them evenly.

Grind a little at first (only when cooking, not at the table). Gradually increase the amount as you grow accustomed to your favorite flavor.

For the Bulk of the Mixture

Black peppercorns: spicy and good with just about everything
White mustard seed: adds a pleasant bitter tang to most any dish
White peppercorns: strong flavor; use only for cooking; good for light-colored foods

For Variety (Use in smaller amounts.)

Anise seed: sweet licorice flavor; don't overuse
Celery seed: popular flavor with some reminiscence of salt
Coriander seed: adds a Latin or Oriental touch; use sparingly
Cumin seed: hot, chili flavor; great with any food, but use sparingly
Dark mustard seed: adds visible dark flecks, but adds a softer spark to food than the bolder white mustard
Dried onion chips: a sweet, pungent flavor of onion
Fennel seed: mellow, sweet licorice flavor; great for meats

Use low-sodium products to replace those that have a high sodium content. Many cheeses, luncheon meats, crackers and other foods are available in low-sodium versions. Try them. If you're making a sandwich or putting cheese on crackers, you probably won't miss the salt.

INTERPRETING FOOD LABELS FOR LESS SALT

Be wary of processed foods that don't have a low- or no-sodium label on them; they probably contain a good deal of salt. The biggest culprits are soups and condiments. Frozen and canned entrees and canned vegetables are also notorious for their high salt content. Sodium labels are appearing on more and more food containers these days and can be very useful in helping you cut down on salt. Here are the five labels most often found and what they mean:

Sodium free: Foods contain fewer than 5 milligrams of sodium per serving.

Very low sodium: Foods contain no more than 35 milligrams of sodium per serving.

Low sodium: Foods contain no more than 140 milligrams of sodium per serving.

Reduced sodium: Sodium content of food reduced by 75 percent. (Data for "before" and "after" the sodium content was reduced must be present on the label.)

Unsalted, no salt added, or without added salt: No salt was added to a product that is normally processed with salt. The number of milligrams of sodium per serving must still be listed.

CREATING LOW-SODIUM, LOW-FAT SALAD DRESSINGS

That low-salt, low-calorie bowl of salad becomes a dieter's nightmare when it gets doused with high-fat, calorie- and salt-laden dressings. To keep your salads lean but tasty, try some of these suggestions.

→ Sprinkle fresh citrus juices on salads just as they are. Or make up blends of fresh lemon, orange, lime, tangerine, grapefruit or ugli fruit (a cross between an orange and a grapefruit) juices.

→ Blend fresh ripe tomatoes or whole canned tomatoes (ones that have no salt added) and let them marinate overnight at room temperature with different blends of minced garlic, onion, parsley, celery, coriander or scallions. Add basil, oregano, marjoram or tarragon leaves. Grind white or black pepper, white or black mustard seed, celery seed, anise seed or fennel seed for some zing and flavor.

→ Peel and puree cucumbers with fresh dill, dijon mustard and yogurt cheese (which is plain yogurt that you have drained in a cheesecloth pouch or cheesecloth-lined colander for several hours).

→ Blend low-sodium, low-fat, cottage cheese with skim milk, garlic powder, chopped red and green sweet peppers, chopped parsley and celery leaves.

→ Blend balsamic vinegar, low-sodium chicken stock and a wisp of tomato paste. Add minced garlic and chopped fresh basil.

Sugar

The average American adult consumes 120 pounds of sugar a year. And judging by the line at the candy counter after school, kids probably consume far more! The price we pay for our sweet tooth is steep—tooth decay, obesity and diabetes are the main results. Although it's easy to spot sugars in things like candy and cake, it's not so easy to identify sugars in the other foods we eat. Here's what to look for and how to satisfy your sweet tooth without sacrificing good nutrition.

CUTTING OUT THE SUGAR IN YOUR DIET

You may find it easy to say no to a chocolate bar, but what about a glass of fruit punch or even a fruit-flavored yogurt? They contain sugar, too. Follow these suggestions for ways to cut down on sugar consumption.

Read food labels for clues on sugar content. If the name sugar, sucrose, glucose, maltose, dextrose, lactose, fructose, corn syrup or any other syrup appears first or near the top of the list, then there is a large amount of sugar in that product.

Use less of all sugars and foods containing large amounts of sugars. This includes white sugar, brown sugar, raw sugar, honey and syrups. Soft drinks, candies, cakes and cookies are obvious foods to avoid, but there's also a lot of sugar in many processed foods such as salad dressings, barbecue sauces and the like.

Reach for a piece of fruit instead of a piece of candy. Melons, berries and other fruits are sweet enough to handle your craving, and they provide nutrition as well as fiber. If you buy canned fruit, buy fruit processed without syrup or with light rather than heavy syrup.

How often you eat sugar and foods containing sugar is as important to the health of your teeth as how much sugar you eat. If you simply must have something sweet to eat, eat it all at once, then brush your teeth or rinse your mouth. The worst thing you can do is snack on sweets throughout the day. The sugar left in your mouth creates the perfect environment for bacteria to flourish. (See "Dental Care" in chapter 1.)

DECORATING CAKES NATURALLY

Homemade cakes need not be trimmed only with sticky, sweet frostings. There are some lovely and delicious things that you can do to add a special finishing touch without weighing down your baked creation with lots of fats and calories.

Try yogurt cheese for frosting. It's easy to make: just take plain yogurt and drain it in a cheesecloth-lined strainer for several hours (you can put the strainer in your kitchen sink) until it takes on the consistency of cream cheese, then refrigerate. It's firmer, sweeter and milder than regular yogurt. If desired, add natural food colorings, sweeten with honey or maple syrup and flavor with vanilla or orange extract.

Pipe borders or flowers with a pastry bag of pureed currants, raisins or other dried fruit. Moisten fruit with a tablespoon of apple juice, if necessary. (To edge a 12-inch cake, use about ¾ cup pureed raisins.)

Find alternatives to dusting with confectioner's sugar. You can lay a doily or other stencil on top of the cake, then sprinkle cinnamon over it and gently lift it off to reveal the pattern. Or use popcorn that has been popped and then ground into a fine white powder in a blender or food processor.

Use frozen skim milk in place of whipped cream. Freeze skim milk until ice crystals form (about 2 hours). Add vanilla, if desired, and whip 5 to 7 minutes. Use like whipped cream but serve immediately because it falls quickly.

Find alternatives to colored sugar decorations. Try sprinkling shredded dried papaya on cakes or cookies. It has a lovely orange color. Or cut decorative shapes out of dried fruit leather.

MAKING SUGAR-FREE BEVERAGES

Stop buying soda and, instead, make these quick and healthy sugar-free drinks.

Serve water with a twist of lemon or lime. It's the best and lowest-calorie thirst quencher. On hot days, keep a quart of it in the refrigerator so it's nice and cold when you want it. Discard and refill daily for freshest taste.

Use water to dilute a higher-calorie fruit juice. You can dilute cranberry (125 calories per 6-ounce glass) or grape (125 calories per 6-ounce glass) juice without losing much flavor. Try using seltzer or carbonated water instead of plain water; it will give your drink a fizz, turning it into a natural soda.

Mix orange or pineapple juice with unsweetened iced tea. Garnish with mint leaves or a slice of orange, lemon or lime.

Combine fruit juices for a change of pace. Try cranberry with orange, or grape with apple. For a hot beverage, heat half pineapple and half

SEVEN SUPER DRINKS

When you're tired of drinking the same old thing, try one of these beverages to perk up your taste buds.

Hot and Spicy Warm-Up

5 cups low-sodium tomato
  juice
¼ cup molasses
4 whole cloves

1 cinnamon stick
1 teaspoon Worcestershire
  sauce

    Combine all the ingredients in a saucepan and simmer for 5 minutes. This makes a delicious hot and spicy warm-up.
    Yields 5 cups

Creamy Fruit Cooler

½ cup pineapple juice
½ cup grapefruit juice
1 cup plain low-fat yogurt

2 tablespoons honey
  mint garnish

    In a bowl or pitcher, combine the juices, yogurt and honey. Pour into glasses and garnish with mint.
    Yields 2 cups

Orange Shake

1 cup orange juice
1 tablespoon sifted powdered
  carob
  dash of vanilla

    Combine all the ingredients in a blender. Serve over crushed ice.
    Yields 1 cup

(continued)

SEVEN SUPER DRINKS — *Continued*

Hot, Spiced Milk

1 cup milk
1 tea bag (any type)

Heat the milk almost to boiling and then steep your favorite tea bag in it. (A good choice is an almond-flavored tea.)
Yields 1 cup

Grape Sparkler

1½ cups white grape juice
2 cups red hibiscus tea

1 cup sparkling mineral water
mint garnish

In a pitcher, combine the grape juice, tea and sparkling mineral water. Serve garnished with mint.
Yields 4½ cups

Peach Cooler

1 sliced, peeled peach
1 tray of ice cubes
1½ cups fruit juice (any flavor)

In a blender or food processor, blend the peach with the ice cubes and fruit juice until slushy.
Yields 2 cups

Five-Fruit Punch

½ cup orange or pineapple juice
½ cup cubed melon
½ cup red raspberries or
    strawberries

1 medium-sized ripe banana
2 cups apple juice

Combine all the ingredients in a blender.
Yields 3 cups

grapefruit juice with stick cinnamon and cloves. You can also try mixing herbal teas with fruit juices, hot or cold.

Spice up your tea with cinnamon and cloves. Use them instead of honey or sugar. Spices offer plenty of flavor but no calories.

Whip up a low-calorie milk shake. Fresh fruit and skim milk can be combined for delicious, potassium- and calcium-rich drinks. Use a touch of vanilla extract; it increases perceived sweetness.

Variety

A healthy diet consists of foods from many sources—whole grains, dairy products, fresh fruits and vegetables. To keep yourself on the right track, and to keep meals interesting, try some of these alternatives to the usual breakfast, lunch and snack fare.

PREPARING BETTER BREAKFASTS

If you're one of those people whose breakfast consists of a hurriedly gulped down sugary doughnut or gooey pastry, you know you're not getting much nutritional value in your morning meal. Try one of these quick breakfasts, instead, and get your day off to a better start.

Make a breakfast milk shake. Blend together yogurt or milk, cut-up fresh, frozen or unsweetened canned fruit, some flavorings, such as almond, vanilla or fresh mint, and a dab of maple syrup or honey. (To add extra calcium, add a few teaspoons of powdered nonfat dry milk.)

Make "instant" hot cereal. The night before, rinse ¼ cup of whole wheat berries, pour into a large thermos and add 1 cup of boiling water. (Make sure there are several inches of headspace left for expansion.) Put on the cap and leave overnight. In the morning, pour the "cooked" wheat into a cereal bowl, add milk or yogurt and fresh or dried fruit.

Make an alternative to pancake syrup. Try a one-minute applesauce made by cubing fresh apples and whirling them in a blender. Or add a few fresh strawberries to the blended apples and whirl again.

Make baked apples for dinner and have the leftovers for breakfast. They will keep for several days and are good heated in the toaster oven or microwave; serve with warm milk and top with granola.

Make juice pops for the kids. If your kids don't like to drink their morning orange juice, they may enjoy a homemade frozen o.j. pop.

Make quick, ready-to-go breakfast foods. If you have a family that doesn't eat breakfast together, have readily available, healthy breakfast foods on hand. Here are some suggestions. Keep these foods in a special corner or special container in the refrigerator so they're easily found:

> bread, for toast
> brown bread and
>   Neufchâtel or
>   low-fat ricotta cheese
> cold leftovers
> cottage cheese
> cut-up fruit
> deviled eggs
> frozen French toast
> frozen waffles
> granola
> raisin bread
> ready-to-eat cereals
> stewed prunes
> sliced cheese
>   (for grilled cheese sandwiches
>   or to eat on apple slices)
> tiny finger sandwiches

Not hungry for breakfast? Drink some juice or eat a piece of fruit before you leave home, and then have a sandwich for a mid-morning snack.

Make breakfast pudding. Start off a cold morning with this warm breakfast pudding: add raisins, milk and maple syrup to leftover cooked rice or vermicelli, then heat. Soups are also quick and comforting for a cold day. Some good ones are corn chowder, cream of chicken, clam chowder, bean and split pea.

Make a breakfast sandwich. Take French toast or waffles and put tomato slices, banana slices, peanut butter and/or cheese between them. Or make cheesy waffles by sprinkling grated cheese over cooked waffles and broiling them for a few minutes.

BRIGHTENING UP BREAKFASTS WITH FRUIT

When you think of fruit at breakfast time, don't limit yourself to a few banana slices on top of cold cereal or a melon wedge on the side. Try some of these more imaginative ways to brighten breakfast with fruit.

→ Serve a scoop of frozen yogurt or ice milk in a fruit juice.

→ Top a cantaloupe half with cottage cheese or yogurt.

→ Try a mug of hot tomato juice or tomato soup flavored with herbs, such as oregano or basil.

→ Mix and chill different fruits, or fruits with a juice, for example, cantaloupe balls with strawberries and orange juice, berries with sliced peaches or sliced bananas with oranges.

→ Broil a grapefruit half topped with a tablespoon or two of fruit juice such as cranberry juice or orange juice.

→ Blend fruit juices such as pineapple juice and grapefruit juice, or cranberry juice and orange juice.

→ Freeze fruit juices in an ice-cube tray to make juice cubes. Then use these juice cubes to chill other fruit juices.

PLANNING HEALTHY BROWN-BAG LUNCHES

For most of us, packing a lunch means just one more peanut butter and jelly or cold cut sandwich. But you can eat healthier food, plus give yourself more energy for the afternoon ahead, if you try one of these ideas instead.

Plan meals so you have leftovers. Many kinds of foods taste as good—or even better—the next day. (See the box "Some Foods Are Better the Next Day" on the next page.)

Pass up lunch meats. Pack the healthier home-cooked sliced chicken, turkey or roast beef instead. You'll be avoiding all that extra salt and you'll save money, too.

Keep your kitchen stocked with "take-out" paraphernalia. This includes sandwich bags and other food wrappings, small plastic dishes with lids, a thermos and other handy-sized thermal containers, plastic utensils and napkins. This way, you've got what you need on hand to pack lunch when you're in a hurry, rather than figure you'll just have to eat out.

Prepare sandwich fillings a day or two ahead of time. Then store them in the refrigerator. You can then make up a quick sandwich in the morning.

SOME FOODS ARE BETTER THE NEXT DAY

If you're always looking for new ideas on how to get more from your leftovers, read on.

Barbecued chicken: Wings and legs are especially good when eaten cold the next day.

Beef: Slice leftover beef to use in sandwiches; purchase frozen puff pastry and make your own turnovers with ground beef; cube beef for adding to salads (beef is particularly good with potatoes).

Breaded baked chicken: Eat cold the next day.

Chili: Package the chili in portion sizes and freeze for later lunches. It can be eaten cold, or warm if the workplace has a microwave for employees.

Hard-cooked eggs: Use in salad as wedges; make deviled eggs or slice or mash with mayonnaise in sandwiches.

Noodle or rice puddings: Eat cold the next day.

Pasta: Make a pasta salad.

Poached chicken: Use in salads.

Poached fish: Use in salads or just eat cold—salmon is particularly good this way. Another alternative is to add a simple oil and vinegar dressing to the cold fish.

Quiche: Eat cold the next day.

Rice, barley and buckwheat groats: Make a cold grain salad.

Shrimp: Serve cold any number of ways, including with a horseradish and tomato sauce.

Stir-fried dishes: Eat cold the next day.

Turkey: Use slices for sandwiches or cut into chunks for salads.

Vegetables: Marinate them and add to green salads, grain salads or potato salad.

Wash lettuce and other greens for sandwiches and wrap in a tea towel. They'll keep for a few days. You can then pull out small amounts for your sandwiches.

Take a frozen food with you. It'll thaw out by midday, and in the meantime keep your packed fruit or drink chilled. This works especially well with yogurt.

Pack a pita bread and a salad separately. Combine them at lunchtime to make a healthy, fresh sandwich that isn't soggy.

Always carry a snack with you. Then when you are enticed by vending-machine food, you are better able to resist because you already have a nutritious snack on hand.

REACHING FOR HEALTHY SNACKS

The next time you get the urge to munch on chips or other junk food, reach for these healthy snacks instead.

Refrigerated snacks can satisfy a craving for something crunchy. Have on hand plenty of washed and sliced vegetables, whole or sliced fresh fruit, fruit canned in natural fruit juices, fresh juices, leftovers that could be eaten cold or warm, salads or low-fat cheeses. Keep them in one section of the refrigerator, possibly on a turntable that can be easily seen and moved by children and adults looking into the refrigerator.

Popcorn is a good low-calorie snack. Made in a hot-air popper and served without butter or salt, a handful weighs in at a mere 6 calories—compare that to 114 calories in 10 potato chips! You can add flavor by sprinkling with garlic powder, grated cheese or chili powder.

Tuna is high in protein and low in calories if packed in water rather than oil. Try it on a bed of low-fat cottage cheese. For a tasty, low-calorie, mayonnaise-free tuna salad, mix some lime juice, low-fat yogurt and a favorite herb with the tuna.

Raw, cut vegetables are great snacks—until you go and dunk them in a sour cream-and-onion dip. To keep the calories and fat down, try a yogurt and fresh herb dip. Take plain yogurt and add your favorite fresh herbs for flavor. (Dried herbs cannot duplicate the taste of fresh ones in a dip.)

Zucchini or carrot sticks get a real flavor lift when marinated in a mixture of soy sauce, rice vinegar, mustard seed, chili pepper, ginger and garlic.

Cherry tomatoes are portable, pop-in-your-mouth snacks. Try them scooped out and stuffed with a combination of cottage cheese, scallion, and parsley.

Quick Cooking

In this hectic, fast-paced world, many of us say we would eat better if only we had the *time* to prepare healthy meals. Well, that's not an excuse any more. Here are nutritious meals you can prepare ahead of time, meals that can be cooked in a flash, quick breads and rice—even timesaving tips for planning those holiday and party meals.

QUICK COOKING FOR ONE

Single cooks have a tough time preparing healthy recipes for one. First, there just aren't a lot of good one-serving recipes around, and second, many recipes seem to be too much bother when there's no one else to share the meal. Here are some shortcuts for preparing quick, healthy meals for one.

Use your freezer. A freezer is a single cook's best friend. It makes eating a variety of good-tasting, homemade foods quite easy. You can avoid the "cook it once and eat it all week" syndrome, as well as the steady diet of commercial frozen entrees. Prepare a recipe for four, wrap each serving individually and freeze. You have created your own single-serving frozen entrees that can be heated in the toaster oven or the microwave. You may wish to try a chicken and vegetable stir-fry dish, a Swiss steak and egg noodle dish, lasagna, a meat stew or vegetable stew (such as ratatouille). Just look in the freezer section of your supermarket for other frozen entree ideas.

Consider buying a microwave oven. Microwaves are a single cook's *next* best friend. Frozen cooked foods heated in the microwave do not need to be thawed first. Freeze or refrigerate leftovers in microwavable containers such as microfreeze bags, freezer-weight zip-locking bags and single-serving microwave cookware with lids.

Purchase fresh produce in small amounts. That way, it doesn't spoil before you get around to eating it all. Or find a supermarket with a salad bar; it's a good way to buy a one- or two-day supply of mixed salad and trimmings.

FIVE TIMESAVING PIECES OF EQUIPMENT

We asked the cooks in the Rodale Food Center to tell us what kitchen tools save them the most time each day. Here are the winners, in order of popularity.

French knife: If properly used and kept sharp, it can make slicing vegetables and cutting and dicing meats very easy. (Use a knife sharpener frequently and don't let the knife sit wet in the sink or on the counter—water will dull its edge.) The French knife is economical, takes up little space, and is easy to clean.

Food processor: Although it can sometimes be an inconvenience to clean, it's wonderful for doing a host of jobs quickly and easily. You'll save cleanup time if you can arrange your cutting, grinding and mixing in an order that doesn't mean cleaning the bowl and blade after each use.

Convection oven: This oven cooks food faster than a conventional oven because heat is actually blown around the food. And, unlike microwaves, it will brown foods. Baked goods, quiches and poultry bake faster and better in the convection oven than in the microwave. A convection oven makes a great second oven.

Microwave oven: This is definitely a shortcut in the kitchen. Foods can be heated in seconds. It is a natural companion to a freezer because frozen meals can be defrosted and cooked in minutes. Reheating leftovers goes quickly, too.

Large cast iron pot with lid or wok with lid: You can whip up quick one-pot dinners by stir-frying sliced vegetables and meats in either. (See "Preparing Quick Stir-Fry Meals" later in this chapter.)

COOKING QUICK MEALS WITH YOUR MICROWAVE

Don't use your microwave oven only when you need to thaw or heat up foods quickly. It's the ultimate time-saver when it comes to preparing full-fledged meals. Here's how to get the most out of your microwave.

Baked Goods

You can do a quick check for live yeast before you bake. Mix the yeast with the recipe's sweetener, the liquid and ¼ cup of the recipe's flour. Then microwave on the lowest power, covered, for 1 minute. If this batter is slightly bubbly and seems to be moving, then the yeast is fine.

You can defrost ingredients quickly. If you're ready to bake but some of your ingredients are frozen, don't invite unwanted microbes by defrosting them slowly. Instead, bring them to room temperature in the microwave.

Fish

You can cook clams and oysters quickly. Place six in a circle with their opening edges facing the center. (Microwaves penetrate the part of the food closest to the perimeter of the oven first, so that part gets cooked the most. You must place the least tender or densest part toward the outside and the tender or thinnest sections toward the inside so they don't get overcooked.) Microwave on full power for about 4 minutes or until all the shells are open.

You can cook eight medium shrimp in their shells to perfection. Set the microwave on full power for about 30 seconds. Let the shrimp stand another 30 seconds before serving.

You can get the most flavor and best texture from frozen fish. First bring it to room temperature for 1 to 2 minutes on low power before you actually cook it in the microwave. Then microwave as usual. If you're microwaving fresh fish, keep in mind that lean fish, such as flounder, microwave better than fatty types. Try smothering the fish with chopped tomatoes and basil, then microwave, covered, on full power for about 4½ minutes.

Fruits and Nuts

You can plump raisins and other dried fruit quickly. Lightly sprinkle 1 cup of the dried fruit with juice or water. Then cover and microwave on full power for 1 minute, stirring after about 30 seconds. Let the fruit stand about 4 minutes before using it in baking, on cereals, in compotes or as a snack.

You can shell nuts easily. Place a handful in a covered dish with enough water to cover them. Microwave on full power for 4 to 5 minutes. Drain,
(continued on page 92)

THE FOUR-CORNER METHOD FOR MICROWAVING HEARTY VEGETABLES

This quick, easy way of preparing whole, dense vegetables such as potatoes, squash and root vegetables guarantees moist, even cooking.

1. Place a single paper towel on the floor of the microwave.
2. Place one whole vegetable on each corner of the towel. If using less than four vegetables, leave extra corners empty. Be sure to position vegetables so the thicker, or denser, end of each is facing out.
3. Check the microwave cooking chart on page 90 for total cooking time. Divide that time into four periods. (For example, if total time equals 6 minutes, each period equals 1½ minutes.)
4. Microwave the vegetables for one time period. Advance them clockwise on the towel (see the illustration), then microwave for another time period. Repeat until the vegetables have been microwaved four times.

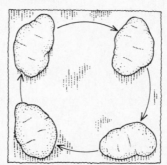

5. As you advance each vegetable, rotate it clockwise from top to bottom one-quarter turn. At the end of four periods, the vegetable will have rolled almost completely over.

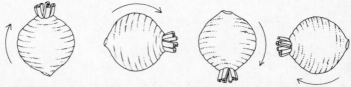

6. Allow vegetables to remain in their final positions for the amount of standing time called for in the chart.

Microwave Cooking Chart

Vegetable	Amount	Approximate Cooking Time on High (100%)	Standing Time
Acorn squash	1 medium (1 lb)	6–8 minutes	5 minutes
	1 large (2 lb)	10-12 minutes	5 minutes
Beets	5-6 medium (1 lb)	8-10 minutes	3 minutes
Butternut squash	1 small (1 lb)	6-8 minutes	5 minutes
	1 medium (2 lb)	10-12 minutes	5 minutes
Carrots	5-6 medium (1 lb)	8-10 minutes	3 minutes
Parsnips	3-4 medium (1 lb)	6-8 minutes	3 minutes
Potatoes (baking)	2 medium (1 lb)	6-8 minutes	4 minutes
Rutabagas (yellow turnips)	2 medium (1 lb)	8-10 minutes	3 minutes
Spaghetti squash	1 small (2 lb)	12 minutes	5 minutes
	1 medium (3 lb)	16 minutes	5 minutes
	1 large (4 lb)	20 minutes	5 minutes
Sweet potatoes	2 medium (1 lb)	6-8 minutes	4 minutes
Turnips	8 small or 4 medium (1 lb)	6-8 minutes	3 minutes

Prep and
Cooking Tips

Rinse; pierce skin; use four-corner method

Rinse; cut stems to ¼ inch; slice off root end. Stand on stem end around perimeter of flat platter. Spin platter clockwise one-quarter turn every quarter of cooking period

Rinse; pierce skin; use four-corner method. *Note:* Place with stem end facing out, and bulb facing in (the bulb is hollow and contains seeds)

Scrub; peel, if desired. Arrange in a radial pattern on a flat platter, pointed ends facing in. Spin platter clockwise one-quarter turn every quarter of cooking period

Scrub or peel; arrange in a radial pattern on a flat platter, pointed ends facing in. Cover with plastic wrap. Spin platter clockwise one-quarter turn every quarter of cooking period

Scrub; pierce skin; use four-corner method

Rinse; cut thin slice off root end. Place stem end up on paper towel; use four-corner method

Rinse; pierce skin; use variation of four-corner method: place squash parallel to and close to oven door. Roll squash clockwise one-quarter turn every quarter of cooking period

Scrub; pierce skin; use four-corner method

Rinse; pierce skin; arrange around perimeter of flat platter. Spin platter clockwise one-quarter turn every quarter of cooking period let them cool and dry, then shell. Shell chestnuts by slitting the shells, then microwaving a handful, uncovered, on full power for about 45 seconds.

Poultry

You can cook odd-shaped meats, such as chicken legs, evenly. Arrange the pieces in a circle with the meaty parts facing the edge. This way, the microwaves will reach the meatiest parts first, so the pieces cook more evenly.

Sauces, Marinades and Flavorings

You can preserve nutrients in your sauces. Heat up sauces in the microwave in a measuring cup (instead of a shallow dish) to cut down on cooking time. The shorter the cooking time, the more nutrients are preserved.

You can reduce salt and fat in your recipes by quick marinating. Instead of marinating overnight, microwave marinated food for 1 to 2 minutes on the lowest power before you cook it.

You can give microwaved foods a quick lift with flavorings. Instead of sautéing fish and vegetables in butter, reduce saturated fats by microwaving them along with fragrant lemon slices and herbs. Enhance flavors by using provocative aromatics such as ginger and scallion with chicken, or grated lime peel and garlic with shrimp.

Vegetables

You can preserve maximum nutrition in vegetables by quick cooking. Vegetables such as broccoli and asparagus should be arranged in a circle with the tender buds facing the middle. This exposes the tough stalks to more intense cooking. Whenever you cook more than one kind of vegetable at a time, cut all pieces the same size. Combining vegetables that have similar textures also helps—for instance, cook root vegetables together.

You can peel fresh tomatoes and peppers quickly and easily. Microwave tomatoes on full power for approximately 1 minute. When you want to remove the skin from a fresh pepper, you can skip the traditional long-roasting method. Simply microwave it on full power for 3 minutes, turning the pepper three times. Then wrap it loosely and place it in the freezer until cool. The skin will peel easily.

COOKING MEAT AND FISH QUICKLY

You don't need a microwave to cook these meats and fish quickly. Just follow the shortcuts outlined below.

Meat/Fish	Quick-Cooking Method
Beef flank steak, whole	Marinate in a mixture of olive oil, ground pepper and mustard seed; broil to medium and slice thinly
Beef flank steak, sliced into strips	Toss strips with soy sauce, sesame oil and garlic; quickly stir-fry with green and red peppers
Chicken breast, whole with bone	Poach in savory bouillon
Chicken breast, deboned	Flatten with mallet, cleaver or pot; marinate 1 hour in Italian or French salad dressing; broil quickly on both sides
Chicken breast, deboned and cut into ½-inch slices	Flatten with mallet, cleaver or pot; dust with seasoned flour; sauté in olive oil
Chicken wings	Remove tip and cut into two joints; marinate overnight in the refrigerator in hot sauce, Worcestershire sauce or vinegar and garlic; drain and broil quickly on both sides; cook the marinade for dipping
Turkey breast, boneless and sliced into steaks or cutlets	Dust with a mixture of paprika; sizzle both sides in a skillet rubbed with oil; serve with taco or enchilada sauce
Fish fillet (bluefish, mackerel, tuna—8 oz per serving)	Top with onion, green or red peppers and lemon slices and sprinkle with paprika; wrap in foil and bake in 450°F oven 8 to 10 minutes OR Mix bread crumbs, mustard and chopped scallions into a paste and spread over fillets; broil 6 inches from broiler for 6 to 8 minutes
Fish fillet (boneless cod, haddock, halibut—6 oz per serving), cut into 1-inch chunks	Bring one can of whole crushed tomatoes and one can of chicken stock or water to a rolling boil; add sliced onion and celery, minced garlic and parsley; simmer for 10 minutes; remove from heat and fold in fish chunks. Steep for 5 minutes. Serve with boiled potatoes or noodles
Fish fillet (boneless catfish, monkfish, tilefish—8 oz per serving)	Poach in half orange juice and half water; chill; blend lemon juice, chopped celery, mayonnaise or yogurt and a dash ground white pepper; pour over fish; serve on greens

QUICK-COOKING BAKED POTATOES

Baked potatoes taste great and are great for you, but they take so long to cook! Here are some ways to cut down on that baking time:

→ Use potato nails.
→ Use potato hooks.
→ Bake potatoes on the floor of the oven, instead of on a rack.
→ Microwave for about 4 minutes per potato on full power.

BAKING QUICK, EASY HOMEMADE BREAD

You don't have to spend all day in the kitchen baking a loaf of bread. Take these shortcuts and you'll be slicing into a fresh, warm loaf in no time.

Measure dry ingredients into a basic mix ahead of time. Keep in a cool, dry spot, or in your freezer. (Be sure to warm up the frozen mix to room temperature before you bake with it; cool mix could make yeast ineffective.) This mix can be used for quick bread or basic yeast bread. You can also vary the additions to create different flavored breads.

Add some unbleached flour or gluten flour to whole wheat bread flour. This makes the dough easier to knead and develops the gluten.

Cut down on the salt in your recipe. Salt slows down the rising process, so cut the salt down to ½ teaspoon per loaf. (If you cut it out altogether, the bread may rise quickly, but it'll also fall quickly.)

Use quick-rise yeast. In the Rodale Food Center, we compared quick-rise and traditional yeasts by making the same roll and bread recipes with each. The quick-rise bread took half an hour to rise; the bread made with the traditional yeast took an hour. Quick-rise yeast is available in your supermarket.

Add sweetener to the yeast-and-water mixture. It will hasten the growing action of the yeast.

Proof your yeast quickly in the microwave. (See "Cooking Quick Meals with Your Microwave" earlier in this chapter.)

Instead of kneading the bread by hand, use a food processor or mixer equipped with a dough hook. There will be no noticeable difference in the texture of the dough whether it is kneaded by hand or machine.

Bake several loaves at a time. Bread freezes well and may be kept for three to four months successfully.

If your family is small, bake mini-loaves. One mini-loaf may be just enough to give you a fresh-baked or reheated loaf for dinner without leftovers or waste.

Make a no-knead bread. Beat the ingredients together, pour into the pan, let rise and then bake. (See the box "Quick-Rise Whole Wheat Bread" below).

Quick-Rise Whole Wheat Bread

4½ cups whole wheat flour
  1 cup wheat germ
  1 package quick-rise yeast
  ¼ teaspoon salt

2 cups hot water (120° to
  150°F)
¼ cup blackstrap molasses
1 tablespoon sesame seeds

Combine 4 cups whole wheat flour, the wheat germ, yeast and salt in a large bowl. Measure the hot water in a glass quart measuring cup and add the molasses to it.

Pour the molasses and water mixture into the flour mixture. With a wooden spoon, stir to combine. Add the remaining ½ cup flour. The mixture will be slightly sticky. When well combined, knead several minutes, adding only enough flour to keep the dough from sticking to your hands.

Cover the bowl with a cloth and allow to rest 15 minutes. Butter two 7⅜ × 3⅝-inch bread pans. Preheat the oven to 400°F.

After 15 minutes, divide the dough in half and press into the bread pans. Top with sesame seeds. Cover with a cloth and allow the bread to rise in a warm place for 15 minutes or until the dough rises just to the top of the pans. Bake for 40 to 50 minutes or until the top and sides are brown and crusty. Allow the bread to cool for 10 minutes, remove from the pans and cool completely on a rack before slicing.

Yields two 7⅜ × 3⅝-inch loaves

TWO QUICK-COOKING WHOLE GRAINS

Many cooks avoid using whole grains because they take so long to cook. Well, here are two grains that you can have ready to serve in no time.

Bulgur

Partially cooked wheat, or bulgur, leads the list here, because it isn't actually cooked at all. You merely soak it in boiling water. Pour at least two parts boiling water or stock over one part grain and let it soak until the texture is right (about 15 to 20 minutes). Drain off the excess water and you're done. If you want to cook it because you're going to be serving it hot, just use the same proportions and boil the bulgur in a pot with the liquid.

Bulgur tastes, not surprisingly, like wheat and resembles brown rice in texture. Served plain or lightly seasoned with butter or margarine, bulgur goes well with foods you'd normally accompany with rice.

Kasha

This dish, made from roasted buckwheat groats, can be ready in about 20 minutes. Make sure you buy the roasted groats for this; they're darker than plain buckwheat groats.

1 egg, lightly beaten
1 cup groats
   cooking oil
2 cups boiling water or stock

Thoroughly mix the beaten egg into the groats. Sauté the mixture in a little oil until the egg just dries. Cover with the boiling water or stock, and simmer until the liquid is absorbed (10 to 15 minutes). The flavor will remind you of made-from-scratch buckwheat pancakes, and the texture will be similar to fried rice.

Yields 1 cup

CUTTING THE COOKING TIME FOR BROWN RICE

Although white rice takes from 12 to 14 minutes to cook whereas brown rice takes up to 45 minutes, brown rice is the more nutritious choice. White rice is enriched just as white bread is, meaning a few nutrients are returned to it after processing, but much of the fiber, fat and other nutrients contained in the discarded bran and germ are lost. If the longer cooking time is the only reason you're not eating brown rice, here are some ways to cut it down.

Bring the water to a boil first before adding the rice. This will cut a few minutes off the cooking time. Use 2½ cups of water for every cup of rice.

Soak the rice overnight in enough water to cover. This will soften the grains and make cooking a little faster.

Precook the rice before mealtime. Bring the rice and its cooking water to a boil in a covered pot earlier in the day, then turn off the heat and let it sit on the stove until a little before mealtime. The rice will continue to cook and soften in the hot water, so the remaining cooking time will be reduced.

Cook up more than you need. Freeze or refrigerate leftovers in convenient portion sizes. Long-grain rice reheats best, especially if you want the grains to remain separate. Rice can be stored in the freezer for about six months but it will keep in the refrigerator only for several days.

You may want to try a commercial brand of quick-cooking brown rice. According to the companies using this process, there are only minimal

---

THAWING COOKED RICE

Frozen rice can be quickly thawed by setting the freezer container in a bowl of hot water. You can also pop it out of its freezer container into a colander and set the colander in a pot or bowl, then pour boiling water over the rice. Let the rice sit in the hot water just until it's thawed, then pick up the colander to drain the rice.

If you have a microwave, there's no reason to thaw the rice before you reheat it. Merely cover the rice and heat it on high for 1½ minutes per cup of rice.

nutritional losses. The final product has more of a flaky texture and costs a bit more than regular brown rice, but it may be worth it to the working cook. Because it is so new, this rice isn't available everywhere. If you can't find it in your supermarket, you can order it from Arrowhead Mills, Box 2059, Hereford, TX 79045.

You can compromise with parboiled or converted white rice. It cooks faster than brown rice and is more nutritious than the regular white. Some commercial brands of brown rice may also come parboiled.

PREPARING QUICK STIR-FRY MEALS

Stir-fry meals are delicious, nutritious and quick to prepare. They are best made in a wok, but a deep skillet is okay, too. Follow the steps here for a perfect stir-fry.

Assemble a dish by choosing ingredients from each column of the table "Mix and Match Stir-Fry," on the facing page. Plan your stir-fry with an eye toward contrasts of color and texture as well as flavor. Try a familiar combination such as chicken, sweet red pepper, mushrooms, scallions and cashews. Or explore the more unusual mingling of slivered duck with carrots, bamboo shoots, mushrooms and shredded bok choy leaves. The amounts in the table will serve four.

Prepare the basic stir-fry sauce. Put ½ teaspoon vegetable oil in a small saucepan, add a clove of minced garlic and sauté about 30 seconds. Add 1 tablespoon soy sauce, 2 tablespoons water, 1 tablespoon sweet wine vinegar and 1 teaspoon honey, and bring to a boil while stirring constantly. Add 1 teaspoon cornstarch that has been dissolved in 1 teaspoon stock or water and continue to stir until the sauce is shiny and thick. Remove from heat and stir in a dash of sesame oil.

Cut all the ingredients you have chosen into uniform, bite-sized pieces. Arrange each category on a separate plate near your cooking surface.

Heat your wok or large cast-iron skillet over medium-high heat for about 1 minute. Then add 1 teaspoon of vegetable oil, swirl it around the pan and allow it to heat for 1 minute longer.

Add the basic ingredient from the left-hand column of the table. Stir-fry by tossing the ingredient quickly. Continue to stir-fry until the food is lightly browned on the outside, which will take 1 to 5 minutes, depending on the ingredient you've chosen. Remove with a slotted spoon and set aside on a plate.

Mix and Match Stir-Fry

Basic Ingredient (choose 12 oz)	Hearty Vegetables (choose 2 cups)	Tender Vegetables (choose 1 cup)	Toppings (choose 2 tbsp)
Beef, slivered; lamb, slivered; pork, slivered	Asparagus, sliced diagonally	Bean sprouts	Almonds, slivered
Bay scallops; sea scallops, halved; clams; firm-fleshed fish, cubed; medium shrimp; oysters	Bamboo shoots, julienned	Bok choy leaves, shredded	Cashews
	Bok choy ribs, sliced diagonally	Lettuce, shredded	Peanuts
	Broccoli florets or stalks, julienned	Nappa cabbage, shredded	Pine nuts
Chicken, cubed or slivered; duck, slivered; turkey, cubed or slivered	Carrots, julienned and lightly steamed	Scallion, cut into matchsticks	Scallion, chopped
	Cauliflower florets	Spinach or kale, shredded	Sesame seeds
Tempeh, cubed; tofu, cubed	Celery, sliced diagonally	Watercress, shredded	
	Daikon radish, julienned		
	Fresh mushrooms, sliced		
	Peas		
	Snowpeas		
	Sweet onion, slivered		
	Sweet or bell pepper, cubed or sliced		
	Tender green beans, whole or sliced		
	Water chestnuts, sliced into coins or quartered		
	Yellow squash, julienned or cubed		
	Zucchini, julienned or cubed		

Source: *Quick & Healthy Cooking* magazine, Spring 1986.

STIR-FRY TIPS

To ensure even cooking and make the most attractive presentation, cut your ingredients to uniform size and shape. If you julienne one ingredient, julienne all the others to the same size. You can leave bite-sized ingredients such as bay scallops, shrimp and clams intact. Here are some other tips for better stir-frys:

→ Sliver or cut meat against the grain. It will be most tender this way.

→ Shred or cut chicken with the grain.

→ Use only firm-fleshed fish such as swordfish, tuna and grouper. Delicate ones, such as cod and flounder, will crumble when stir-fried.

→ If you prepare your ingredients a few hours (or a day) in advance, use the basic stir-fry sauce, uncooked and minus the cornstarch mixture, as a marinade for the basic ingredient (but not for the vegetables). When you're ready to cook, drain the marinade well and use the liquid to complete the basic sauce as usual, adding the cornstarch mixture.

→ You can prepare ingredients up to a day ahead and store them in the crisper (vegetable) drawer of the refrigerator, wrapped separately in plastic.

→ Dry the vegetables thoroughly after washing so they don't splatter when added to the hot oil.

→ Be sure your pan is large enough to cook your ingredients quickly. If there's more than an inch of food in the pan it will start to steam and become soggy.

→ Sauté tofu instead of stir-frying it so it won't crumble. (Shake the wok or skillet instead of tossing the tofu.)

→ Stir-fry all foods in mild vegetable oils such as peanut, safflower, sunflower or corn. Avoid olive oil because its fruitiness doesn't blend well with oriental flavors. Don't ever stir-fry with sesame oil because the flavor will get too strong; instead, stir in a dash as a seasoning just before serving. Avoid butter, too, because it will burn during stir-frying.

→ *Never* cover the wok or skillet with a lid or your crisp stir-fry will turn to mush.

Drizzle another teaspoon of oil into the pan. Allow a few seconds for the oil to heat, then add your choice of hearty vegetables from the second column in the table and stir-fry for about 3 minutes. The vegetables are done when slightly tender.

Immediately return the first ingredient to the pan along with one or more tender vegetables from the third column. Add the basic stir-fry sauce and your choice of toppings from the right-hand column. Toss all the ingredients quickly to coat them with the sauce, remove from heat and serve.

NOTE: When you want to make a stir-fry calling for a pound or so of meat, plan to make the recipe a day or two after serving a large roast of the same meat. This saves time because the meat is already cooked. It also saves money because you are paying less per pound for the bigger cut. A good example of this is having pork loin or boneless pork roast one night, then saving the leftovers for pork fried rice later on in the week.

CREATING FAST AND EASY GARNISHES
Colorful garnishes can really add eye appeal to your foods. But many of us don't bother with garnishes because they look like they take a lot of time and know-how to create. Here are 13 garnishes that are quick and easy to make and will add beauty to any dish.

- → Dress up a dish with sprigs of fresh herbs.
- → Use lemon, lime or orange half-moons as simple garnishes for fish, fruits, vegetables, beverages—even grain dishes and soups.
- → Use a vegetable scorer or canelle knife to carve vertical stripes in cucumber, zucchini or citrus. Then slice the vegetable or fruit into decoratively striped rounds.

➔ Use long chive greens to tie together bundles of carrot and celery batons.

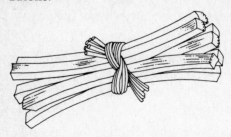

➔ Use scooped-out grapefruit, orange, lemon or lime halves as baskets to hold sauces, dips, berries or hot breakfast cereal.
➔ Slice a bell pepper into thin rings. Then make a tiny cut in half of the rings and link them together in a chain to line a platter. This is especially attractive if you use two or three colors of pepper.

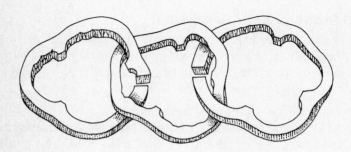

➔ Cut a cucumber into thin slices. Make a cut from the center of each slice to the outside, then twist half of the slice forward and half backward. Do the same with limes, lemons and oranges and use to garnish platters, individual plates or whole grilled fish.

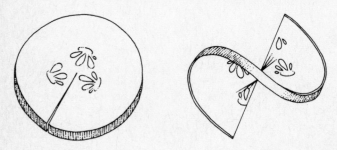

➔ Alternately skewer red and green grapes on a toothpick and use to garnish desserts, entree platters and individual plates.

→ Make carrot ribbons to toss over salads: scrape away long strips of carrot with a swivel vegetable peeler, then use a chef's knife to cut the strips lengthwise to form thinner ribbons.

→ Use hollowed-out watermelon, cabbages, pineapple, squash or round bread loaves as containers for salads, dips and spreads.

→ Use flower- or heart-shaped cookie cutters to make decorative shapes from carrot and turnip slices. Use to garnish salads, platters and soups.

→ Use a crinkle-cutter when slicing hard vegetables and fruits such as carrots, turnips, sweet potatoes, pears and apples.

→ Try edible flowers such as nasturtium, calendula and chive flowers for beautiful garnishes.

PLANNING FOR HOLIDAYS AND PARTY MEALS

Cooking for holidays and parties can sometimes be overwhelming. And usually the last word that applies is "quick." But we've come up with some tips that *will* cut down your time as well as make these special events run a bit smoother.

Keep a notebook or card file of holiday or party menus that you particularly like. Include shopping lists and schedules of things to do. This way, you don't have to start with a new plan every time you do special entertaining. This will keep frazzled nerves to a minimum.

Choose your menu well in advance. You can prepare and freeze dishes weeks, or even months, ahead of time, thus avoiding that last-minute rush to get it all done.

Keep menus simple. Using hard-to-find or out-of-season items will cut into your preparation time because of time-consuming shopping trips.

When planning a meal, choose dishes that use the same oven temperature, give or take 25°F. This will allow you to cook all the food at the same time, helping to save on both time and utility bills.

Use tried-and-true recipes. Trying something new for company may backfire.

Keep all basic ingredients on hand. Most basics, if stored properly, will keep for long periods of time. Keep favorite beverages or beverage ingredients in stock, as well. You'll free up time that you would have spent in the grocery store.

Keep appetizers and hors d'oeuvres frozen and ready to bake or reheat. This also applies to desserts and bread. Having these parts of the menu on hand will allow you to devote more time to the entree.

Keep paper supplies on hand for informal gatherings. Buy them on sale and store them for future use.

EASY FREEZING IN BOILABLE BAGS

The gadgets that can heat-seal special boilable plastic food bags for freezing are very handy. You can prepare uncooked dishes or pack individual portions of leftovers in the boilable pouches so you have convenient, quick dinners in your freezer. The advantages of freezing in boilable bags instead of casserole dishes or freezer containers are:

→ You won't have to add any fat or oil in the cooking.
→ Foods cooked in bags are moist and flavorful.
→ Cooking odors are confined in the bag.
→ It's easy to clean the pots afterward.

Here are some tips from the Rodale Food Center on cooking in boilable bags.

→ Use only bags specifically recommended for boiling in water.
→ Don't overfill the bags; they should be as thin as possible—never more than about two inches thick.
→ Try to squeeze as much air out of the bag as possible before you seal it.
→ If ingredients are added to the bag in layers they tend to stay separate and look pretty when served.
→ Always put the bag into water that's already boiling, and regulate the heat to maintain a very gentle boil, partially covering the pot with a lid.
→ Large pots such as shallow stockpots are the easiest to use with boilable bags. Fill with water to a depth of four to five inches.

→ If the food is ready before it's wanted, remove it from the pot. It will stay hot for a reasonable time—10 to 15 minutes in the unopened pouches—and can easily be warmed up if necessary.

→ If you have a microwave, slash or puncture the bag and microwave for 5 to 6 minutes.

Grilling

Everyone loves a barbecue. Outdoor grilling is a favorite American warm-weather pastime, but, unfortunately, what usually gets grilled are high-fat steaks, or other meats just dripping with high-calorie sauces. Here's how to grill *healthy* foods, along with some tips that will make the task easier so you can get on with the eating and outdoor fun.

GRILLING LOW-FAT FOODS

You can grill chicken, fish, leaner cuts of beef and even vegetables with great success. Part of the secret to grilling such low-fat foods is to marinate them prior to cooking. Marinades impart flavor and moistness to food, and they also are excellent for basting foods while you grill them.

Create your own no-fat marinades. Use stock instead of oil or butter. The tougher the cut or type of meat, the more acidic the marinade should be. For red meats, add a flavored vinegar, lemon juice or cider to the stock. Yogurt, or buttermilk, works well as a marinade with poultry. Then add minced aromatics like onion, garlic, shallot, celery, ginger, carrot, fennel or leek. Strong spices such as curry, saffron, chili powder and turmeric will add flavor and color.

Marinate beef, pork and lamb overnight. Poultry with skin can be marinated overnight, as well. More delicate foods such as skinned poultry and fish should be marinated for only about an hour before grilling.

MAKING BETTER GRILLED CHICKEN

Chicken is an excellent low-fat food for grilling, provided you omit the heavy barbecue sauce. Here are some tips that will turn out the best grilled chicken.

Precook chicken in the oven or microwave before grilling. This way, it will cook through without burning when grilled. If you can't precook, grill for about 30 minutes, then cover the chicken with a foil tent, continuing to turn and baste, until the chicken is cooked through.

Grill the chicken about six inches from the heat source. To ensure a juicy texture, leave the skin on while the chicken is grilling; you can remove it before serving.

Grill whole chicken and other small fowl with a superb method the French call *crapaudine*. Split the bird down the backbone, flip it breast-side up, spread the cut sides out and flatten. Then smack the breastbone so that it breaks and the bird lies flat. The bird's shape now resembles a toad, or *crapaud,* and will cook more evenly than in its original form.

Baste chicken about every 10 minutes, using its marinade or some stock. Never baste with a sauce that contains sugars or fats (such as traditional barbecue sauce) not only because it's unhealthy, but also because it will burn the chicken. Try to get used to low-fat flavorings. If you must use barbecue sauce, lightly coat the chicken during the last 10 minutes of cooking, or serve the sauce on the side.

CREATING SUCCULENT GRILLED FISH

Have you ever tried grilling fresh fish? If not, you're in for a taste treat. Here's how to successfully prepare fish on the grill:

- → For even cooking, each piece of fish should be the same thickness.
- → Very thin fillets, such as sole or flounder, don't need to be turned.
- → If the points of thin fillets are extra thin, turn them under so the fillet will cook evenly.
- → To preserve a moist texture, whole fish should be grilled with heads and skin on; they can be removed before serving. When grilling split fish, leave the backbone in.
- → Grill fish four to six inches from the heat source, for about 10 minutes per inch of thickness.
- → Choose fish steaks 1½ inches thick or less to retain a tender texture when grilled. Thicker steaks should be baked or poached.

MAKING DELICIOUS GRILLED MEAT

If you're cutting your fat intake, you don't have to forego grilling meats. Just remember that lean meat is healthier than fatty meat. Start by choosing a lean cut and then trim away all outer fat before grilling. Then follow these steps for delicious grilled meat:

- → For even cooking, each piece of meat should be the same thickness.
- → Meat should be grilled about six inches from the heat source.
- → Large pieces of meat such as roasts should be precooked in the oven prior to grilling. If this is not possible, cover with a foil tent

or the barbecue lid, if your grill comes with one, after about 30 minutes of grilling and baste frequently until the meat is cooked through.

MAKING YOUR GRILLING EASIER

Although outdoor cooking can be enjoyable, it can also be frustrating if the charcoal won't light, the fire takes forever to get hot enough or your food ends up a blackened mess. Read on for tips on hassle-free grilling.

Choose a reputable grade of charcoal. Actually sniff the bag; if it smells strongly of petroleum products (reminiscent of oil or gasoline, for instance), pass it up and buy a brand that doesn't.

Be sure the area of charcoal that you lay in the grill is larger than the food you're going to cook. This ensures even cooking. Note that the closer together the coals are, the hotter the fire will be.

Give the charcoal enough time to heat up. It takes about 30 minutes for charcoal to become hot enough to cook food. You can tell it's ready by the coating of white ash. For maximum heat, knock this coating off with long tongs before grilling. Check the temperature of coals by carefully holding the palm of your hand just above the grill surface on which the food will be cooked. If you can say "Shortcut Cook" twice, figure the coals are "high"; 5 times, "medium"; and 7 to 10 times, "low." (Low is too cool to cook on.) The instant your palm is uncomfortable, *move it*.

Keep the grill rack super clean and lubricated. Otherwise, food will stick and tear when removed. A no-stick spray is handy for "oiling" the grill.

Avoid dangerous flare-ups. Slightly prop one end of the grill rack so dripping juices will slide down the rungs rather than onto the coals.

Baste frequently with marinade or stock. This helps keep the food moist. Reserved marinade can be used as a sauce if heated to a boil before serving.

Be flexible with your time schedule. Grills differ slightly in temperature from use to use; wind and other weather factors cause recipe times and temperatures to vary. Make note of the various cooking times for the future.

Add aromatics during the last few minutes of cooking. To avoid flare-ups, soak them in water for about 15 minutes, drain, then toss onto the fire. Some aromatics you may like to try include hickory, mesquite, fruit-woods, grapevine, tea leaves and herbs.

4

Shortcuts to

A Better You

Sometimes we could all use a little help with our personal and work lives. There just seem to be days when all we do is argue with our loved ones, or we feel down in the dumps or we have a hard time making a decision. Maybe we worry too much or feel a lot of stress from our jobs. In this chapter we'll talk about some of the things that can cause stress or unhappiness and show you positive steps you can take to help yourself.

The "Blues"

Ever have one of those days when you just feel "blah"? When nothing anyone can say or do can put you in a better mood? You can't rely on others to get you out of your emotional slump, but there are some things *you* can do to cope with the blues.

LEARNING TO BEAT THE BLUES

When you're feeling depressed, the last thing you probably want to do is pull yourself up and get on with things. But that's exactly what you must do—nothing gets accomplished by moping about. Try these suggestions to perk yourself up.

Do something you're good at. Occasional bouts of depression are often caused by fluctuations in your feelings about yourself. The lower your self-esteem, the more you blame yourself for things you should or should not have done and the more depressed you feel. You can combat these bad feelings by doing something that you're good at. Doing something well makes you feel virtually better. If you're a good piano player, for instance, take some time now to play (instead of watching TV or eating, which doesn't always raise your self-esteem). Don't think you're not good at anything. *Everyone* is good at something, such as making a nice meal, repairing something that is broken or dressing nicely.

Learn something new. Read a book or an article in a magazine that you normally wouldn't have bothered with. Ask another person to teach you something: how to cook a different meal, how to play a game you've always been curious about, how to sew or knit or how to repair a car—anything you think you might be interested in. Learning something new will help lead to higher self-esteem.

Exercise. Even if you believe that you don't have the energy to do anything but lie in bed, you'll be surprised at how even minimal activity can get the blood moving. A brisk walk is often a good way to get started. Besides burning calories and providing good feelings because you did something good for yourself, exercise helps to rid your body of the toxic effects of anxiety, and anxiety often goes hand in hand with depression.

Think about whether you're angry at someone. Bouts of depression often coincide with incidents that have made you angry. In fact, one of the definitions of depression is "anger turned inward." If someone important to you (parent or spouse) has done something to make you mad, and you don't feel that it's all right to be angry at that person, you may end up feeling depressed. Try to get your anger out in some way, such as discussing it with the person or a friend or even writing it down.

Contact someone who would be surprised to hear from you. Why not call up an old friend from high school or college or even a relative with whom you've spent little time? If the idea of making a phone call is too threatening, try writing a letter. If you don't feel that you know anyone you'd like to contact at this point, there are millions of people—especially older ones—who would welcome a visit or correspondence from a stranger.

Do something cultural. Are you the type of person who takes advantage of what your hometown has to offer only when you're showing guests around? Why not show some of that same consideration to yourself? Go to a park, a museum, a play, a concert or anywhere else you would normally take a tourist.

Do something nice for yourself. Take the time to dress yourself impeccably and finally get out of those pajamas. Or take a warm bath, with bubbles. You could also take the time to make yourself a nice meal, complete with candlelight. If you begin to act as if you're important, you'll begin to feel that way as well.

Try to spend some time in the sun. Research suggests that there may be a relationship between lack of sunlight and depression—called the Seasonal Affective Disorder, or SAD. The National Institute of Mental Health conducted studies that indicate that exposure to bright light at regular intervals may help to lift depressive feelings. Others, however, believe that exposure to light itself may not provide the answer, but that getting outside may ward off feelings of loneliness or social isolation. Although there are no conclusive data about sunlight and depression, why not try to get outside when you see the sun shine? It certainly can't hurt.

If things don't seem to improve, seek professional help. The suggestions mentioned above are designed to help lift you out of a temporary depression. Everyone gets the blues at some point, and with effort you can tackle those feelings and start to feel better about yourself. However, if you feel depressed most of the time or feel that your depression is adversely affecting your job, marriage or other relationships, it is important to seek professional help. A qualified mental health practitioner can determine whether or not your problem is serious and whether you need additional assistance.

FEELING BETTER THROUGH HUMOR

How much do you laugh each day? Heard any good jokes recently? Over the past 10 years, researchers in the medical and psychological fields have found that humor is one of the best ways to help us feel better. Physical illness as well as psychological stress are affected by humor and our ability to laugh. Although life issues can be serious, a humorous look at life situations can help establish a better frame of mind. Just like daily exercise, daily doses of humor can release stresses and concerns and help chase away the blues (see "Dealing Successfully with Stress" later in this chapter). Here are five ways to get a regular dose of humor.

Collect amusing items. If it makes you laugh, make it available. Collecting cartoons, jokes, video movies, stories, books or records or even writing down funny things you've heard is a way to have a library of material you can use. Take time each day to go over some of what you've collected for some comic relief.

Go to places where you can get a good laugh. Schedule a time and place to laugh into your routine. It doesn't matter where you go—whether to a movie, a comic club, a friend's house or even a street corner.

Look for humor in every situation. Of course there are serious concerns in life; however, even the most serious and troubling event may have an element of humor. Look for it.

Explore new avenues of humor. Frequently there are only a few things we find humorous. But there may be other types of comedy or humor that we haven't even noticed. Read a new magazine or book. Watch a different show. What wasn't funny to you a few years ago may be funny to you now. With the increase in comic clubs in many areas, and television and movie comedies, you may find opportunities to discover new humor.

Participate in the humor. This is probably the most important step. Whether you act in a humorous manner, converse in a humorous way or laugh heartily at something amusing, you can be involved in the fun. Healthy humor is not restrained. Allow yourself to feel the laugh and the amusement, and allow others to share that feeling.

Making Decisions More Easily

Most people make difficult decisions at some point in their lives. For some people, however, even the most trivial decisions can be magnified to overwhelming proportions, all but paralyzing the individual. If you have a hard time making decisions, read on.

EIGHT STEPS TO EASIER DECISION MAKING

Psychologist Harold Greenwald developed "Direct Decision Therapy," a procedure by which patients are helped to overcome psychological conflicts by being taught how to make *decisions*. Here's how to discover what kind of decision-maker you are and how you can learn to make decisions more easily.

Determine what kind of decision-maker you are. There are several types of decision-makers, including those people who just can't seem to make a decision at all! See the box "Decision-Maker Types" on the next page to determine where you stand.

Think about what you lose by avoiding independent decision making. Did you recognize yourself in any, or several, of the characterizations listed above, except for the last one? If so, it may benefit you to think about what you lose when you avoid making a "real" decision. The most important loss, perhaps, is the opportunity for increased self-esteem and an enhanced sense of identity. We are who we are because of the choices

DECISION-MAKER TYPES

What type of decision-maker are you? Check below, then read on to see how you can learn to make decisions more easily.

The procrastinator: The procrastinator is an individual who continually postpones making a decision, often to the point where a decision is no longer called for. For example, Karen talked constantly about her dilemma of deciding whether to work harder to get ahead in her current job or to take the time to look for a better position elsewhere. As it happened, Karen "accidentally" became pregnant, necessitating a temporary retreat from the working world and at the same time, successfully avoiding the decision.

The waffler: The waffler often looks as though she or he has made a decision, and then *whoops!* suddenly the waffler attempts to choose the alternative. Often the waffler can go back and forth between alternatives so many times that the result is some hazy, less-than-satisfying compromise that is usually worse than simply making a firm decision in the first place.

The throw-in-the-toweler: An individual who throws in the towel in the face of a decision leaves herself or himself at the mercy of everyone and everything else and simply abdicates all power in the decision. Faced with conflict, a throw-in-the-toweler beats a hasty retreat, hoping that the decision will either go away or that someone more powerful (or fate, or the gods and so forth) will intervene.

The depender: The depender is a decision-maker who is similar to the throw-in-the-toweler in that the depender virtually hands over all power to determine her or his own fate to another. Relationships are sometimes built on the tendency of one to maintain powerlessness and the other to compensate by appearing quite powerful. In actuality, however, both depender and "dependee" reveal enormous lack of self-esteem (the powerful one needing such a dependent person as much as the depender needs her or him).

The reactor: The reactor is actually the flip side of the depender. The reactor will carefully solicit other opinions and then when

(continued)

faced with a decision, intentionally go against the others' advice. The reactor maintains the facade of independence while actually being quite dependent upon having another's opinion to go against.

The impulsive: The impulsive decision-maker gives little rational thought to any decision and is carried along by whim or impulse in making choices. Impulsive acts are not real decisions because they often stem from unconscious motivations and feelings, which are not under the control of the decision-maker. Instead of gaining control and power through a decision, the impulsive decision-maker has actually lost control and has usually courted major or minor disaster.

The "real" decision-maker: The real decision-maker is one who is able to freely choose one of possibly several alternatives, taking personal responsibility for that choice. The decision is a "healthy" one, involving both intellect and feelings, or rational and irrational components. A real decision-maker often listens to the advice and opinions of others but at the time for decision, determines her or his own opinion independently. Not that real decision-makers have it easy; a real decision often involves realizing the potential losses of having to choose one option over others.

we make. The feeling of power and sense of control over ourselves and our destiny is impaired by the avoidance of decision making. Rather than feeling inner calm and peace, the lack of decision making often produces feelings of anxiety, fear, unsettledness and stress.

Decide on a decision to be made. The first step toward independent decision making is to make the first decision: What issue will I make a decision on? For your first decision, choose one that is relatively unimportant to you but one that is still causing you some difficulty. In other words, don't choose to decide upon getting a divorce, going back to school or other such "big" decisions at first.

Make a list. Suppose you have decided to decide whether to buy a new sofa or reupholster the old one. Make a list with two columns, headed "new sofa" and "old sofa." Under these headings list all the reasons you can think of for buying a new sofa versus all the reasons why reupholstering the one you have would be better. You may come up with reasons such as opportunity for different style and extended warranty versus cost savings and being able to pick out the exact fabric you like. Once you have made your list, go back over it and number the reasons in each column by order of importance. In this way you will have an ordered, logical list that you can refer to during your process of decision making.

Take time to think about any hidden factors influencing your decision. Now that you've made a list of all the reasons for picking either one or the other of your alternatives, take some time to reflect on your feelings. For example, are you emotionally attached to the original sofa? Or, was it given to you by your mother-in-law and you've just been waiting for the chance to get rid of it? In essence, what you're doing is giving yourself the chance to let your unconscious get involved, an important part of any decision-making process. Decisions based entirely on logic and devoid of feelings often end up making you feel empty and unfulfilled.

Determine whether a compromise is possible. Careful here—don't take too much time to search for compromise or you'll perpetuate the avoidance of decision making. Another avoidance tendency to watch for is the halfhearted acceptance of an alternative that seems like a compromise but is actually a choice that makes you unhappier than either original choice would have. However, if you can honestly say to yourself that you'd truly be happy with your compromise, then that is a reasonable decision.

Motivate yourself to act. A good way to motivate yourself is to imagine what might happen if you *fail to act.* This technique often works best when you're faced with deciding between two evils rather than between two things you'd like to do. In her book *Pathfinders* (William Morrow & Co., 1981), Gail Sheehy tells the story of a woman trying to decide whether to divorce her alcoholic husband or continue to live with him, fearing the effects that divorce would have on her children. The woman reported that by concentrating on the evils of staying in limbo, she was able to motivate herself to make a decision and then act on it. Another way to motivate yourself is to think about the relief you'll feel once you've finally decided.

Resolve the conflict by making the decision. Suppose you decide that you just can't stand that old sofa any more and resolve to buy a new one. Although you'll probably experience feelings of relief, elation and freedom once the decision has been made, don't expect that entire post-decision period to be a bed of roses. Often those who have struggled and have finally made a decision experience doubts about whether or not they've done the right thing, such as "Can I *really* afford it?" or "Will my mother-in-law be angry with me?" There may also be feelings of loss, mirroring the reason the conflict was apparent in the first place—fear of losing other alternatives. Eventually, however, the decision should result in a psychological boost because you'll feel good about taking charge and asserting yourself.

Marriage and Family Life

No matter how happy your family life is, there are bound to be times when stresses and strains take their toll. Marital problems, family arguments and divorce all create bad feelings among family members. Here's how to cope.

IMPROVING THE QUALITY OF YOUR MARRIAGE

Almost everyone has heard that one in every two marriages ends in divorce, but did you know that there are more marriages taking place now than ever before? Those who choose to marry these days are more fortunate, perhaps, because more is known about how to make and keep a happy relationship than ever before. Leading experts have suggested several ways to improve the quality of your relationship. Here are 10 proven suggestions for a better marriage or intimate relationship.

What you see is what you get. This rule is the cornerstone for the rest. How many times have you heard someone say something like "Oh, George would be perfect *if only* . . . ." Perhaps you thought that your own mate was ideally suited to you except for that one habit of hers or his that was just driving you crazy. Entering a relationship with the expectation that you will be able to change your mate is setting yourself up for frustration and disappointment. No one can change another person. Instead, you might try to focus on changing your own feelings about what is bothering you. For example, if you can't stand Mary's nail biting, no amount of pleading, cajoling or threatening will get her to stop unless she's ready. You *can* think about why it bothers you, move to another room or try to stop focusing on what Mary's doing and think about what you're doing instead.

Focus on the positive aspects of your mate. When two people marry, they each marry a whole person—for better or worse. Admittedly, you may only be attracted to some aspects of your mate, but they are part of a package deal. For example, Joan loved Eric's calm, easygoing manner but was constantly irritated that it took Eric longer than her to do things.

Joan had a choice: she could either focus on his slowness or she could delight in his not getting ruffled about relatively trivial matters. Joan chose the latter and found that when she stopped criticizing Eric, their relationship became more positive.

Divide duties in a way that is comfortable for each of you. When people live together there are certain responsibilities that have to be met, such as cooking, cleaning, shopping and balancing the checkbook. Often one person takes on the bulk of these tasks, much to her or his resentment. It is important when entering a relationship to discuss who will do what, based on which partner is the more efficient, has more time or has more desire. If you haven't talked about these matters yet, it is important to take the time now to do so.

Know when to compromise. Issues are seldom black and white; everyone has conflicting feelings about even their most dearly held beliefs. What happens during a fight is that each person gets cornered, so that she or he ends up defending something that she or he doesn't even believe in that strongly. When you find yourself "digging your heels in" during an argument, realize what is happening and begin to look for solutions that are on "middle ground" and are more pleasing to both of you.

Welcome conflict as an opportunity for growth. Therapists are always suspicious when someone tells them, usually smugly, about how well they get along with their mate because "We haven't had a fight in years!" When any two people live together, conflicts are bound to arise, giving you opportunities to find creative solutions to changing your relationship. It's truly amazing how, when you set your mind to it, seemingly unresolvable differences can be negotiated, often resulting in a solution that's exciting to both of you.

Learn effective ways to express your feelings. An expression during the '60s was "Let it all hang out," which referred to showing your feelings whenever it "felt right." Many people discovered that simply spewing forth feelings (especially angry ones) was only satisfying in the short term, and usually turned out to be destructive to the relationship. For instance, Mary got into the habit, when angry with John, of yelling at him until he couldn't stand any more. This style of arguing wasn't satisfying for either of them because they were never able to discuss the original problem. Eventually, Mary learned to control her angry outbursts by taking "time-outs" between the time she first felt angry and when she attempted to communicate this to John. She could then calmly discuss with John what had made her angry and he, not feeling attacked, could listen and respond to her, making them both feel better.

Talk to each other. This suggestion sounds so obvious, yet so many people *assume* they know their mates without ever bothering to check out their assumptions by *talking*. For example, it wasn't until George filed for divorce that Rita discovered that George never liked going to his in-laws' house for Sunday dinner. Far more serious misunderstandings were involved, but Rita had no idea that George was unhappy in the marriage because she mistook his silence for contentment (when actually, George was silently fuming with resentment). Talking to your mate is guaranteed to surprise you. You'll surely find that the person you married is a lot different (and more interesting) than you assumed she or he was!

Take time to listen to your mate. Of course, no amount of talking to your mate will help make a happier marriage unless you *listen* to what she or he says. How many times have you caught yourself not really paying attention—your mind wandering to your own problems, daydreams or fantasies—and then trying to figure out what your partner was just telling you? If you would like to become a better listener, here's an exercise that you and your partner can practice together. First you make a statement. Then your partner repeats what you said *using her or his own words.* Next, you decide whether the message heard by your partner was actually the same as the one you intended to send. Now reverse roles. You'll be surprised at how easily even one-sentence statements can be misinterpreted!

Accept—do not fight—change in your mate. Look at your relationship as an adventure whereby your mate will become many different people throughout the course of your time together. What you can expect are subtle changes, such as new interests appearing and old ones fading and different attitudes toward many things. When people sense changes in their mate, they often attempt to deny that the changes are occurring. Instead of ignoring or fighting your mate's changes, delight in discovering the newly emerging qualities in her or him. These changes, along with your own, are the food that keeps the relationship growing and alive.

Build on your relationship's specialness. Just as no two people are alike, no two relationships are equal; each has a special quality that distinguishes it from all the rest. This specialness refers to that particular combination of people and circumstances that makes some marriages thrive. A vital way to enhance your own relationship's specialness is to resist nervously comparing your relationship to other ones. Instead, work on developing self-confidence in your own relationship, realizing that you've chosen your mate and relationship based on what *you* need. After all, there are reasons why you've chosen your mate over the hundreds of other people you've met!

DISCOVERING THE SECRETS TO A HAPPY MARRIAGE

What are the ingredients of a happy marriage? This is a question couples and those wishing to be couples have been asking themselves for a long time. Many myths abound, but recent studies have shed new light in this area. The results show that the secret to a happy marriage is not necessarily what your mother or grandmother may have once told you! Here are the answers to some commonly asked questions about marriage.

Is frequency of sexual intercourse an ingredient to a happy marriage? Believe it or not, research, dating to 1938, has shown little or no relationship between frequency of sexual intercourse and marital satisfaction. For happily married couples, frequency of sexual intercourse ranged from less than once a month, for some couples, to one couple who reported daily activity. Moreover, one-third of these men and two-thirds of these women reported a sexual problem such as an inability to relax or a lack of interest in sexual activity. Despite the fact that these couples reported being unhappy with their sex lives, they still felt their marriages were happy ones.

Is how happy a couple was before marriage related to how long their marriage lasts? Again the answer is no. Some researchers believe that compatibility is not as important in a marriage as how you deal with the *incompatibility*. In other words, how do you and your partner deal with the problems that arise in the marriage? Do you deal openly with difficult situations and express your feelings respectfully to your spouse or are problems shoved under the rug?

Is how well a couple communicated before they were married predictive of marital success? Yes! The ability to communicate is crucial in working through any problems that may arise during the course of a marriage. Happily married couples seem to develop a private language. Researchers at the University of Illinois found that husbands in happy marriages were much better at understanding exactly what their wives meant than were strangers. But in distressed marriages, strangers were as adept at understanding messages from wives as were their own husbands. This was also found to be true for more subtle feelings. Wives in happy marriages were aware of stress even when it was not readily apparent to others. In unhappy couples, husbands seemed oblivious to the hostility of their wives although objective observers noted it. Good communication is one of the cornerstones of a good marriage.

Is responsiveness to your partner related to marital happiness? "Yes," says John Gottman, chief of a research team at the University of Illinois. Gottman found that being responsive in sharing the events of the day with one's spouse distinguished happy and unhappy couples. The friendship built up through such day-to-day exchanges appears to make couples willing to go through the difficulties of repairing their relationship when it becomes strained.

Does sharing similar personality traits lead to a better marriage? This idea has also been investigated for many years. It was believed that if individuals shared the same traits such as "easygoing" or "stubborn" they would get along better as a couple. No clear relationship between personality traits and good marriages was ever found, however. In fact, the whole notion of "personality traits" has come to be questioned.

What are the ingredients to a happy marriage? They can be boiled down to the three *Cs:* caring, concern and communication. If you genuinely care for and are concerned about your spouse, and can communicate this, you are on the road to a happier marriage.

DEALING WITH TWO-CAREER-COUPLE SYNDROME

Over the past 15 years economic conditions have forced a majority of families to have two full-time breadwinners. This situation places a great strain on all involved. When both incomes are needed, the couple may feel as if they are trapped in a situation they cannot change. They usually have little free time with each other, and when they are together, those moments can become increasingly stressful and unsatisfying if frustrations, complaints and resentments build up without being openly communicated and constructively resolved.

The following steps are intended to help improve a relationship that is in this situation. In some cases, however, the problems in communication have become so serious that the relationship may need professional help if it is to survive. Certainly in cases involving major behavioral problems, alcohol or drug abuse, violence or an extramarital affair, consulting a professional should be the first step.

Recognize that a problem exists. Both members of the relationship must recognize and openly admit that a difficult situation exists and that changes need to take place to correct the problem. If one person believes the relationship is in serious trouble but the other denies that a problem exists, this is often enough reason to seek professional help.

Make a commitment to resolve the problem. Both members of the relationship must communicate a strong sense of commitment to each other. For many couples, this open renewal of commitment to each other is enough to restore energy and freshness to a stale relationship and may actually lead to positive, permanent changes.

Schedule periodic "summit" meetings. Set aside a block of time seven or eight hours long every six months. This time should be free of interruptions—no children, visitors or phone calls. At this meeting, each partner should have an agenda to be discussed. Topics should include problems to be solved rather than just complaints about each other. For example: "We need to arrange our schedules to have more time with each other" versus "You are never home. You don't care about me." (See the box "Topics for 'Summit' Meetings" below.) A leisurely lunch or dinner at a favorite eating place is recommended as a reward for progress being made.

The couple should come to the meeting prepared to listen to suggestions as well as to propose them. Both must be willing to compromise. The more cooperative the couple is feeling toward each other, the more that can be accomplished.

TOPICS FOR "SUMMIT" MEETINGS

Once you decide to initiate regular summit meetings, make sure you have an agenda, and make sure your talk is a productive one. It won't do any good just to complain. Here are some suggestions for topics.

Discuss ways to find time each week to be together. The key here is time *by yourselves*, engaging in an activity you both enjoy. It does not have to involve a lot of time or expense—consistency is the primary factor. Meeting for lunch once a week to share a pizza can work wonders. Other activities may involve watching or participating in sports or going to a concert, to a movie, or for a walk in the woods.

Discuss ways of making each other's regular weekly schedule as efficient as possible. A fresh look by the other partner may find ways of cutting corners and saving time.

Discuss and plan major household projects. This can help your relationship by having both of you share in a mutually agreed-upon venture.

Take time to objectively look at the family budget. Much frustration and tension is often caused by a difficult financial situation. In a
(continued)

meeting where both partners are being cooperative, some major unnecessary expenses can be done away with and some new ways of generating income can be arrived at.

Review your child-rearing practices. Discuss discipline methods. Hearing how your partner views your dealings with the children can have a sobering and profound effect. It is important that your critique of each other is done in a nonjudgmental and nonattacking manner.

Discuss how to improve upon the format of these meetings and tentatively schedule the next one. It is important to remember that just as with the summit meetings of international leaders, the primary purpose of these discussions is not to solve *all* problems, but to start a dialogue on some major issues.

AVOIDING FIGHTS WITH LOVED ONES

Fighting, arguing and hitting are usually a result of frustration. We take the frustration out on another person—often a loved one, such as a child, spouse, parent or friend. Most of us don't really want to fight, but when everyday problems or tensions get to us, what can we do? Here are 10 alternatives to try. One or two should work for you if you really want to avoid a fight.

Stop and take a breath of air. Take a deep breath and concentrate on your breathing. Count how many breaths you take in two minutes.

Make a phone call. It doesn't matter who you call. Call a friend, family member or even a local store for information. The idea is to talk with someone who is not involved in your current dispute.

Stop and look in a mirror. Spend a few minutes in front of a mirror talking out what's bothering you.

If you feel you have to hit someone, hit some*thing* instead. For example, punch your bed. Better still, go out and walk around for 10 minutes. Look at your neighborhood and notice what's around. If you're angry enough to kick a tree, fine, kick it—just be careful of your toes. Physical activity is one of the best alternatives for getting rid of frustration for some people.

Sit down and write about your thoughts and feelings. Write as much as you can about how you feel and what you'd like to do about it. You're the only one who is going to read it, so write whatever comes to mind without censoring. Try to get out the frustration so it doesn't have to be expressed in a fight or in a physical way.

Grab a magazine and rip it up. Rip a few pages at a time, then sit down and read what you ripped. If the pages are in pieces, put the pieces together like a jigsaw puzzle and then read the pages.

Lie down on the floor and do some simple exercises. A few sit-ups or push-ups would be helpful. Doing some aerobic exercises would help direct the frustration into a more positive activity, even if you're not feeling positive.

Go into the bathroom. Often the bathroom is the only place to get some privacy and quiet. Have some magazines or books there, possibly even a radio or television. Sit and relax for 10 to 20 minutes. This would be a time to think about what your feelings are. Maybe you're frustrated by your child, but how is hitting going to help? Maybe your spouse makes you angry, but destructive fighting will only make the situation worse. Take some time to look at the situation and think of ways to make it better.

Get something to eat. Sit down alone and chew on an apple or a sandwich. For some people, chewing helps relieve tension and frustration.

Call a counselor or therapist. If the frustrations are so great that no matter what you try you can't get relief, then some professional assistance would be helpful. Having a trained professional available to help you talk out your feelings and to look at other alternatives could give you a better way of dealing with the anger than your old habits of fighting or hitting. Sometimes counseling can help prevent a battle from starting or a situation from getting worse.

HELPING YOUR FAMILY SURVIVE DIVORCE

When we think about the family members who will be affected by divorce, we tend to think of the children ranging in age from toddlers to teenagers and usually don't give much thought to infants and adults. But family members of all ages can have trouble adjusting to new marital situations. Here's how to help them cope with divorce.

Infants: Children at this stage in life are learning whether or not they can trust both themselves and the world around them. The building of trust is dependent upon how well the infant is being cared for. Thus, the utmost concern should be to ensure that there is at least one constant caretaker in the infant's life during the divorce. Infants should not be shuttled back and forth between custodial and noncustodial parents, if at all possible, but should stay in one place and have the parents visit there. Another practice to guard against is the over- or under-parenting of the infant caused by the parents' stress over their own situation. If the parents are having a difficult time with the divorce, it is preferable to have the infant temporarily cared for by someone consistent and reliable than to expose the infant to extreme parental distress.

Preschool children: According to noted psychologist Erik Erikson, the preschooler is at a stage in which she or he begins to develop a "conscience" and feels guilty about being responsible for things that have gone wrong. Preschoolers, then, should be told about the divorce in such a way that they will not feel as though they are to blame. Ideally, both parents should sit down with the children and tell them about an impending divorce so the children don't assume that one of the parents is at fault. Parents should allay fears of abandonment by spelling out exactly what will happen to the children, for example, "Mommy will have dinner with you tonight and then Daddy will make you breakfast tomorrow." The most important task for parents of preschoolers is to reestablish the sense of security and consistency in separate households as soon as possible. Although young children are initially apt to react very badly to a divorce, with proper care, the effects can be substantially reduced in as little as two years.

Prepubescent school-age children: Children at this stage in life are developing confidence in their ability to master the world. Having fairly free access to both parents at this age seems to lessen their fear of fragile relationships with each parent as well as the resulting feelings of inferiority. Ideally, the parents should live close enough to each other so that there may be frequent visits with the noncustodial parent. Younger children may benefit from an abundance of activities to distract them from their sadness; older school-age children, in particular, should be encouraged to talk about their feelings regarding the divorce (the predominant one is often anger at the unfairness of things). It is especially important to avoid bad-mouthing the other parent. Some thought might also be given to same-sex custody, particularly with boys, because research indicates that boys of divorced parents are affected much more than girls and that a father's influence on his son has a calming, esteem-enhancing effect.

Adolescents: During this stage the adolescent is typically struggling to develop a personal identity and often is much more dependent on friends than on parental figures. For this reason, it is easier to ease an adolescent through divorce than younger children. Divorce may even be positive for teenagers if the result is a closer and more understanding relationship with each parent individually. It seems especially important for parents to be honest with the children about the reasons for the divorce; adolescents are able to understand the gray areas of life and can relate to what the parents are going through. Not only can they relate, but adolescents can be reassured by learning that parents also experience what the adolescent herself or himself may be currently experiencing with first love relationships. When being honest, however, it is important to avoid heaping blame or responsibility on the other parent (however justified). Teenagers, especially, need role models, and viewing both parents in a relatively positive light eases the search for identity. It is also important for parents to make histories and mementos from childhood available, particularly from those events involving the intact family; this provides the teenager with a sense of grounding to bounce off from. And finally, many teenagers who have witnessed an unhappy marriage and divorce may need special encouragement to risk any close involvement of their own.

Young adults: The successful young adult will have formed her or his own solid identity and can risk involvement with others without having to fear loss of the self. Those with a more fragile identity may become self-interested and self-indulgent, however, leading to a growing sense of isolation from the world. As a parent, then, the most important help one can give at this stage in life is to talk to the young adult about who she or he is and to support this emergent being in a positive manner. Any developmental arrests from earlier periods may become clearer at this age, and difficulties in forming close interpersonal relationships signal the need for possible professional help.

Grown children: For years it was mistakenly believed that grown children whose parents were divorcing had mercifully escaped all of the pitfalls of facing divorce in the younger years. There had been little research to date on the impact of these later-life divorces, but therapists in clinical practice point to the following effects:

> a greater danger of alienation from one of the parents
> an often unconscious reevaluation of the grown child's own marital relationship, leading to increased divorce rate
> more stress from the increased emotional and financial support that grown children are often asked to provide
> anger and resentment caused by remarriage and inheritance changes

Thus, a divorcing parent of grown children needs to be especially sensitive to the increased responsibilities often felt or assumed by their children and must make every effort to not look to them for such support. The impulse to get the grown child on one's side, or worse, to ask her or him to be the go-between, should be resisted as well. It is important to keep in mind that divorce adversely affects offspring of any age and, as with earlier stages, it is best to approach an impending divorce with as much sensitivity as possible toward all affected.

Relaxation

Relaxation is one of the best methods for combating the effects of stress. Deep relaxation, if practiced regularly, can produce a host of valuable physiological changes. But not everyone knows how to truly relax. Here's how to get started, and some of the positive results that relaxation will bring.

LEARNING TO RELAX AND FEEL BETTER

The sympathetic nervous system reacts to stress by secreting hormones that mobilize the body's muscles and organs to face a threat. This is sometimes called the fight or flight response, and includes shifting blood flow from the limbs to the organs and increased blood pressure. This stress response can be triggered merely by everyday worries and pressures. In contrast, the relaxation response releases muscle tension, lowers blood pressure and slows the heart and breathing rates. The particular type of relaxation technique that one uses is unimportant—any method that involves deep muscle relaxation is fine. However, this is not the same as sitting quietly, sleeping, reading or watching TV. One good program for relaxation is given in the box "One Relaxation Technique" on the next page. If you practice this technique a few times and find it effective, read the list into a cassette recorder or have someone whose voice you find particularly soothing read it for you. Another good source for relaxation techniques is Herbert Fensterheim and Jean Baer's book *Stop Running Scared* (Dell Books, 1978). In the back of their book is a script that you can read word for word into a tape recorder. There are many other tapes and books available to guide you in learning to relax.

UNDERSTANDING THE CHANGES RELAXATION CAN BRING

Here are some of the changes you may experience through deep relaxation. The researchers who performed the studies mentioned here caution that intensive training followed by regular use of the relaxation techniques may be required before any medical benefits appear. Also, not everyone is

ONE RELAXATION TECHNIQUE

This is just one of several relaxation techniques you can practice. Here's what you do: Lie face up on a bed or reclining chair with your arms at your sides and your legs uncrossed. Close your eyes and focus on your internal sensations. Now, first tense and then relax the muscle groups listed below so you begin to learn the difference between feeling tense and feeling relaxed. Tense the muscle for approximately 5 seconds; relax for 10, then go on to the next muscle.

> right hand and forearm (make a fist)
> right bicep (pull elbow in toward body)
> repeat for left hand, forearm and bicep
> right upper leg and thigh (try to lift it up off the bed and push it down at the same time)
> right calf and lower leg (pull toes toward head)
> right foot
> repeat for left leg and foot
> abdomen (make stomach hard)
> chest, shoulders, upper back (take a deep breath, hold it, pull shoulder blades together)
> lower back (arch back away from bed)
> shoulders and lower neck (hunch shoulders)
> neck, sides and front (pull chin downward and at the same time, try to prevent it from actually touching chest)
> back of neck (look behind you by bending head backwards)
> forehead and scalp (lift eyebrows as high as possible)
> eyes, cheeks and nose (squint eyes and wrinkle nose)
> jaws and lower cheeks (bite teeth together and pull corners of mouth back)

After completing this exercise, you should feel very relaxed. Next imagine a pleasant scene, one that you can recall at other times of the day. Just recalling this scene may create a relaxed feeling without your going through the entire exercise. To successfully learn to relax, have a friend talk you through the muscle groups at the optimal pace. Or read the steps into a tape recorder. Using commercially available relaxation tapes is another alternative. Regardless of the method, the key is practicing the technique.

helped by relaxation training. Some people change a little, some change a lot and there are a few whose lives turn around totally. Why there is such variability in results is not known, but in order to get the maximum benefit, learning the relaxation techniques well and then practicing them on a regular basis are essential. If you do that, here are some of the benefits you may find.

Strengthening of the immune system: Along with relaxation, there are some shifts in hormone levels that seem to produce beneficial effects on the immune system. For example, relaxation training of medical students was found to increase the level of helper cells in the blood that defend against infectious disease.

Control of blood pressure: Patients who were able to achieve a deep state of relaxation lowered their blood pressure and were able to maintain that reduction up to four years.

Lowering of cholesterol levels: Research performed at the Preventative Medicine Research Institute in San Francisco found that patients who practiced relaxation regularly were able to lower their cholesterol levels.

Lessening of severe angina attacks: Those suffering from angina were able to lessen the severity of those attacks through relaxation. These findings, also from the Preventative Medicine Research Institute, reflect relaxation's role in improving blood flow to the heart.

Control of diabetes: Studies performed at Duke University Medical Center found that relaxation improved the body's ability to regulate glucose in patients with the most common type of diabetes. It is the body's inability to control glucose that ultimately leads to the damage done by the disease.

Relief from asthma: Paul Lehrer of the Rutgers University Medical School found that relaxation training can bring significant relief to chronic asthma sufferers in two ways. First, relaxation can lessen the emotional stress that often brings about an attack. And, second, if an attack should occur, relaxation can diminish the constriction of air passages that chokes breathing.

Help for chronic pain: In a study performed at the University of Massachusetts Medical Center, patients trained in relaxation reported a sharp decrease in pain and related symptoms. Pain derived from backache, from chronic migraine or tension headaches, from cancer or even from the outcome of operations to control pain was found to be significantly diminished or even eliminated following relaxation training. A follow-up study conducted four years later found that the majority of the patients were still practicing relaxation and that, overall, there was a decreased reliance on medication to control pain.

Stress

Each of us, at some time, encounters a period of high stress as a result of some change in our lives. Whether caused by a job change, a loss of someone close, a new relationship or even a financial setback, the stress can feel overwhelming. To cope with the changes that confront us and to adapt in a positive manner, it is helpful to:

→ Secure adequate information (get to know as much about a situation as possible so as not to misjudge).
→ Maintain a positive self-image (don't demean or blame yourself).
→ Maintain autonomy (in other words, stand on your own two feet—it's up to you to make the final choice).

Here are other tips on how to recognize and cope with stress.

CHECKING YOUR STRESS LEVEL

Did you know that people exposed to too many stressful events in a relatively short period of time run a high risk of developing physical complaints? Thomas Holmes, M.D., and Richard Rahe devised the "Social Readjustment Rating Scale" to determine just how much stress is too much—the amount that might later lead to major illness. Use this scale in the table "Social Readjustment Rating Scale" on the facing page to measure your own life stress level.

The numbers in the right-hand column represent "stress units" (SU). If you have recently experienced the event in the left-hand column, write down the corresponding SU. Read through the entire list and then total your SU score. If your SU score adds up to 300 or above, you have a high risk of developing illness within the next two years. For methods that you can employ to relieve stress and thus decrease your chances of future stress-related physical complaints, see "Learning to Relax and Feel Better" earlier in this chapter.

DEALING SUCCESSFULLY WITH STRESS

Untreated stress can lead to a host of problems, including physical illness such as ulcers, heart disease, psoriasis and high blood pressure. It was

Social Readjustment Rating Scale

Event	Stress Units	Event	Stress Units
Death of spouse	100	Son or daughter leaving home	29
Divorce	73	Trouble with in-laws	29
Marital separation	65	Outstanding personal achievement	28
Jail term	63		
Death of close family member	63	Begin or end school	26
		Change in living conditions	25
Personal injury or illness	53	Revision of personal habits	24
Marriage	50	Trouble with boss	23
Fired at work	47	Change in hours or conditions at work	20
Marital reconciliation	45		
Retirement	45	Change in residence	20
Change in health of family member	44	Change in schools	20
Pregnancy	40	Change in church activities	19
Gain new family member	39	Change in recreation	19
Sex difficulties	39	Change in social activities	18
Business readjustment	39	Small mortgage or loan	17
Change in financial state	38	Change in sleeping habits	16
Death of close friend	37	Change in number of family get-togethers	15
Change to different line of work	36		
Change in number of arguments with spouse	35	Change in eating habits	15
		Vacation	13
High mortgage	31	Christmas	12
Foreclosure of mortgage or loan	30	Minor violations of the law	11
Change in responsibilities at work	29		

even estimated that stress-related illness in 1984 cost the nation approximately $77 billion in lost productivity! People exposed to stress over long periods are also prone to develop depression, feelings of hopelessness and inferiority, loss of sexual interest, memory problems — the list is virtually endless. Here are seven ways to deal successfully with stress and thereby decrease your risk of developing other complaints.

Identify and address the problem producing the stress. Often those who are under stress first attempt to relieve the stress by attacking the symptoms: taking medication, getting more sleep or changing eating habits. Although sometimes helpful in the short term, these methods can actually prolong the stress by leaving the underlying cause untreated. Instead, take time to identify the stressful situation, which may be some aspect of your job, your relationships with others or another similar circumstance. Once you have determined the source of your stress, you can take control and address the problem. For instance, if your work situation is causing you stress you may decide to discuss possible solutions with your boss. By taking charge, you reduce the feelings of helplessness and being "out of control" and take an important step in relieving the source of your stress.

Learn to relax. What if you've identified what you believe is the source of your stress and yet decide that it's impossible to change? Then you can take steps to reduce the effects such situations have on you by learning to relax. One of the easiest ways to learn to relax is to deliberately try to make yourself tense and then relax specific body areas slowly, one by one. (See the box "One Relaxation Technique" on page 126.)

Exercise. Not only does exercise make you feel better by doing something positive for you, but recent studies indicate that such activity can help your body release its own natural opiates, called endorphins. Why not avail yourself of your own natural healing powers? (See chapter 2, "Shortcuts to a Fitter You.")

Devote time to hobbies and outside interests. Immersing yourself in hobbies and other outside interests can often reduce the intensity of the stress by taking your mind off the stressful situation. Worrying only increases your stressful feelings.

Talk to someone. Talking about your problems often helps to put things into perspective. In this way, you may realize solutions you never thought of or at least gain a better understanding of whatever is bothering you. Often simply airing your feelings to someone else brings immediate relief.

Laugh. Amazingly enough, a good belly laugh can sometimes relieve tension and indicate that you've come to terms with the problems that are causing the stress. If you can laugh at the situation, you are that much closer to being ready to do something about it. (See "Feeling Better through Humor" earlier in this chapter.)

Concentrate on having fun. A survey conducted by Dr. Martin Snyder at the United States International University indicates that engaging in pleasurable activities may actually reduce symptoms of stress. The survey suggests that in order to combat the effects of stressful living, one should participate in more social events and, simply, have more fun! Exposed to the same degree of stress, those people who enjoy themselves more report fewer symptoms associated with stress than do those without pleasurable activities. So if you can't beat the stressful situation, at least alleviate its effect on you by going out and having a good time.

Work

Many of us spend the greater part of each day on the job. Because we spend so much time working, it's important that we learn to get along with our bosses and coworkers and understand the impact our work life has on our private life.

COPING WITH THE HIGH COST OF SUCCESS

Things are finally looking up. You've just gotten that big promotion, and things are going well on the job. Yet just when you've had your biggest accomplishment, you find that coworkers and those who are close to you begin to move away emotionally. Your friends are there to congratulate you, but soon after you notice that something is different. No longer are you considered "one of the gang." Why have things changed? Social psychologists offer two possible explanations:

→ Envy. You've done something that your coworkers or friends haven't done, or you now have something they don't have, and so they may be envious.

→ Group identity. When you're promoted, you usually leave a group of coworkers. Those people must still continue with their work despite the fact that most of them would really like to be in your position. In order to better tolerate their own positions, your former group casts out everyone who is no longer "one of them." It's a way of saving face and maintaining the group identity.

Once you understand these principles, what can you do to try to improve your relationship with your coworkers?

Be sensitive to the needs of the group you have left behind. The salesperson who has become a manager, for example, might be able to minimize the effect of the promotion by helping the other salespeople achieve managerial positions themselves. She or he could also be particularly sensitive to the needs of salespeople and use the new position to make the sales jobs more pleasant.

Reassure people that you're not rejecting them. People who are promoted leave their coworkers behind almost as often as their coworkers cast them out. Just because you've moved up the ladder doesn't mean you can no longer associate with your former "gang." Try to stay in touch, and let people know you still respect their values.

GETTING AHEAD AT THE OFFICE

Why is it that some people plod along in the same jobs, year after year, while others seem to follow a meteoric rise to the top? Many dismiss the successful employee's efforts with comments such as, "Well, he must have been in the right place at the right time," or "Wish I were that lucky." Others insinuate that sex must have somehow been involved; how else does a male explain a female's promotion over him? In fact, researchers have discovered that although fate and luck may play a part in success, successful people are more likely to create the opportunity for luck to strike *them*. Also, sex at the office is more likely to derail a career rather than enhance it. So how do some people get ahead more quickly than others? Here are 10 steps you can take to maximize your own career opportunities.

Show initiative and creativity. Most people try to do their jobs as best they can, but a special few not only take care of their own responsibilities, but actively look for other things to do. Although you may decide simply to offer to help others with their work, a better way to get noticed is to be creative; for example, aren't there more productive means to accomplish a lot of the tasks that you do every day? Many companies even formally recognize such initiative by offering cash bonuses to employees who find better ways to do things.

Make your boss(es) look good. Some people make the mistake of blatantly parading their talents in front of top management in the hopes that they'll be recognized for the star that they think they are. What they're showing, however, is an extreme lack of loyalty and respect for their own boss in the drive to get ahead. Rather than trying to outshine your boss, direct your efforts toward making your boss look good. Unless she or he is extremely insecure, your boss will appreciate your efforts on her or his behalf (as well as your loyal, "team" approach) and will help you rise to meet your potential.

Handle criticism well. No one likes to be criticized, but those who are more likely to get ahead listen to criticism and try to learn from it. Suppose your boss points out a mistake you made on a customer's account. Instead of arguing, crying, defending yourself or taking it personally, think about the mistake you made and ways to prevent such errors in the future. You may even be thankful that your boss pointed out your mistake before it spread throughout the company! Above all, separate yourself from your work—a mistake on the job does not mean that your very value as a person is at stake, and it should have no relation to self-esteem.

Don't be a workaholic. In mistaken attempts to advance in their careers, some people will devote more and more hours to the office at the expense of relationships, leisure time and so forth. What usually happens is that the workaholic eventually suffers from massive job burnout, ceasing to feel any pleasure or energy in relation to the job. Make sure that you plan time to truly leave your job, totally forgetting about work. Such periods actually will rejuvenate you so that you'll be able to be even more productive when you return.

Determine your long-range goals. Take some time to assess where you are and where you would like to be some years from now. In this way, you'll establish a path for yourself and know what you're working toward. Perhaps you'll decide that your present career is not the right one for you, or even that you're happy where you are and don't want to invest more time and energy in your work than you already are. Whatever your goals, you'll be better able to measure your progress rather than feel defeated by some vague notion that you should be getting ahead in some unspecified way.

Don't rely on your boss to be your friend. Women, especially, are vulnerable to the notion that they have to like the people they're working with. In their book, *The Managerial Woman* (Doubleday, 1981), authors Margaret Hennig and Anne Jardim discuss differences in the ways males and females are raised: "Boys learn how to put up with each other and how to use each other to a degree that girls hardly ever find necessary. For men, friendship may be a valued outcome of interaction on the job. For women, it too often tends to be a prerequisite." Remember that you don't *have* to like the person you work for; you simply need to be able to work together. Look outside the office for friendships.

Avoid interoffice romance! Not only should you look elsewhere for friends, but you should look elsewhere for romance. Such a relationship rarely goes unnoticed by coworkers and provides a convenient outlet for others' frustration and anger. An office romance will *always* affect your work in some way and usually in a negative one. Often it results in you or the other person involved having to leave the company. Think about what happened to Mary Cunningham and Bill Agee at Bendix if temptation ever threatens to get the better of you!

Try to find a job that you enjoy. Prior to the turbulent '60s, work was often viewed as a means to an end—a way to pay for all of the material things that were supposed to lead to happiness. Since then, however, work is seen more and more as something you should *enjoy.* Although it's impossible for *everyone* to enjoy her or his job, it's important to like what you do if you want to get ahead. You know how hard it is to motivate yourself to do something that you don't want to do! If determination of your long-range goals indicates that you may enjoy something else, don't be afraid to move. Statistics from the U.S. Labor Department and the National Bureau for Economic Research indicate that the typical American will work for 10 employers, stay in each job only 3.6 years and switch careers three times! Moreover, today's employers are less likely to frown on frequent job changes.

Dress the part. Although clothes don't "make the man," they can certainly help. Newspapers recognize the importance of proper work attire when they include such advice columns as regular features. Witness also the recent proliferation of books along the theme of "dressing for success." In order to know what style would best suit your particular position and geographical location, look at the way your bosses dress. But be careful not to overdress. Consistently "outdressing" the boss may be viewed as a sign of disloyalty—not something that you want to convey! If you're a woman, try not to dress too provocatively. Studies show that employers tend to judge a woman's job performance negatively if she looks dressed for the bedroom.

Be persistent—but know when to quit. One-time efforts or sporadic attempts to get ahead are rarely successful. What is called for is persistence—the ability to stick with something long after others have thrown in the towel. People admire persistence because it is such a rare quality; the ability to stick with something may also compensate for other career deficits, such as lack of brilliance or creativity. Be realistic about your efforts, though; don't put in 20 years at a dead-end job waiting for that one promotion. Above all, don't mistake persistence for stubbornness, indecisiveness or inertia. But if what you want seems clearly and reasonably within your reach, continue to go for it!

Worry and Fear

We all have times when we think we're worrying too much or we have fears that we know are groundless. These feelings are usually caused by a stressful event and, once that event is over, our worries and fears subside. But if you find yourself constantly worrying, or afraid of many things most of the time, here's what you can do to help yourself.

LEARNING TO STOP WORRYING

According to a survey conducted by the National Institute of Mental Health, worriers are those who worry more than 90 minutes a day. Worry becomes a disorder when a person wants to stop worrying, but cannot. Worry is classified as an anxiety disorder. It can be looked at as a chain of negative and relatively uncontrollable thoughts and images. Now there may be help for worriers who are unhappy with their condition. Researchers at the Pennsylvania State University have come up with a way to treat people who worry too much. The technique works by associating worrisome thoughts with particular places and times. In this way, worriers can isolate their worries and spend the rest of their day productively. Here's Penn State's five-step technique:

→ Establish a 30-minute worry period that occurs at the same time and in the same place every day.

→ Learn to identify the early signs of worry, such as the inability to concentrate, a sinking feeling in the stomach or sweaty palms. Record the worries in a journal to read later.

→ Immediately replace worrisome thoughts by focusing attention on something else, such as completing a task or taking a walk.

→ Do not look at your list of worries until the worry period.

→ During your worry period, pull out your journal and think through the worries on the list. Try to come up with solutions.

The researchers found that worriers trained in using this method reported, on average, spending 35 percent less time worrying than previously. Results, however, appear to vary widely. Although this technique can benefit some people, it may not be as effective for others. Motivation to stop worrying and the ability to set aside a specific time period every day to practice the recommended procedure may influence the outcome. But if you are a worrier who has the time and inclination to bring your anxiety under control, your technique may be right for you.

CONTROLLING YOUR FEARS

Fear is actually a protective mechanism, helping us assess danger in all kinds of strange and unfamiliar situations. All of us are constantly bombarded by fearful thoughts and feelings. A problem arises, however, when the fear response itself threatens to take over, causing us to avoid certain challenges and actions, even contact with others. Left unchecked, fear becomes more and more pronounced so that eventually situations that were once easy to handle can become terrifying. To break out of this negative spiral of fear/avoidance/more fear/more avoidance, begin to get the upper hand on your fears.

Realize you are not alone. Often people think they are the only ones in the world suffering from fear. Such negative self-appraisal only worsens the problem because the person weakened by fears is further weakened by lowered self-esteem. In actuality, millions suffer from some fear or a combination of fears that interferes with their ability to live fully functional lives.

Know that fears don't have to be "rational." Obviously, it is perfectly reasonable to feel fear when faced with dangerous situations: a rattlesnake slithering toward you, debilitating illness or even the headlights of an approaching car coming too close to you. All fears, though, are not so rational. The sudden onset of terror when driving a car, for example, can occur apart from any identifiable reason. The person even *knows* that such fear is ridiculous, but is still unable to drive. Such irrational fears are all the more difficult to control as they can appear at any time and without warning.

Begin to identify your own unique fears. Take some time and make a list of everything you can think of that you're afraid of. Include in this list all situations that you currently avoid just in case you might feel that uncomfortable panicky feeling coming on. Make a second column where you designate these fears as either 1, doesn't bother you too much; 2, causes you moderate discomfort or 3, a fear that really interferes with your day-to-day functioning. Try to make this list as complete as possible; once you've gotten all your fears down on paper it will be easier to begin to take control over them.

Pick one level-1 fear from your list. Trying to overcome too many fears at one time is at best confusing and, more often, overwhelming and unsuccessful. Look over your list of fears and pick one that you wish to tackle. The fear that you choose should be one that causes you some discomfort but not one that would be too difficult to work on the first time. The idea is for you to gain mastery over a lower-level fear, building up your confidence to tackle a more terrifying situation the next time.

Further analyze this one fear. Suppose you decide to tackle your fear of driving. Determine the specific conditions and circumstances that cause you fear in this situation. For example, are you able to drive anywhere during the day but you panic at night? Do passengers in the car help? Does it make a difference at what speed you are traveling? Do specific routes or areas cause special difficulty? Once you have specified your fear, list the driving conditions least fearful for you, going in order of difficulty so that you end with that situation most likely to cause you the greatest difficulty. If you primarily fear driving with passengers at high speeds in unfamiliar territory, your list may begin with a half-mile trip by yourself to the local grocery store and end with taking a group of people a long distance.

Actually DO the things on your list. Beginning with the least frightening situation, actually carry out the items on your list. Make that trip to the local grocery store and continue to do so until you can drive there with no discomfort. After you have mastered the easier situation, go on to the next. It is important to remember that you will most likely be frightened at first, but the fear will fade in intensity as you repeat the action. Repeat this step as many times as you need to feel totally comfortable. If the next level of action is too much for you, simply perform the easier task until you're ready to try again. *Don't* give up and start over!

CALLING IN THE PROS

Sometimes, despite all your best efforts, personal problems can become overwhelming. That's when it's time to seek professional help. Unfortunately, it is impossible to give an exact formula for finding the perfect therapist. Someone you find to be comforting may be found grating or overbearing by someone else. There are, however, some general guidelines by which all therapists should conduct themselves. As a potential consumer of mental health services, you have a right to know these guidelines. You also have the right to information about the differences among mental health professionals that will allow you to make an informed choice. Here are the questions that people seeking a therapist frequently ask.

How do I know if I need to seek professional help? Many times an individual will be required to see a therapist. Courts, schools and employers often compel individuals to seek professional help for a problem. If you feel very depressed or feel like hurting yourself or others, then it is time to seek help. Otherwise it is usually a matter of personal choice. You don't *have* to see a therapist just because your marriage is in trouble or you're afraid to ride in airplanes, but therapy could probably help in situations such as these. Some people who don't have any major problems go to a therapist just to have a little time to themselves and reflect upon their own lives for a while. The basic rule is this: Therapy should improve the amount of pleasure you feel in life. This is true regardless of the problem or even if you don't have a problem.

(continued)

CALLING IN THE PROS—*Continued*

There are so many different kinds of "doctors" out there—what do all of those letters behind their names really mean? Individuals with varied backgrounds call themselves therapists or mental health professionals. It's not possible for the average person to be familiar with all of the different degrees and training programs that are available. See "Alphabet Soup—What Those Letters Really Mean" on page 141 for a list of the abbreviations you are most likely to encounter.

What's the difference between a psychologist and a psychiatrist? A psychologist is someone trained in the study of human behavior and personality. This training is obtained in graduate school and leads to the degree of M.A. or Ph.D. Many psychologists become involved in psychological research. Others obtain a license to practice psychotherapy. Psychologists cannot prescribe medication.

A psychiatrist goes to medical school and becomes an M.D. Following medical school, a training program is completed with courses in psychiatry and psychology. A residency in psychiatry usually follows. A psychiatrist can prescribe medication. Some psychiatrists also practice psychotherapy.

What's a psychoanalyst? A psychoanalyst is someone who uses a particular therapeutic technique, that of psychoanalysis. Because this person has received special training in using this technique and applies it to most of her or his patients, she or he can be called a psychoanalyst. Anyone (psychiatrist, psychologist, layperson) who identifies with this approach can call themselves a psychoanalyst.

What is "testing"? Who should do this? Testing, or assessment, covers a number of different areas. There is achievement testing, vocational testing and psychological testing, among others. Achievement testing is usually performed in schools and is designed to find out how much information a person possesses. Vocational testing is also meant to find out how much a person knows or how she or he performs, but in this case it is work-related. Psychological assessments are done to better understand the individual's personality. If done properly they can give the therapist a great deal of information,

(continued)

and they help the therapist focus on the important problems. As a result, this information may actually shorten the amount of time spent in therapy. Psychological assessments are almost always done by a psychologist.

How much will therapy cost? What if I can't afford it? As a general rule, psychiatrists charge the most money for their time, followed by psychologists. Their fees are usually based on an individual session lasting approximately 50 minutes. Most health insurance plans pay part or all of the fee charged by a licensed social worker, psychologist or psychiatrist. You should check your particular insurance plan to be sure.

If money is a consideration, when you call for your first appointment ask what the charge will be for that session. Then discuss the fee for future sessions during your initial interview. Many therapists have a sliding scale. If you cannot afford to pay anything, help is often available from community clinics and hospitals or from county mental health agencies.

Is a male therapist better than a female therapist? The most important consideration when choosing a therapist is whether you get the feeling that you can talk honestly and that the therapist cares about your concerns. The gender of the therapist is only important if it affects your ability to feel comfortable with that person.

Should I see more than one therapist before deciding whether I want that one or not, or whether I should continue at all? Most helping professionals agree that it is usually better to meet with at least two and possibly three therapists before deciding to continue with one in particular. In this way you can get a feel for what most therapists have in common and what is unique to each. You will also learn which one makes you feel the most comfortable.

How do I find a therapist? Looking in the yellow pages, asking a friend or your family doctor or calling your local board of mental health are all ways of finding a therapist. Recommendations from friends or other professionals who have knowledge of the therapist are usually most informative and helpful. The psychology department of a nearby university may also be a source of information.

(continued)

CALLING IN THE PROS—*Continued*

Group, family, couples or individual therapy—which is best? The type of therapy depends on the nature of the problem as well as the therapist's orientation. Many times a problem with an adolescent or child will involve the family. Marital problems nearly always involve the couple, providing both people are willing to attend. Groups can be helpful to those who have a common problem, such as trying to quit smoking. It is best to ask the therapist which type of therapy she or he recommends and why.

Short-term versus long-term therapy—how long should therapy last? Some therapists believe that most problems can be resolved within a specified period of time, and usually state this at the outset. That is, they will tell you before you begin that your therapy will last 10 sessions, or whatever they believe the number of sessions will be. Most therapists, however, do not operate in this way. For them, the length of therapy is not predetermined because they believe that each person is unique and that it's impossible to know how long it will take to resolve their particular problem. Rather, the issue of termination is part of the therapy and can be discussed at any time. You should feel free, therefore, to discuss the length of therapy with your therapist at any point during your course of treatment. Remember that, unless you have been mandated to therapy by the court or some other agency, the final decision to remain in therapy is yours and yours alone. If your therapist believes that it is in your best interest to continue and you disagree, get another professional opinion.

What should I expect during the first meeting, and how much should I disclose? Your therapist should be someone whom you trust, yet you must decide how much you wish to reveal about yourself. A therapist should not coerce you to reveal information. During the course of therapy you may wish to discuss areas of your life that are very private, such as your feelings about yourself, your spouse, your dreams or your sexual attitudes. Anything can be talked over with your therapist, but *you* are the one who should decide what is revealed about yourself, not the therapist.

(continued)

During your first meeting the therapist may ask you some general information about yourself such as your address, phone number, occupation and so on. She or he may also ask what is bothering you or why you have decided to come for treatment. In general, the therapist should create an atmosphere in which you feel comfortable to discuss whatever concerns you may have.

What if my therapist wants me to take medication? Medication can be a valuable asset to therapy. It may help you feel better and make better use of your therapy time. If you feel you may need medication and are not currently receiving it, discuss your feelings with your therapist. If you are already taking medication and you feel it is not helping or you want to stop, tell your therapist immediately. Although you can't be forced to take medication, you should continue to take the medication until your doctor tells you to stop. Remember that only a medical doctor (M.D.) can prescribe medication.

ALPHABET SOUP—
WHAT THOSE LETTERS REALLY MEAN

Therapists and other mental health professionals come from a wide background of knowledge. As a result, there are confusing strings of letters after their names. Here's a rundown of the abbreviations you're most likely to encounter when seeking professional help.

Ed.D., Doctor of Education: This person has earned her or his doctoral degree in education. If you are considering someone with this degree as a therapist, make sure they have had advanced training in the applied areas of psychology.

M.A., Master of Arts: A master's degree usually consists of one or two years of study past the bachelor's degree (college). The master's degree can be awarded in many areas and so it is best to check in which area your potential therapist has obtained her or his degree.

M.D., Doctor of Medicine: An M.D. has completed four years of medical school in addition to receiving an undergraduate degree.
(continued)

ALPHABET SOUP—*Continued*

An M.D. has usually had a residency at a hospital and training in a specialization. An M.D. who is a therapist should have had specialized training in psychiatry or a closely related field. M.D.s are permitted to prescribe medication.

M.Ed., Master of Education: The M.Ed. has a similar educational background as an Ed.D., but only up to the master's-degree level.

M.F.T., Marriage and Family Therapist: There are many states that license marriage and family therapists. If you live in one of these states you can be sure that the therapist has at least a master's degree and extensive experience in dealing with couples and families. In other states you have no assurance that these individuals are adequately trained.

M.S.W., Master's Degree in Social Work: Social work programs usually consist of two years of training beyond college. A large portion of this training is in actual work settings, so individuals with this degree often have a great deal of experience. They also have a greater knowledge of the social agencies that may be present in a community.

Ph.D., Doctor of Philosophy: The holder of this title has attended graduate school and obtained the highest degree possible. She or he usually received a master's degree prior to this and has written a dissertation (an original piece of research). A therapist's Ph.D. should be in psychology or a related area.

5

Shortcuts to

Good Parenting

It's not easy bringing up children these days, and there's plenty of advice in books and magazines and on television shows, each one pointing the way toward better parenting. Here we take a look at a variety of child-rearing situations, including health care, feeding, relationships and common problems, and how you can best cope with them. Although we don't offer all the answers, what we do offer is what parents, educators and child-care professionals have found to work well for them.

EDITORS' NOTE: We recognize the importance of bias-free text but, for the sake of clarity, we have chosen to use the pronoun "he" when talking about a single child.

Child Care

Whether you're caring for your children at home or having someone else look after them during the day, child care is an awesome responsibility. To make the way a bit smoother, we offer tips on how to avoid the most common child-raising mistakes, how to be effective working parents, how to find the best caregivers for your children and other sanity-saving ideas.

AVOIDING THE MOST COMMON CHILD-RAISING MISTAKES

Raising children has to be one of the toughest jobs around. What makes child rearing even more difficult is that there is so little preparation for what's in store—few people are "taught" how to be good parents! You can be a better parent, however, by simply *not doing* some things that are virtually guaranteed to cause problems. Here are ten of the most common mistakes that you can avoid when raising your children.

Failing to respect your children's privacy. Having a "place of their own" becomes especially important as children reach adolescence. This "place" could be as seemingly insignificant as a purse, a diary, a shoebox of notes or a drawer in a desk. The important part is that your children understand that this is their private place, and that you will not look through this without their express permission.

Not setting appropriate limits. Children of all ages need limits set regarding such issues as house rules, time to be in for the night, how to treat other family members and so forth. It is often difficult for parents to do this, however, for fear that the children won't like their parents as a result. On the contrary, children need to feel that parents are in charge, and children become anxious and afraid when they sense parental weakness. Clear, consistent limits teach children to control themselves, what is right and wrong and what is acceptable or unacceptable behavior. Without appropriate limits, children lack the means to develop self-control and often increasingly misbehave out of frustration and unhappiness.

Not following through on rules and punishments. The consequences of not following through on rules and punishments are usually similar to not setting appropriate limits: Your children will feel out of control, behave worse than before and, in general, will feel frustrated and bad about themselves.

Betraying your children's confidences. At a very basic level, children need to feel that they can trust their parents. Such trust forms the foundation for good self-esteem and, later, trust in others and in the world around them. One way to earn your child's trust is to respect your child's "secrets" unless, of course, to do so would be to endanger your child or someone else.

Relinquishing control of your children to someone else. There are fewer and fewer children today being raised by two parents in a traditional family home. It is quite common for both parents to work or for a single parent, who must work, to raise children on her or his own. In both situations, outside child care is a necessity. Although child care can work out quite well for all involved, there is increased potential for confusion on the children's part as to who is really in charge—the parent(s) or the substitute caregiver. If the parent(s) obviously relinquishes her or his control, it can be quite confusing and distressing to the children. Children need to feel that their parents are strong and in control in order to feel good about themselves.

Constantly criticizing your children. Ironically, parents can often be critical of their children because they love them so much. Such was the case with John. John was worried that his son Michael was very sensitive and would get hurt too easily. In order to "help" Michael, John constantly belittled him in an attempt to "toughen him up." John's behavior had the unfortunate effect of increasing Michael's doubts and insecurities about himself and, in addition, made him furious at his father. A better way to help Michael would have been to show him support and love, enhancing his self-image and helping him to be more sure of himself.

Trying to substantially change your children's personalities. Seldom do we meet the perfect person; we often think to ourselves, "So and so would be great *if only . . . .*" The impulse to change our children more to our liking is particularly strong, especially if we see them imitating something in us that we're not all that proud of. Sue, for instance, would always tell her shy child, Michelle, that she should speak up more often and talk louder. In essence, she embarrassed Michelle in front of others. Worse, she would continually tell Michelle that she could "change if she wanted to," implying that Michelle was shy out of spite for her mother. Sue's continuing effort to try to change Michelle had the reverse effect—Michelle felt worse about herself for not being able to change, and she resented her mother for not accepting her as she was.

Disciplining your children by using inappropriate statements. When your children do something that you find unacceptable, avoid using the following statements:

- → "You're bad." The child isn't bad, the behavior is.
- → "Wait till Daddy comes home." Try handling the situation yourself and not delaying punishment until it's no longer meaningfully related to the transgression.
- → "Because I'm the mommy (daddy), that's why." This statement doesn't teach your children about right and wrong and gives little guidance about how to act in the future.
- → "Your sister (brother) doesn't do that." Comparison with other children fosters increased feelings of resentment and competition.
- → "See if I care." You don't want your children to think you don't care if they misbehave—you do. Also, don't tacitly dare your children to misbehave again.
- → "You never do anything right." This statement is particularly painful for children to hear and damages self-esteem.

Fostering dependence long after it's realistic. Successful parenting ideally prepares children to make their way in the world as well as they can. As your children mature, the growing process is marked primarily by increasingly independent behavior: walking, being toilet trained, going off to school, sleeping over at a friend's and ultimately, leaving home for work and/or college. If your children's efforts at independence are thwarted in any way, they will have that much more difficulty in establishing an independent existence.

Giving your children the message that they are incapable, irresponsible, unreliable or incompetent. This mistake is related to several of the others presented here and probably has the most devastating effects. Children are very attuned to your feelings for them, and usually try to act accordingly. You communicate feelings for your children not only through what you say to them but, equally important, through your behavior toward them. For instance, if Jimmy starts to do something and you continually rush in to help him, you are giving him the message that you have little faith he can do it himself. After enough similar experiences, Jimmy will also doubt his abilities. A good parent wants to enhance their children's self-esteem and feelings of confidence, not diminish their belief in themselves. Indeed, many parental "mistakes" can be tolerated without harm to the child as long as a basic loving and supportive attitude prevails.

SETTING RULES FOR YOUNGER CHILDREN

Doris Durrell, a child psychologist, has suggestions for giving rules to your children. Her ideas appear in *The Critical Years* (New Harbinger Publications, 1984).

Give explanations for your rules. For example, when you ask your children to straighten up their toys, don't give a simple order with no follow-up, and don't answer your children's request for an explanation with, "Because I told you so." Instead, offer an explanation such as "Because I don't want to trip over the blocks," or "I like to have the room straightened before we go to bed." Such a response will improve your children's reasoning and ability to make logical connections. These, in turn, will help them improve their own self-control. Also, children will be much more likely to follow a rule if they understand the reason for it.

Make rules as simple as possible. Children are naturally baffled by the adult world's contradictions. Keep rules simple and direct. Make exceptions to rules only after the children have learned the rules.

Be consistent. Children don't understand subtleties. Throwing a sponge across the room is the same to them as throwing a baseball across it. If you do not want your children to throw things, then make sure you don't throw anything, either.

If you lay down a rule, enforce it. Don't let your children think they can break rules and not pay consequences. Provide the consequences immediately, and they will learn self-control more quickly.

BECOMING A BETTER WORKING PARENT

Juggling a job and parenting can make you feel like you are being pulled apart on a torture rack. But there are some shortcuts to easing the strain. Sally Olds, a noted author on parenting and childhood, accumulated some tips in a book called *Working Parents Survival Guide* (Bantam Books, 1983). Here are a few suggestions.

On the Job Front

→ Try to persuade your employer to let you work flexible hours, work part-time, share your job with another worker or perform part of your job at home.

→ Ask your employer to refrain from asking you to work late on short notice.

→ Ask your employer to allow paid leave for you to take care of sick children at home.

→ Explore the possibility of establishing a day-care center at work.

→ Try to concentrate on work at work and on home life while at home.

→ Prove your worth and dedication to an employer before you ask for time off. Save special time-off requests for when it's really important.

→ Every now and then take your children to lunch during your workday, even if a sitter has to drive them in.

→ Listen carefully to your children. Take time off from work for the activities your children most want you to attend, not the ones that are most convenient for you.

Sick Days

→ If a child is sick, and you cannot otherwise get off work, use one of your own sick days to care for him.

→ Take a half-day off and have your spouse take a half-day off so you can split nursing duties.

→ Develop two or three emergency-care people in case a child is sick and you have an important meeting at work. These may be neighbors, friends or relatives. You and your child should get to know them before an emergency arises.

Between Job and Home

→ Move closer to work or change jobs so that you can diminish commuting time and devote the saved hours to your family.
→ Use commuting time to unwind from a job and prepare yourself for home life. Get off the bus a stop early and walk the extra distance—the exercise will help you feel fit and clear your head.
→ If you still need some transition time when you arrive home, ask for 15 or 30 minutes to yourself. Then take the time to nap, bathe, exercise or otherwise relieve stress.

At Home

→ Don't fall into the trap of thinking that you can do everything, that you can be a superparent.
→ Make friends with other working parents. Exchange problems, ideas, sympathies and solutions.
→ Learn to handle the stresses and little hassles of life. Put them in perspective. Attack one problem at a time. Then give yourself one treat a day—a special food, a long bath, a talk with a good friend.
→ Plan family time. Push back dinner an hour if need be. Devote Saturday or Sunday to family activities.
→ Because time is precious, try to get the family to act as a cooperative. Encourage each member to help when work needs to be done—where everyone in the room helps when just one person spills, for example, or where each shares in the cooking and cleaning.

CHOOSING AN IN-HOUSE CAREGIVER

Selecting a person to come into your home and care for your children all or part of the workweek is never an easy task. Here is some advice compiled by Gloria Norris and JoAnn Miller in *The Working Woman's Complete Handbook* (New American Library, 1984).

Consider hiring a relative. A relative is okay, as long as you can talk frankly with her or him about matters of child raising. A person committed to old-fashioned techniques or who does not take suggestions well will be troublesome. Insist on paying, even if it's a small sum—it will be appreciated.

LETTER OF AGREEMENT BETWEEN PARENTS AND IN-THE-HOME CHILD-CARE PROVIDER

In addition to the points included here, you may also want to spell out nap and feeding times, appropriate disciplinary action the provider can take with the child, general household rules, other household duties required of the provider, specific emergency procedures and the like.

Dear _____:

Please regard this as a letter of agreement between us concerning care for our child. If you find anything inappropriate or missing in this agreement, please call us so that we can discuss it. Otherwise, we'd appreciate it if you would sign one copy and return it to us. The other copy is for you. Thanks.

You have agreed to care for our child in our home _____ days a week from _____ A.M. to _____ P.M. for a total of _____ hours a week. You will be paid every week on _____ at the end of the day.

You agree not to take our child out in your car, to your house or to the house of a friend unless you get our permission first. You will take our child outside daily for a walk, to the playground or to play in our backyard. You are not required to do any housework, except to clean up your own dishes and those that our child used during the day and to leave the house as you found it. You will feed our child breakfast and lunch. You are to provide your own transportation and your own meals and snacks.

In case of an emergency you are to call _____ at work at _____-_____. The names and numbers of our pediatrician and neighbor as well as emergency numbers are posted near all telephones.

For this care we will pay you $_____ each week, minus what we withhold for income tax, FICA and FUTA. Should we ever need you to stay later than _____ P.M., we will pay you $_____ for each additional hour we are late from work and you stay with our child. We agree to increase your hourly rate by at least _____ percent after the first _____ months.

We will pay you for a full week even if one of your workdays falls on a holiday that one of us is also paid for and will be home.

(continued)

LETTER OF AGREEMENT—*Continued*

The same will be true for those days that we ask you not to come because one of us chooses to stay home with our child for whatever reason. However, you will not be paid for our vacations or for yours. (And as we discussed, we will be taking one week in _____ and one in _____ and we understand that you will take a vacation sometime in _____ and _____.)

　　　　Should you become ill and not be able to come to work, we'd appreciate knowing as early as possible so that we can make other arrangements. Because such an occasion will usually mean that one of us will have to stay home or pay for another sitter, we would expect that you would do your best to make up the missed time by coming in an extra day or days as soon as you are well. If you are unable to make up a sick day, we agree to pay you for your sick day, for a maximum of ____ sick days a year, starting after the first ____ months.

　　　　You will be caring for our child ____ days per week. On occasion, either you or we might request another day be substituted for one of these. A change in days is fine once in a while, as long as it is discussed in advance so that arrangements can be made by all of us.

　　　　This agreement shall be in effect until one of us chooses to terminate it. It's understood that a minimum of 2 weeks' notice is required for termination.

　　　　Let us end by just saying that we are delighted that you'll be caring for our child. All three of us look forward to getting to know you better.

Sincerely,

_____

(Parents)

Agreed to by:

_____

(Child-care Provider)

Check the "Situations Wanted" advertisements in newspapers and on bulletin boards, and place your own ads there as well. In your ad, say that you require recent references. It is also a good screening technique to add the ages of your children and whether light housekeeping is to be part of the job. Work the grapevine—ask parents where you work, at dinner parties or in playgrounds if they have recommendations.

Screen applicants by telephone first. Determine if they understood the ad. Describe the job, making certain to mention its most difficult aspects.

When an applicant comes to your home for an interview, ask specific questions. For example, ask "What would you do if Jane began throwing her blocks at our ceramic collection?" rather than "What is your philosophy on discipline?" Have your children present for at least part of the interview and observe the feelings between the children and the applicant. Look for genuine enthusiasm in an applicant, a real appreciation of children and signs of flexibility and intelligence, which the caregiver will need to have to cope with the antics of children.

Consider hiring a man, especially if your bent is to break down society's stereotypes. You may find that some men are less reluctant to do light housework than a woman who regards herself as a professional child raiser. And you may find that men are often less set in their ways about child rearing and will accommodate their actions to your views.

CHOOSING A DAY-CARE CENTER

Day-care centers, including nursery schools and preschools, are not all the same. When selecting one, do your research. Here are some steps you should take.

Define the center's orientation. Day-care centers have differing philosophies. Some tend to concentrate on intellectual development, emphasizing nascent abilities in dealing with numbers and letters. Others concentrate more on emotional and social development. Either type is fine, but the one you select should have elements of the other woven in and also should include a wide range of physical, artistic and musical activities. The least desirable type is one that considers its task to be mere "baby-sitting" and tolerates a certain amount of boredom and unhappiness.

Day-care centers that are cooperatives or parent-run organizations tend to be good because the parents want stimulating and wholesome activities for their children. Often the cost of these is lower because the parents themselves act as teachers or teacher-helpers on a rotating basis. In addition, an organization of this type forms a kind of support group for you because you come to know and learn from parents who have problems similar to yours.

Visit the center first. Before you decide on a day-care center, visit it, preferably unannounced. Be sure to get past the front office and observe the room in which the children will play. Later, interview the teachers. When you get a chance, ask the teachers about their training. Ask how long teachers remain at the center—the better centers keep teachers longer. Questions you should ask yourself during your visit are:

→ What is the "feel" of the group?
→ Are the children relaxed?
→ Do the children seem to trust their teacher?
→ Do the children cooperate with each other?
→ Is the atmosphere aggressive or subdued—how would it please your rambunctious youngster or your shy one?
→ What is the attitude of the teacher?
→ Does the teacher deal with the children as individuals or as a group? (Don't be alarmed if a teacher appears to be doing little— many of the best ones don't rule with a heavy hand but subtly guide the play.)
→ Is there one teacher for every four or five children?
→ How are the physical facilities?
→ Is there an outside play area?
→ What kind of outdoor equipment is there?
→ Does the equipment look safe?
→ Is there a good fence?
→ Are the bathrooms adequate and clean?
→ Are there fire detectors, fire extinguishers and fire exits?
→ What provisions are made for medical emergencies?

Don't make a hasty decision. After your visit, take some extra time to consider your choice. Don't choose simply on the basis of your own convenience—close to work or home, for example—but consider the needs of your children. Do not equate expense with quality. Probably the most important factor in day care is the attitude of the teacher, so recollect what you observed about this aspect. And talk with other parents who have had children in the day-care centers you are considering; their opinions are based on experience.

KEEPING KIDS AMUSED INDOORS

It's a Saturday afternoon and you had hoped the kids could play outdoors, but the weather is lousy. What can you do? Here are six ways to keep children happy indoors.

LETTER OF AGREEMENT BETWEEN PARENTS AND DAY-CARE CENTER PROVIDER

Because a center has its own house rules and cares for several children, you may not be able to add all the conditions and considerations that you'd like to in this letter of agreement. The day-care center you choose may very well have its own forms for you to fill out and sign. Even if this is the case, you may find points in the sample here that you like and can add to a standard form.

Dear _____:

As we have discussed, you will provide day care to our child beginning around _____ when the child is approximately _____ months of age. A fee of $_____ per week, in effect until at least _____, will be paid to you to provide care beginning at _____ A.M. and ending at _____ P.M., _____ through _____. This fee will be paid each _____ by check, even if our child misses days because of sickness, holidays, or vacations. For the _____ weeks per year when you are on vacation, it is your responsibility to provide alternate care for the child, which has my advance approval.

Infant equipment, including crib, high chair and so forth, will be provided by you. We will provide food and diapers for the child. Instructions will be provided to you regarding feeding.

When the child becomes ill during the day, you will inform us as soon as possible, and we will mutually decide on the best action to take.

Any trips that are taken by the child during your care must be approved by us in advance.

Enclosed is a nonrefundable application fee of $_____. Also enclosed is a check for $_____ for the first week's fee. These two fees register the child and assure us a position in your day-care facility.

Please sign below to establish agreement with the above information. Keep the *copy* for your records and return the original in the enclosed envelope.

Thank you.

SIGNED:_____   SIGNED:_____
    (Child-care Provider)   (Parents)

Put nonskid mats on the floor of the bathtub. Then, with a shaving cream can, squirt the tiles around the tub and let the kids "fingerpaint" the tiles. Hose the kids down later—the shaving cream will clean them.

Get out old stationery and stamps or stickers so the children can play at post office. Let them write letters to one another and send them via different locations around the house to their final destinations. (If you are lucky, they may even write letters to their grandparents!) You can add play money and receipt forms to the game to give it a business dimension.

Hand out old magazines. Have the kids make a scrapbook of cutout photographs.

Have children take turns lying on a large piece of paper. Trace around them; then let them use crayons, bits of old cloth and glue to fill in the outline with eyes, clothes and so forth.

Fetch old boxes of various sizes, plus crayons, felt-tip pens, string, paper clips and paste. Let the kids make houses and stores from the boxes.

Let the kids dress up in what they can find around the house. For example, let them make crowns out of cardboard rolled into cylinders, and ponchos out of grocery bags.

Health

Keeping your children healthy goes beyond treating the usual childhood diseases, colds and flu. It also means feeding them well and offering a safe home environment. Here are some tips for keeping your children in the best of health.

KEEPING CHILDREN HEALTHY

Keeping children healthy is not a matter of luck. Families can take definite steps to promote health and happiness. Dr. Herbert Haessler and C. R. Harris, authors of *How to Make Sure Your Baby Is Well—and Stays That Way* (Rawson Associates, 1984), have these ideas on sustaining good health.

Start with the basics. Provide a clean, safe, warm environment. Dress your children in adequate clothes. Practice childproofing and accident prevention.

Offer a nutritious diet. Keep nonnutritious foods out of the house and don't let your children see you eating them yourself. Make snacks of fruit pieces, graham crackers and milk and the like. Discourage relatives from giving sweets as gifts or rewards.

Keep an up-to-date medical history of each child. This should include immunizations, medication records, allergies, injuries and any family traits that in the future may be useful to a doctor. Keep records in a safe, but easily accessible, place.

Provide a stress-free environment. Everything goes better when a family is relaxed. Dr. Mike Samuels and his wife Nancy, authors of *The Well Child Book* (Summit Books, 1982), are especially enthusiastic about the idea that emotional well-being is a leading contributor to physical well-being. "Family life can be patterned to create healthy children," they proclaim. And "evidence points to the fact that over half of childhood illnesses and accidents can be eliminated merely by managing stress better . . . . Children should learn to relax and do things they enjoy."

EASING A CHILD THROUGH ILLNESS

Dealing with a sick child is no fun, but there are some things you can do to make the way smoother for both of you.

→ Give medicine matter-of-factly, as if you would never think your child would not like it.

→ When you give medicine in liquid form, make it a drink your child usually doesn't have, such as cranberry juice or lemonade, so he will not detect a funny taste.

→ If the medicine is a crushable tablet, grind it up and put it into some coarse food such as chunky applesauce, but only in a small helping in case your child doesn't eat much.

→ Use a lollipop for a tongue depressor.

→ Give toys or games that keep him occupied—puzzles, stringing beads, weaving pot holders, making a scrapbook or building a model town or circus. Other time-passers are new library books, musical instruments, activity books with mazes and games and a doctor kit. Bring home sing-along and story tape recordings or records from the library.

→ If your child misses his friends, let him call them on the phone.

CHILDPROOFING YOUR HOUSE

Accidents around the house are a frequent cause of childhood injuries, yet many of them are preventable. Note these important shortcuts to keeping your children healthy and safe from accidents.

Put away objects that can cause harm. These include pens, pencils, electric fans and space heaters. Put vases, statues and other objects that might tip over out of reach. Get down on your hands and knees to look at the house in the way a crawling baby does. Search for buttons, pins, paper clips, bottle caps and the like that a child could swallow.

Lock up all medicines and hazardous substances. Put away detergents, cleansers, plant food, fish food, insecticides, furniture polish and similar substances.

Install childproof safety latches on cabinet doors and drawers. And make sure latches and locks on exterior doors, basement doors and the like work and are beyond the reach of little hands.

Use gates at the tops and bottoms of stairs. Avoid those, though, that have wooden, accordionlike rails. Children can get their heads stuck in the diamond-shaped openings.

Put all plastic bags out of reach. And watch what you put into wastebaskets —children can pull things out again.

Plug up electrical outlets. You can purchase plastic outlet safety covers in hardware stores.

Deactivate privacy locks. These can be found on bedroom and bathroom doors. You don't want your child locking himself inside.

Review first-aid procedures. Keep emergency numbers near telephones on all floors. Include the telephone numbers for police, fire, ambulance and the local poison information center.

Keep a bottle of syrup of ipecac to use in case of poisonings. Use it only if a poison information staffer advises you to induce vomiting or you know for certain that induced vomiting is the proper first-aid procedure.

Buy products that show they have met safety standards. But also use your own critical eye and knowledge of your child's strength to evaluate products.

Keep bathroom doors shut. Bathrooms can be dangerous places for small children. They can climb into the tub or toilet, open a cabinet door or slip on a wet tile floor.

Lower your water heater's thermostat to 125°F or less. Hot tap water can easily burn a child's tender skin. To avoid the possibility, never leave a child alone at a sink or in the bathtub.

Kids and Food

It's not easy getting kids to eat what's good for them. From fussy toddlers to junk-food-loving teens, children frustrate their parents with their bad food habits. Here are some tips to help you win the nutritional battle.

FEEDING A FUSSY TODDLER

Toddlers can put up fierce resistance to what is placed in front of them. But if you are clever early on and practice some elementary psychology, you can usually head off finicky habits.

Be alert to food allergies your children might have. Introduce solids slowly, especially if your children have been bottle fed. Rotate their diet so that you don't repeat serving the same food within a four-day period. Watch for a rash, fussiness or wakefulness. Eliminate any foods that seem to cause problems.

Keep mealtimes pleasant times. Let your children think of food as something they enjoy.

Don't insist that your children eat a particular food item. Remember that over the course of several days children eat all that they need, including food from all the proper nutrition groups. Your children's diet may end up being unbalanced at one meal or for one day, but it usually balances out over several days. Once your children have refused a particular food, your requests will only set their minds against it.

Serve small portions. Dice or cook vegetables, which are difficult to chew raw.

Keep meals attractive and occasionally fun. Offer a new place mat from time to time and new utensils. Serve alphabet soup. Make food visually appealing.

Work fruit pieces into gelatin desserts. If your fussy eater doesn't like the fruit chunks, puree them before you add them to the gelatin. Also try working vegetables into soups.

If your toddlers prefer to use fingers instead of a spoon, let them do so. Don't make meals a time for discipline, or they will turn into battles.

Don't stock nonnutritious food, such as cookies and candy, as temptations. Even if sweets are initially offered as rewards, your children will soon want them before eating anything else.

(continued on page 160)

HOMEMADE BABY FOODS

Almost anything you prepare for yourself can be made for your baby, so long as it's not too spicy, does not contain foods that give some people gas (such as beans and cabbage) and is not too acidic (such as lots of citrus fruit or lots of tomatoes). Grind up baby's portion in a baby-food grinder, a blender or a food processor. As your baby grows, you'll find that he can handle minced pieces of food mixed in with smoother foods, which will add variety to the puree usually recommended by pediatricians when babies begin solids. Check with your doctor about when to start solids and then when baby can handle minced foods and finger foods. (See the box "Healthy Finger Foods and Snacks for Toddlers" on the facing page.)

For convenience, make up several baby-sized portions at a time and freeze them. You can put individual portions into ice cube trays or spoon portions onto cookie sheets, freeze and then place into plastic bags.

Some foods and combinations of foods that work well for babies include the following:

apple sauce and other pureed fruits
banana-yogurt blender drink
chicken, split peas and tomatoes
combinations of steamed and pureed foods, such as beef, carrots, chicken, corn, fish, green beans, pork, spinach, squash, sweet potato, veal
cooked oatmeal with fruit
cooked rice and barley
cottage and ricotta cheese
egg custard
egg salad
macaroni and cheese
mashed avocado
mashed hard-boiled or scrambled egg
mashed potatoes and spinach
plain yogurt with pureed fruit
pureed chicken livers
smooth, mild-flavored soups, such as cream of potato and spinach

HEALTHY FINGER FOODS
AND SNACKS FOR TODDLERS

As your children get older, they will start to get interested in feeding themselves finger foods. Discuss food options for this age with your doctor and explore your children's likes and dislikes. But watch out for any foods you think they may choke on. Popcorn and nuts are definitely out, and grapes, raisins, apple slices, hot dogs and other small, round, hard, solid foods are questionable.

Here are some good finger foods to consider:

any of the baby foods listed in the box "Homemade Baby Foods" on the facing page, chopped instead of mashed or pureed
baked apple with sweet potato
brown rice pudding
chopped chicken livers
cut-up baked potato, stuffed or plain
deviled egg
fish sticks, cut-up fish cakes
French toast
granola (avoid the very sweet kind and those with nuts)
mashed tofu cooked in broth, plain or with vegetables
mild cheese
oatmeal cookies, whole wheat peanut butter cookies
omelet, quiche
pasta and tomato sauce (shells, ravioli and tortellini are neater, spaghetti more fun)
pieces of fresh fruit (avoid hard fruits such as apple slices until baby is older because it might be hard to swallow and lead to choking)
pieces of meat loaf
pizza, cut-up
rice, barley or mashed potatoes with any chopped meat, fish or vegetables
small pieces of cooked ground meat, fish, chicken
small sandwiches made on cocktail bread
soups
toast, bagel, muffin or crackers, with cream cheese
tuna fish, plain or salad
vegetables, plain or spread with cream cheese
waffles and pancakes enriched with cottage cheese, shredded

Don't let your children fill up on milk first. Give food first and let them fill up on milk after.

Be alert to your children's feeding limits. When your children begin to play more than eat, assume they are no longer hungry and allow them to leave the table.

GETTING CHILDREN TO EAT WHAT'S GOOD FOR THEM

Older children can drift toward eating too much junk food, especially when away from home. Here are some ideas on how to return them to a better diet.

Get children involved in foods. Take them grocery shopping. Talk to them about the foods you select, what nutritional groups they belong to and how such foods help people stay healthy.

Have older children plant a garden. They can watch the food grow, and they should be able to taste a big difference between fresh foods and processed foods.

Involve children in cooking. Older ones can prepare whole meals. Younger ones can add vegetables to soups or assemble into salads the nutritious items you have selected and cut.

Have children chart their food habits. Tell them to keep a record of everything they eat and drink for several weeks and then to analyze both the strong and the weak points of their diet. Then encourage them to gradually improve their selections of foods. Have them concentrate on one type of food at a time: fruits the first week, for example, green vegetables the second and so on. Mark success with stars on a chart.

Be a model. Don't lapse into poor eating habits yourself.

Relationships

Sibling rivalry is probably one of parenting's biggest challenges. How many times have you heard yourself plead, "Why can't you children learn to get along?" And there are other relationships to deal with outside of those at home. Perhaps your child is aggressive toward other kids, or the reverse—shy and retiring. Either can present problems. Here's a look at helping your children, and you, cope with relationships.

HANDLING SIBLING RIVALRY

Sibling rivalry can be a maddening disruption to any family. But there are some measures you can take to ease the conflicts. Lea Brammick and Anita Simon, educators and authors of *The Parent Solution Book* (Penguin Books, 1983), have these suggestions.

Show love for each child as an individual. Assure each child that you love him and that he need not compete with siblings for your affection. Focus on each child's strengths and individual accomplishments.

Help each child build affection for the other. As a parent you should try to encourage affection between siblings that will overshadow any short-term flare-ups of competition. Have them enjoy things in common, such as camping trips or visits to relatives, in order to build shared experiences and memories. When one goes away alone to a party or on a trip, encourage him to bring home a present for the other. Encourage the older one to use his expertise to help the younger one, showing how to take the bus, for example, or how to use a vending machine. Commend any caring attitudes and acts that you see.

Consider causes. When rivalry erupts, look for causes that may lie below the surface. One child may really be angry at a teacher or friend and is taking it out on his sister or brother. Try to discover such sources and disarm them with understanding talks.

DEALING WITH AGGRESSIVE BEHAVIOR

Aggressive behavior in children is always troublesome. Psychologists and experts have worked for years developing ideas on how to curb this all-too-natural instinct. Here are some of their guidelines.

Be careful not to let your child think aggression is acceptable. Don't be aggressive yourself, but rather always maintain your self-control. Do not subtly condone violence by not setting strict enough limits on behavior.

Prevent aggressive action before it arises. Then reinforce alternate behavior. For example, when you see a child about to grab a toy from another, run to the child and say, "No, Tricia. Jim is playing with that puzzle. We'll find another one for you." If Tricia still wants the puzzle, try to work out a trade or compromise that involves getting another toy or waiting for the first one. Close supervision is paramount. It is far easier to prevent grabbing and to reinforce sharing than to halt aggressive behavior once it is seen by children as a way to get results.

Cut down on discipline. This may seem odd, but if a child becomes habitually aggressive, it may be because he is receiving too much discipline and is reacting in a hostile manner. If a child seems frantic much of the time, try to calm him with more relaxing activities. Sometimes aggressive behavior develops because a child has had too little chance to get used to other children and imagines they are a threat; see that such a child gets more supervised play with others.

Explain to a child in very clear terms that violence will not be tolerated. Explain that it hurts. When you see aggressive behavior, intervene immediately. Be consistent.

Help a child to understand that there are outlets other than harmful aggressiveness. Say that you will allow him to get angry and shout, or complain at length to you, but that the child must not hit or bite. Tell the child he can punch pillows, clay or a duffle bag to vent violent feelings. Explain that everyone has ways of channeling violent feelings into other actions. Give your child some examples of how you, other members of the family or the child's friends deal with the problem.

HELPING YOUR CHILD OVERCOME SHYNESS

Edna LeShan, author of *When Your Child Drives You Crazy* (St. Martin's Press, 1985), has accumulated thoughts on dealing with shyness. Basically, she suggests that you probe for the sources of the shyness and treat these rather than the shyness itself.

Shyness may result from a distorted self-image. Examples are "I am ugly" or "I am uncoordinated." The solution is to try to correct the perceptions involved.

Shyness may be a way of avoiding reality. A child may have convinced himself that he will fail and so retreats from people. The solution is to build up your child's self-confidence. Have him tackle one task at a time. Show your child he can succeed at numerous jobs, and build self-esteem on these.

Shyness may grow upon feelings of hostility and it can actually be a means to cloak such feelings. A child may be retreating from certain peers because he is, in fact, angry with them. If such is the case, allow your child to vent his anger. Then teach your child that he can avert many such hostile feelings if he becomes more assertive in relationships with others.

Shyness may actually stem from a stage of maturation. An outgoing 2-year-old may become an introverted 3-year-old simply because he is more aware of complex social customs, but does not really understand them. The child is puzzled and needs time for reflection to figure things out. Give a child like this time, a sympathetic ear and a reasonable explanation of social mores.

Provide your child with opportunities for socialization. Dr. Barbara Powell, author of *The Complete Guide to Your Child's Emotional Health* (Franklin Watts, 1984), adds that shyness may often be handed down from shy parents. In addition, she says, shyness establishes a vicious cycle: a child doesn't have social skills, so is not exposed to situations in which he might learn them and as a result doesn't have them at an even older age. Dr. Powell suggests going out of your way to provide such a child with opportunities for socialization.

EASING SEPARATION ANXIETY

Until a child is 6 months old or so, the child does not particularly care who looks after him. Beyond this age, the child can become very attached to his parents and doesn't really understand that a separation will not be permanent. At 1½ or so, he probably understands that a departure will eventually be followed by a return, but the child may be upset nonetheless. To ease separation anxiety, try some of the methods outlined below.

Explain what's going to happen. If your child is old enough to understand, explain in advance the approaching separation, telling your child when you will leave, who will stay with him and when you will return. Explain that the separation is not a punishment. If the separation will be a particularly long one—for days—make a calendar for your child to X through the days, or a picture book that tells the story of your departure and your happy return.

Have a prospective sitter come over and play with your child while you remain at home. Make subsequent leaves short to begin with, then gradually longer. If your child is going to a day-care center, take him on a day before the sessions begin, introduce the child to the teacher, if possible, and point out toys you think your child will enjoy.

Plan something special that your child can do with the sitter. It could be playing a game, doing some craft work or opening a new toy.

Whenever you leave, use the same words and gestures. Similarly, whenever you return, use the same words and gestures. Your child will come to understand that departures are temporary and that returns are not brief interludes between departures.

When you return, spend time with your child. Allow your child to express his feelings—they may be negative toward you, but this is common. Reassure your child that your time away was not because you were angry with him, and tell your child that you love him more than ever. And be careful not to make the time you spent away from him sound too interesting.

School

School plays a big role in your children's lives. They will spend more time during the day there than with you. So it's important to start them off right and then make sure they stay on track. Here are some tips for helping your kids make the most of school, from preparing them for that first school year to helping them improve their grades.

PREPARING FOR THE FIRST SCHOOL YEAR

Child psychologist Charles E. Schaefer, author of *How to Talk to Children about Really Important Things* (Harper & Row, 1984), has these ideas about easing a child's entry into schooling.

Familiarize the child with the school. Before opening day, tour the building. If possible, introduce him to the teacher. Tell your child how long school will last, what the routines will be and what behavior is expected of him. Answer all of your child's questions—uncertainty will make him anxious. Encourage your child in the weeks and days before school begins to "play school," using what he has learned about it from your visit.

Expect success. Talk about school as something everyone does. Do not suggest there are alternatives. Be confident of your child's success and he will pick up on your attitude.

Be supportive. Encourage your child to talk about school. Assure him that you and many others have had apprehensions about school but that talking about them helps.

Encourage independence. The more dependent a child is on you for feelings of security and happiness, the harder it will be for him to duplicate these feelings in school. Long before opening day, build your child's self-reliance in thinking, playing and having fun with others. Gradually increase your child's time away from you with sitters, playmates or relatives.

Be positive. Take an upbeat attitude about school and encourage your child's older siblings to do so, too. Equate school with independence, growing up, adventure, making new friends and learning fascinating things.

Here are some thoughts on the subject from other child psychologists and educators:

→ Don't push a child into school because he is bright or because you want your child to be academically advanced; it is more important that he is ready socially.

→ Try to have your child play a number of times with a child who will be in his class; that way your child will at least know someone when school begins.

→ If your child will walk or take the bus to school, go over the route with him several times in advance of opening day so that your child need not be apprehensive before he even gets to the schoolhouse door.

GETTING KIDS OFF TO SCHOOL

Are mornings always a rush at your house, with parents getting ready for work, kids getting ready for school and no one knowing where anything is? If this sounds familiar, take heed of the advice below.

Make a list or chart of each day's needs for each child. For example, Joseph: Monday, gym shorts; Tuesday, violin and so on. Post it on the refrigerator or other conspicuous place and have the children check it before they leave.

Plan morning chores ahead of time. Make sure everyone knows who will clear the breakfast table, who will clean the dishes and so forth.

Plan breakfasts that are easy to fix and easy to clean up. For example, make large amounts of waffles or pancakes in advance and heat them in a toaster each morning as needed.

The night before, ask your children to talk to you about school events of the following day. Help them to think of things they will need. Gather as many items as practical and place them next to the front door. If they can't be placed at the front door, make a note about them and tape it to the door. It's also a good idea to make lunches the night before.

Have children awakened with their own alarm clocks. About 10 minutes after the alarms go off, play loud music that the children enjoy to make sure they're up and moving. If your bathrooms are limited, stagger wake-up times.

Get up half an hour earlier yourself. You may find this unthinkable, but you'd be surprised by the difference it can make—the rest of the morning will not be so hectic because you've had some time to yourself.

IMPROVING YOUR CHILDREN'S GRADES

Does your style as a parent affect the grades your children receive in school? Is there anything that you, as the parent, can do to help your children improve their grades? The answer to both these questions is a definite *yes*. According to a recent Stanford University study by researcher Sanford M. Dornbusch, there is a relationship between parents' actions and their children's school performance. Parents can, and do, have an influence on their children's grades. Here's what you can do to help your children get higher grades in school.

Be firm, yet encouraging. Set reasonable guidelines for your children and stick to them, but also take the time to explain the reasons for the rules. Try to give your children the sense that you have confidence in their capabilities and that you know they are trying. Even if they aren't always trying their hardest, they may put more effort into their work knowing you think so highly of them.

Communicate. Talk with your children in terms they can understand. Explain to them why you think school is important and why they need to do their homework. It may not make arithmetic any easier, but at least they know that you value what they are doing. And take time to really listen to what they have to say. You can let them know you're listening by giving a one-sentence summary of what they said before going on to what you want to tell them.

Let them play. Unlikely as it may seem, participation in school sports is associated with better grades. This is because children use play as a way of *learning*, rather than just as a diversion, as most adults do. They also have more energy than most adults and need a constructive outlet for it.

Praise your children. Low-key support, such as praise and encouragement, works better than material rewards or big, exaggerated emotional responses. Creating rewards and punishments is not effective because children become more concerned with them than with their schoolwork. Try to help them understand that though they may not always enjoy what they're doing, it's important that they persevere. There is an exception, however, to low-key support. When a child's grades are very poor, stronger intervention is necessary. The school and parents should work together to find out what is causing the low grades and take steps to correct the problem. You must keep in constant contact with the school to demonstrate your concern. Don't wait for them to contact you if you sense a problem.

Don't overreact. If your children bring home poor report cards, don't get visibly upset because this will only worsen the situation. Your distress will upset your children more and this will lead to poorer grades over time. Follow the guidelines listed here.

Don't be too responsible. When all is said and done, you can't control everything that happens to your children. There are many factors beyond your reach that may influence school performance. Your children's friends, teachers and neighborhood all have an impact. Don't take too much responsibility for what goes wrong. You have a responsibility to try to help your children do the best they can in school, but you are not responsible for the results.

COPING WITH A LEARNING DISABILITY

Learning disabilities have mystified parents and professionals alike for years. The typical learning-disabled youngster is usually of average or above-average intelligence, so that he (70 to 80 percent of learning disabled children are boys) may be able to discuss complex topics while at the same time, has great difficulty spelling a simple word. It is precisely this wide variation in abilities that is all the more confusing to anyone dealing with such a child. Diagnosis is not easy for the professional, either. The definition of learning disabilities includes a wide range of problems such as deficits in attention, speech, reading, writing, memory, maturity and coordination. What, then, can you do if you suspect your child may be learning disabled?

Watch for specific early-warning signs that may signal the presence of a learning disability. All children pass through developmental stages in a jerky, uneven manner, mastering some tasks that appear much more difficult before the tasks that seem relatively easy. But if your child shows several of the following "symptoms," you may wish to consult a learning disabilities specialist:

> short attention span, unable to concentrate on any task for any length of time
> low frustration tolerance
> difficulties getting along with other children
> problems with schoolwork (most notably, obvious reversal of letters and numbers, difficulties with reading, writing, spelling and calculations; in general, performance below what would be expected)
> poor coordination

difficulties with speech, such as delayed onset of speech or difficulty expressing himself

little understanding of the concepts of time and space

memory deficits—difficulty concentrating, unable to remember the days of the week, numbers and the alphabet in the correct order

poor organizational ability

If you notice behavior that might indicate a learning disability, take immediate action. If your child is already in school, he is guaranteed by law the right to a free evaluation. Various tests can determine the presence of a learning disability and even pinpoint the exact area(s) of the deficit(s). If he is a preschooler, you can take him to a family physician at regular intervals in order to have growth and development monitored. A psychologist can also tell you whether or not there appear to be deficiencies in task mastery. Above all, don't let a suspected learning disability in your child go undetected; the more failure he experiences early on, the greater the damage to self-esteem.

Persist if the symptoms continue despite a negative diagnosis. Oftentimes a professional may mistakenly attribute the source of the problem as being a parent's overreaction. Don't be deterred by such a response to your concerns; you know your child better than anyone else. Trust your instincts. If you do not get satisfaction from one professional, persist until your child has received a thorough examination, with special consideration given to the developmental lags that are apparent to you.

Understand what a positive diagnosis really means. If your child is diagnosed as having a learning disability, this does not mean that your child may not be bright and talented in many areas. Although the exact cause(s) of learning disabilities has yet to be discovered, most theories speculate that problems only affect specific areas of the brain, leaving other areas unaffected. Several famous and talented people such as Leonardo da Vinci, Thomas Edison and, more recently, Bruce Jenner have been diagnosed as learning-disabled. It is important not to get mired in denial and rage but, instead, take a positive approach to finding what can be done for your child.

Know what your child's rights are. You should know at the outset that your child is guaranteed by law an education equal to that of other children. It is vitally important for you as parents to develop a working relationship with your child's school to make sure that his right to an equal education is being protected. Most schools conduct "resource classes" in addition to their regular classes, where such areas as reading, spelling and math are taught by specially trained learning specialists. Your learning-disabled child will most likely be in as many regular classes as it is felt he can handle, and will receive special instruction in problem areas via the resource classes. In this manner, his education should be enhanced rather than limited in any way.

Play "games" at home. If you learn that your child has specific difficulties with perceiving numbers, for example, you can devise several games at home that will teach him numbers without the pressure of failure. You may want to ask your child to help you dial a telephone number or even play a board game where number recognition is part of the game. For children with organizational difficulty, setting the table can be an excellent exercise that combines shape recognition as well as understanding what goes where. Many sports activities, such as playing catch, help youngsters with coordination deficits. It is most important to remember that your child is a child, and to let him explore and discover what he is good at, even though he may never be a top-notch speller.

Know where to turn for additional assistance. There are several organizations that can provide valuable additional information and support:

ACLD (Association for Children and Adults with Learning Disabilities)
4156 Library Road
Pittsburgh, PA 15234

FCLD (Foundation for Children with Learning Disabilities)
99 Park Avenue
New York, NY 10016

The Orton Dyslexia Society
724 York Road, Department M
Baltimore, MD 21204

Trials and Tribulations

Along with the joys of raising children come the problems. Many parents are all too familiar with the "terrible twos," thumb sucking, bed-wetting and childhood fears. Although we can't make them go away, we can show you how to best deal with these trials and tribulations. Just remember— childhood doesn't last forever, though in trying times it may certainly seem so!

DEALING WITH "THE TERRIBLE TWOS"

First-time parents who have heard about the terrible twos are quite surprised when the little monster they were expecting to appear the day after his second birthday remains a fairly stable individual. Unfortunately, this is the calm before the storm. Most children from 24 to 30 months generally behave in a fairly cooperative and pleasant manner. By this time they are more confident of their motor and language skills. They can communicate and get along with the world more effectively than ever and seem pleased with themselves. Parents should try to enjoy this time because the nature of human development is such that at about 2½ years of age that same child will be undergoing major changes that could turn the parents' world upside down if they are not prepared for it.

What You Can Expect

The parents of a 2½-year-old must first realize that their child, at this point in his life, is not an easy person to be with. They did not cause this; kids are made this way. Here are some typical characteristics of this age group.

They are rigid and inflexible. They demand order and sameness. Things must be kept in the "right" place. Routines and rituals must always be followed exactly the same way. Stories must be read over and over again. The world is a very confusing place for children this age and they are just not capable of adapting to even minor changes.

They are oppositional. They not only want the opposite of what you want but will actually seem to have arguments with themselves. Children this age are incapable of making clear choices and can vacillate back and forth forever: "Me want hot dogs—me want peanut butter!" and "Me want red—me want blue!"

They cannot control themselves. They are unstable. They can flip from one extreme mood to another without any warning.

They are possessive. They will kill for a piece of scrap paper they think belongs to them or should belong to them.

They demand freedom. Children this age will usually rebel vigorously against physical restrictions. They develop an intense dislike for clothes, shoes and diapers. Only complete nudity will do. The outdoors is the place to be, come rain or come shine. Car seats are seen as racks left over from the Spanish Inquisition—they'd prefer to do the driving themselves. The idea of taking naps is considered insulting.

What You Can Do

Now that you know what to expect from your 2½-year-old, is there anything you can do to prepare yourself for the ordeal? Yes—here are steps you can take in dealing with your child.

Accept it—these are times that try parents' souls. The child is not "bad." You are not "bad." Your child will not hate you forever. Your child is acting his age—it just happens to make it very difficult for you.

Realize there is light at the end of the tunnel. These difficult periods of disequilibrium for children are only temporary. The child who turns 3 is much easier to manage.

Look for support. Spouses must support and communicate with each other. Join a local parenting group or seek out neighbors and friends who have 2-year-olds.

Lose a battle to win a war. Avoid conflicts if at all possible. Go with what the child wants if it is not a major issue. Try to minimize the ways in which he can get into trouble. For example, put breakables out of reach. If a temper tantrum starts and the child cannot stop himself, avoid bodily injury and ride it out.

Take time off. It is all right to take breaks from parenting. Use baby-sitters or barter for time with other parents. Let the other spouse take over if one of you is experiencing burnout.

Create diversions. Try to avoid locking horns by changing the subject or the scene or by introducing something different such as a toy or a distracting remark ("Look at those birds out there, I think they have hats on!" Then proceed to help your child find those birds.)

Don't hurry. Assume you will be late for appointments and will only accomplish half of what you would like to. If you hurry 2½-year-olds, paralysis sets in their legs.

Do not give choices when it really matters. If your child hasn't had a bath in three weeks don't ask if he would like to take a bath. Try: "Let's get your toys and fill the tub." Also, at this age you may not want to give a choice of foods if your child says "No" to everything you offer.

Accept your angry feelings. Raising a child can be extremely frustrating. It is normal for all parents to feel anger, even rage, at their children, especially during the more difficult stages of development. The more parents feel comfortable with their feelings, no matter how intense they may be, the more likely they will act appropriately and allow healthy growth.

DEALING WITH THUMB SUCKING

All children are born with a strong instinct to suck, and with good reason—it is necessary for their nourishment. Beyond the age of 6 months to a year, however, sucking at a thumb is not part of a reflex to eat but rather a comforting technique, according to Dr. Benjamin Spock in his famous *Baby and Child Care* (Pocket Books, 1985). Thumb sucking itself is not a sign of maladjustment. Nor does it lead to any physical harm—even if baby teeth become tilted, the permanent teeth will grow in straight, and by this time, around age 6, thumb sucking has usually been dropped.

A parent should only be concerned under two circumstances: (1) If a child sucks a thumb in conjunction with withdrawal-type behavior, such as watching children play but not playing with them himself, he may be overly introverted and (2) if the child still sucks his thumb when permanent teeth appear, he may tilt them. Both circumstances are rare and should be brought to the attention of a doctor. The following are other thoughts on how to deal with thumb sucking.

Breast-fed babies are less likely to become thumb suckers. Mothers tend to let their babies suck longer at the breast than babies spend with a bottle, which empties to air and loses its special appeal. Breast-fed babies, therefore, satisfy to a greater degree their urge to suck than bottle-fed ones, who take to sucking other objects between feedings.

Babies who suck pacifiers are less likely to end up sucking their thumbs. Babies tend to suck either a pacifier or a thumb, but not both. At age 1 or 2, most babies who suck pacifiers get tired of them and give them up, but don't necessarily take up sucking their thumbs.

Look for the reasons your child sucks his thumb, and deal with these. Note the times and circumstances of sucking. If it's when your child is tired, try an earlier nap or bedtime. If it's when he is hungry, try a snack. If it's when the child is bored, play with him. If it's when he seems to be under stress, try to make your child's life happier and tension-free.

Naggings and scoldings usually increase a child's determination to suck a thumb. Scoldings in public are especially unproductive—they increase a child's anxiety, a cause of sucking to begin with.

Stay away from physical deterrents. Arm restraints, mittens, bitter-tasting applications and bandages do not cure thumb sucking.

Cuddle your child more. What he wants is more security and less stress. Then be patient—your child will grow out of it, usually before he is 5.

DEALING WITH BED-WETTING

Bed-wetting is a common ailment, especially among boys. Its cause is poorly understood. Formerly, many doctors thought the source was psychological, but now the prevalent theory points to a lag in the development of muscle and nerve control. Here are ways to help the problem.

Accidents don't really constitute a problem. Don't consider bed-wetting a problem at all until a child has mastered daytime control for a lengthy time or even until he is about school age. Up until this time, accidents may happen, but should not be cause for concern.

Give a boy encouragement. This is especially important coming from the father. Bed-wetting is often twisted into a vague sense of inadequacy. A boy needs to know that he is a competent person and that he will grow out of his problem. Tell him that many people were troubled with the same ailment but all outgrew it.

Take a low-key attitude. When you see evidence of bed-wetting in the morning, act naturally and assure your child that he will have dry nights soon. Scoldings and shamings are counterproductive; your child is not doing the wetting on purpose; he is sound asleep, perhaps having a bad dream, when the bed-wetting occurs.

Restrict drinks before bedtime, but only within reason. It is more important for your child to maintain a proper fluid level than to make early conquest of his problem.

Lay a rubber mat under the bottom sheet to prevent moisture from reaching the mattress. Encourage an older child to change his own pajamas and sheets if he wakes up at night; you get more rest and your child takes on a measure of responsibility for himself.

Alarms and drugs should be used only under the supervision of a doctor. Alarms that sound when mats attached to them become wet are meant to develop eventually in the child a reflex that wakes him up just before he wets. These are known to work sometimes, but usually only in children who are old enough to really want to master their problem. Drugs that constrict bladder muscles also have been known to work, but both of these techniques should be used only with a doctor's approval.

Praise every success. Downplay the lapses. And have patience—the problem will eventually go away.

EASING YOUR CHILD'S FEARS

Children quite naturally suffer many fears as they grow older. These might include a fear of dogs, swimming or dragons. Sometimes such fears can become overwhelming. Jonathan Kellerman, author of *Helping the Fearful Child* (W. W. Norton & Co., 1981), suggests a three-part method of easing your child out of fears.

Help your child develop a positive attitude. Let your child know that he has strengths of his own, that he is competent and will in time overcome this fear. Give upbeat messages such as the following:

→ "It's okay to be afraid." Fears are normal; everyone, including parents, has them, but everyone learns to overcome them.
→ "Being afraid doesn't last forever." This message diminishes the sense of helplessness and increases the expectation of success.
→ "It's okay to talk about being afraid." Sharing the feelings will help diminish them, and you can correct any distorted and exaggerated ideas your child has developed.
→ "You can handle it, and you can proceed at your own pace." Tell the child you will not force the issue but instead will let him maintain a measure of control.

Help your child learn a new feeling to replace the old one. Fear can be displaced by other emotions. Anger is one. You can tell your child that he can get mad at a dog or dragon or whatever. You can suggest that your child draw a picture of a witch or dragon and then X through it, supplanting fear with a sense of mastery. Or have your child imagine he is a knight who confronts the feared object and masters it. In this way, the fear is replaced by a better emotion.

Give your child positive reinforcement. Do not be too supportive when a child shows fear; that is, do not give hugs, treats and such or you are actually reinforcing his reaction. Instead, give attention, praise and hugs when your child does not show fear, especially when he confronts his problem and shows improvement.

DEALING WITH A COMFORT OBJECT

Around age 6 months, babies begin to feel that they are individuals, and the thought can be a bit scary. They want to assert their independence but are anxious about separation from their parents. Some children deal with this transition by clinging to a teddy bear, blanket or other comfort object. The object, really a kind of parent-substitute, allows these children the freedom of independence but with the illusion of security. A comfort object, which a child may carry around in one form or another for years, is not a sign of significant insecurity, but an appropriate coping mechanism. Parents need not be concerned as long as the child has a good home environment and has social skills appropriate for his age.

Still, there are ways parents can ease both themselves and their children through the comfort-object stage.

If you see your child becoming attached to a particular object, restrict its use. Lay down certain rules. Tell your child that he can cuddle it only at home or only at bedtime, for example, and do not let your child begin to use it in public.

Do not take an object away from your child. It will only increase his desire for it. Remember that eventually, at any time between ages 2 and 5, he will outgrow the attachment.

Let others know about it. Tell baby-sitters about the object and any rituals that go with it.

Try to keep the object clean from the beginning. If you don't, your child may get as attached to its grubbiness and smell as to the object itself and will howl when it smells clean. Try to wash it at night or buy a duplicate and wash each of the two objects alternately.

If the object is a blanket, you can cut part of it away occasionally. Your child will get used to the smaller remnant and soon you can reduce it to the size of a handkerchief.

Nagging does not help. Instead, twice a year, remind your child that when he grows older he will not need the special object. Have patience. Your child will forget all about the blanket or bear in time.

→6

Shortcuts to

Home Management

Home management goes beyond housecleaning. There's caring for your furnishings, understanding insurance, managing your money, shopping wisely, organizing storage spaces, and a host of other daily concerns to keep a homeowner busy. Here's a look at how best to manage—and clean—your home.

Cleaning

Whether you live in a small apartment or a large house, you can't get away from housecleaning. Some of the most troublesome spots are the bathroom and the kitchen along with the fixtures and appliances they contain. Of course, there are also walls and floors, and, when things become too much, there is the option of hiring some household help. Read on for tips and techniques to make your cleaning chores easier.

CUTTING CLEANING TIME IN THE BATH

Cleaning the bathroom doesn't have to be a dreaded, all-day affair. Follow these steps to cutting your cleaning time there.

Cut down on scrubbing. You can eliminate virtually all weekly scrubbing by drying the shower walls after each shower. You'll be wiping away the moisture and soap film that mildew positively thrives on. A squeegee does a terrific job here, but if you don't have one, a sponge is fine.

Put a halt to ring-around-the-bathtub. Wipe the waterline right before letting the water out. If you have hard water that leaves a gummy soap ring, you'll find that a white nylon scouring sponge (the type safe for nonstick cookware) removes the ring with a light rubbing. In homes with soft water, an ordinary cellulose sponge or a terry dishcloth is all you need.

Protect your finishes. Apply a thin coat of car wax to basins and shower walls after cleaning (but not to tub bottoms because it will make them too slippery). Buff with a soft cloth. The wax will both protect the finish and make it easier to wipe away soap film in the future.

Fight mold and mildew. After your bath or shower, hang the wet rubber bath mat over the shower rod or a towel rack to dry with the underside facing out. This will help fight mold growth on the underside of the mat. Stretch wet shower curtains full width to prevent mildew from growing in the folds. If the mildew's already there, remove it by washing the curtain in the washer, along with some terry bath towels for scrubbing action. Use ordinary detergent, chlorine bleach and warm water. Line dry.

Be prepared. Pour diluted disinfectant or mild detergent in a janitorial-type spray bottle and keep it handy for quick cleanups. White vinegar and water kept in another spray container is handy for cleaning bathroom mirrors.

REMOVING STAINS FROM FIXTURES

Here's how to clean stains from bathroom and kitchen fixtures.

Dirt that has accumulated in cracks: Cover the surface of the crack with a powdered abrasive cleanser. Moisten the powder until it has the consistency of paste. Allow the paste to stand for several hours. Scrub the paste into the crack with a stiff-bristled brush, then rinse the crack thoroughly with clean water.

Hard-water deposits: Use full-strength vinegar on them, then rinse the surface thoroughly.

Rust stains on porcelain: Naval jelly, muriatic acid and diluted phosphoric acid are all good for removing rust stains. These solutions can be found in most hardware stores. CAUTION: These preparations are extremely strong. Follow the manufacturer's instructions carefully, for your own safety. Also, make sure your timing is right. Don't leave these preparations on the porcelain surface any longer than is necessary, or you may damage the porcelain.

Rust on unporcelainized surfaces: Remove this type of rust (such as the rust that forms on the exterior of an old-fashioned, claw-footed tub) with a wire brush. Coat the surface with a rust-resistant primer, then apply an oil-alkyd-based finish paint.

CLEANING TILE

Follow these steps to cleaner tile in the bath or kitchen.

1. Wipe down the tile with a mop or sponge dampened with a mild detergent and water.
2. Apply a paste of hot water and a nonabrasive scouring powder to any area that has accumulated dirt. (Use a white powder to avoid discoloring white or off-white grout, and test the powder paste on a sample tile to make sure it won't scratch the tile surface.)
3. Wait 5 to 10 minutes, then scrub with a plastic pad.
4. Rinse off the paste and wipe dry.

CLEANING AN OVEN QUICKLY

The best time to clean your oven, including the racks, is when it's slightly soiled. Once every few months is about right if you use it mostly for baking breads, cakes, cookies, muffins and the like. An immediate cleaning is a good idea after you've roasted a turkey, rack of lamb or other meat because roasts are messy, spitting and spattering in the oven's heat.

Non-Self-Cleaning Ovens

1. Remove the racks and wash them, by hand, in hot soapy water. If necessary, use a soapy steel-wool pad to remove stubborn soil. Rinse well.
2. Place a shallow pan filled with ammonia in the oven, close the door and leave it overnight. Fumes from the ammonia will soften the baked-on grease, making cleanup easy the next day.
3. The next day, wash the oven walls with ammonia and hot water. To remove tenacious soil, scrub with a soapy steel-wool pad. Rinse repeatedly; otherwise, as soon as you turn on the oven, soap

residue will burn, producing an acrid smoke and leaving behind brown-black streaks.

4. Leave the oven door open until the interior is dry. Give yourself a reward—the job's done!

Self-Cleaning Ovens

1. Remove the racks and wash them (see step 1 above).
2. Wipe up loose, heavy soil in the oven with a clean, damp sponge—never use abrasives or a commercial oven cleaner. Following the instructions that came with your oven, run the cleaning cycle.

KEEPING YOUR OVEN CLEAN

Once you've cleaned your oven, you'll want to keep it as clean as possible to avoid undertaking that chore again. Here are some ways to keep that newly cleaned oven clean.

Wipe spills and spatters after each use. Acidic spills require attention because they can permanently ruin the finish; others are simply easier to remove when they're fresh.

Bake with lower oven temperatures. Lower temperatures, plus the use of covered pans whenever possible, will reduce spits and spats.

Fill casserole dishes only three-fourths full. This allows room for bubbling and lowers the chances of them boiling over.

Use a casserole ring under a casserole or pie pan to catch spills. The ring is inexpensive and can be found in the cookware section of many stores.

Wash the broiler pan every time you use it. It needs the same type of care you give other pots and pans and should be stored in a cabinet, where it will stay clean when not in use.

MAINTAINING A SPOTLESS RANGE TOP

Everyday use can make your range top look like a mess. But you can do a few quick cleanups as you go along to help keep it spotless.

Cover pans with lids or spatter screens whenever you can. Either will work to reduce spattering—a clean range's number one enemy. Spatter screens, which allow steam but not grease or food droplets to escape as foods cook, are inexpensive and readily available in gourmet cookware shops and in the cookware sections of many hardware stores, department stores and supermarkets.

Wipe up spills and spatters as soon as practical. Left where they fall, both will be a nuisance, hardening and ready to scorch the next time you turn on the stove. Acidic spills can be double trouble, not only scorching but also nibbling away at the stove's finish.

Wash the reflector pans on an electric stove frequently. That can mean as often as after each use if food has spattered or spilled. With just a quick swipe of a soapy sponge followed by a swoosh in clean water, you can send spills floating down the drain. If you let spills become old, cooked-on spots, it will take quite a bit of elbow grease—and sometimes soaking plus an abrasive—to remove them.

Remove dust and other debris from the area near the pilot light and the air vents on a gas stove. Do this at least once a week. An accumulation of debris is unsightly and hazardous as well.

Clean the crevices around the nameplate, temperature settings and push buttons. A toothbrush dipped in warm soapy water works well for this. Then rinse and dry. Do this when things start to look dingy or feel tacky.

CLEANING A MICROWAVE OVEN

If not cleaned regularly, food in a microwave can develop an unpleasant odor when it becomes rancid. In addition to spills on the floor of your oven, you'll find that food particles can accumulate around the door frame and interfere with the seal. Here's how to clean your microwave:

→ Wipe the oven with a sponge after every use using a solution of dishwashing detergent and warm water. Never use abrasives or commercial oven cleaners.

→ Boil a cup of water in a 2-quart glass measuring cup in the microwave. The steam will soften cooked-on food.

→ Boil ½ cup lemon juice and 1 cup water in a 2-cup glass measuring cup in the microwave to eliminate odors.

→ Make a paste of baking soda and water to remove stains from the ceramic oven floor. Allow the paste to remain on the surface a few minutes with the oven off, then wipe off with a sponge and rinse well.

KEEPING YOUR REFRIGERATOR IN TIP-TOP SHAPE

The best way to clean a refrigerator is to maintain it each day, but it's also a good idea to give it a semiannual cleanout. Here's how.

Wipe up drips and spills right away. Acidic foods may ruin the finish and strongly colored foods—beets, grape juice, tomatoes, those seasoned with turmeric—may stain the finish. Some foods, such as garlic marinades or milk, may leave lingering odors.

Thoroughly clean the interior at least twice a year. When the contents are low, turn off the refrigerator and remove everything—the food, the shelves, the meat bin and the vegetable drawers (also called hydrators or crispers). Wash the interior with a dilute solution of warm water and baking soda; rinse well. Wash the shelves and bins by hand in warm, sudsy water; rinse. (If the parts are dishwasher safe, by all means, use the dishwasher.) With a damp, soapy sponge, wipe the gasket. Rinse and dry it. Leaving the refrigerator door open, let the interior dry. Line the vegetable drawers with a single layer of fresh paper towels to absorb moisture and drips if you store lots of fresh vegetables and fruits, then restart the refrigerator. After a few minutes, replace the food, inspecting and wiping each package as you go. Discard old or spoiled items.

Defrost and clean the freezer section of a manual-defrost model twice a year. (See "Defrosting and Cleaning a Freezer" later in this chapter.) Clean the freezer in a frost-free model at the same time and in the same way that you do the refrigerator section.

Vacuum the condenser coils once a month to remove accumulated dust. Depending on your refrigerator's style, you'll find the coils in the back of or underneath your refrigerator. Use your vacuum's crevice or brush attachment for this. If the coils are located underneath your refrigerator, you'll need to remove the air-intake grill in the front to get at them.

Clear the drain in the freezer and the tube that goes from the drain to the drip pan under the refrigerator twice a year. Found in frost-free units, the drain and tube carry away the water from the defrost cycle. If either becomes clogged, the water will escape to wherever it can—usually to the bottom of your refrigerator. To dislodge food particles or ice from the drain, use a piece of wire or a screwdriver. To free the tube, force water through it with a baster.

Empty the drip pan and wash it in warm, sudsy water several times a year. Let it dry; then slide it back in place. Given the chance, molds will flourish on the dust and moisture that collect here.

Wipe the exterior frequently. Use mild dish detergent and warm water and immediately rub the surface dry and smear-free with soft terry toweling.

DEFROSTING AND CLEANING A FREEZER

Your freezer runs most efficiently (maintaining 0°F or less) when the interior is virtually ice-free, so defrost your freezer when the ice buildup is about ½ inch thick. How quickly does the ice reach a ½-inch thickness? It takes 6 to 12 months, depending mostly on your climate and on how often you open the freezer door. When you're ready to defrost and clean your freezer, follow the steps outlined here.

1. Turn the freezer to its coldest setting the day before defrosting. Food that's frozen solid has the best chance of staying frozen for the hour or so that's needed to defrost and clean a freezer.
2. The next day, remove the food from the freezer and work quickly to reduce the amount of thawing. One option here is to put the food in the refrigerator. Another is to wrap it in several layers of newspaper, then cover the bundles with a blanket. Or you could pack the food in picnic coolers and move them outdoors if the temperature is below freezing.
3. Set the "flash defrost" switch, if your freezer has one; pull the plug; or turn the freezer off once you've emptied it. To hasten the ice's melting, leave the freezer door open and aim a fan or hair dryer at the interior. Pans of hot water set inside will speed things along, too. As chunks of ice loosen, remove them from the freezer with a rubber spatula. Remember not to scrape the finish with anything sharp, or you may puncture the liner.
4. Clean and deodorize the interior with a dilute solution of warm water and baking soda after removing all the ice. Rinse well and sop up any water on the freezer floor. Before putting your sponge away, wipe the gasket and the exterior with clear, warm water. Dry with soft terry toweling.
5. Allow the freezer to dry thoroughly before restarting it; otherwise, you risk lining the freezer with a thin layer of ice at the outset. Once dry, start the freezer and let it run about 30 minutes before adding the food.
6. Wipe each food package dry as you return it to the freezer. Any water left on the packages as they freeze will act like mortar— binding the packages together in a huge lump.

CLEANING HARD-SURFACED FLOORS

Hardwood, no-wax vinyl, tile and linoleum floor coverings have a luster that's easily maintained. The trick is to stop soil from dulling the surface.

Place mats in entranceways. These will catch dirt and grit that can scratch—and eventually wear away—even the toughest of flooring finishes.

NEW APPLIANCES COST LESS TO OPERATE

If your appliances are very old, replacing them can make good economic sense. Even if your appliances were manufactured within the past 10 or 15 years, you can save money on the annual cost of operating them if you purchase new ones. According to the May/June 1986 issue of *Appliance Letter* (Association of Home Appliance Manufacturers, 20 North Wacker Drive, Chicago, IL 60606), here's what various appliances manufactured in 1985 could save you annually, compared to their peers manufactured in 1972 (based on the 1984 average residential electricity cost of 7.56¢ per kilowatt-hour):

- Clothes washers use nearly 34 percent less energy (508 fewer kilowatt-hours), saving $39.94.
- Dishwashers use 36 percent less energy (459 fewer kilowatt-hours), saving $36.51.
- Freezers use 45 percent less energy (661 fewer kilowatt-hours), saving $49.95.
- Refrigerators use 34 percent less energy (588 fewer kilowatt-hours), saving $44.43.
- Room air conditioners use nearly 19 percent less energy (238 fewer kilowatt-hours), saving $17.91.

Use a vacuum or dust mop frequently. This will remove soil before it's ground into the flooring.

Apply wax to clean floors. A good coat helps keep dirt from sticking, protects the finish and makes routine vacuuming easier. For hardwood floors, select a spirit-solvent wax in paste or liquid. You'll need to polish or buff after applying. For other surfaces, use one of the water-based types. Today, many are self-polishing. When wax begins to yellow or feel tacky, remove it with a solvent, but don't sand. Sanding goes too deep, rubbing away more than just the built-up wax.

Wipe up spills promptly. Besides making the surface dull and sticky, some liquids stain. That's especially true of water left on hardwood.

Clean vinyl, linoleum and tile with gentle cleansers. All you need is a mop, cloth or sponge wrung out in cool water plus a little white vinegar, all-purpose cleaner or mild detergent. Never use harsh abrasives or strong alkaline cleaners; both can damage the flooring's original finish. What about using a scrub brush instead of a cloth or mop? Don't. Brushes can scratch floor surfaces, particularly the no-wax vinyls. And put as little water as possible on the floor, especially if the floor has numerous seams. Puddles take hours to dry and standing water can seep through the seams to the subfloor, causing the wood to warp and rot.

Put plastic or metal glides on table and chair legs. This will prevent furniture from scratching the floor. Use pieces of adhesive-backed felt as temporary stand-ins until you can buy the glides.

CLEANING WALLS AND WOODWORK

Before you go to the trouble of repainting dingy interior walls and woodwork, try this method to see if a simple cleaning will do the trick.

1. Vacuum the surface to remove dirt and dust.
2. Mix a pail of water with 2 to 3 tablespoons of a gentle cleanser, such as Ivory soap.
3. Dip a sponge into the solution, squeezing it gently so that water won't drip from it when you wash the wall.
4. Test the cleaning solution by gently rubbing a portion of the wall. Rinse the clean section thoroughly with fresh water, then dry with a cloth or paper towel.
5. If the patch test is satisfactory, proceed to clean the entire painted surface. Some people recommend washing the lowest part first, claiming that the dirty water that drips from above wipes off more easily from a clean wall than it does from a dirty one.
6. After the wall is clean, repair minor scratches in the existing paint surface with touch-up paint.
7. Inspect all your walls and woodwork for signs of deterioration. If the paint is badly chipped, peeling or cracked, a new paint job is your best bet.

SELECTING A VACUUM

There are three basic vacuum styles—upright, canister and canister with power nozzle. Here's a look at each one, to help you decide which is best for your cleaning needs.

Upright

In these vacuums, rotating brushes in the nose do most of the cleaning; suction serves mainly to pull the dirt into a bag on the handle. Uprights are terrific for cleaning large expanses of carpet but only do so-so on bare floors. These models are also difficult to maneuver in tight spaces, under furniture and on stairs. Here's what to look for in an upright vacuum:

> dust bag that's easy to remove and replace
> height adjustment for different carpet piles
> quiet motor
> reasonably long cord
> rubber bumper that protects furniture and woodwork
> suction control

Canister

Operating with suction only, canisters excel at cleaning bare surfaces, but do poorly on carpets. Generally speaking, they can sit comfortably on stairs, and maneuver around furniture well. They're good for poking into tight spots. Here's what to look for in a canister vacuum:

> attachments for cleaning a variety of surfaces: rugs, bare floors, crevices, fabrics, upholstery
> compactness
> dust bag that's easy to replace
> positive method of locking hoses, wands and tools
> rubber bumper that protects furniture and woodwork
> strong suction
> suction control
> swivel front casters for easy maneuvering
> wheels that are large enough for easy handling

Canister with Power Nozzle

These vacuums combine the best features of the uprights and the canisters. The power nozzle has better brushes, driven either by air or a separate motor, for deep cleaning carpets. Here's what to look for in a canister vacuum with power nozzle:

> attachments for cleaning a variety of surfaces: rugs, bare floors, crevices, fabrics, upholstery
> height adjustment for different carpet piles
> large-capacity dust bag that's easy to replace
> positive method of locking hoses, wands and tools
> power overload indicator on the power nozzle
> reasonably long cord
> rotating brush and bar
> rubber bumper that protects woodwork and furniture
> strong suction

suction control
swivel front casters for easy maneuvering
two-speed motor—one for vacuuming carpets with the power noz-
    zle; one for using the other attachments
wheels that are large enough for easy handling

HIRING HOUSEHOLD HELP

If you've decided that the housework is just too much to handle by
yourself, you may be considering hiring household help. But before you
put that ad in the paper, consider this advice.

Outline the ground rules for the job. Do this before starting to look for
help. You should already have decided: what you will pay, what the
hours are, how many days a week, what the job responsibilities are, if
transportation is needed, if a driver's license is necessary, if you will
provide meals and so forth. If you don't have a plan formulated, writing a
help-wanted ad, interviewing and hiring just the right person for the job
will be difficult.

When determining how much to pay household help, take the
following into consideration: the minimum wage, what you can afford,
the going rate for similar work in your neighborhood, fringe benefits such
as meals or room and board, job responsibilities and extra skills the
housekeeper or child-care worker may bring to the job.

Plan to give some paid days off. Usually employers who include paid
benefits have a better chance of cutting down on employee turnover.
You'll probably want to give your worker these days off: Christmas, New
Year's Eve or New Year's Day, Good Friday, Labor Day, July 4th,
Memorial Day and Thanksgiving, plus a few days of sick leave, personal
leave and vacation.

Use a post office box number instead of your home address. If you place a
classified ad in the help-wanted section of your local paper, ask applicants to send a resume and letter of application to a post office box
number. This process will allow you to screen applicants without
interviewing every one. It also prevents people from stopping by or
calling instead of writing.

**During the interview, carefully and thoroughly explain the job and what you
expect.** Don't gloss over any aspect of the job. For example, the prospective employee must be told if she or he will be responsible for child care
plus housework. False and inadequate expectations on the part of the
employee can only lead to employee dissatisfaction.

Ask a prospective employee for references. Then be sure to call or write the references and ask plenty of specific questions. Is the prospective employee reliable? Did she or he arrive punctually every day? Why did she or he leave your employment? Were you happy with her or his performance? Don't be embarrassed to ask for details—after all, you'll be leaving the care of your home and perhaps even that of your children or elderly parents to this individual.

Give the employee a one- to two-week trial period. That will help you know whether the employee is right for your job.

Prepare a daily schedule for your help to follow. A written schedule leaves little doubt about your expectations.

Keep good payroll records. You, as employer, are required to remit some or all of the following: Social Security (FICA), federal and state personal income tax withholding, state disability, unemployment insurance and worker's compensation.

If you're unhappy with the employee's performance, let her or him know. Then explain what changes you want to see. If, after several discussions, warnings and a trial period, things don't straighten out to your satisfaction, there must be a parting. Handle everything in a calm, businesslike manner. Above all, be firm and specific. If appropriate, give the employee one or two week's notice of dismissal.

Furniture and Furnishings

Furniture and other home furnishings are expensive investments, and ones that deserve care and attention to keep them looking their best.

CARING FOR WOOD FURNITURE

Wood furniture looks beautiful when it's new, or recently refinished, but scratches, burns, fingerprints and other marks really take away from its appearance. If your wood furniture looks like it's seen better days, follow these suggestions to getting it back in shape.

Dust wood surfaces fairly often. Just how often depends on the traffic in the room, but don't wait until you can write your name in the dust. Accumulated dust will scratch a polished surface. When all you want is a quick once-over, the brush attachment on your vacuum does a reasonable job, otherwise, use a flannel cloth. Smooth-finish cloths push the dust around; feather dusters scatter it in the air where it quickly settles back on the furniture. Every few strokes, shake your dust cloth outdoors.

Banish smudges and sticky fingerprints. Firmly wipe wood surfaces with a dry, soft flannel cloth. If that doesn't do the trick, wash them away with a terry cloth dipped in warm, dilute soapy water and then wrung nearly dry. Wipe immediately with a cloth wrung out in clear water and quickly dry with a clean, soft terry towel. Let dry for 30 to 40 minutes, then lightly polish with lemon oil or wood preservative.

Cover small nicks and scratches. Shell a walnut or pecan, then break the meat and rub it lightly over the surface. It will stain the wood. Repeat until the cover is dark enough to match the wood's finish.

Polish with oil or wood preservative once or twice a year. For best results, avoid polishes and waxes containing silicon or beeswax, both of which can rob the wood of its natural patina and instead leave it with a hard, almost harsh, shine. The purpose of polishing is to protect the finish and restore moisture. But don't overdo a good thing. Polish applied too frequently is difficult to buff, feels sticky and looks dull. Once you've selected a product, stay with it because few products are compatible. To remove built-up polish, wipe the surface with mineral spirits or turpentine, then polish.

Sponge up spills—including plain water—quickly, before they result in white marks and other discolorations. If you don't catch the spills in time, gently rub the wood's surface in the direction of the grain with pumice or very fine steel wool dipped in linseed or mineral oil. Wipe dry with a clean cloth, then polish with the product you've been using. An alternative is to sprinkle the discolored area with salt or rottenstone, then rub gently with a cloth dipped in oil. Finish by wiping dry and polishing.

CLEANING WOOD FURNITURE
Follow this procedure when your furniture needs a good cleaning.

1. Mix a neutral detergent, such as Orvus or Igepal (available at tack shops) with a good amount of water (the solution should be fairly weak).
2. Dampen a soft, cotton cloth with the detergent solution and apply it to a small, hidden area of the furniture to test it. If it doesn't harm the finish, proceed to wipe down the piece of furniture with the solution.
3. Dry the furniture immediately with a soft, dry cloth.
4. Remove any waxy or greasy dirt with mineral spirits on a soft cloth.

REFINISHING WOOD FURNITURE

Homer Formby, president of Formby's, Inc., a company that manufactures refinishing products, offers these tips for refinishing furniture.

Check for dirt buildup on the finish by rubbing the dirtiest spot with a cotton cloth and a little furniture cleaner. If you can remove the grit and reveal the grain, you may not need to refinish the piece at all.

If the wood needs to be stripped, use a fine steel wool pad and an old paint brush trimmed to a stubby length to work the stripper into carved areas. Follow the directions on the can for the amount of stripper to apply and the length of time it should set.

Work when the temperature is between 65° and 85°F; you'll get the best results then.

After you're done, rub a fresh coat of refinisher from one end of the piece to the other (going with the grain) to remove any swirls and streaks.

Wipe the piece with a clean cotton cloth and allow it to dry for about half an hour. Then buff with dry steel wool.

MAINTAINING LEATHER FURNITURE

To keep leather upholstered furniture looking its best, follow these guidelines:

➡ Position the furniture so that it's kept out of direct sunlight, otherwise the color will fade.
➡ Keep the room temperature moderate or on the cool side; if it's too hot, the leather will crack and dry out.
➡ Make sure the room is dry; if the room is overly humid or damp, the leather can rot.
➡ Dust leather furniture regularly.
➡ Oil the leather upholstery regularly using a special preparation called hide food to keep the leather supple.

CARING FOR UPHOLSTERED FURNITURE

Getting a piece of furniture reupholstered is both expensive and time-consuming. To make sure your upholstered furniture lasts as long as it can, follow these suggestions.

Vacuum frequently to pick up surface soil before it works its way deep into the fabric. Once there, soil particles act like hundreds of tiny razors cutting away at the fibers. For flat areas, vacuum with the small upholstery attachment; for between the frame and padded spots, use the crevice attachment.

Turn the cushions over regularly. If you can, change their positions to help distribute wear. Do this after vacuuming.

Use arm and back covers. These protect your upholstered furniture from skin and hair oils. Furniture manufacturers often include the covers when you buy a sofa or chair—if you have them, use them. If you don't have furniture covers, they can be easily made from matching fabric.

Blot up spills immediately while they're still beaded on the surface of the fabric. If a liquid has already soaked into the fabric, treat the stain as soon as you can; you'll have much better luck removing it. Once a stain has set, it's usually permanent.

Shampoo the upholstery when it looks dull and shows some, but not much, soil. For a couch or chair that gets a lot of use, you can expect to shampoo every year; for furniture that gets much less use, you can put off the task for three, four or even five years. When shampooing, you have two options: do it yourself or call in a professional. If you decide to go the do-it-yourself route, first test the upholstery in an inconspicuous spot. (It's a good idea to keep some leftover fabric scraps from a newly upholstered piece for just this purpose.) If the color runs, you'll have to have it dry cleaned. Once you've cleaned your upholstery, spray it with a dirt-repellent compound.

Once or twice a year, inspect the upholstery for wear and tear. Patch large holes with a piece of matching fabric either by sewing it on by hand or by ironing it on using a piece of double-faced, iron-on interfacing (available at most sewing stores) to affix it. Snip any loose threads that are likely to snag.

REVIVING A BUTCHER BLOCK FINISH

It's best to use a nontoxic, vegetable oil finish on your butcher block counter or cutting board, especially if food will come into contact with it. The oil will keep the wood looking good, but from time to time, you'll need to take these two simple steps to renew the finish.

1. Lightly sand the counter.
2. Reapply the oil (olive or mineral oil are two possible choices, but plain vegetable oil is fine) by wiping it into the wood with a soft cloth.

EXTENDING THE LIFE OF YOUR CARPETS

You can expect a good-quality carpet to last 10, 15 even 20 or so years, given reasonable care. To get long life from your carpets, follow these guidelines.

Use "dirt-catcher" mats inside as well as outside entranceways. Inside, carpet remnants are well-suited to this purpose and can be fairly unobtrusive, especially if you use leftover pieces of your carpeting. When that's not possible, check carpet outlets for complementary bound remnants. For the outside, get a tough mat, such as one of straw or rubber, that'll stand up to lots of scraping from dirty shoes. A mat with a rough surface for cleaning the bottom of shoes is a good choice.

Vacuum carpets often to remove surface soil. Once imbedded deep in the carpet pile, soil works like sandpaper, wearing away the fibers. To stay one step ahead of the soil, thoroughly vacuum moderate- and light-traffic areas such as bedrooms once a week. Tackle heavy-traffic areas—halls and family rooms—several times a week. What's a thorough vacuuming? Seven to eight passes over a single carpet area. Generally speaking, you'll get best results with a rotating beater brush.

Rejuvenate flattened carpet pile with a carpet rake. You can find these inexpensive rakes wherever other carpet-care supplies are sold.

Catch spills before they become permanent stains. Use the technique outlined here:

1. Blot the spill with a dry, clean towel and avoid using any liquid that might spread the stain.
2. Test any chemical remover in an inconspicuous area to make sure it won't damage or discolor your carpet.
3. Work the cleaner into the carpet from the outer edge of the stain toward the middle of it. To avoid spreading the mess, don't rub.
4. Dry excess moisture with a clean, *white* terry towel (the dye in a colored one might transfer to your carpet).
5. Brush the carpet's nap to a standing position and let it dry completely before walking over the area.

Shampoo or deep clean your carpets when they become grubby. Other indicators that it's time for shampooing include when your carpets look matted, feel sticky, show grimy spots or send up puffs of dust when you walk across them. If you've been vacuuming and removing stains religiously, this may not be necessary for five or more years.

Apply a soil retardant to your clean carpets. It will help keep stains and soil on the surface of the carpet fibers.

STORING RUGS

When storing a rug, it's best to roll it onto a pole instead of folding it; the fold lines will weaken and mark the rug. Follow the steps outlined below.

1. Clean the rug with a liquid carpet shampoo (follow the manufacturer's directions for appropriate application).
2. Darn any holes or catches.
3. Lay the clean, repaired rug out flat on the floor with the pile face down.
4. Put a heavy, wooden pole at one end, and roll the rug up onto the pole, with the pile facing out.

CARING FOR CURTAINS AND DRAPES

A few extra minutes spent caring for curtains and drapes will add years of life to them.

Curtains

Launder curtains when they look dingy and limp. You'll probably need to do this once or twice a year, depending on their location and the type of heating system you have.

Shake curtains outdoors to remove dust accumulated between launderings. Or you can tumble them in the dryer on the fluff cycle. This should probably be done every two to three months.

Drapes

Vacuum drapes weekly, on both sides, to remove dust. If your drape panels are small, you may prefer to remove the dust, and fluff the drapes at the same time, in the dryer. Use the no-heat cycle. Do this every two to four months.

Dry-clean drapes only when they are truly soiled. It's not a good idea to routinely clean them, say every 6 to 12 months, because professional dry cleaning is expensive—at least 20¢ a square foot. (Coin-operated dry cleaning is less expensive, but you do the pressing if any is needed.) And the results may be less than you hoped for—the linings, the stitching or the drapes themselves may shrink, or previously unnoticed sun-rot may cause parts of the drapes to disintegrate during the cleaning process.

Insurance

Whether you're insuring your home, your life, your health or your car, there are things you should know that can save you money on your policies while giving you the best coverage for your dollars.

CUTTING THE COST OF HOMEOWNER'S INSURANCE

Your home is your most valuable asset, and to protect it you probably have homeowner's insurance. But are you paying too much? Here are some tips for cutting the cost, but not the coverage, of your insurance.

Don't overinsure. No matter how much insurance you carry, you won't be paid more than replacement cost of any loss.

Repair hazardous wiring, roofs and chimneys. With some companies, such repairs will earn you a lower rate.

Take as large a deductible as you can comfortably afford. Over the long haul, you'll usually save.

Pay for replacement-cost coverage. Most policies pay the depreciated value rather than the replacement cost of any losses. In other words, if five years ago you spent $150 for a storm door and it was broken by vandals last week, the insurance company will pay a depreciated value, say $35. But if you have replacement-cost coverage, you'll get the amount it will cost to replace that door today. This is one case when an extra premium may be well worth its price.

Obtain a policy that runs for three to five years before renewal is necessary. A long-term commitment generally costs less than a short-term one. And, if you can, pay the entire annual premium at once, avoiding expensive monthly charges that often accompany monthly or quarterly payments.

Determine if you qualify for special discounts. Many insurance companies offer discounts under certain circumstances, including the following:

> your home has one or more smoke detectors in good working order
> you are a nonsmoker
> you've installed a heat-sensitive fire detector and it's working
> you are 65 years old or older

GETTING LIFE INSURANCE FOR LESS

You see the ads in newspapers and magazines and the commercials on television. Insurance is big business and every insurance company wants *you* as its customer. But how do you know what to look for? There are

LIFE INSURANCE: HOW MUCH DO YOU NEED?

Here are some obligations to consider when determining your life insurance needs.

Your home. To leave it free and clear to your family, you'll need enough insurance to pay off the mortgage. You should also have enough to pay off any other outstanding debts.

Your income. To give your family time to readjust to the loss of your income, you should cover one to two years' salary.

Children's education. If you want to provide funds toward college tuition, be generous. Costs will surely go up.

POLICY RIDERS YOU CAN DO WITHOUT

When purchasing life insurance, consider saying no to these four policy riders.

Accidental Death Benefit (ADB), also called double indemnity. Most policies have many tricky exclusions here so be very careful and learn what you are and aren't covered for. Though the additional cost is usually minimal, it's rarely a good investment. The reasoning is this: Your family won't need twice as much money just because you die by accident rather than from illness.

Cost of Living (COL). This lets you increase your coverage without taking a physical. It's usually overpriced because most companies assume that only people in poor health will opt for the rider.

Guaranteed Insurability. This is only available to people over 40 and it's extremely expensive.

Waiver of Premium (WP). With this, the insurance company pays your premiums if you become disabled. Generally, this is very expensive and you'd be better off buying disability income insurance.

Life Insurance Basics

Term	Whole-Life	Endowment
Protection for a specific period of time	Protection for life	Insurance plus rapid cash accumulation
Low initial premium -	Higher initial premium than term	Higher premium than term or whole-life
May be renewable and/or convertible	Growing cash value	You can arrange the policy to coincide with future events
Premium rises with each new term	Fixed premium	
You or your dependents get nothing back if you survive the term	You or your dependents always receive benefits	
	Available as universal, variable and adjustable life	
	Should be purchased with the intention of keeping it for life or at least for a long period of time	

lots of life insurance policies out there—which are right for you? Here's a checklist for smart insurance shopping.

Shop for the best coverage at the best price. Once you've found what seems to meet your needs, read all the fine print in the policy, check the company's reputation for quick and easy payoff and determine if the company has assets to cover its obligations.

Ask about discount rates. Some companies offer lower premium rates on life insurance to nonsmokers and other people with healthy life-styles. If you think you're eligible, be sure to ask about these rates.

Think twice if someone tells you to replace your whole-life policy. Remember, you are now older than when you first purchased your policy, so a new one will cost more. Also, some older policies may have provisions not duplicated in new ones.

When comparing policy costs, you can make the most accurate comparison if you use a special life insurance cost index. The index will provide you with a number that reflects the price of the policy. Generally speaking, the smaller the index number, the better the buy. An agent or insurance company can provide more information about its index.

Consider not carrying life insurance at all. If you fall into one of these categories, you may be wasting money on life insurance:

> married with no children and your spouse earns a salary roughly
>   equal to yours
> single with no responsibility for children or parents

Consolidate your policies if you have several of them. Generally speaking, you'll pay much less in premiums. And if you have more whole-life than you need, switch to a universal-life policy for a better return on your money.

Pay your premium annually. Some insurance companies will allow you to pay the premium annually rather than quarterly or twice a year. By paying once a year, you may save a substantial amount.

Buy convertible policies. If you buy term insurance, make sure it's convertible to whole-life (ordinary or straight) without your having to take a medical exam. Someday you may want to switch, and if your health isn't what it used to be, you may be denied.

BUYING MEDICAL INSURANCE

Many workers don't have to worry about medical insurance because their employer picks up all, or a good part, of the tab. But if you're self-employed or find that your employer no longer covers you after you retire, you may find yourself in the market for medical insurance. Here's how to buy wisely.

Shop for the best coverage for the least money. Be sure you understand what you're paying for.

Take part in group coverage, if you can. Group policies are usually cheaper and often better. Many travel organizations and credit card companies offer low-cost group insurance.

Stay away from specific disease coverage. You're far better off with more general insurance that covers any illness or condition.

Opt for a higher deductible. If you can afford to pay some of your own medical expenses, go for a high deductible, say $250 to $500, on major medical. In the long run, you'll save.

Ask about a nonsmoker's discount. With companies that offer such discounts, you can often save almost 10 percent.

Pay your premium annually if you can. Without the carrying charges that are added on to extended payments, you can save about 5 percent.

DETERMINING YOUR AUTO INSURANCE NEEDS

As with the other types of insurance, it pays to shop around for your auto insurance. Here's some other advice.

Drop collision and comprehensive coverage on older cars if you can afford to pick up losses yourself. Your insurance won't pay to repair damages that run higher in cost than the resale (depreciated) value of the car. *Collision* pays for damages to your car if you hit another vehicle or object; *comprehensive* includes losses caused by fire, theft, wind, vandalism, explosions, flood and collision with animals. It also covers some loss for personal property left in the car.

If you don't want to drop collision and comprehensive coverage, go for the highest deductibles you can afford. In many cases, you can save 30 to 50 percent. If you're 65 years old or older, check on a senior's rate. In many states, rates are considerably lower for people in this age bracket.

Include any additional family cars under the same policy. Keeping all the coverage together will entitle you to a multicar discount—often up to 20 percent.

Check if your insurance company offers a safe driver plan. You may be eligible for substantial savings on premiums if you have an accident- or violation-free driving record. Also ask if the company offers a good-student discount for young drivers ranking in the top 20 percent of their class. In some states, you can qualify for a discount if the young drivers in your family have passed a driver-training course. Encourage your son or daughter to take such training.

Keep track of your mileage. Do you drive fewer than 7,500 miles a year? If you're not sure, keep track of those miles. You may find you use the car less than you think and are eligible for a low-mileage discount.

When you're in the market for a new car, buy one with a low repair history. Ask your insurance agent or broker or check consumer magazines for an up-to-date list of cars with histories of high repair costs, then seriously consider not buying those models. Some insurance companies will charge a higher premium for cars with a reputation for costly repairs.

Check for other discounts. Many auto insurance companies offer discounts for some of these:

> → Theft protection. Some companies will give you a 15 percent break if you install a theft-protection device.
> → Five-mile-an-hour bumpers. If your car has them, you may qualify for a lower collision rate.

→ Nonsmoking and nondrinking. Sometimes called a good-driver deduction. On some policies, you can get up to a 20 percent reduction if you qualify.

→ Defensive driving course. If you take a certified course and graduate, you may get a 25 percent discount.

→ Pleasure use. If you never drive to work but commute by bus, train or van instead, let your insurance company know. You could save as much as 30 percent. And don't forget, if you're retired, inform your insurance company. You'll be eligible for a reduction now that you're not using the car to commute.

→ Car pool. Do you drive to work fewer than two days a week? You may qualify for a savings of 20 percent.

Money

Running a smooth household includes handling and budgeting money, keeping financial records and watching out for credit debt. It also involves saving money on your utility and grocery bills. Here are some suggestions for smart money management.

MAINTAINING A MONTHLY BUDGET

With this down-to-earth approach to budgeting, you can track your income and expenditures from the 1st to the 30th of each month on a single sheet of paper. The approach is flexible, allowing for individual needs and minimizing record keeping. Here's what you need to start figuring your budget-at-a-glance: pencil or pen, a blank 8½ × 11-inch piece of paper and your past year's spending records.

1. Identify all of your fixed spending categories—taxes, phone, insurance, mortgage, rent, trash, electric, heat. Then determine the average monthly amount spent in each category. This means, for example, that you'll need to look up the past year's electric bills and then average the year's total over the 12 months. The purpose here is to arrive at fairly predictable spending amounts for this year based on what you spent during the past year.

2. Take your sheet of paper and rule off columns for each of your categories plus an extra column for miscellaneous spending. Reserve an area on the right for income sources and other notes. Next, having identified your spending categories, write an appropriate heading over each column—electricity, real estate taxes, mortgage, auto insurance, food and so forth. Under each heading,

MONTHLY BUDGET

SPENDING CATEGORIES   INCOME ALLOCATIONS

CREDIT BALANCE	CREDIT PURCHASES	MORTGAGE PAYMENTS	ELECTRIC	WEEK #1	WEEK #2
290.81		563.92	125.00	140.00 REAL EST TAX	210.28 MORTGAGE
				84.00 INSURANXE	70.00 FOOD
				70.00 FOOD	25.00 MEDICAL
		PHONE	**GARBAGE**	32.00 PHONE	16.00 AUTO REP.
		32.00	26.00	10.25 GIFTS	10.00 RECREATION
				10.00 RECREATION	6.50 GARBAGE
			REAL ESTATE TAXES	6.50 GARBAGE	6.25 GIFTS
		INSURANXE		51.47 MISC.	57.69 MISC.
		84.00	140.00	404.22	401.72
		AUTO REPAIRS	**MEDICAL**		
		49.00	25.00		
		GIFTS	**RECREATION**	WEEK #3	WEEK #4
		33.00	40.00	125.00 ELECTRIC	241.28 MORTGAGE
				112.36 MORTGAGE	70.00 FOOD
				70.00 FOOD	15.00 AUTO REP.
		MISCELLANEOUS		18.00 AUTO REP.	10.00 RECREATION
		224.46		10.00 RECREATION	8.25 GIFTS
				8.25 GIFTS	6.50 GARBAGE
				6.50 GARBAGE	57.19 MISC.
		FOOD		58.11 MISC.	408.22
		280.00		408.22	
	SEARS 128.10 J.C. PENNEY 23.31 VISA 12.27 VISA 108.45 SEARS 14.81 VISA 3.87				

enter the average amount that you calculated from the past year's records. This will be your monthly budget.

3. Divide your weekly net income by categories and, each week as you receive income, add the appropriate amount to each category. At the end of four weeks, your totals should equal your requirements.

In a five-week month, you can use the fifth week's income as a buffer for larger spending categories that don't call for frequent payments, such as auto insurance. If your income is monthly, simply allocate the funds monthly rather than weekly.

4. Subtract the money you actually spend from the budgeted amount as you pay incoming bills. Your budget will tell you what funds are still available and whether you are running ahead of or behind your estimates.

5. Set up a credit column if you want to use your new budget to keep a watchful eye on credit card spending. In the credit column, list both the amounts of card purchases and the cumulative amount due. At the same time, subtract each purchase amount from the appropriate budget category—let's say medical or clothing—and add them to the cumulative credit amount. This way there are funds available to pay card balances when they're due. At the end of the month, simply subtract the payment from the cumulative amount column and delete the corresponding purchase amounts.

6. Use the miscellaneous column for nickel-and-dime expenses usually paid in cash. Whenever you obtain pocket money at the bank, subtract the amount from the miscellaneous category. You needn't make further budget entries and don't calculate leftover money in your monthly audit (see item 8 below).

7. Adjust your income allocations when you notice some categories running a surplus and others, a deficit. And feel free to "rob Peter to pay Paul," on a short-term basis. As long as your monthly audit confirms that expenses match your income, moving money from category to category gives flexibility.

8. Audit your budget amounts against the actual available funds at the beginning of each month. The audit is simple: Add up all remaining amounts in your spending categories; then match the totals to those in your checking account (or whatever account your spending funds are held in). Then set up a new budget sheet, making appropriate adjustments to fit changing financial circumstances. You're ready to go again!

KEEPING FINANCIAL RECORDS

For good records, you'll need three storage files: a crucial file in a safe-deposit box at a bank, an active file in a metal box or two-drawer filing cabinet at home and an inactive file in a carton stored in the basement, attic or closet. Here's what each should contain.

Crucial File

Keep these papers in a safe-deposit box:

adoption papers

automobile titles and any other vehicle titles, such as boats, planes and so on

birth, death and marriage certificates

citizenship papers

copies of wills (Don't put your original in a safe-deposit box. Upon notification of death, the bank must "lock" your safe-deposit box, even if it is also in your spouse's name. Your family will be without access to its contents for several days or weeks, so your will should be kept with your lawyer.)

copy of household inventory plus photos and receipts for insurance purposes

divorce decree

insurance policies

leases, property titles, property deeds, mortgages, contracts and other legal papers

major bills of sale, patents, copyrights and other court-recorded papers

military records

professional licenses and certificates

stock and bond certificates; certificates of deposit and any other bank savings certificates

Active File

Organize these items in a metal box or file cabinet for easy access:

canceled checks and bank or money market statements for the past three years

copies of insurance policies; records of bills paid by insurance, names, addresses and phone numbers of insurance agents

copies of past three years' tax returns

copies of wills with note as to location of originals

credit card contracts, statements, account numbers

education bills, receipts, diplomas, degrees

home improvement records

immunization and other health records

investment records including brokers' confirmations of sales and purchases; brokers' names, addresses and phone numbers; records of capital gains and losses

lists of items in safe-deposit box
net worth statement and financial plan
paid receipts
paycheck stubs and W-2 forms for the past three years
records of all loan agreements; loan payment books; loan statements
records of business and professional expenses
records of casualty losses
records of charitable contributions
Social Security and pension statements
warranties, service contracts, appliance operating instructions

Inactive File

Store these papers in file folders or envelopes, boxed and put away in the basement or attic:

active file papers more than three years old

Items You Can Discard

There's no need to keep these around:

expired warranties and warranties and instructions for appliances you no longer have
paycheck stubs that you've checked against your W-2 forms
receipts for items not tax deductible such as home improvements and receipts that have no sales tax

HELPING YOUR MONEY GROW

Most passbook savings accounts offer low interest rates, and many checking accounts don't offer earned interest at all. This means that your money isn't earning you very much. To keep your money growing for you, check out some of these alternatives.

Open a NOW account instead of a checking account. That way, you'll earn interest on money you've set aside for bill paying. The interest earned may not seem like a lot, but over the course of a year, that interest can easily offset other account expenses such as service fees and the cost of the checks themselves. Many banks offer NOW accounts for a minimum balance that's often as low as $200. Shop around for the best interest rate and lowest minimum balance, even if that means going to an out-of-town bank.

Arrange for direct deposit of your paycheck or Social Security check. There are two reasons for doing so: your money earns interest immediately, without your making a trip to the bank; and some banks will waive the service fees and minimum balance requirements.

Establish a passbook savings account for convenience. Open your account in a conveniently located bank with a 24-hour-access, automatic teller machine. The key term here is *convenience*. You want this account for holding spending money if the bank with your NOW account is located across town or otherwise inconveniently situated. Every time you need cash, make a withdrawal and replenish the funds in the savings account by writing a check against your NOW account.

Start a mutual fund money market account. Your money will earn 1 to 3 percent higher interest than it would in a NOW or passbook savings account. Typically, money market funds require a $1,000 minimum balance and limit check writing to $250 and up. Some have limits on the number of checks a month you can write. In your money market fund, accumulate amounts needed to pay large expenses: mortgage payments, car loan payments, insurance. For addresses and phone numbers of financial institutions offering money market accounts, check the financial magazines or the financial section of newspapers. Read the prospectuses carefully so you understand how the account works.

Use credit cards with discipline. That means only purchasing items you've planned for in your budget; then paying the *entire* balance due by the date specified in your statement to avoid stiff finance charges. The advantage? Your money—assuming it's in a NOW, passbook savings or money market account—will continue earning interest from the date of purchase until you pay the balance due, a 7- to 30-day float. If you do this often enough, the interest earned can outstrip your annual card fee.

ESTABLISHING A CREDIT HISTORY

If you've never taken out a loan, you don't have a credit history. That means you may run into problems when you go for a big loan such as a car loan, school loan or mortgage. Here's what you need to do to establish your credit history.

Open checking and savings accounts. Make regular deposits into the accounts, and take care not to overdraw the checking account.

Open a retail charge account. Use the card for small purchases you would have otherwise paid cash for. When the bill arrives, pay it promptly.

WHAT'S YOUR CREDIT WORTHINESS?

Potential lenders seek answers to the following questions of capacity, character and collateral before granting any loan or credit card.

→ Does your employment record show you can hold a job and earn enough money to pay off your debts?

→ Have you promptly paid off previous credit card accounts, charge accounts and other loans?

→ Does your present list of creditors and amounts owed indicate you haven't borrowed beyond your means to repay?

→ Have you lived in the same apartment for several years?

→ Do you own your home? If so, how long have you lived there?

→ Do your assets in savings, stock, life insurance and so forth exceed your liabilities?

Generally, there is no finance charge on these accounts if they're paid within a specified time—usually 30 days.

Apply for a bank card. These cards usually have an annual fee and a limit on the amount you can charge. If you pay the balance promptly each month, there's often no interest charge.

Take out a small loan, such as a personal loan. Make regular, prompt payments. After six months, you can repay the entire amount, if you wish.

PROTECTING YOUR GOOD CREDIT HISTORY

Once you've established a good credit rating, you'll want to keep it. Here's how:

→ Be truthful when applying for credit.

→ Use credit only in amounts you can easily repay.

→ Fulfill all the terms of the credit agreement.

→ Pay promptly.

→ Notify creditors immediately if you can't meet the payments as agreed.

WHEN TO USE CREDIT
AND WHEN TO PAY CASH

It's probably okay to use credit . . .

> to buy something you really need when it's on sale. But only use credit if paying cash would seriously deplete your cash on hand

> to improve your home rather than moving to a more expensive location

> to obtain cash instead of turning in securities and incurring heavy penalty fees for early withdrawals

> to pay for schooling that would potentially increase your earning power

It's best to pay cash . . .

> to make routine purchases for things like groceries

> to pay for entertainment

> to sustain a life-style you can't afford because of a changing income

> to take a long-deserved vacation so you won't still be paying for last year's vacation as this year's rolls around

KEEPING THE PRICE OF CREDIT DOWN

Paying with borrowed money, whether it be from a loan or by credit card, can be an expensive proposition. Firms that offer credit differ in terms, interest rates and annual fees. Shop around for the best deal, but make sure you're working with a reputable outfit. In most cases, banks and credit unions offer the best terms. Follow this advice to keep the costs down.

Make a large down payment. The smaller the loan, the less paid in overall interest charges.

Repay the loan in the shortest time possible. The longer the loan is outstanding, the more you'll pay. And if you can receive a refund by prepaying, by all means, do so. This also applies to monthly credit card bills. Pay all or as much of the balance as you can to reduce overall interest charges.

Limit the number of credit cards you have. That way, it's easier to keep track of your spending. If you're a "credit-cardoholic," take scissors to your cards and deal strictly in cash.

Curb impulse buying. If you don't need anything, stay out of stores and eliminate window shopping. Also, try throwing out special flyers and other tempting ads.

RESOLVING CREDIT WOES

Here's what to do when early warnings or credit disaster loom in the distance:

→ Don't take on any new obligations. If need be, cut up charge cards so you can't make any new impulse purchases.
→ Concentrate on paying your bills and reducing credit balances.
→ When you have a clean slate, cautiously take on new debts.

Here's how to handle the situation when you see disaster is about to strike:

→ Immediately stop adding to your debts and figure how much you can afford to pay each creditor once a week or monthly.
→ Set up a repayment plan and discuss it with each creditor, or go to a community credit counseling service. You can usually get recommendations for reliable services from your employer's personnel office, your church, The National Foundation of Consumer Credit or family service agencies. The counseling service will help you with your budget and intercede with creditors.

Once you've come face-to-face with credit disaster, you'll need to do the following:

→ Get a lawyer and try to work out a "wage earner plan." Such a plan calls for submitting a 36-month repayment schedule to the court. Though you'll have to live a frugal life-style, this route may be preferable to declaring bankruptcy.
→ Declare bankruptcy as a last resort. It's a blot that can stay on your credit record for 10 to 14 years.

REDUCING YOUR LIGHT BILLS

If your monthly budget includes a whopping total for your electric bill, you should consider ways to cut the amount of electricity you use. One way is to make sure the lights you use are efficient and cost-effective. Follow these light-saving tips:

→ Dust light bulbs regularly—dust-free bulbs produce 20 percent more light than dusty ones.

→ Check the wrapper when you buy new light bulbs to make sure you're getting the most lumens per watt.

→ Use lower wattage bulbs when you can—a 60-watt bulb can often replace a 100-watt bulb without a marked difference.

→ Use dimmers—they allow you to use the amount of light needed, not the amount of light a bulb automatically supplies.

→ If you do need a lot of light somewhere in your house, opt for a single, higher-watt bulb rather than several lower-watt bulbs; one 100-watt bulb produces more light than four 25-watt bulbs for the same amount of electricity.

→ Reduce your lighting load by turning off lights when you don't need them, using sunlight when you can, placing lamps close to work areas and painting the walls a light color to make the most of available light.

MAINTAINING HOUSEHOLD APPLIANCES

Often it's just a simple repair that's needed to get your balky appliances up and running again. Check the list below for some do-it-yourself tips that will save you the expense of having to haul your appliances into the repair shop.

Blenders

→ Clean the blender after you use it by putting a cup of water in the vessel, adding a little detergent and running the blender for about 10 seconds. Rinse the blender in the same fashion (but this time using two cups of plain water).

→ If you use your blender frequently, wash the cutting blade assembly in warm water with a little dish detergent about once a month.

Dishwashers

→ Clean the spray-arm holes regularly. Remove the arms (most lift out; some must be unscrewed) and poke a piece of wire into each hole. Then turn the arm upside down to shake out any particles of dirt.

→ Scrub the filter and filter trap with a stiff-bristled brush. If you're lucky, the filter and trap will be plainly visible at the bottom of the dishwasher. If they aren't, your appliance manual should tell you how to get to them.

Irons

→ To remove sediment buildup in the ports of a steam iron, unplug the iron and clean out the ports with a straightened paper clip (check your manufacturer's instructions first).

→ Flush sediment residue, dust and so on from the interior channels by filling them with a half-and-half solution of water and vinegar and turning the iron on a low-steam setting until the sediment has all come out (again, check your manufacturer's instructions first).

→ Buff out scratches in the soleplate with fine steel wool (on metal) or a plastic pad (on nonstick models).

Juice Extractors

→ Use a stiff brush to loosen accumulated pulp when washing the disc and shaft of the juice extractor.

→ Soak the strainer and the grating disc in cold water and a mild dish detergent for 24 hours, then scrub them with a stiff-bristled brush, to remove stains caused by mineral buildup.

Portable Electric Heaters

→ Lubricate the fan motor shaft and oil ports at the start of each heating season. (Check the manual that came with your unit to find out where the motor shaft and oil ports are located on your particular model.) Use a light oil—a heavy one isn't necessary.

→ On a periodic basis, vacuum, or with a clean cloth wipe, any accumulated dust from the heater. CAUTION: Always unplug the heater before performing routine maintenance tasks.

Room Humidifiers

→ Periodically clean the water pan by scrubbing it with hot, soapy water. If that doesn't get rid of any existing mineral deposits, soak the pan with a solution of vinegar and hot water.

→ If your unit has an evaporating drum (check your owner's manual), periodically soak it in hot, soapy water or vinegar and water to clean it.

Toasters

→ Unplug the toaster, then open the crumb tray (usually located at the base of the toaster). Brush the crumb tray and the inside of the toaster with a soft-bristled toothbrush, and close it. CAUTION: Don't use a metal tool, such as steel wool, to clean the inside of a toaster. If a stray metal strand gets caught inside the toaster, it could create an electrical fire hazard.

→ Replace worn or defective cords with a similar cord. Make sure the new cord is the same size and has the same rating as the old one.

SAVING ENERGY WHEN YOU'RE AWAY

Just because you're away from home, that doesn't mean your house isn't using up energy. Follow these suggestions to save on your utility bills while you're gone:

→ Disconnect any appliances that won't be in use (for example, clocks, heaters for water beds, water heaters, air conditioners and so on).

→ If you want to keep a heater on, turn the thermostat down to the lowest possible temperature; if you plan to keep the air conditioner on, turn it up to a higher level than you normally would.

→ Close curtains and drapes; they'll keep out the summer sun and prevent the place from overheating. Open attic and crawl space vents, too.

CHECKING OUT CHEAPER AT THE SUPERMARKET

Once you enter the supermarket world with all its tempting displays, you can easily spend $100 to $200 in an hour. That's a quick way to run your family budget off the track! Here's how you can get more for your dollars, and save time, too.

Before You Shop

Make a list. Research has shown that shopping from a list saves you minutes and dollars. Arrange your list so like items are together: baked goods, dairy products, meats, produce and so forth. On shopping day, take inventory of supplies, read the food circulars, thumb through your coupon file and then complete your list.

Clip and redeem coupons for products you regularly use. Don't be lured into using coupons for unnecessary products. Whenever you can, combine coupons with specials and go for the double-coupon offers. With a little practice, you can save $5 to $10 on a single order. Arrange your coupons to match your grocery list; that is, all cereals together and so on. You'll spend less time fumbling with the coupons in the store.

Avoid refunding. Get into refunding only to save on products you would normally use. Large-scale refunding calls for super organization and lots of time.

Eat before you shop. Studies show that food shoppers who are hungry buy more goodies on impulse when they are hungry.

When You Shop

Go to the market only once a week. Or, better yet, once every two to three weeks, except for perishables such as milk and produce. (Freezers are indispensable for storing meats, baked goods and so on, which allows you to shop for these items only one or two times a month.) Shoppers who run to the store frequently buy more impulse items.

Try to shop only when you feel rested and alert. You'll be better equipped to calculate bargains and watch for errors at the checkout counter. And shop alone, if you can. Babies will distract you and older children will want everything they see except, of course, the staples you need.

Bring a pocket calculator. Use it to keep a running total of what you're spending. That way you won't get a nasty surprise at checkout time.

Shop in one place. Unless the bargains elsewhere are great, stick to one store. Running all over town costs dollars and minutes.

Shop midweek. That's when the sales are likely to be on. And to zip through the store with the greatest of ease, try going early, late or at mealtimes.

Keep you visit short. Try to keep it under 30 minutes, though the super-market would love for you to stay longer. Market surveys indicate that shoppers spend an extra 50¢ a minute for every minute over 30 in the store.

Stay in the perimeter aisles. That's where you'll find food with the least processing: produce, meats, dairy. Minimal processing means lower prices, with only a couple of notable exceptions—frozen orange juice and powdered milk are both cheaper than their less-processed counterparts.

Look for specials, but be careful. Not all so-called specials are special. You have to study prices in order to spot the good buys. Search high and low for bargains, literally. Most times, the best buys are on inconveniently high or low shelves—eye-level space is reserved for premium-priced goods.

Frequent the day-old bread section. Sometimes you'll find your favorite bread marked half price. Over-the-hill produce, on the other hand, is best avoided unless, for instance, you want to puree bananas that very day. Don't buy any goods in damaged cans. Although these canned goods may be offered at bargain prices, it's no bargain to find bacteria in your food!

Compare unit prices across brands and sizes. Not so long ago, it was up to you to figure the price per ounce or pound. Now, however, nearly all supermarkets have done the calculating for you and clearly display unit pricing on the front of the shelves. Take advantage of the service.

Be willing to try house and generic brands. Most times, they're less expensive and their quality is just fine. Be aware that sometimes generic brands and items found in bulk bins are more expensive than brand name items that are on special.

Pick up quantities of staples when the price is low. But don't go hog-wild. For quantity buying, you need storage space and you must be able to use the items within a reasonable period of time. There will always be other specials.

Get the "large-economy" size when the unit price indicates it's really economical. Be sure it's also something that'll keep until you can use it up. In most instances, you pay a premium price for foods packaged in single-serving sizes.

Buy fresh produce in season. Why pay for refrigerated shipping of strawberries in September when local ones, juicy and sweet, are available for less in June?

Choose meats carefully. Consider the amount of lean meat in a serving as well as the price per pound when selecting meats, fish and poultry. Often a slightly higher priced meat will yield more edible servings in a pound because there's less waste from fat, gristle and bone.

Request a rain check when the store runs out of an advertised special. Some stores habitually run out; obviously, their ploy is just to get you into the store.

Check your register tape. Research shows that unintentional mistakes are commonplace, especially on large purchases.

Bag your order yourself. Put all perishables on top and all frozen and cold foods together in plastic bags. All too often, harried clerks carelessly pile heavy cans atop ripe peaches and delicate lettuces. And keeping cold foods together will help them stay cold longer than if they are separated.

Moving

Moving from one residence to another truly tests the organizational abilities of home managers. If there's a move in your future, follow this advice to make your experience a pleasant one.

MAKING YOUR MOVE GO SMOOTHLY

Moving is disruptive to anyone's routine, to be sure. But armed with these strategies, you can smooth out many of the would-be rough spots.

Develop a master plan. Include a timetable for doing everything from calling the mover for estimates to deciding which things to discard. A checklist works nicely here. Divide your plan into sections indicating what needs to be done when, and leave plenty of room for notes.

Get a change-of-address kit from the post office. Use it to notify doctors, schools, insurance companies, banks and others of your new address. To let publications know of the change, send your new address along with their mailing labels for easy identification. Many businesses, especially publishers, will need six to eight weeks to process your change.

Contact your utility companies. Make arrangements to turn services off in your old home and turn them on in the new one.

Use up food in your refrigerator, freezer and pantry. If you're hiring movers, it will be very costly to move canned goods and a full freezer.

Consider selling major appliances along with the house. They're heavy and expensive to move. If you're taking them with you and you aren't sure how to properly disconnect them, arrange for a service person to disconnect and prepare them for the move. Don't depend on your movers—they aren't trained to disconnect and prepare appliances and, therefore, usually won't do it.

Obtain necessary moving permits. Some locales and many apartment complexes require them as evidence that local taxes and rents have been paid.

Take your old phone book with you. It will come in handy if you ever need an address or phone number from your former town.

Investigate sending, instead of moving, books and other heavy items. You may save a considerable amount of money by using the mail or a common carrier instead of the movers.

Have a moving sale to dispose of items you no longer use. Then donate whatever's left to Goodwill, the Salvation Army or other charity. School and hospital libraries will often welcome fairly new books in top-notch condition.

PACKING EFFICIENTLY

Packing is one of the least enjoyable activities associated with a move. Although we can't make it more fun for you, we can offer these seven best packing techniques.

Obtain clean, sturdy cartons in a variety of sizes. These are usually available from supermarkets, liquor stores or your workplace. You can also buy new boxes from a mover. Use small boxes for heavy items, such as books, and large boxes for light, bulky objects. Secure all seams and closings with tape and *label every box* by either naming the room the items belong in, or listing all the items themselves (or better yet, do both).

Stand plates on end. If you stack them, you risk having the bottom ones broken from the weight of those above.

Use linens—towels, sheets, pillowcases, tablecloths—instead of newspapers to protect packed dishes and glassware. This eliminates washing dishes to remove the newspaper smudges when you unpack. Another alternative is to use paper towels. Expensive? Yes, but if you save the towels for other household chores, you'll have a supply that will last for months. There's still one more way to avoid inky newspaper smudges — buy newsprint from a mover. It's ink free and fairly inexpensive, though you'll still have to wash the dishes because it's not meant to be used near food or food-holding items.

Pack the contents of each kitchen drawer separately. Put items in plastic bags, then close with a twister. When you get to your new kitchen, simply slip the contents of each bag into an appropriate drawer. You save yourself the time and aggravation of sorting through boxes of jumbled utensils.

If your dresser drawers are full of unbreakable items, leave them in place. The mover will position the furniture so the drawers won't slide open during travel.

Secure large mirrors between two mattresses for a short move. All mirrors should stand on end. For a long move, buy a mirror carton from your mover.

Move hanging clothes in a wardrobe. You can purchase these sturdy cardboard "closets" from the mover. They eliminate the need for folding and packing clothes that are normally on hangers. When you get to your new home, just move clothes from the wardrobes to the closets.

CHOOSING AND USING A MOVING FIRM

If you decide to let someone else do the moving for you, follow these suggestions to get the best moving help and make the most of their services.

For local moves, check with the Better Business Bureau in your area for a list of reliable movers. For interstate moves, call your local office of the Interstate Commerce Commission (ICC). Complaints about interstate movers should be sent to ICC, Office of Compliance and Consumer Assistance, Room 6328, 12th and Constitution Avenues NW, Washington, DC 20423 (203-275-7844).

Schedule your move during the mover's slack time. This is usually November through March. Ask for a discount for doing so. The busiest moving months are April through October, with the peak coming in June through September, when school is out for the summer. Delays are common during those months. Obtain price estimates from at least three movers and get all agreements in writing.

Supervise the packing. If the mover is packing your belongings, watch the packing closely to make certain the boxes aren't left half full, then stuffed with packing material. This practice is called short, or balloon, packing and is all too common. You'll have to pay for the extra cartons and packing materials plus their weight.

Examine the mover's inventory carefully. See that it lists all your belongings and that it describes them accurately. Make notes on the inventory where you disagree.

Accompany the mover to the weigh station. This helps prevent outright cheating. You shouldn't be paying for four or five 200-pound moving men

---

SOME VERY MOVING QUESTIONS

When you call a mover for an estimate, ask plenty of questions, such as these:

→ What *won't* the mover take?
→ Will your belongings be the only ones in the van?
→ What's the charge for packing boxes and insurance?
→ Will the mover insure your belongings if you pack the boxes?
→ Will your antiques be covered by insurance?
→ How will the total cost be figured? By the pound? By the hour?
→ How are damages compensated? And how quickly?
→ What are the arrangements if the mover is late? Who pays for delays?
→ How long will the entire move take?

---

aboard the van. If there's no scale for your move, you may be charged at the rate of seven pounds to every square foot of van space used. (The weight of your belongings would be estimated by the firm.) This only works to your advantage if you're moving a ton of books and other heavy items.

Inspect the van when the movers say everything has been unloaded. You don't want any small, expensive items to be left in the van.

Sign the receipt only after inspecting all your goods. Make note of any misplaced or damaged items. If you must sign before unpacking, note "approved subject to unpacking boxes" above your signature and add the date.

Organization

Every good housekeeper knows that the key to keeping things in order is organization. But that seems to be one area where a lot of people just let things fall apart. Your house may be clean, but you can't find anything! From closets to bedrooms to basements, if you've got a place for everything and everything in its place, you'll be ahead of the game.

ORGANIZING CLOSETS AND STORAGE AREAS

The best place to start organizing your house is in the closets and storage areas. After all, that's where things are often the hardest to find! Take these steps to put things in order:

→ Put seldom-used items toward the back of closets and drawers and often-used things near the front.

→ Group clothing in closets according to length. That way, there will be space below shorter items for a shoe rack or extra shelves.

→ Store out-of-season clothes in garment bags at the back of the closet. Better yet, if you can, store these clothes in the attic or basement.

→ To make good use of dead space near the top of the closet, install another shelf above the existing one. Use the uppermost shelf for seldom-used items.

→ Empty storage areas and take inventory. Then dispose of any items you haven't used for a year or two.

→ Outfit storage areas with some of the many space-saving accessories on the market, such as plastic-coated wire bins and shelving.

→ Keep papers and booklets that you refer to often in file folders or notebooks.

→ Label all boxes of stored items. That way, it's easy to find something when you want it.

→ Use cutlery trays in desk or kitchen drawers to organize pens, pencils, stamps, tape, scissors, paper clips and the like.

MAKING THE MOST OF YOUR CLOTHES CLOSET

Here are a few other tricks to help you get the most out of your closet space.

Cover the doors with full-length mirrors. That way, you can see how you look from head to toe, even when you're in a hurry. (Mirrors have the added benefit of making your bedroom look twice as large as it actually is.)

Install bifold doors. They'll give you access to the entire closet while using less space than conventional closet doors.

Install a fold-down ironing board. You'll have it handy for those last-minute touch-ups and you'll cut down on the number of trips you have to make between the laundry room and your closet.

ORGANIZING THE KITCHEN

Ever spend too much time searching in kitchen drawers or cabinets for that item you "just saw the other day"? If this sounds all too familiar, take these steps to clean things up:

→ Use a lazy Susan in corner cabinets. It will be easier to reach things.

→ Attach small baskets to the inside of kitchen closet doors to hold envelope mixes and small cans.

→ Hang a heavy-duty rack on the inside of a pantry door for storing large cans or boxes of foil or plastic wrap.

→ Install wire slide-on shelves in cabinets for storing dishcloths, towels, pot holders and sponges.

→ Mount towel racks in the cabinet under the sink. These are terrific for storing damp towels and dishcloths between uses.

→ Keep boxes of foil, plastic wrap, waxed paper and plastic bags in a large rectangular dishpan in the cabinet under the kitchen sink.

ORGANIZING THE BATHROOM

If your bathroom is a jumble of toiletries, kids' toys and piles of damp towels, try some of these suggestions:

→ If your bathroom didn't come with a toothbrush holder, install cup hooks on the wall or under a cabinet.

→ Put shelves over the toilet tank for towels, hand lotion, tissues and extra toilet tissue.

→ Install hooks on the back of the door for shower caps.

→ Keep a rectangular dishpan under the vanity to store cleaning supplies in. Place another pan next to the bathtub and use it to hold children's bath toys.

→ Install as many towel racks or hooks as you can without cluttering the room. Extra space for hanging towels is always welcome.

ORGANIZING THE BASEMENT AND GARAGE

After the attic, the basement and garage seem to be favorite places for storing everything people want to save but don't know what to do with. If you're one of these people, here's how to put some order into that chaos:

→ Build shelves under the basement stairs for extra storage space.

→ Nail empty coffee cans to the wall for clips, nails, small tools and other items.

→ Install a pegboard for hanging tools.

→ Baby food jars are great for organizing nails and screws of all sizes. Nail the caps to a wood base or wall plaque; then screw the jars in place.

→ Install large hooks to hang bikes from the basement or garage rafters. This will also help preserve the bike's tires by keeping the weight off them.

→ In the garage, build a storage platform over the car. Such a spot is ideal for stashing off-season storm doors and other seldom-used bulky items.

GETTING THE CHILDREN'S ROOMS IN SHAPE

If you shudder at the thought of trying to keep order in your children's rooms, use these tips to help them get organized:

→ Use bins, boxes and shelves, at heights that are accessible to your children, for housing toys and books. And teach your children to pick up after themselves.

→ Put closet rods and hooks down low so young children can reach their own clothes.

→ Put hats, mittens, sweatshirts and scarves in bins or boxes on the floor of the closet so young children can grab what they need.

→ Make a shoe bag with oversized pockets and hang it behind the door in a child's room. Use the bag for storing stuffed animals and other odd-shaped toys.

→ Utilize the space under the beds. Use flat, pullout bins for storing toys or bed linens.

→ If your children are budding artists, hang bulletin boards in their rooms for displaying artwork. Bulletin boards are terrific for organizing messages, schedules and other reminders, too.

7

Shortcuts to

Home Maintenance and Repair

From repairing a door hinge to building a deck, being a homeowner means you have plenty of repair and maintenance jobs to keep you hopping, not to mention those occasional big remodeling projects. Whether you're tackling an electrical or plumbing problem, repointing brick or repairing a plaster wall, here are shortcuts to getting them done quickly and economically.

Doors and Windows

Whether you're about to hang a new door or are wondering what to do about window condensation, here are tips to help you solve some of the most common door and window dilemmas.

REPAIRING A DOOR HINGE

If your door doesn't hang properly, it could be because a hinge is loose or undone. First, examine the screw holes. A common cause of loose hinges is a screw hole that has become enlarged over time. If your inspection turns up a hole that's too big for the screw, follow these steps for a quick and easy remedy.

1. Prepare the screw hole. The hole should be at least one size larger in diameter than the screw itself. If it isn't that large, use a drill bit one size larger than the screw to enlarge the hole.

2. Cut a piece of wooden matchstick or dowel to the same length as the hole. (Use matchsticks for small holes and dowels for big ones.)

3. Glue the matchstick or dowel into place with wood adhesive. Allow it to dry, then reattach the hinge, using a new screw.

REPLACING A DAMAGED DOOR

Replacing a door is not difficult; just follow these five steps for a professional-looking job.

1. Hold the new door up to the opening to gauge how well it fits.

2. Plane the door at the top and bottom until there is a proper clearance at both ends. (On the top, the clearance should be about $\frac{1}{16}$ inch; on the bottom, about $\frac{3}{8}$ inch.) Always work from the ends of the door in toward the center; otherwise the action of the plane could cause the corners of the door to chip off or splinter. Plane the sides of the door so there will be a space of about $\frac{1}{16}$ inch on either side.

3. Prop the door into its correct position in the opening, using scrap wood to raise the door to the right height.

4. Holding a double-edged knife parallel to the floor, stick the blade into the crack between the door and the jamb to mark the location of each of the hinges. Using this method, you'll have marked both leaves of the hinge at the same time.

5. Remove the door. Stand the door on its side and trace the outline of the hinges at the appropriate locations. Then attach the hinges to the door and hang it in the opening.

UNSTICKING POCKET DOORS

Pocket doors—doors that slide in and out of a cavity in the wall—are often found in older homes. Sometimes they stick after years of use. Here's how to get them moving freely.

1. Remove the door from its pocket. To do this, lift the door up toward the ceiling until the rollers are off the track, and then pull out the bottom of the door. (Pocket doors can be quite heavy, so you may need someone to help you lift it up.)

2. Using a narrow attachment, or simply the end of the vacuum itself, vacuum out any plaster or debris that may have collected in the pocket.

3. Examine the studs that frame the pockets for any signs of warping. If the studs are warped, the door may no longer slide easily past them. In this case, insert a piece of wood the same width as the door into the opening to determine where the door is binding. If you can reach the stud that's catching the door, plane it down. (If you can't reach it, you'll have to open up the wall and then replace or replane the stud.)

4. Examine the track for dents. Use pliers to bend a dented track back into shape. Inspect the rollers on the bottom of the door. Clean the good ones of dust and dirt, and oil them with an all-purpose household lubricant. Replace any broken rollers. Rehang the doors.

INSTALLING WEATHER STRIPPING

Although installing weather stripping in doors and windows is a fairly easy job, it's also easy to install it improperly, resulting in a loose fit. Here's how to do it right.

1. Measure the gaps to be weather-stripped and choose a product that will fit. If you install a gasket that's too thick for the space, it will be difficult to open and close your door or window. If the product is too thin, you'll have a loose fit.

2. Make sure doors and windows are plumb and square, and clean all surfaces thoroughly.

3. Apply a thin bead of high-quality caulking compound along the line where you plan to install the weather stripping. (The caulking will prevent gaps from occurring between the strip and the mounting surface.)

4. Lay the weather stripping on top of the compound and staple or nail it to the mounting surface. (Make sure you don't stretch the vinyl or plastic weather stripping while you fasten it, because the flexible gasket can shrink after exposure to heat and cold.)

UNSTICKING WINDOWS

It's the first day of spring and there's a warm, gentle breeze. Time to open the windows and let in the fresh air—but they're stuck! If this has ever happened to you, you know what a pain it can be to get windows to open again. Here's the best method.

1. Remove the window stops (the vertical strips of wood that are nailed or screwed along the inside of the window frame that the sash rubs against). Remove the window.

2. With a heat gun and a scraper, remove any built-up paint on the window sash and frame. If paint isn't the problem, the problem may be that the window sash does not fit properly because it's warped. Plane the warped edge smooth.

3. Wax the sash along the edges that come into contact with the frame. Replace the window.

4. Install the stops a hairbreadth away from where they were previously located, to give the window sash ample room to move up and down.

PROTECTING YOUR WINDOWS FROM AGING

An ounce of prevention is worth a pound of cure. Here are ways to protect your new *or* old windows from deterioration so they will remain problem-free for years to come.

→ Install a roof overhang or gutter system to protect your windows from rain.
→ Make sure the exterior sill of your window slants *away* from the window so water won't collect near the lower sash.
→ Inspect wooden sills periodically for signs of termites and carpenter ants.
→ Replace any deteriorated glazing compound to prevent water from leaking into the groove that holds the glass.
→ Secure loose window flashing or loose drip caps (the sloped caps above your windows that allow rainwater to run off).

CUTTING GLASS

Cutting a piece of glass to replace a broken window pane isn't difficult; it just takes a little practice. Here's the best technique.

1. Lay a cardboard template or straightedge on the piece of glass. Holding the glass cutter between your index and middle fingers with the thumb supporting it behind and the teeth facing you, run the cutter along one side of the pattern, scoring the glass.

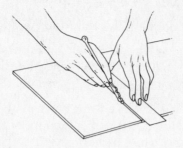

2. Tap gently underneath the glass with the end of the cutter and the glass should break along the score line with a cracking sound. If the glass is broken through but still holds together, you can bend it over a table edge to break it. Alternatively, you can break the excess glass off with pliers.

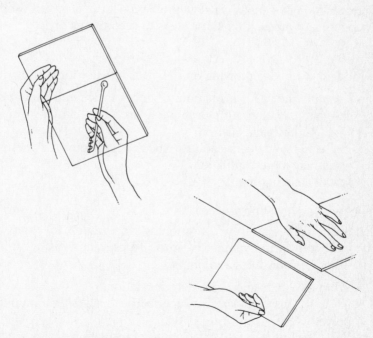

3. Smooth any rough edges on the glass by breaking the nibs off with pliers or by rubbing them with a file or sandpaper.

CURING WINDOW CONDENSATION

Window condensation is unsightly and can eventually lead to the rotting of a wooden sill. Here's the cure.

1. Make sure all of your windows are tightly caulked and weather-stripped.

2. Install exterior storm windows. If you already have storm windows, make sure the weep holes—small holes usually found drilled into the bottom of the storm window frame—are not stopped up.

3. Reduce the humidity in your home by cutting down on the amount of moisture being generated by daily activities. For example, make sure that you run ventilating fans when you take baths or showers, that you cover

---

CURING HOUSEHOLD CONDENSATION

Condensation isn't just a window problem—it can occur on walls, ductwork and pipes. Take these steps to keep things dry.

Walls

If mildew or mold is growing on the walls inside your house:

→ Examine the wall's insulation. Chances are, there's either not enough insulation or the insulation has settled, leaving a cold spot. Add more insulation.
→ Exchange solid doors leading to the area with louvered ones, to encourage more ventilation.
→ Install a circulating fan.

Ductwork and Pipes

Cold-water pipes and air conditioning ducts often fall prey to condensation during warmer weather. To prevent moisture from collecting on your ducts and pipes:

→ Wrap the ducts and pipes with insulation.
→ Cover the insulation with a vapor barrier such as aluminum or polyethylene.
→ Seal all joints between the sections of insulation with a water-proof duct tape.

pots and pans when you cook and that you water houseplants only as they need it.

4. As a last resort, install a dehumidifier.

Electricity

Many people are not comfortable doing their own electrical repairs, and with good reason: a mistake could be fatal. But there are some simple repairs that a homeowner can tackle—such as replacing existing outlets and receptacles. In this section, we'll take you step-by-step through these repairs. Just be sure to start by following the safety rules.

REPAIRING ELECTRICAL SYSTEMS SAFELY

If you make a mistake while attempting to repair your electrical system or when adding an outlet, *it could be fatal. Never* attempt to work on your house's electrical system without following the safety rules listed below.

Never assume the power is off. Be absolutely certain that the power is turned off before you touch any part of your electrical system. Never assume that it is off—always use a voltage tester to make sure wires aren't "live."

Don't touch any metal pipe when you're working with electricity (this includes plumbing and gas system piping). You could get a serious shock if you accidentally touch a pipe and a live wire at the same time. Even if you are certain the wire is dead, don't take chances!

CUTTING THE COST OF
HIRING AN ELECTRICIAN

To save money rewiring your house, you can fish wires (pull them) through the walls yourself, leaving the final wiring jobs—such as installing outlets, receptacles, light fixtures and switches—to a professional electrician. Fishing wires is an easy but time-consuming job. By cutting the hours a professional electrician spends on the house, you can save substantial amounts of money.

ELECTRICIAN'S TOOLBOX

For minor electrical repairs, you'll want the following tools.

Continuity tester: A device that checks a circuit to make sure electricity can flow through the circuit. It looks like a penlight or a flashlight. A penlight tester has a needle point at one end and a wire with an alligator clip at the other. The flashlight tester has two alligator clips. A continuity tester has a low-voltage lamp that lights up when current flows from the alligator clip to the tip of the probe.

Always test the continuity tester before using it to make sure that it works. To test the continuity tester, touch the tips of the alligator clips or the wire and the alligator clip together. The light should then go on. If it doesn't, the bulb, the battery or the tester may be worn out.

Fish tape: A type of tape used for pulling wires through finished walls, so the wires will be invisible from a room's interior.

Fuse pullers: A tool that's used to pull cartridge fuses safely out of a fuse panel.

Lineman's pliers: Heavy-duty pliers used to cut cable and wire, to bend heavy wire and to work with electrical components.

Neon voltage tester: A device designed to tell you whether a circuit is live, or hot. Always test for live wires. The voltage tester consists of a holder that houses a neon lamp. Two wires ending in test leads extend from the holder. When the leads touch live power lines, the bulb will light up.

Always test your voltage tester before using it to make sure that it works. To test the voltage tester, plug it into a live receptacle, touching one of the test leads to the screw on the cover plate exterior (or the ground in a three-slot outlet) and the other to each slot. If the voltage tester is working, the bulb should light up.

Romex cable: A nonmetallic, sheathed cable (commonly identified by the trade name Romex) that consists of insulated wires enclosed in plastic. This is the most commonly used cable in residential wiring today.

Wire nuts: Used for wiring splices.

Never stand in water, on a damp floor or on the ground when working on your electrical system. Instead, put down a dry board, cover it with a rubber mat and stand on that. That way you won't get a shock if you should touch a live wire.

Follow the National Electrical Code when doing any electrical wiring or repair projects. Make sure to contact the local authorities to see if there are any local code requirements that differ from the national code. Have any work that you do yourself checked by your local inspector to make sure that it is safe.

REPLACING AN EXISTING SWITCH

Replacing an existing switch or receptacle is a fairly easy task: basically, you just take out the old switch or receptacle and wire in the new one just as the old one was.

1. First study the illustration showing a typical single-pole switch.

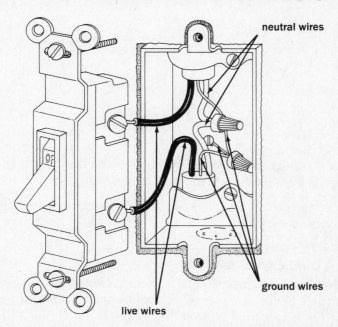

2. Turn off the switch and turn off the electrical power to the switch. Remove the cover plate and unscrew the two screws holding the switch into the junction box. Tug on the ends of the mounting strap to pull the switch out of the box.

3. Using your voltage tester, check from each brass screw to the metal junction box and "across" the brass screws to make sure that the power is really off.

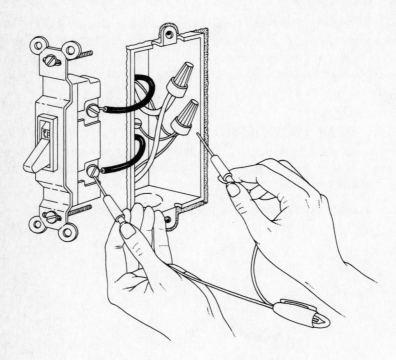

4. Unscrew the brass screws on the old switch. Transfer the wires from the brass screws on the old switch to the brass screws on the new switch.

5. Insert the new switch in the junction box and secure it with the screws. Replace the cover plate.

REPLACING A DUPLEX RECEPTACLE

In most cases, replacing a duplex receptacle is just as simple as replacing a single-pole switch. However, if you live in an older home, your existing receptacle may not have a third hole on the bottom for grounding, the way the modern receptacle in the illustration does. If such is the case, and you replace your old receptacle with the modern three-hole version, you'll need to run a new bare ground wire to the metal junction box with BX cable (a trade-name cable that consists of insulated wires encased in spirally wound, flexible steel armor). Check with an electrician or your local zoning authorities to make sure you understand the procedure.

1. Study the illustration of the duplex receptacle.

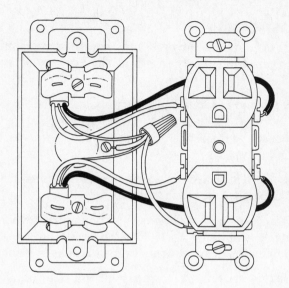

2. Turn the power off to the receptacle. Check the receptacle with your voltage tester to make sure there's no live electrical current.

3. Remove the cover plate. Remove the receptacle from the box by unscrewing the two screws holding the duplex into the junction box and tugging on the ends of the mounting strap.

4. Place one end of the voltage tester on a brass screw and the other on a silver screw to make sure that the power is turned off. Then unscrew the brass and silver screws. Remove the wires.

5. Transfer the black wire(s) to the brass screw(s), the white wire(s) to the white screw(s) and the green or bare wire to the green screw.

6. Insert the new receptacle into the box, and screw it securely in place. Replace the cover plate.

Exterior Walls

No matter what the age of your house, at some point you will have to do some work on its exterior walls. You may find yourself simply changing the color of the paint or getting into more involved work, such as repointing brick, repairing stucco or waterproofing exterior basement walls. In this section we'll show you the best ways to get these exterior chores done.

PAINTING A HOUSE EXTERIOR

Painting the outside of your house involves a bit more than just climbing up the ladder with a can of paint and a paintbrush in your hand. Here are some tips for a successful job.

Check for any openings that moisture can infiltrate. Caulk small cracks or holes in the siding and around windows, replace rotten siding and countersink nails and fill the holes with putty. Replace or repair deteriorated trim around windows and doors.

Prepare the surface. Wash it, scrape away loose or peeling paint and then sand it. Prime any exposed, bare wood surfaces.

Schedule your painting for a dry, windless day. Paint will dry best when the temperature is between 60° and 70°F. Avoid painting on an overly humid day. Lay drop cloths under you and over sidewalks or plants.

Work from the eaves down. That way, drips will run onto unpainted surfaces.

PREVENTING EXTERIOR PAINT PEEL

Peeling paint on the exterior of a house is usually the result of water vapor being generated inside the house and not being able to escape through the walls. To prevent exterior paint from blistering, you need to tighten up your interior walls and loosen up your exterior ones.

→ Seal any cracks on your interior walls. Caulk over any seams.
→ Paint the interior walls with a couple coats of oil-based paint or a special vapor-barrier paint.
→ Remove the chipped, peeling paint from the exterior.
→ Refinish the siding with a vapor-permeable stain or a latex paint.

PAINTING EXTERIOR METALWORK

Gutters, chimney flashings and exterior house trim are often made of galvanized iron or steel. Painting these surfaces prevents them from rusting and deteriorating.

Clean the metal surface. An easy-to-make cleaning solution consists of 1 pint of vinegar to 1 gallon of water. Scrub the metal surface with this solution, then rinse thoroughly with water. (If you don't remove all of the vinegar, it can cause the new coat of paint to fail sooner than it would otherwise.)

Prepare the surface for priming. If the metalwork is old and rusty or has been previously painted, apply a commercial stripper to the surface, rinsing thoroughly after each use. If the metalwork is new, sand it gently.

Prime the metal. For best results, use a zinc dust paint (a special paint recommended by the experts for use on galvanized metal). Allow the primer to dry.

Paint the metal. Apply a top coat of a high-quality, acrylic latex exterior house paint. (But first check with the manufacturer to make sure the top coat you choose is compatible with the primer.)

CHOOSING THE RIGHT PAINT

Are you confused by paint terminology? Don't be. Study the list below before you go to the paint store and you'll be prepared to buy what's right for you.

Acoustic tile paint: This is a paint that is especially formulated so it won't clog the holes in acoustic tile. Acoustic tile is sound-deadening tile. It's able to deaden sound in a room because it has many little holes in its surface. If you tried to paint an acoustic tile ceiling with an ordinary paint, the holes would fill up and the tile would lose much of its sound-deadening properties.

Alkyd: This is an oil-based, solvent-thinned paint that has a strong odor and takes longer to dry than latex paint. Alkyd paint is a good choice for areas that are subject to wear and tear, especially in the form of abrasion. It creates an exceptionally smooth surface and can help to replenish an old, dried-out wood surface. To clean paintbrushes that have been used with an alkyd paint, you must use a solvent such as mineral spirits.

Enamel paint: A latex or an alkyd paint can be called an enamel paint. The term enamel means that the paint contains a high percentage of resin and therefore has a highly durable, stain- and scrub-resistant gloss finish. Use enamel paint in areas where there's a lot of traffic or where you plan to wash the painted surface frequently.

Epoxy coating: This is a two-part coating that has qualities similar to baked-on enamel. It is highly moisture resistant and is ideally suited to areas where there's a lot of humidity, such as bathrooms.

Floor-and-deck paint: This is a heavy-duty paint especially formulated for high-traffic areas. It also resists the onslaught of foul weather. Two versions of this paint are available: a high-gloss finish that's easy to keep clean and a low-gloss finish that's designed to resist chipping and to be less slippery when wet.

Latex: Latex, or water-based and water-thinned, paint is the most convenient paint to use. It is resistant to alkali—an important consideration when it comes to painting a surface that has a high alkali content such as freshly formed concrete. You can use latex in most areas around the home. Latex paint cleans up with soap and water and dries quickly, too. It also tends to have less of a paint odor than oil-based paints.

Latex flat enamel: This paint has the benefit of a latex paint—it is water-soluble and, therefore, easy to clean up. It also has the benefits of enamel paint—it is more durable than regular latex paint and it resists scrubbing. It has a flat finish.

BUYING PAINTBRUSHES

Don't skimp on paintbrushes; most professionals say that the extra money spent buying a good brush is worth it. To find out how good a brush is, try:

> brushing the bristles against your fingers; they should feel flexible
> pressing the bristles against the palm of your hand; they should spread easily
> pulling the bristles gently; they should remain firmly attached to the handle
> reading the label to find out what the bristles are made of. Nylon bristles are preferred by most experts for use with water-based paints; natural bristles are preferred for oil-based paints

UNCLOGGING GUTTERS

Clogged gutters are the source of many home moisture problems. When gutters are clogged, water backs up under the roofing and into the walls. Here's how to unclog gutters safely.

1. Position a ladder so that its top is six to eight inches away from the gutter. Using a trowel or a gloved hand, remove all twigs, leaves and other debris from the gutter.

2. Locate the downspout strainer (it's a wire-cage strainer located just above the downspout) and clean it out.

3. Caulk any rough seams or joints.

4. Pour a bucket of water in the gutter or use your garden hose. The water should flow smoothly and quickly toward the downspout; if it doesn't, adjust the gutter slope.

REPAIRING PERFORATED GUTTERS

If your gutters have some holes, don't rush out to buy replacements. Instead, try patching them yourself.

1. Using a wire brush, clean the area around the hole. With a paint scraper or trowel, apply a generous coat of roofing cement to the area of the gutter surrounding the hole.

2. Cover the hole with a square of flexible metal sheeting or fiberglass screening, then cover with a patch made from the same material as the gutter.

3. Coat the patch with more roofing cement. Smooth it out using the scraper or trowel.

REPOINTING BRICK

If the mortar between the old bricks in your wall is crumbling, it's time to have it repointed. There's no need to shy away from doing it yourself — just follow the steps outlined here.

PREPARING MORTAR

All your brickwork will be for naught if you don't properly prepare your mortar. After all, it's the mortar that's holding it all together! Here's the best way to do the job.

1. Roll the unopened bag of mortar mix on the ground to combine the ingredients, then pour the mortar into a wheelbarrow or pan and mix the ingredients with a hoe.

2. Pile the mortar in the middle of the pan and make a fist-sized indentation in the mix. Pour a small amount of water into the indentation, then begin mixing the dry mortar with the water.

3. Continue to add a little bit of water at a time until all of the ingredients are moist. When the mortar is firm enough to form ridges when you run a trowel through it, but not so stiff that it sticks to the trowel, place a batch on a board and you're ready to go. (Keep the rest of the mortar out of the sun until you need it.)

---

1. Chisel out the existing mortar between the bricks, leaving a flat-bottomed channel about ¾ to 1 inch deep.

2. Wet the area. (If the joint isn't damp, it will tend to draw the water from the mortar and dry mortar won't cure properly.)

3. Mix the mortar. For old bricks, use a mix consisting of 1 part portland cement, 2 parts hydrated lime and 7 or 8 parts fine sand. Add water until the mixture is wet but stiff enough to keep its shape when squeezed. Mortar made primarily of portland cement should be used only on modern brick—portland cement will damage soft, older brick. If you're not sure how old your brick is, check with your local historical society.

4. Fill the channel with a layer of newly mixed mortar. Allow it to set about an hour, then fill it with a second layer.

5. When the mortar is stiff, run a joint tool down the joints to create a concave surface or to even off the mortar with the surrounding brick. Use the surface shape of the original mortar as a guide when you decide how to finish the new mortar.

6. Dampen the new mortar periodically so it takes two to three days to dry—a slow curing period will encourage a stronger bond.

REPAIRING STUCCO

You can't repair a large hole or crack in a stucco wall unless the lath—the wire mesh or wooden boards that the stucco is applied to—is in good condition. If the lath isn't intact, it will need to be replaced, and you may want to leave the job to a professional. However, a do-it-yourselfer can easily repair stucco that's slightly cracked.

1. Enlarge the crack with a knife or a chisel. Undercut the crack so that the bottom is wider than the top. Wet the crack thoroughly with water.

2. With a trowel or pointing tool, pack the crack with a ready-mix mortar. Tamp it down firmly.

3. Over the next three days, periodically moisten the patch so that it will cure properly.

COMBATING WET BASEMENTS

To combat a leaky basement, you must prevent water from building up in the soil around your basement walls. The best way to solve a wet basement problem is to excavate the house foundation and lay drain tile (clay or plastic perforated pipe) around the foundation at the depth of the footings, then paint the foundation exterior itself with a waterproofing compound. Unfortunately, this method is also the most expensive way to deal with a leaky basement. Before going through the expense and trouble of an excavation, try some of these methods first:

→ Inspect the ground around your house foundation to make sure it slopes *away* from the basement.

→ Dig shallow drainage ditches around the foundation of your house to collect and divert the runoff. (You can either work these ditches creatively into your landscape or you can plant them with grass and allow the grass to grow to a height that's even with the rest of your lawn so the ditches won't show.)

→ Check rain gutters and downspouts to make sure they're not clogged.

→ Add a downspout extension to carry water farther away from the house.

→ Coat the interior walls of the basement with a good waterproofing compound. (See "Applying Basement Waterproofing Compounds" later in this chapter.)

Floors

No matter if your floors are wood, vinyl or slate (or if you have a bit of each in your home), you may find yourself faced with some minor flooring repairs. Whether it's installing carpeting or sanding wood floors, there's no need to call in the professionals—here's how to do a first-rate job on your own.

REMOVING WALL-TO-WALL CARPETING

If you've ever tried ripping up old wall-to-wall carpeting to restore the hardwood floors underneath, you may have found that the foam carpet backing remained stuck to the floor. Here's how to remove stuck-on backing.

1. Scrape up the backing with a putty knife or other scraper.

2. Wipe down the floor with mineral spirits and 0000 steel wool. (Make sure the room is well-ventilated and that you are wearing gloves.)

3. When the backing is removed, allow the floor to dry, then proceed with refinishing the floor.

INSTALLING CARPET ON A STAIRCASE

1. Measure the steps from the crouch to the nose (see the illustration). Just to be safe, add one extra inch to this step measurement. Add up the length measurements for all the steps, then measure the width.

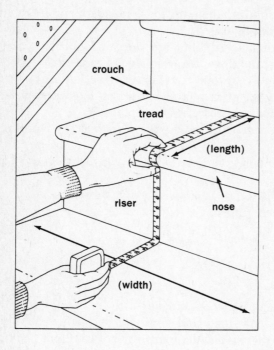

2. Buy a piece of carpet. If you buy more than one piece, mark the direction of grain on the back of the pieces so you'll be able to lay the carpet with the grain of both pieces running in the same direction.

3. Cut and lay the padding. The padding should be positioned so that it lies at least one inch from the crouch (the corner where the tread meets the riser) and so that it overhangs the nose by an inch. If your carpet won't be covering the stair's entire width, cut the padding an inch short on either side. Staple it along the back and sides.

4. Starting at the top of the stairs at the first crouch, cut a piece of carpet large enough to cover a single stair tread, plus wrap around the nose and run down the riser.

5. Pull the back edge of the carpet to the crouch and staple it to the tread. Then pull the carpet taut and staple it underneath the nose.

6. Pull the rest of the carpet down over the riser and staple it at the bottom. Trim it at the next crouch with a utility knife.

7. Repeat the procedure until you've reached the last tread. Then cut a piece of carpet that will cover the last tread from the crouch to the bottom of the nose.

8. At the top of the stairs, cup a piece of carpet to fit the top riser from the crouch to the bottom of the nose. Don't run the carpet over the nose unless the carpeting is continuing down the hall.

REMOVING A DAMAGED FLOORBOARD

Sometimes a floorboard is so badly damaged that the best thing to do is remove and replace it. Here's how.

1. Drill a large hole in the center of the damaged board. Starting at the hole, drive a chisel down the center of the board, making a nice, straight crack to the end, then return to the hole and work toward the other end.

2. Insert the chisel or a prybar into the crack. Wriggle the tool until a piece of the board pops out. Remove the remainder of the board in the same fashion.

3. Cut a new piece of floorboard to fit the space left by the old. Test the board to see if it fits. Use the chisel to make any necessary adjustments so the new board will mesh with the existing tongue and groove boards.

4. Coat the new floorboard with a wood adhesive and insert it into the space. Countersink nails on either end of the board. Fill the holes with putty for a finished look.

REMOVING AN UNDAMAGED FLOORBOARD

If you're removing wood flooring to replace it with something else—tile, for example—there's no need to ruin the wood while taking it up. You may want to save it to use somewhere else, or you may be able to sell it. Here's how to remove an undamaged floorboard so that it can be used again.

1. Insert a prybar into the space between the floorboard and its neighbor. Manipulate the prybar until the corner of the board is lifted; then slide a second prybar or a broad chisel under the other side of the board.

2. When both sides of the floorboard are lifted, slip a metal ruler under the end of the floorboard. Work it down the length of the board, until the whole board is forced up and out of its slot.

SANDING A WOOD FLOOR

When the time comes to have your wood floors sanded, consider doing the job yourself. Here's how.

1. Inspect the floor for any raised nails or carpet tacks. Using a hammer and nail, tap any exposed nail heads until they are below the wood surface. Pull out any nails or tacks that can't be hammered below the surface. Mend all split or cracked boards.

2. Rent a professional belt sander (available at many tool rental shops). It's an impossible task to sand a floor with a small finishing sander or with a drill with a sander bit.

3. Equip the sander with a coarse- or medium-grade paper. The more uneven the floor is, the coarser the paper should be.

4. Position the belt sander on the floor. Tilt it back onto the rear wheels so that the sanding drum—the revolving cylinder that holds the sandpaper—is several inches above the floor.

5. Turn on the sander. Gradually lower it into place and begin moving it across the floorboards at a 45° angle to the boards, making sure to overlap each stroke by two or three inches.

6. Once you have given the boards a pass, switch to a fine sandpaper and sand them again, this time running the sander parallel to the direction in which the boards were laid. *Never* sand at right angles to the floorboards or allow the sander to stand still at any time; the sander will gouge the surface and you will never be able to get the deep scratches out.

7. Use a hand sander to do the edges of the floor and any small nooks or crannies that the large floor sander can't reach.

RENEWING A WOOD FLOOR

Your old floor is a disgrace, but you'd prefer not to sand the floor down to the bare wood and refinish it from scratch. Try following these steps instead.

Clean the floor. Mineral spirits, scrubbed on the floor with a brush or fine steel wool and wiped with clean rags, will, in most cases, remove wax and dirt buildup. (CAUTION: When using mineral spirits, work in a well-ventilated room, away from open flame.) *Never* wash or wet-mop a wood floor; even if the finish is water-repellent, the water can seep between the floorboards, leaving dark stains and sometimes even warping the wood.

TYPES OF WOOD FINISH

There are many kinds of finishing products for wood flooring. Here's a rundown of what's available.

Irradiated polymer: A durable finish that is applied in the factory and primarily used for commercial flooring.

Lacquer: Lacquer dries quickly, but it needs a master touch to apply it correctly. Often lacquer is applied in layers—really fine furniture can have dozens of layers of lacquer comprising the finish. The lacquering process creates a rich, glossy surface finish, but the finish can be difficult to maintain and shows scuff marks.

Penetrating sealers: Sealers soak into the pores of the wood and harden, sealing the floor against dirt and some stains. Sealers have a low-gloss appearance. A penetrating sealer that has worn in spots may be repaired by applying more sealer to the worn areas. The new sealer will blend into the old, without any wear marks.

Polyurethane: A blend of synthetic resins and plasticizers that forms a moisture-resistant surface finish on wood. It's extremely resistant to spills and stains, but it cannot be spot-repaired. Instead, you must take off the entire coating of polyurethane and apply a new one. It's available in both matte and gloss finishes.

Shellac: Shellac is a surface seal. It dries quickly, but water will create white spots or marks on it. If it is subject to daily wear—as a floor is—it will soften, permitting dirt to enter and giving the floor a grainy, cloudy appearance. To protect a shellac finish, you need to apply a coat of wax.

Varnish: Like polyurethane, varnish is a surface seal. It's usually darker in color than polyurethane and gives wood a low-, medium- or high-gloss finish. It takes a long time to dry and cannot easily be touched up. A high-quality varnish is very durable; a poor-quality varnish will become brittle and will scar easily.

Wax: Wax enhances the beauty of wood. It's often applied over a penetrating sealer, to further enhance the floor's appearance. It's relatively easy to reapply wax to a floor in the places where it has worn off.

Camouflage water spots. Use an oil stain that matches the color of the rest of the floor. (Experiment with the stain in an out-of-the-way corner first, to make sure the color will match.)

Sand minor scratches by hand. Begin by sanding them with a coarse paper, then finish with a finer paper. Apply varnish.

When the varnish patches are dry, vacuum up remaining dust and grit. Wipe down the floor with a tack rag, a cloth that's designed to pick up dust and grit and which can be found wherever furniture refinishing items are sold. Periodically wrap a push broom in a cotton rag and wipe down the floor with a small amount of oil of cedar to keep it looking great and to avoid wax buildup.

SILENCING A SQUEAKY FLOOR

If your wood floor squeaks, follow these steps to a quick cure.

1. Locate the exact boards that are squeaking by having someone walk on the floor while you listen and watch the boards closely for movement.

2. Inspect the floor for protruding nail heads. Sink raised nails by covering them with a piece of carpet remnant, placing a wood block on the remnant and striking the block with a hammer.

3. Coat the joint between adjacent floorboards with furniture polish, mineral oil or talcum powder to lubricate it.

4. If the floor still squeaks, inspect it to see if the squeak might be caused by the floor separating from the joists (the beams that support it). If the problem is on the first floor, go down to the basement and eye the floor from below to find out whether the joists have pulled away from the subfloor (the flooring—usually plywood—that the finished floor is nailed on top of). If the joists and the subfloor have separated, try pulling them together by driving wood screws into the finished flooring from below.

5. If step 4 won't work, try shimming the subfloor by driving thin pieces of wood between the subfloor and joists. The shims should be snug— not extremely tight.

6. If you can't see the subfloor to inspect it, try countersinking screws into the floor from the top. Camouflage the holes by filling them with wooden dowels or wood filler colored to match the existing floor finish.

RESTICKING A VINYL TILE EDGE

The corners of vinyl and linoleum tiles sometimes curl up because the adhesive that once held them flat has lost its holding ability. Here's how to restick them.

1. With your electric iron on a low setting, "iron" the tile. The heat will melt the adhesive, and you can spread some of the melted adhesive over the area that was not properly glued before. If there is not enough excess glue to do this, once the adhesive is softened by the heat you can peel the entire tile up from the floor.

2. Coat bare patches on the bottom of the tile with a vinyl adhesive. Re-lay the tile in its old space.

3. Cover the tile with a couple of old boards and some concrete blocks or other heavy objects until the glue is dry.

PATCHING SHEET FLOOR VINYL

It's always a good idea to save some sheet vinyl flooring when you have a new vinyl floor installed. That way, you have some to use as patches if you should ever need to do so. Here's how to patch a vinyl floor.

1. Cut a new piece of vinyl larger than the area that needs to be patched. Place the new piece of vinyl over the damaged floor area.

2. Manipulate the patch so the pattern on the patch aligns with the pattern on the floor. Then, with a sharp utility knife, cut through the vinyl patch and into the existing vinyl floor covering.

3. Remove the patch and set it aside, then remove the damaged piece of flooring.

4. Place the new patch in the hole to make sure it fits; then glue the patch into place with a vinyl adhesive. Using a wallpaper roller, smooth the seams of the vinyl patch so they'll lay smooth. Wipe off any excess adhesive and weigh down the patch for several hours until the adhesive sets.

Interior Walls

Drywall or plaster, your interior walls need care just as your exterior walls do. Here's a rundown of some common interior wall maintenance projects, from wallpapering to waterproofing.

WALLPAPERING A ROOM

For a professional-looking wallpapering job, follow these tips from wall-paper manufacturers.

To get an accurate estimate of the wall space to be covered, multiply the entire distance in feet around the room by the height of the walls.

To find out how many rolls of paper to order, divide the total square feet of wall area by the number of square feet in a roll.

For best results, begin wallpapering in an inconspicuous place, such as a corner.

When cutting the paper, line the pattern up at the ceiling, not the floor (the floor is less visible). Next, cut the paper, allowing at least two extra inches at the top and bottom of the sheet to ensure that there's enough paper to cover the full length of the wall and to match patterns.

Before you paste, establish a plumb line on the wall. Hang a heavy object from a string rubbed with chalk. When the object stops dangling, snap the string to make a chalk line on the wall. Make the plumb line as far away from the starting corner as the paper is wide, and use both it and the corner wall to align the first sheet of wallpaper.

Wet the paper thoroughly, if it's prepasted, by allowing it to sit for a couple of minutes in the paper tray or by swishing it around. If you're using an adhesive, make sure the paper is evenly and thoroughly covered.

To apply the paper to the wall, lay it against the wall and smooth it down lightly with a soft-bristled brush. While the adhesive's still damp, you can move the paper around until you've got it lined up correctly.

Smooth out all air bubbles with a hard-bristled brush—air left underneath the paper usually results in the paper buckling or peeling.

Mop up the excess glue at the edges with a damp (not wet) sponge or rag as you go. Seal the edges by rolling them with a wallpaper roller (an inexpensive tool available at most hardware stores).

For corners, always hang the paper in two parts. Measure the distance from the corner to the previous sheet. Cut a strip of paper ½ inch wider than that distance. Hang the strip so that the paper overlaps the corner. Take the remainder of the sheet you cut the strip from, measure its full width and mark a plumb line that far in on the new wall. Now paste up the remnant strip in the same way you did the first sheet.

REMOVING WALLPAPER

It's best to strip off old wallpaper before applying new wallpaper, otherwise the seams and pattern of the old wallpaper could show through the new.

1. Scrape off as much of the old wallpaper as you can. In most cases, a knife or a wallpaper scraper, applied to a corner where the old wallpaper has already loosened, will do the trick. However, if the paper has been painted, you'll need to cut or sand through the painted paper to create an opening.

2. If the wallpaper doesn't come off cleanly, you'll have to try a wet method of stripping. The simplest wet method is to sponge the walls of the room with hot water. When the wallpaper has become thoroughly soaked, take a wallpaper scraper and run it across the wall in a horizontal motion.

3. If the paper still won't come up, you'll have to resort to using a wallpaper steamer. You can rent this tool at many tool rental shops. Hold the steamer against the wall, allowing the steam to penetrate and soften the paste behind the wallpaper. With a knife or a scraper, loosen the remaining wallpaper.

PATCHING DRYWALL

Patching drywall doesn't have to be a messy, time-consuming task. For small holes or large ones, try the techniques outlined here.

Small Holes

1. Draw a square around the damaged area. Using a keyhole saw, cut out the damaged part. You should be left with a clean, square hole.

2. Cut a drywall patch to fit the hole.

3. Take a strip of scrap lumber that is at least two inches longer than the width of the hole in the drywall and drill a hole in the center of it that is large enough for your finger to fit through.

4. Coat the ends of the wood strip with glue. Insert the strip into the hole in the wall, then put your finger in the hole in the wood and pull gently but firmly to make the glue adhere to the back of the wall. (You may have to hold it for a minute or two until the glue starts to set.) Let the glue dry.

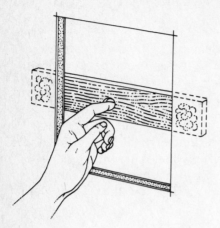

5. When the glue has dried, coat the wood strip with joint compound, press your drywall patch into place and smooth over the edges of the patch with more compound. (You can tape the seams first, if you wish.)

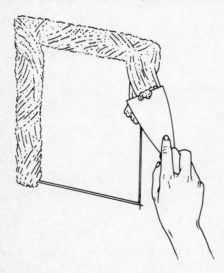

Large Holes

1. Draw a rectangle around the damaged area. Make sure the sides of the rectangle are each located on the centerline of a stud.

2. Saw out the old drywall and cut a drywall patch to fit the missing section.

3. Nail or screw the drywall patch to the studs. Smooth over the edges of the patch with joint compound.

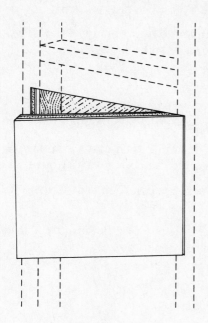

REPAIRING PLASTER WALLS
Plastering a wall from scratch is a job best left to a professional, but you can take care of most minor repairs.

Hairline Cracks
1. Brush the crack with a soft brush to remove any debris or crumbling plaster. Enlarge the crack to a depth of $\frac{1}{16}$ inch using a pointed tool, such as a chisel or screwdriver.

2. Fill the crack with joint compound and allow the patch to dry thoroughly.

3. Sand the patch smooth and proceed to paint or paper the wall.

Large Cracks
1. Follow steps 1 and 2 outlined above for hairline cracks.

2. Sand the patch smooth, then with a brush, apply a thin coating of wallpaper sizing.

3. Cut a piece of rubberized paper tape (available in hardware stores) long enough to cover the crack. Saturate the tape with water (the water should be about room temperature) and lay the tape over the crack, smoothing it with a damp sponge. Allow the tape to dry.

4. Trowel a thin layer of joint compound over the tape. Allow it to dry thoroughly, then sand the compound smooth. Finish the wall with paint or paper.

Discolored Walls

1. Fix the leak, if that's what has caused the discoloration.

2. Make sure the plaster wall has dried out, then coat the surface of the wall with a thin layer of joint compound. Smooth it with a trowel or float.

3. Allow the compound to dry for 24 hours, then coat it again in the same way.

4. Wait another 24 hours, then take a piece of wet burlap and run it across the wall, smoothing over the joint compound.

Small Holes

1. Pack the holes with joint compound.

Large Holes

1. File the edges of the holes so that they are either smooth and vertical or angled in toward the back of the hole.

2. Moisten the edges of the plaster with a wet sponge. With a trowel, apply a plaster patch.

3. If the hole is deep, allow the patch to set until it's relatively firm but not completely dry. Using the edge of your trowel, score the top of the patch, then apply another layer. Keep applying layers until the hole is filled. (If you fill the hole with a deep layer of plaster all at once, the plaster is likely to bulge or run out of the hole.)

4. If the hole is more than a foot wide, use joint compound instead of plaster to patch the hole. The plaster will harden too fast for you to be able to fill the crack in layers as described above.

REPAIRING BROKEN LATH IN PLASTER WALLS

You can repair broken lath in your walls if you can get to it easily. Here's what to do.

1. Enlarge the hole until the wall studs are visible. Nail new wood or metal lath to the studs.

2. Proceed with patching the hole, following the steps outlined above for repairing large holes in plaster walls.

PAINTING A NEWLY PLASTERED WALL

Once you've finished your plastering job, it's time to paint or paper your finished wall. But when it comes to painting, you shouldn't just get out the brush and go to it. Your new wall will need some preparation first. Here's how to get the the job done right.

1. Run a wallpaper scraper over the wall to remove any nibs or irregularities. Be extremely careful not to gouge or scrape the delicate plaster finish.

HOW MUCH PAINT DO YOU NEED?

Take these steps to figure out the amount of paint needed to cover an entire room (including the ceiling).

1. Measure the room. (Use a metal or a wooden ruler instead of a cloth one; you'll get more accurate measurements because these materials "give" less.)

2. Add together the width of all of the walls.

3. Multiply the total width of all of the walls by the height of the walls.

4. Multiply the ceiling length by its width.

5. Add the figures calculated in steps 3 and 4 together and subtract 10 percent (for door and window openings) from the total figure. The result will tell you the estimated number of square feet in the ceiling and walls.

6. Divide the square footage by the square-foot coverage shown on the back of the can of paint you want to buy. The result will tell you how many gallons you'll need of that particular paint.

GETTING THE MOST FROM YOUR PAINT ROLLERS

Paint rollers make the job of painting interior walls go much faster. But many people discard rollers after one project because they just don't seem to stand up to much more use. Here's how to get the most from your paint rollers.

→ Before you begin painting, "prime" the roller cover by dipping it into the paint and rolling it back and forth on a piece of cardboard or newspaper. This will press out any air as well as get the paint worked into the fabric of the roller cover.

→ Your roller cover will last longer if, every now and then, you reverse it on the roller frame.

2. Seal the plaster surface by washing it with a paint mixture consisting of equal amounts of water and a latex or other water-based paint. Allow it to dry.

3. Fill in scratches or chips with an all-purpose filler (for best results, use a vinyl-based filler) and allow it to dry.

4. Using fine sandpaper, sand the filler so that it's smooth, and even with the wall surface. (Be careful not to gouge the surrounding area; if you do, you'll have to fill and sand the surface before proceeding to the next step.)

5. Coat the repaired spot with the paint and water sealer. After the sealer has dried, apply the finish coats of latex paint.

REMOVING WOOD MOLDING

At some point you may need to remove wood molding, perhaps to get to the wall behind it to replace an outlet, or maybe because you want to replace the molding with one of another style. Here's how to remove wood molding without damaging it.

1. Fit the end of a prybar or small crowbar into the crack between the molding and the wall. Hammer the bar gently.

2. Slip a thin piece of wood between the wall and the crowbar to protect the wall against further damage.

3. Using the wall as a support for the crowbar, slowly and carefully work the molding away from the wall. Stop when you've exposed a nail (the molding should be about ¼ inch from the wall at this point). Then move the crowbar up a few inches and work at the molding again until another nail comes into view. Continue this for the length of the molding.

4. When all of the nails are exposed, gently tap the molding back into place, leaving the nails raised. Remove the nails with the crowbar or by pulling them out of their holes with pliers.

5. Label molding as you remove it so you won't forget where it goes if you want to reassemble it at a later time.

FILLING SPACE BETWEEN BASEBOARD AND WALL

In older homes, after the flooring and walls have settled, unsightly gaps may appear between the baseboard and the wall. Here's how to fill them in.

1. Fill the space between an existing baseboard and the wall with a clear-drying wood glue. Smooth the glue with an ice cream stick and allow the glue to set.

2. If the glue shrinks or doesn't fill the entire crack, repeat step 1 until the crack is filled.

3. Paint the glue to match the baseboard.

REGROUTING CERAMIC TILE

Discolored grout lines around ceramic tiles are an eyesore. Use this method to regrout existing bathroom or kitchen tile walls.

1. Examine the ceramic tiles. The tiles should be in good condition and firmly mounted to the countertop or wall surface. Replace any missing or cracked tiles.

2. Using a dental pick or other sharp instrument, scrape out the old grout to a depth of at least ⅛ inch, forming a flat-bottomed channel. Vacuum the channel to remove any remaining grout flakes or chips.

3. Mix the grout according to the instructions on the package. For best results, use a grout specially formulated to resist acid and alkali stains, such as a non-cement product like sanded epoxy grout.

4. Apply the grout, using a trowel or float to work the grout into the channel, and squeegee off the excess. The remaining grout should be flush with the tile edge. (Professional grouters apply grout with a lightweight float designed especially for this purpose; you can pick one up at a hardware store.)

5. When the grout has become firm, wash down the surface with a damp sponge or cloth. Cover the newly grouted area with cut-up grocery bags and allow it to cure for at least three days.

6. With a dry cloth, remove any grout residue from the tile surface. Avoid cleaning the regrouted tile with harsh detergents for at least 30 days.

REPAIRING SCRATCHED CERAMIC TILE

Scratched ceramic tiles don't necessarily have to be replaced. First try repairing them, as outlined here.

1. Scrape the surface of a scrap piece of the same tile as the one you want to patch. Then grind the scrapings to a fine powder (if you have a mortar and pestle, you might try using them here).

2. Put the powdered tile in a dish and mix it with a clear varnish until it has the consistency of paste.

3. With an ice cream stick, palette knife or other similar instrument, fill the scratch with the mixture. Allow the patch to dry, then smooth it with a fine-grade garnet paper, fine-grade sandpaper or steel wool.

RESTORING MARBLE

Marble is expensive to replace. If you have an antique washstand, a countertop or any other type of marble surface that has been chipped, use the following method to fill in the chip and make the surface look like new.

1. Scrape the bottom or back of the counter (or piece of marble) with a diamond-edged saw blade to generate some marble dust. Or check with your local quarry or tombstone maker to see if you can obtain some dust. The dust should be the same color as the surface you're patching.

2. Mix the marble dust with a clear epoxy adhesive. The mixture should be stiff enough so that it doesn't run or flow out of the crack.

3. Fill the crack with the mixture. Depending on where the crack is, you may have to apply several coats of the patch material.

4. Smooth the final coat with a putty knife. Allow to dry.

APPLYING BASEMENT WATERPROOFING COMPOUNDS

A basement waterproofing compound can help keep a leaky basement dry, but only if it's applied properly. Here's how to do it right. (See "Combating Wet Basements" earlier in this chapter.)

1. Brush the basement wall briskly with a wire brush to remove dirt, scale, crumbling mortar and so on. Remove any wax, grease, oil or soap with a heavy-duty cleaner. Rinse thoroughly.

2. Check for any signs of efflorescence (when whitish crystalline material collects on the inside of masonry walls as a result of salts carried to the surface by passing water). Remove the powdery crust by washing the wall with a 20 percent solution of muriatic acid (available where waterproofing products are sold).

3. Repair visible holes or cracks by chiseling out a channel about ¾ inch wide and 1 inch deep, making sure the back is wider than the front. Fill the trough with hydraulic cement—a fast-setting cement that expands when wet and will plug holes even while water is leaking through them.

4. Apply the waterproofing compound with a stiff nylon or polyester brush. Make sure you "scrub" it into all of the pores and cavities. Apply two coats of the compound even when the manufacturer says one coat will do, especially if the concrete blocks in your basement wall appear very porous.

Plumbing and Heating

Before you call in a plumber for minor repairs, take some time to get to know your home's plumbing and heating systems. You'll find that it's not all that difficult to perform simple plumbing and heating repairs and maintenance.

KNOWING YOUR HOME'S PLUMBING SYSTEM

If you've ever wondered what all those pipes are in the basement ceiling, here's a visual tour of a typical home's plumbing. It doesn't hurt to know these things—you'll be able to hold up your end of the conversation the next time you need to call the plumber, or better yet, you may find that once you know where to look, repairs become simple do-it-yourself tasks.

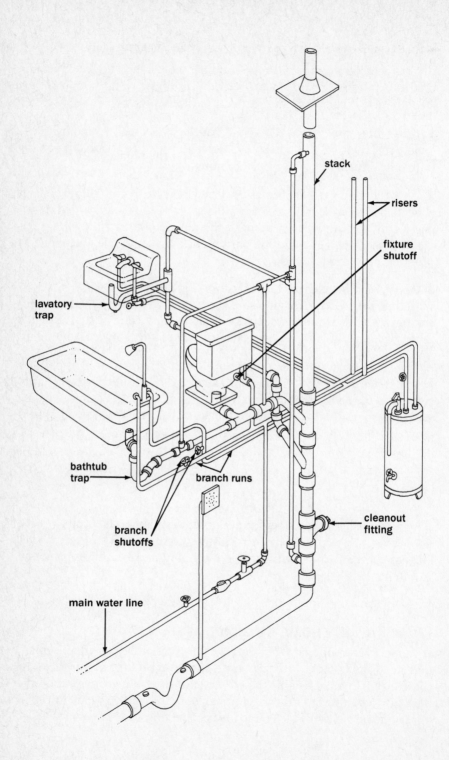

stack

risers

fixture shutoff

lavatory trap

bathtub trap

branch runs

branch shutoffs

main water line

cleanout fitting

Main water line: If your house has municipal water, the main water line comes into the house at the water meter. The pipe for the main water line is usually at least ¾ inch in diameter. Near the point where the pipe enters the house, you'll find a valve. Called the shutoff valve, this is the valve that you turn to shut off the water from the entire house.

Branch runs: Branch runs are usually made of pipe that's ½ inch in diameter. They're called branch runs because they branch off from the main pipeline. Each branch run delivers water to one section of the home's plumbing system, and one branch run feeds the hot water heater directly.

Risers: Risers are branches of pipe that run vertically through the house, through one or more floors. One riser will feed water to all of the fixtures that are located directly over one another.

Branch and riser shutoffs: Each branch and riser is equipped with a shutoff valve. These shutoff valves are generally located near where the branch splits off from the main line.

Fixture shutoffs: Each fixture is equipped with a valve that you can use to shut off the water going into that fixture only. Look behind the U-shaped pipe under the sink for the shutoff valve; the valve for the toilet is behind the bowl, just below the tank.

Drains: There are basically two types of drains: those with U-shaped traps that run from such fixtures as sinks, toilets and free-standing tubs through the walls and out; and the waste lines from toilets, built-in tubs and shower stalls. Generally this second category of drain exits straight through the floor.

Stacks: Stacks are vertical pipes that vent waste odors. Usually they start at the level of outgoing sewer lines and run up through the house and out the roof. In older homes, there is often only one vent stack; in modern homes, there may be more.

Cleanout fittings: These are fittings—usually some kind of bolt or screw cap—located in drainpipes (usually at the base of a trap). By removing these fittings, you gain partial access to the drain and any clogs that might be preventing water from flowing out freely.

CLEARING HOUSEHOLD DRAINS

Clearing sink, shower and tub drains is a relatively easy task when you've got a "plumber's helper" (plunger) on hand. Just follow these steps.

Troubleshooting Plumbing Problems

Problem	Usually Caused By	Solution
Ill-working spray hose	Nozzle plugged Worn or defective valve	Clean head; if that doesn't work, replace the unit
Leaky faucet	Worn washer Worn O-ring Damaged stem packing	Replace worn part
Leaky pipe	Loose fitting	Remove and inspect fitting for worn threads; if threads are okay, apply pipe-joint compound to fitting and tighten the fitting with a wrench
	Rust and corrosion	Cut out corroded section and replace with new piece of pipe
	Pinhole leak	Wrap a piece of rubber tubing around pipe and secure it with a metal clamp, or patch the leak with a two-part epoxy
Loose sink stopper	Dirty or damaged stopper valve	Clean valve; if that doesn't work, replace the stopper
Low water flow from faucet	Clogged filter screen or aerator	Clean or replace
Low water flow from spray hose	Kinked hose	Replace hose
	Clogged spray hose nozzle	Clean or replace nozzle
Water runs in toilet after flushing	Leaking flush valve (ball cock)	Replace assembly

The Kitchen Sink

1. Fill the sink with hot water to within two inches of the top. If you have a double sink, you must plug up one drain before you plunge the other. To do this, ball up rags and wrap them in a plastic bag or plastic wrap. Stuff the ball into the drain hole. Have a helper hold the plug in place, or fill the plugged sink with the same amount of water as is in the clogged sink. The water will hold the plug in place.

2. Place the plunger cup over the drain opening and pump vigorously up and down for a few seconds.

3. Lift the plunger from the drain. The drain should now be clear and the water should drain out quickly. If not, repeat the procedure.

PLUMBER'S TOOLBOX

A well-equipped toolbox is a homeowner's best friend, especially when it comes to doing plumbing repairs yourself. If you're already used to doing a good bit of work around the house, you probably have a propane torch and some multipurpose wrenches. The following list is limited to those tools that an all-purpose toolbox is not likely to have.

Basin wrench: A wrench with a head that swivels 180° and that can be stopped in a number of different positions. This type of wrench is useful if you have to get into a lot of tight spaces.

Faucet seat wrench: A seat wrench enables you to turn the seat of the faucet. Basically, there are two kinds of seat wrenches: a *right-angle* seat wrench that you can manipulate by hand; and a *straight* seat wrench that you turn with an adjustable wrench. Either kind of seat wrench can turn any type of faucet seat because they both come equipped with a hexagonal end and a square end.

Flaring tool: This is a tool designed to allow you to connect pieces of copper pipe without having to use solder. Although this is an expensive tool, it's worth buying if you plan to do a lot of work with copper pipe.

Stilson wrench: Similar to pipe wrenches, Stilson wrenches have a separate housing and an adjustable nut that provide excellent bite and grip. (A pipe wrench has a solid, one-piece housing.)

Strap wrench: This is a wrench that uses a heavy fabric strap instead of teeth to grip the pipe. The strap protects the pipe surface from being marred. They're especially useful when working with brass, aluminum or plastic pipe.

Tube bender: A tube bender prevents pipe from kinking when it's bent. The tube bender simply slips over the pipe you're going to bend.

Tube cutter: This is a tool that cuts plastic or copper pipe accurately. You could cut these pipes with another cutting tool, such as a hacksaw, but you wouldn't get the clean, precise right-angle cut that you want and that a tube cutter provides.

The Bathroom Sink

1. Fill the sink with hot water to just below the overflow drain (the opening near the top of the basin).

2. Stop up the overflow drain with either rags or plastic, as described above for the kitchen sink. If there is a series of holes in the ceramic, stop them up with a piece of plastic wrap covered by a small sponge that is pressed with a piece of wood. (You'll need a helper to hold this stopper in place.)

3. Place the plunger cap over the drain opening and pump vigorously up and down for a few seconds. The drain should be clear. If not, repeat the procedure.

The Tub and Shower

1. Unscrew the overflow fitting (located just below the bathtub faucet) and press a plastic-covered rag into the tube to plug it.

2. If the overflow tube contains the mechanism for your tub's pop-up stopper, pull the assembly out and set it aside. This assembly is removable, though it may take some tugging to get it to come out. Then put your rag plug in place.

3. Place the plunger cap over the drain opening and pump vigorously up and down for a few seconds. The water should begin to drain. If not, repeat the procedure.

In a shower stall, simply fill the shower base to within a few inches of the top and plunge vigorously over the drain hole in the floor.

SEALING THE BATHTUB PERIMETER

If the caulk seal between the rim of your bathtub and the tub surround has become cracked, chipped and discolored, it should be replaced. Here's how to do the job.

1. Clean the area around the seam with a mild detergent and hot water. Be sure to rinse thoroughly. Make sure that no soap film remains.

2. Scrape out the old grout or caulk. Vacuum up any debris.

3. Fill the tub with water. The weight of the water will force the seam to open up, enabling you to fill it with caulk when it's at its widest.

4. Fill the crack with a high-quality silicone caulk that contains a fungicide. Run the end of a toothbrush down the joint to remove excess caulk and to smooth the joint.

5. Allow to set. Scrape up any drips with a scraper or a razor blade. Drain the water from the tub.

REFURBISHING OLD CERAMIC BATHROOM FIXTURES

Before you go to the expense of replacing your old bathroom fixtures, first try refurbishing them. You may be quite pleased with the results.

Give the fixtures a good cleaning. The cleaning method will vary with the fixture, but it's best to begin by scrubbing the fixture with hot water and a nonabrasive cleanser (such as Bon Ami) to remove any surface grime and stains without damaging the porcelain. Rinse the fixture thoroughly. If stains or dirt still remain, you'll probably have to use a specialized technique to remove them. (See "Removing Stains from Fixtures" in chapter 6.)

Make sure the fixtures are caulked and sealed. Remove any deteriorated caulk. Clean all dirt and mildew from the joint, then run a new bead of fungicidal silicone caulking between the fixture and the surrounding tile floor or tile walls.

Evaluate the results, and take further action if necessary. If you're not satisfied with your sparkling-clean fixture, you might want to consider having your fixtures resurfaced. A professional tub refinisher will come to your home, strip the tub or sink with acid and spray it with an epoxy resin paint for about $200 to $250. You can expect this kind of finish to last from two to five years. Tubs and sinks with cast iron or clay bases *can* be reporcelainized—but this process is extremely expensive because the fixtures must be removed from your house, stripped and then put into a heated kiln for a new glazing to be baked on. It may be less trouble and less expensive for you to just buy a used fixture that's in good shape and install that instead. Check your local yellow pages and your local newspaper's classified ads for sources of old fixtures and tub refinishers.

SPRUCING UP RADIATORS

Many owners of older homes are in despair about their old hot-water or steam radiator heating system—not because it doesn't do its job, but because it's often so unsightly. It's not uncommon for these radiators to be painted gray or silver—colors guaranteed to have them stick out like a sore thumb! Often, the paint on these radiators will be chipped, making them even more unsightly, but there are ways to "hide" ugly radiators.

Enclose them in decorative casings. Most casings are hardwood frames with open backs and metal grills in front and on the sides. If your home has a lot of woodwork, matching wooden radiator casings add a nice decorative touch. Keep in mind, however, that any kind of casing will decrease the efficiency of the unit because the radiated heat will be blocked, to some degree, by the casing.

Freshen them up with a new coat of paint. Just make sure you're not building up too many coats of paint; the more coats of paint on the radiator surface, the less efficient the heat flow into the room will be. And you can't just walk up to your radiator and start painting. Follow these steps:

1. Drain the radiator system and remove the radiator. (See the box "Draining and Removing a Radiator" below.)
2. Clean the radiator by scouring off any rust spots with steel wool.
3. Paint the radiator by spraying it evenly with a thin coat of heat-resistant paint. Coat it a second time if the first coat is too thin. Make sure the room is well-ventilated before you start.

DRAINING AND REMOVING A RADIATOR

Before moving a radiator, you must first drain it. It's not as difficult as it may seem; just follow these steps.

Draining

1. Turn off the water supply valve at your boiler.

2. Attach a garden hose to the boiler drain cock, then run the hose to a floor drain or out a window or door. Open the drain cock at the boiler and the bleeder valve at the radiator. Water will start to leak from the radiator; catch it with a pan.

3. When all the water is out of the system, (when it stops flowing from the hose at the boiler) you are ready to remove the radiator.

Removing

1. With a pipe wrench, loosen the union between the radiator and the elbow pipe on either side of the radiator.

2. Plug the openings with rags, then disconnect the elbows from the riser pipes coming through the floor and lift the radiator onto a bed of newspapers. (Radiators are *very* heavy—you'll probably need help here.)

FINE-TUNING A RADIATOR

Radiators need to be "bled" prior to the heating season to keep them running smoothly throughout the winter. The procedure is as simple as 1-2-3, and should be done before you turn on the heat. Start with the radiators furthest away from the boiler and work your way down to those closest.

1. Examine the top of the ends of the radiator. You will find a small valve at one end. Directly below this valve, position a pan to catch drips.

2. If you're lucky enough to have the key to the radiator, insert it in the valve and turn it to allow any air in the pipes to escape. (If you don't have the key, try using a wrench or a screwdriver.)

3. You will probably hear a hissing of air that is followed by some drips of water. Keep the valve open until all the air is out and the little drips of water become more of a stream. The escaping water means that all of the pipes are now full of water and that any air that has built up in the pipes has been expelled. Now you can turn on the heat.

If no water comes out, it means your system has been drained and you must go to the boiler and fill the water tank to build up pressure again.

Remodeling

Remodeling can run the gamut from changing the look of a room to putting an addition on your house. We won't go into any major construction here, but we will show you how you can improve less-than-perfect space, make a small room look larger, use color to your advantage, lay walkways, install fences, build decks, buy wood, find a contractor and more.

IMPROVING LESS-THAN-PERFECT SPACE

You can improve dreary or inefficient rooms by following these suggestions.

Camouflage obvious faults. Fabric, color and strategic furniture arrangements can help conceal architectural eyesores such as heating pipes, uneven walls and odd-shaped spaces.

Alter the existing structure. By installing new partitions or altering existing ones, you can create a "space-within-a-space" that will suit your needs better than the original room.

Tear down and rebuild the interior from scratch. Gutting a structure and rethinking the entire interior gives you ultimate control over a room's design and layout, but do this only as a last resort because this option is the most expensive; if you can, try to avoid making any large structural changes.

MAKING A SMALL ROOM SEEM LARGER

Don't be dismayed about small rooms that you can't seem to do anything with. Try some of these ideas to create the illusion of space:

→ Extend the flooring from an adjacent room into your too-small room.

→ Paint the ceiling a lighter color than the walls; the ceiling will appear to recede.

→ Go with a neutral or pastel color scheme; the lighter the colors, the larger the space will look.

→ Wallpaper the walls with a small-figured pattern, preferably a dark figure on a light background. This will give the viewer a sense of space extending beyond.

→ Increase the amount of natural or artificial light coming into the room; light is a great room expander.

→ Run mirrors into corners or from floor to ceiling to expand the viewer's impression of space.

→ As a last alternative, open up the wall between the small room and an adjacent room, creating one large room.

MAKING A LARGE ROOM SEEM SMALLER

Sometimes having lots of space is not an advantage—especially when you feel as though you have a room that people can get lost in. Here's how to give it a cozier feeling.

Group furniture to create zoned areas. Each "zone" can be used for a specific activity, such as watching TV, sewing or entertaining.

Lower the ceiling over one part of the room. This helps define a special place. Or paint the ceiling a shade darker than the walls to make it look lower. Another technique is to bring the ceiling paint down a foot or so on the walls to make it look closer. Add molding where the wall and ceiling paints meet, if you wish.

Apply a strip of molding around the room. A good example of this is a chair rail. The molding will help to draw in the walls.

Change the floor height in part of the room. You can do this by installing a platform. A change in floor height cuts a single room in two.

MAKING THE MOST OF TOO-LONG ROOMS

Long, narrow, rectangular rooms are not only psychologically uncomfortable to be in, they are seldom useful for living, eating or sleeping in. To make a too-long room work better, try one or more of the following suggestions.

Paint the far end of the room a bright, warm color. The wall will appear to advance, thus making the room seem shorter than it actually is.

Choose a flooring with a distinctly striped pattern. If you install the flooring so that the stripes run across the width of the room, the walls will appear to be farther apart than they really are.

Run a window seat, alcove, bookcase or closet across one end of the room. You'll shorten the room visually and supply useful storage space as well.

Consider installing a bay window or a greenhouse addition. Of course, you can only do this if one wall of the room is exterior. Often you only need these few feet of extra space to relieve the "tunnel vision syndrome."

WORKING WITH COLOR

When it comes to picking paint for a room, many homeowners become frightened, rather than inspired, by the vast number of colors available to choose from. But you can use color to make the most of your rooms by following these guidelines.

Bear in mind the personality of the individual that will most often occupy the room. Although red may cheer up a despondent person, it can irritate someone who's prone to nervousness. Similarly, most people find blue calming, but a sad person may become further depressed in a blue room.

Add visual relief. Most people don't feel comfortable in a room that's all one color. To provide some visual relief in a room that's done mostly in warm colors such as coral or red, choose accent pieces—lamps, pillows or wall trim—in a cool color such as turquoise or blue.

Take advantage of color interactions. Warm colors appear to "advance" and cool colors appear to "recede." You can create a sense of depth on a flat surface by exploiting the way warm and cool colors interact with one another.

Play it safe with neutrals. If you plan to move soon, or if you want to make sure the color you choose for a particular room won't offend anyone, it's best to choose a neutral color scheme with such colors as beiges and tans. But choose textured wallpaper, carpeting, upholstery and so forth to prevent a neutral color room from becoming boring.

Test the color first. Once you've decided on a color, paint a small patch of it on the wall or paint a piece of paper with it. Tack the paper on the wall of the room you plan to use that color in and live with it a while. It may look very different on your living room wall than it did in the store, especially if your home lighting scheme is different.

CHOOSING A COLOR SCHEME

Color affects how we feel, how we think and how we perceive space and time. Used properly, color can be one of the most effective, and least expensive, tools for bringing out the best of any room. Keep these in mind when choosing a color scheme:

→ Red and orange will warm up a chilly room.
→ Pink helps to relax the inhabitants.
→ Hospital green is soothing to your eyes.
→ Blue encourages calm efficiency—try it out in your home office.

REDUCING NOISE IN A ROOM

You can control excess sound in a room by choosing the right finish materials. For walls, cover with cork, cloth or textured wall coverings. For floors, use thick carpeting (hard materials such as wood and marble reflect sound, causing an echo effect). For windows, use heavy drapes or thick, quilted fabric shades. If a room in your house is suffering from noise pollution, try one or more of these methods to remedy the problem:

→ Insulate the floor.
→ Build up mass in the walls by adding another layer of drywall.
→ Finish the ceiling, walls and floor with sound-absorbent materials such as cork, rubber tile or carpeting.
→ Cover windows with heavy drapes or some other form of movable insulation.
→ Finally, if the noise is coming from the outside—from a nearby road or highway, for instance—consider landscaping with earth berms, shrubbery or fences to create a sound buffer. (See "Planting to Reduce Noise" in chapter 9.)

LAYING BRICK WALKS OR PATIOS

Don't be intimidated by the fancy brickwork of the professionals. With a little time and patience, you can lay walks or patios that look just as good. Follow these steps.

1. Excavate the site to four to six inches below the surface area, removing any grass or weeds presently growing there.

TAKE A TIP FROM A BRICKLAYER . . .

When laying brick, never interrupt the job for more than half an hour at a time, or the mortar may set. If you must stop working for a longer period of time, finish the joints with a joint tool first. Then, when you go back to work, brush off any dried mortar with a wire brush before continuing to lay brick.

2. Smooth the ground by filling in any holes or cracks, evening out bumps and removing rocks. (You may wish to rent a heavy roller from a tool rental shop to help you create a firm, smooth surface to lay the brick on.)

3. Define the area you plan to cover with bricks by stretching twine between stakes. The twine should lay on the ground; use a level to make sure the twine lies level. If the twine is not level, the site isn't either, and you may have to build up one end of it with dirt or gravel.

4. Spread a two-inch layer of sand or gravel over the site and tamp it down. If you use sand you'll be able to lay the bricks closer together and will get a smoother, more even finish.

5. Lay the bricks on top of the sand or gravel bed in whatever pattern you like best. (Use bricks designed for exterior paving—they'll wear the best.) Leave a one-half-inch space between the bricks.

6. Spread sand over the bricks, brushing it into the cracks between them. You can leave the bricks just like this, or move on to steps 7 and 8 below for mortaring the cracks.

7. Mix cement with an equal amount of sand. Add water until the mixture has about the same consistency as cake batter. Fill the cracks between the bricks with this mixture.

8. Spread sand over the joints, then brush the newly laid brick with a broom.

INSTALLING A BETTER FENCE

Good fences make good neighbors, but good fences aren't always easy to make. Here's how to get the most from your new fence.

Check local zoning laws to find out if your town or city has regulations regarding the height, style or setback of fences.

Have your property surveyed to find out where your property line is. To avoid disputes with neighbors, set the fence two or three inches inside your property line.

Choose a fence style that's suitable for your location. For instance, a solid board fence installed at the bottom of a hill traps cold air and can kill frost-sensitive foliage on the uphill side of the fence; installed on the south side, it will block the sun. In both cases, a wire or lattice fence would allow more air circulation.

Paint or stain a wooden fence *before* you put it up.

Support the fence with wooden fence posts made from pressure-treated or rot-resistant wood (such as cedar, black locust or redwood).

Set each fence post so that at least one-third of its length is in the ground. If you sink the post into a concrete footing, make sure the top of the footing slopes toward the ground to prevent rainwater from collecting around the wood, speeding rot.

Buy a lightweight gate and equip it with strong hinges to prevent it from sagging.

BUILDING A LONG-LASTING DECK

If you decide to build your own deck, make sure that you build one that's low on maintenance and built to last. Here's how.

Build with a naturally rot-resistant wood, such as redwood or cedar. For in-ground posts, wood that's been treated with at least 0.40 pounds of pressure per cubic foot is your best choice. The pressure will be marked on the lumber. If it isn't, don't buy the wood—it's not made by a reputable manufacturer.

Use concrete footings that extend at least six inches below the frost line. Anchor posts to the footings with metal connectors embedded in the concrete before it drys. Use corrosion-resistant hardware.

Grade the ground so that it slopes away from the house. Protect the ledger (the wooden board attached to the house that holds up the deck's joists) by flashing it with aluminum and by using two or three washers on the bolts between the ledger and the house; the washers will create a space that water can drain away through.

Wait before you stain. If you plan to stain the deck, wait at least two months before applying the stain. As the wood weathers, it becomes rougher. The rougher the surface of the wood, the more stain it will absorb.

BUYING AND USING WOOD STUDS

It's a fact: Lumber is almost never straight. Even quality lumber may have a slight twist or bend to it. If you've ordered a load of lumber for a large project, take the following steps to ensure that you get your money's worth.

Examine the lumber carefully. Do this once as soon as it arrives at the site— *before* it leaves the truck. Refuse to accept any sorry-looking specimens.

Once the lumber you've accepted has been deposited, look it over carefully. No matter how good the lumber is, it will have some defects. Divide the lumber into three categories: ones that are as straight as they can be, ones that are slightly bent and ones that have other defects.

Select from the three piles according to the job. Use *straight studs* around windows and doors. Use *slightly bent studs* where walls intersect. Use *studs with other defects* between the corners and the windows, inside the walls.

WORKING WITH PRESSURE-TREATED WOOD

Many people prefer to use pressure-treated wood for fence posts and supports in areas where the wood is likely to come into contact with water and insects. Although pressure-treated wood resists rot better than most natural woods, this chemically preserved wood can be dangerous if it's not used properly. Follow these guidelines for safe use.

Inspect the wood carefully, before you buy it. If the wood has any white, crusty residue on it, don't buy it; the residue could be arsenic-based.

Wear heavy, protective clothing while you're sawing or drilling into the wood. This includes heavy coveralls, vinyl-coated gloves, a respirator or dust mask and goggles. (Never saw or plane pressure-treated wood indoors; it will release preservative-laden dust into the air.) When you're through working, wash your work clothes separately from the rest of your laundry.

Don't burn pressure-treated wood. If it has any arsenic in it, burning the wood will release the arsenic particles into the air. Instead, bury the wood or dispose of it through conventional trash collection means.

A RESOURCE GUIDE FOR HOMEOWNERS

Homeowners often have questions or concerns about maintenance and repair, and they are always on the lookout for helpful information about techniques and products. Below is a listing of just some of the organizations that can provide information and answer questions.

American Home Lighting
  Institute/The Cultured
  Marble Institute
435 North Michigan Avenue
Chicago, IL 60611
(312) 644-0828

American Institute of
  Real Estate Appraisers
430 North Michigan Avenue
Chicago, IL 60611
(312) 329-8559

American Plywood Association
7011 South 19th Street
Tacoma, WA 98466
(206) 565-6600

American Wood Council
1250 Connecticut Avenue NW
Suite 230
Washington, DC 20036
(202) 265-7766

Association of Home Appliance
  Manufacturers
20 North Wacker Drive
Chicago, IL 60606
(312) 984-5800

BOCA (Basic Building Code)
4051 West Flossmoor Road
Country Club Hills, IL 60477
(312) 799-2300

CUTTING WOOD QUICKLY

To save time cutting joists or other wooden boards, cut them all at once.

1. Stack the boards on the ground so that all of them are flush and square at one end.

2. Measure the length of the top board; mark the line that you plan to cut on with a pencil.

3. Set your circular saw so that it will cut deeper than the thickness of the top board by ⅛ inch.

4. Cut the top board. The saw will automatically make a surface cut in the board just below. Mark and cut the next three boards in this fashion.

5. Remeasure when you reach the fifth board to make sure you haven't inadvertently moved your cutting line. Continue until you've cut all of the boards.

California Redwood Association
591 Redwood Highway
Suite 3100
Mill Valley, CA 94941
(415) 381-1304

CARIERS (Energy Hotline)
P.O. Box 8900
Silver Springs, MD 20907
(800) 523-2929
(800) 233-3071 (in Alaska and
  Hawaii)

Consumer Product Safety
  Commission
5401 Westbard Avenue
Bethesda, MD 20207
(800) 638-2772

Gas Appliance Manufacturer's
  Association
P.O. Box 9245
Arlington, VA 22209
(703) 525-9565

National Association of Home
  Builders
15th and M Streets NW
Washington, DC 20005
(800) 368-5242

National Association of the
  Remodeling Industry
1901 North Moore Street
Suite 808
Arlington, VA 22209
(703) 276-7600

National Fire Protection
  Association
1110 Vermont Avenue NW
Suite 1210
Washington, DC 20005
(202) 667-7441

Portland Cement Association
5420 Old Orchard Road
Skokie, IL 60077
(312) 966-6200

OBTAINING CONSTRUCTION BIDS

By asking several subcontractors to bid on a remodeling project, you could save yourself a bundle of money and time. Here's how to go about obtaining bids.

Start by contacting and setting up appointments with several subcontractors. Lend each subcontractor a set of plans and specifications. At your meeting with each subcontractor, discuss the plans and specifications in detail. Make sure you cover all of your expectations for the job.

Visit the job site with each of the subcontractors. This is especially important if the job requires major alterations of the site, such as excavating.

Work out the contract. Make sure the contract describes the full extent of the work to be accomplished; any materials or other items the subcontractor will be supplying; what the subcontractor can charge extra for (and how much); what the agreed-upon hourly rate will be; whether the subcontractor is allowed a markup on the materials he supplies and, if so, what percent the markup will be; and how the subcontractor will be paid.

Evaluating the Bids

Compare the bid prices. Do they differ greatly?

Compare the details of the proposal as they are specified in each bid. Do they all include the same scope of work and supply equivalent materials?

Make sure you understand how each subcontractor arrived at her or his estimate. If there is a wide spread, discuss the job with each bidder again, to find out why.

Make your choice. Once you've made your decision, send the unsuccessful bidders a thank-you note for their time and effort.

FINDING A GOOD SUBCONTRACTOR

It's not a good idea just to go to the yellow pages when you're looking for a subcontractor. You want to make sure that the person you choose is reliable and will do a good job.

Ask your bank to recommend one. Your bank will have helped to finance many other home renovation projects, and they'll know which contractors are financially sound and which can be trusted to get the job done on time.

Ask the manager of your local lumberyard or building-supply store. The manager will know which subcontractors have steady work and which are the most established. You can also get recommendations from other homeowners.

Check out their reputations. Find out if your state has a law requiring subcontractors to register with a state board; if so, you can find out about the reputation of the people you're thinking of hiring. Other organizations you might contact are the National Association of Home Builders (15th and N Streets NW, Washington, DC 20005) and the National Association of the Remodeling Industry (1901 North Moore Street, Arlington, VA 22209). The members of these groups subscribe to a code of ethics.

DECIDING ON MAJOR HOME REMODELING

If your family has outgrown your existing home, or your own housing needs have changed, you have two choices: you could spend time and money remodeling your existing home, or you could sell your existing home and buy a new one better suited to your needs.

Remodeling is your best bet if you agree with the statements below. If you don't agree with the majority of them, then selling your present home and buying a new one is probably the better idea, if you can afford it. Remodeling is a good idea if:

→ You like your neighbors.

→ Your house has steadily appreciated in value over the past five years or your house is worth more today than it was one year ago.

→ You like your community; the properties that surround you are kept in good repair.

→ You get good services in return for your tax dollars.

→ The schools in your area are known for giving kids a quality education (especially important if you have school-age children).

→ You are within a convenient commuting distance to work, school, shopping centers, public transportation and recreational activities.

8

Shortcuts to

A Terrific Garden

From preparing your soil to harvesting your first crop, there's plenty to learn about making your garden grow. We've compiled the best gardening tips and techniques to help you on your way.

Compost

Compost is the fuel for growth in a garden. It returns rich nutrients to the soil, ensuring healthy plant growth. In this section we'll take a look at how to make and store this gardener's gold.

LEARNING THE SECRET TO BETTER COMPOST

Every gardener seems to have a secret recipe for making compost. Although their claims might be valid, the real secret to good compost is understanding these five "musts."

Size: Make the pile at least three feet wide, three feet long and four feet high.

Carbon and nitrogen: These two elements should be present in a ratio of 25:1 to 30:1 for fast composting. Too little nitrogen is a common reason for slow decomposition. (See the table "Carbon/Nitrogen Ratios of Organic Materials" on the facing page.)

Air: Oxygen is needed for good decomposition. You can provide it by turning the pile or inserting perforated pipes.

QUICK COMPOST

Any mixture of ingredients that averages out to the ratio of 25:1 to 30:1 carbon to nitrogen will compost quickly. Here are a few examples. (The amounts are measured by weight, not volume.)

→ Equal parts garden debris, kitchen scraps and leaves.
→ Four parts garden debris to one part manure.
→ One part fruit wastes to two parts grass clippings or manure.
→ Equal parts kitchen scraps, grass clippings, rotted manure and leaves.
→ One part straw to two parts chicken manure.
→ Equal parts hay, grass and chopped cornstalks.

Carbon/Nitrogen Ratios of Organic Materials

High-Nitrogen

Material	Ratio
Alfalfa	13 to 1
Chicken manure, fresh	5 to 1
Clover, green	16 to 1
Clover, mature	23 to 1
Garden debris, green	30 to 1
Grass clippings	19 to 1
Hay, legume grass	25 to 1
Kitchen scraps	15 to 1
Manure, rotted	20 to 1

High-Carbon

Material	Ratio
Cornstalks	60 to 1
Fruit wastes	35 to 1
Leaves	40-80 to 1
Paper	170 to 1
Sawdust	290 to 1
Straw	80 to 1
Wood	700 to 1

Water: A 50 to 60 percent moisture content is ideal (as wet as a squeezed-out sponge). Water the pile as you build it.

Cover: A tarp or sheet of plastic over the top keeps moisture in and sheds rain, which leaches valuable nutrients.

COMPOSTING THE TRADITIONAL WAY

Although many compost methods exist, two in particular are the most well-known and are used successfully by thousands of gardeners every year.

The Indore Method, Developed by Sir Albert Howard

1. Spread out a six-inch-deep layer of plant wastes (use hay, straw, sawdust, leaves, grass clippings, corncobs, cornstalks or kitchen garbage) over an area at least three by three feet.

2. Add a two-inch layer of manure mixed with straw or sawdust.

3. Sprinkle a thin (⅛-inch) layer of topsoil or soil from a barnyard.

4. Top this with a dusting of rock phosphate, greensand and/or wood ashes.

5. Repeat the layering process, watering each layer, until the pile stands three to four feet high.

6. Turn the pile twice—once after three weeks and again three weeks later, mixing the ingredients together. Depending on the materials used, the compost will be ready in three to six months.

Fast Composting, Developed by Dr. Clarence G. Golueke

1. Layer or mix together raw materials in a well-balanced carbon to nitrogen ratio, wetting them down as you go. The greater the variety of materials, the better. Shred or chop bulky materials so they'll break down faster.

2. Build the pile at least three feet wide and four feet high. (The finished compost will measure about half this volume.) A compost bin makes a tall pile easier to manage.

3. Turn the compost every second or third day. Depending on the composition of the pile, it will be finished composting in as little as two to three weeks.

COMPOSTING WITH THE PROS

Most veteran gardeners have settled on a favorite compost-making method, based on locally available materials. Here are three gardening pros' favorite recipes.

Eileen Weinsteiger, Rodale Research Center Horticulturist

1. Make four- to six-inch thick layers, about four by four feet, of equal parts of straw, garden refuse with soil on the roots and grass clippings.

2. Water each layer thoroughly and keep building until the pile is 4½ feet tall.

3. Turn the pile with a pitchfork, mixing layers, every three weeks. The compost will be finished in about three months.

Mark and Carol Ramus, Hemlock, Michigan; 1984 Organic Gardener of the Year Winners

1. Spread one pickup-truck load of fresh horse or cow manure to a 6- to 10-inch-thick layer. Cover it with a load of vegetable trimmings (available from produce markets) and mix thoroughly with a garden tiller.

2. Spread straw over half the pile, and shovel or rake the other half onto the straw.

3. After about two weeks, run the tiller over the pile, add another load of vegetable refuse and till it in.

4. Rake up the pile so it's about half as wide and twice as high as it was when you started. It will be ready to use in two to three months.

Ron and Sherry Foreman, Manns Harbor, North Carolina; 1983 Organic Gardener of the Year Finalists

1. Start with a four-inch layer of leaves about 3½ feet in diameter, then add ½ inch of chicken manure.

2. Repeat the layers of leaves and chicken manure—mixing in some kitchen scraps, garden trimmings and seaweed—until the heap is four feet tall. It will be ready to use in three to four months.

MAKING YOUR OWN COMPOST BINS

You don't *need* a bin to make compost in, but it can make the task of building and turning the compost easier, not to mention how grateful your neighbors will be when they see a neat bin instead of a messy pile. Here are three basic bin designs you can make.

Collapsible Bin

1. Form 11 feet of four-foot-high snow fence, chicken wire or hardware cloth into a circular bin. Hold together with wire or twine.

2. Tie or wire the bins to stakes made of metal or conduit.

3. When the pile needs to be turned, remove the stakes, untie the ends of the bin and pull the fencing away from the pile. Then set it up next to the compost heap and turn the compost into it.

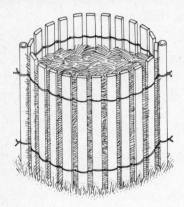

Wood Frame-and-Wire Bin

1. Cut 24 three-foot lengths of 1×2 lumber. Using threepenny box nails, tack together six lengths for each of the four panels that make up the sides, as shown in the illustration. Staple chicken wire over the inside of each panel.

2. Cut five 38-inch lengths of 1×2 lumber and use four lengths to make a square frame for the lid. Tack the fifth 1×2 straight across the middle of the lid. Staple chicken wire over the top of the lid frame and cover it with plastic.

3. Hold the whole affair together with hooks and eyes. You can quickly dismantle and move the bin each time you turn the pile.

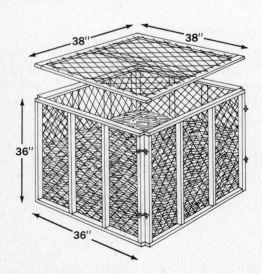

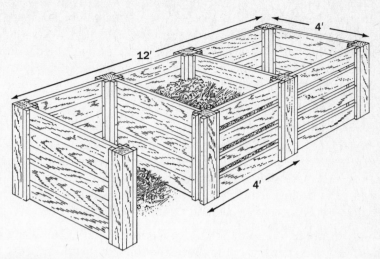

Triple Composter

One bin accumulates organic materials as you collect them, while the second contains the active pile. When you turn the compost, it goes into the third bin. The front is open in this design, but you could add doors for a neater appearance.

1. Set four pressure-treated 4- × 4- × 6-foot posts two feet deep into the ground. Set them in a straight line at four-foot intervals for the front of the bin. Set four more posts in a parallel row four feet away for the rear.

2. From ground level to the top of the posts, nail pressure-treated lumber to form the sides, rear and two dividers. You can add doors to the front, if you'd like.

3. Cover the bins with a tarp when in use.

Garden Techniques

Whether you've got a huge yard to fill with vegetables, or just a windowsill, here are the techniques that can help you make the most of the space that you've got, and also give you some of the best produce you've ever grown.

MAKING A RAISED-BED GARDEN

Depending on how intensively you plant, raised-bed gardening can yield two to four times the amount of food that row gardening can, so you can drastically cut down on the amount of space—and time—devoted to a garden. You can often plant two weeks earlier in raised beds because the soil dries out sooner, you'll use less fertilizer because none is wasted on paths and raised-bed gardens can be very attractive, too.

There are three basic styles of raised beds: tilled-and-hilled, double-dug and filled. The sides of the beds can be enclosed with wood for a neater appearance.

Tilled-and-Hilled

1. If you're starting a new garden, till the entire area with a rear-tine tiller. If you're converting an existing garden, loosen the soil with a spade, hoe or garden fork. Use stakes and string to lay out beds measuring 4 feet wide and the desired length (5- or 10-foot-long beds are convenient), leaving 18- to 24-inch-wide pathways in between. Till the bed areas.

2. Shovel the loose soil from the pathways onto the beds. Or, if your tiller has a hiller attachment, use it to divert the soil from paths to beds.

3. Using a metal garden rake, rake the beds smooth so the top of each bed is flat and the sides are gently sloped toward the paths. Beds raised with this method will be about six to nine inches higher than the paths. Manure or compost added to the bed areas before tilling will make higher beds as well as richer, more friable soil.

Double-Dug

1. After marking off the bed as described above (step 1), stand on a board one foot or so from the end of the bed to avoid compressing the soil. Use a spade to dig a trench at the end of the garden area that's one foot deep, one foot wide and four feet long.

2. Put the soil into a wheelbarrow or garden cart and wheel it to the opposite end of the bed.

3. While standing in the trench, loosen the soil an additional foot with a spading fork. This is called subsoiling.

4. Move the board back a foot, and when you dig the next trench, throw each spadeful of soil onto the area just subsoiled.

5. Repeat the digging and subsoiling, trench by trench, until you reach the end of the bed. Fill the last trench with the soil from the wheelbarrow.

6. Finally, shape the bed with a rake and add compost and fertilizers.

Double-dug beds won't be raised as high as tilled-and-hilled beds, but the loose, friable soil allows water and roots to penetrate it easily, and often raises yields dramatically.

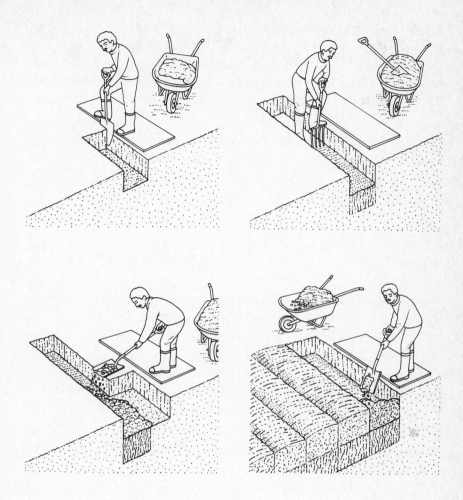

Filling

Filling is an easy alternative to tilling or digging, and may be your only option if the soil is too poor or compacted for vegetable growing. All you need is enough soil, compost and manure to build a raised bed about six inches high. You can make it right on top of the lawn or ground. Within a week or so, all the grass and weeds underneath the bed will die and decompose.

1. Mark off the bed area and water it for several hours.

2. Spread the soil and organic amendments in a six-inch-thick layer, and rake smooth. That's all there is to it!

ENCLOSING RAISED BEDS

No matter which method you choose to make a raised-bed garden, you can frame the beds in wood, landscape ties or concrete blocks—primarily for aesthetics, but also to contain rambling perennial plants and to keep the soil on the sides from drying out. Here's how to make a wooden frame.

1. Cut four pieces of one-foot-wide by one-inch-thick shelving pine the length and width of the bed. Paint the pieces with two coats of copper naphthenate wood preservative.

2. To assemble, lay the boards in place and attach two three-inch-long metal brackets to the outside of each joint with ¾-inch screws.

SAVING ON GARDEN SPACE

You don't need a lot of room to grow a terrific garden. Follow these suggestions for saving on space.

Plant in beds. When you plant intensively in four-foot-wide beds instead of rows, you can grow the same amount of vegetables in as little as one-quarter of the space.

Ignore traditional spacings. You can usually reduce the recommended spacings on seed packets by one-third to one-half without crowding plants too much (see the box "Intensive Spacings for Vegetables" on the facing page). Divide each bed into blocks and space plants equidistantly instead of planting in rows.

Trellis tomatoes. Use one of the following methods:
- → Buy or make wire cages from 3½-foot-high wire fencing rolled into 2-foot-diameter cylinders. Leave 10 inches between each cage and attach each one to a stake in the ground for stability. Plant one tomato plant per cage.
- → Prune plants to one stem, like vines, and attach with twist ties or soft cloth strips to 8-foot bamboo poles driven into the ground 18 inches apart.
- → Drive two sturdy 6-foot metal or wooden posts into the ground, up to 14 feet apart. String two lengths of heavy wire between them at the top and bottom. Attach baler twine to the wires vertically at 18-inch intervals and train tomatoes pruned to one stem up the twine.

Trellis winter squash and cucumbers. Use a tepee trellis:
- → Start with four wooden poles or saplings at least eight feet long and two inches in diameter. Tie two of the poles together about 10 inches from the top by wrapping sturdy twine around both poles.

INTENSIVE SPACINGS FOR VEGETABLES

3 inches: carrots, radishes
6 inches: beets, onions, peas, snap beans, spinach, turnips
9 inches: leaf lettuce, lima beans, Swiss chard
12 inches: Chinese cabbage, head lettuce, sweet potatoes, white potatoes
15 inches: collards, peppers
18 inches: asparagus, broccoli, brussels sprouts, cabbage, cauliflower, corn, cucumbers, okra
24 inches: eggplant, melons, summer squash, tomatoes
36 inches: pumpkins, winter squash

→ Tie the other poles together the same way, except place the twine 6 inches from the top of the poles.
→ Spread the first pair of poles apart so they form an X over the hill of squash or cucumbers, with the bases about three feet apart. Stand the other two poles so they straddle the first pair of poles and the hill, with their bases also three feet apart.
→ Attach the end of a ball of twine near the bottom of one of the poles. Loop the twine around the other three poles in succession, and spiral it up the trellis until it reaches the top. Then cut the twine, tie it to a pole, and your vines will be ready to climb.

Succession plant. Plant new crops in spaces left by harvested crops (see the table "Successful Successions" below).

Successful Successions

Plant This Vegetable	After Harvesting This Vegetable
Carrots	Peas
Chinese cabbage	Beans
Lettuce	Corn, cucumbers, onions, turnips
Radishes	Carrots, lettuce, onions, peas
Tomatoes	Broccoli, cabbage, cauliflower

Interplant. Plant more than one variety within a block of space. Usually, one will be a quick-maturing variety that is harvested before the other one fills in the space. Try planting:

> beans with carrots, corn, cucumbers, onions or squash
> lettuce with corn, peas, radishes or tomatoes
> radishes with carrots, melons, onions or peas
> zucchini squash in the same hill as yellow or another summer squash

GARDENING IN CONTAINERS

Container gardening is for you if you'd like to increase the productivity of your garden without tilling up another bed, if you don't have the space for a big garden or if you'd like to add some bright spots of color to your front porch, back patio or deck. And because soil in containers warms up fast in the spring, you'll have flowers sooner as well as an earlier vegetable harvest.

Select containers that will give roots plenty of room and have drainage holes in the bottom. They can be made of just about anything, including clay, plastic, concrete, fiber—even wooden half-barrels make good containers.

Prepare potting soil mix. There are many recipes, but one all-purpose mix is made by combining equal parts of sharp sand, topsoil and peat moss or compost. Water the mix well and fill the containers with the mix.

Plant seeds or seedlings, spacing them the same as you would in an intensive garden. Most vegetables can be started from seed directly in the containers, but a few vegetables and many flowers need to be started in smaller containers and then transplanted as seedlings. You can grow these yourself or you can purchase young plants at a garden center.

Water faithfully, when soil is dry, to a depth of ½ inch. In hot weather, this may mean every morning or even twice daily. For lower maintenance, install drip irrigation with a timer.

Mulch with a one-inch layer of white stones to hold in moisture and keep roots cool.

Fertilize once every two weeks with fish emulsion.

Stake or cage tall varieties of tomatoes and peas.

GETTING A JUMP ON THE SEASON

You *can* fool Mother Nature, at least a little bit. The trick is to trap the sun's warmth during the day and protect plants from the cold at night. By

WHAT SIZE CONTAINER?

Small (4- to 6-inch diameter, 6- to 8-inch depth)
Vegetables: Lettuce
Flowers: Ageratum, begonia, candytuft, coleus, dianthus, gazania, marigold, pansy, petunia, primrose, sweet alyssum

Medium (8- to 12-inch diameter, 9- to 12-inch depth)
Vegetables: Carrots, lettuce, onions, radishes, spinach
Flowers: Ageratum, aster, balsam, calendula, carnation, creeping zinnia, daisies (many types), gazania, geranium, impatiens, marigold, phlox, salvia, schizanthus, snapdragon, zinnia

Large (12- to 14-inch diameter, 14- to 16-inch depth)
Vegetables: Beets, broccoli, cabbage, cauliflower, celery, Chinese cabbage, eggplant, melons, peas, peppers, tomatoes (cherry and dwarf)
Flowers: Geranium, schizanthus, zinnia

Extra-Large (14- to 16-inch diameter, 16- to 18-inch depth)
Vegetables: Beans, corn, cucumbers, potatoes, squash, tomatoes (standard)

Hanging Basket (at least 8-inch diameter)
Vegetables: Celery, Chinese cabbage, lettuce, spinach, tomatoes (cherry and dwarf)
Flowers: Begonia, coleus, creeping zinnia, fuchsia, geranium, impatiens, morning glory, nasturtium, pansy, petunia, sweet alyssum, sweet pea, vinca

using one or a combination of the techniques outlined below, you'll be able to plant 7 to 10 days sooner and harvest vegetables up to a month earlier. In some cases, you'll end up with higher yields, too. The same plant protectors also work well to extend your gardening later into the fall.

Plant Protectors to Make Yourself

Milk jugs: Cut the bottom off one-gallon plastic milk jugs and place one over each plant. The caps can be removed on warm days and replaced if a

SEEDS OR SEEDLINGS?

Direct-Sow as Seeds

Vegetables: Beans, beets, broccoli, cabbage, carrots, cauliflower, Chinese cabbage, corn, cucumber, lettuce, melons, peas, potatoes, radishes, spinach

Flowers: Marigold, morning glory, sweet pea, zinnia

Transplant as Seedlings

Vegetables: Celery, eggplant, onions, peppers, tomatoes

Flowers: Ageratum, aster, balsam, begonia, calendula, candytuft, carnation, coleus, creeping zinnia, daisies, dianthus, fuchsia, gazania, geranium, impatiens, pansy, petunia, phlox, primrose, salvia, schizanthus, snapdragon, sweet alyssum, vinca

cold night is expected. You can use one-gallon glass jugs the same way by removing the bottoms with a glass cutter.

Barn cloches: Popular in Europe, cloches are made from four pieces of one-by-two-foot double-strength glass held together in a barn shape by a special set of heavy-gauge wires. Cloches can be arranged end to end to protect a bed of any length. To close off the ends, place a piece of glass vertically in front of the opening. Glass is heavy enough to stand up to wind and with care will last a long time. The wire fittings are available from Walter Nicke, Box 667RP, Hudson, NY 12534 (catalog 50¢).

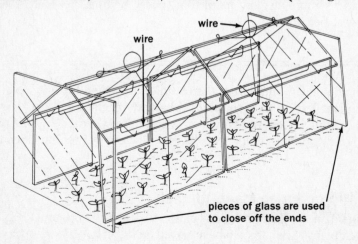

wire

wire

pieces of glass are used to close off the ends

Rumsey clips: These are small, ingenious devices that hold together two panes of double-strength glass (up to 12 by 18 inches) to form a tent. They won't be able to accommodate plants as large as the barn cloches can, but otherwise the two cloche designs are similar. Walter Nicke supplies these clips (see address above).

Cold frames: A well-built cold frame is not only a place to start seeds and grow transplants, but can provide you and your family with carrots, Chinese cabbage, lettuce, spinach and other cold-weather vegetables throughout the winter in all but the coldest regions of the United States. Perennials and biennials started the previous summer or fall will also overwinter more reliably in a cold frame.

Plant Protectors You Can Buy

Cold frames: There are several ready-made products on the market. One of the most clever is the Juwel, made in Austria and available from several major mail-order nurseries and garden suppliers. The framework is aluminum, and the glazing is tough double-walled polycarbonate. Plastic clips lock the lid open or shut easily, and pins hold the 34-by-39-inch unit in place. Worthwhile options include an add-on unit and an automatic vent opener. (Available from The Kinsman Co., River Road, Point Pleasant, PA 18950.)

Wallo' Water: This 18-inch-high cloche is open at the top and bottom and has sides made up of individual cells that hold water for solar heat storage. In cold weather it can be set up in a cone shape with the top closed. (Available from Terra Copia, Inc., 2365 South Main Street, Salt Lake City, UT 84115.)

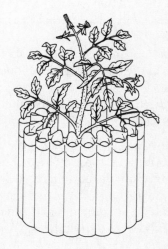

DESIGNING A COLD FRAME

There are many ways to design a cold frame. One simple design uses seven bales of hay or straw and six old window sashes arranged as shown. After moving the plants to the garden, dismantle the frame and mulch the plants with the hay or straw.

You can make a more permanent frame using old windows and a half-sheet (4 × 8-foot) of plywood, cut as shown.

1. Cut one 4-foot-long, 18-inch-high piece for the back.
2. Cut one 4-foot-long, 6-inch-high piece for the front.
3. Cut two side pieces 18 inches high at the back and 6 inches high at the front. The length of these pieces (which represent the width of the frame) will be determined by the size of the windows you use.

Fiberglass cones: They stand about two feet tall, are 30 inches in diameter at the base and have an opening at the top to allow excess heat to escape. Two tabs on the bottom provide an easy way to peg down the cones. They're durable, nest together for easy storage and can be found at retail outlets.

Hotkaps: Nothing more than little domes made of waxed paper reinforced with tape, these hotcaps hold up surprisingly well, even after heavy rain. Bury the bottom edges with several inches of soil to hold the hotcaps in place. As the plants grow, slit the tops of the hotcaps. The Hotkaps brand comes in 6-by-11-inch and 9½-by-11-inch sizes. You can find them in mail-order catalogs.

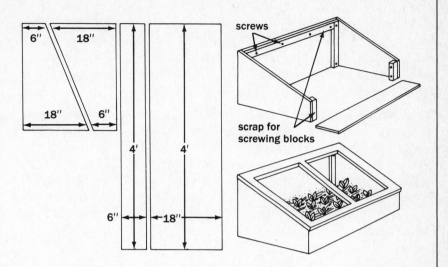

4. From scrap lumber, cut two pieces ¾ inch wide and 4 feet long (shorter scraps are all right as long as they add up to 8 feet), two more pieces ¾ inch wide and 18 inches long, and two pieces ¾ inch wide and 6 inches long.

5. Screw the 4-foot-long strips to the inside and even with the top edge of the front and back pieces. Screw the 18-inch-long strips to the inside of the longer side of each side piece, and the 6-inch-long strips to the inside of the shorter side of each side piece.

6. Assemble the frame, using eight screws, and give it two coats of exterior latex paint. When dry, lay the windows in place.

Guard'N Gro Cloche: Made from rigid, translucent plastic and shaped like a mini-greenhouse, this cloche is 18 inches wide and 40 inches long. At each end of the peak is a two-inch ventilation hole. The units lock together and are held in place with anchoring rods. (Available from Guard'N Gro Company, 104 Arlington Avenue, St. James, NY 11780.)

Slit plastic row covers: These covers are available through mail-order catalogs and retail stores under several brand names. They are constructed of a single layer of slit, clear polyethylene to be stretched over wire hoops, and most come with a sheet of black plastic for mulch. The slits open for ventilation when temperatures rise and the plastic becomes more flexible; at night, the covers stiffen and the vents close to keep the heat in.

Instant Greenhouse and Keylite: Both of these products are rolls of heavy plastic film reinforced with wire mesh. You can cut them to make either individual cloches or long row covers. Two lengths can be held together with clothespins to form an A-frame. The wire holds the shape you give it, but to span more than two feet, it needs support. Secure the edges with stones and/or homemade hooks pushed into the ground. These products are distributed through garden centers.

Spunbonded row covers: Made of polyester or polypropylene fibers, these covers are translucent and so lightweight that the plants underneath support the covers. Their edges are buried to hold them in place, allowing enough slack in the material for plant growth. Moisture, light and air can pass through, but insects, birds and animals are screened out. In cool weather, venting isn't necessary, but when temperatures outside reach 75°F, the covers should be partially removed. They are available at garden centers.

ROTATING YOUR VEGETABLE PLANTINGS

Planting the same vegetables in the same location year after year can deplete soil nutrients. By rotating your plantings, different levels of nutrients will be used, and you'll also help keep some insects and diseases from increasing to harmful levels.

Four-Year Rotation

1. Divide your garden into four equal parts.

2. Divide your vegetables into four groups so they will fit into these four quadrants, including successions, based on the amount of each vegetable you need. Because the same diseases and insects tend to attack all the vegetables within the same family, it's often convenient to divide them this way.

3. On a piece of graph paper, record which vegetables you planted this year in each of the four plots. Next year, move plot A's crops to plot B, plot B's to plot C, and so forth. After four seasons, you'll be back where you started.

Two-Year Rotation

1. Divide your garden into two equal parts.

2. Divide the vegetables into two groups that require the same amount of space. Make a note in your record book of the locations of the crops.

ROTATION SYSTEMS

Here are two ways to plan your garden for the healthiest plants.

Four-Year Rotation
Plot A: Corn, cucumbers, melons and squash, with early lettuce and spinach planted along the borders
Plot B: Beans, broccoli, cauliflower, peas, radishes
Plot C: Eggplant, onions, peppers, tomatoes
Plot D: Cabbage, carrots, lettuce, potatoes, spinach

Two-Year Rotation
Plot A: Beans, eggplant, peppers, potatoes, tomatoes
Plot B: Beets, broccoli, cabbage, carrots, cucumbers, lettuce, onions, radishes, spinach, squash

---

3. A garden divided into two plots will have a two-year rotation system. In year three, when the crops return to their original plots, you can plant the vegetables in slightly different locations than they were previously. High levels of compost in the soil will help to compensate for the short rotation by providing balanced nutrients and thwarting certain soilborne diseases.

CHOOSING A MULCH

Do you need a mulch to conserve moisture, keep down weeds or add nutrients? Or what about a decorative mulch to offset ornamental plantings? Here's a rundown of some of the most common mulching materials and how to use them.

Alfalfa hay: This is easiest to handle when freshly cut, but dry, spoiled hay may be cheaper. High in nitrogen, it will supply enough of this nutrient for fruit crops and most vegetables and ornamentals.

Black plastic: Plastic is a good choice where persistent weeds are a problem. It can speed the maturity and increase yields of warm-weather crops such as tomatoes, peppers and melons. You can also save on decorative mulches by covering the soil with plastic and topping it with two to three inches of mulch. Poke a few holes in the plastic to let water through. Add manure or other organic fertilizers to the soil before planting. Heavy plastic is reusable.

Cocoa bean hulls or shells: Hulls or shells make a fairly fine-textured and attractive mulch that holds 2½ times its weight in water; though these materials are relatively expensive.

Corncobs: Ground into one-inch pieces, corncobs are coarse in texture and should be applied four to six inches deep. Apply a source of nitrogen to the soil before mulching with corncobs.

Garden refuse: Refuse composed of shredded stemmy materials, such as cornstalks, make an excellent mulch. It's easiest to shred when green.

Grass clippings: Clippings are one of the most abundant, least expensive and easiest materials to work with. Because of its high nitrogen content, a grass-clipping mulch renewed several times during the season may be all the supplemental feeding most plants need, but it also breaks down quickly, so apply at least three to four inches in several thin layers to avoid matting and anaerobic decomposition. Avoid clippings from lawns treated with weed killers or pesticides.

Leaves: Shredded, partially composted leaves are ideal. If using raw, unshredded leaves, mix them with straw or grass clippings to keep them from matting. During windy weather, dry leaves sometimes blow away.

Newspaper, cardboard: These paper products are low on nutrients, but they improve soil tilth when turned under at the end of the season. Either weigh down with stones, or combine with another mulch such as grass clippings or wood chips. New information says that colored newspaper no longer contains heavy metals and is perfectly fine to use in the garden.

Peat moss: This has a high capacity for retaining moisture. However, once the surface dries, it is difficult to rewet. Breaking up the crust with a rake helps water penetrate. Peat moss is low in nutrients, but worked into the soil, improves tilth.

Pine needles: Needles keep crops such as strawberries clean. Apply two to four inches deep and renew yearly. They can be a fire hazard during a drought.

Salt hay: This hay grows in saltwater marshes. It is sometimes available in garden centers. Used as a thin layer applied over a newly seeded lawn, it helps the grass seed germinate. It's also a good mulch for strawberries — especially for winter protection.

Sawdust: This is a long-lasting mulch because it has a low nitrogen content. Apply nitrogen to the soil first. When dry, a thick layer of sawdust can block water from reaching the soil.

Stones: They have no nutritive value, but stones help keep the soil cool and conserve moisture. They're most practical around perennial plantings. For weed control, put plastic down first, then the stones.

Straw and hay: Straw is what is left over after a grain such as oats, wheat or barley has been harvested, and it contains no weed seeds. It will last a full season and then can be composted or turned under with manure. Hay is made up of grasses and/or legumes (such as clover) and usually has some weed seeds.

Weed control mats: There are several new mats on the market, made of heavy-duty fibers such as polyester. Some are designed to let water and air through without allowing weed growth. The mats can be topped with wood chips around ornamental plantings.

Wood chips, bark: These are attractive and long-lasting and are sometimes available free from electric and telephone companies. They add very little nitrogen to the soil, however.

REAPING A YEAR-ROUND HARVEST

With a little planning and a taste for the unusual, you can grow and harvest fresh vegetables 12 months of the year, whether you live in Pennsylvania or southern California. Of course, by storing and preserving your produce, you can further extend you garden's contribution to meals. See "Getting a Jump on the Season" earlier in this chapter for ways to protect crops in early spring and late fall.

For fall-maturing or early winter-maturing crops, add a week or two to the "days to harvest" figure on the seed packet to compensate for cooler weather. For example, if you want to plant a variety of beet that matures in 56 days, you will have to plant your beets two weeks earlier; then they'll be ready to harvest in 70, not 56, days.

A Northern Garden (About 170 Frost-Free Days)

Winter: Belgian endive, carrots (under mulch), collards, kale, leaf lettuce (grown indoors under fluorescent lights), parsnips (under mulch), spinach (in a cold frame)

Spring: Asparagus, Chinese cabbage, leaf lettuce, parsley, peas, radishes, spinach, Swiss chard (new growth from fall-grown plants), turnip greens

Summer: Asparagus, beans, beets, broccoli, cabbage, carrots, corn, cucumbers, eggplant, kohlrabi, lettuce, onions, peas, peppers, summer squash, tomatoes, zucchini

Fall: Beets, brussels sprouts, cabbage, carrots, cauliflower, Chinese cabbage, escarole, kale, leaf lettuce, leeks, parsnips, rutabagas, spinach, Swiss chard, turnips, winter radishes, winter squash

A Southern Garden (About 270 Frost-Free Days)

Winter: Beets, broccoli, cabbage, cardoon, celery, Chinese cabbage, kohlrabi, lettuce, Swiss chard

Spring: Broad beans, carrots, kale, kohlrabi, mustard, onions, parsley, parsnips, peas, potatoes, radishes, salsify, shallots

Summer: Corn, cucumbers, eggplant, garlic, melons, peppers, summer squash, tomatoes, zucchini

Fall: Beets, broccoli, cabbage, carrots, green bush beans, kale, kohlrabi, late corn, lettuce, Swiss chard

NOTE: Heavy nutrient demands are made on the soil in any year-round garden, therefore a good soil-building program is essential. In southern gardens, this is particularly essential.

PICKING VEGETABLES AT THEIR PEAK

Sometimes it's difficult to tell when vegetables are ready to be harvested. If picked too soon or too late, they're bound to be disappointing. Here's a rundown of the most common garden vegetables, and when to pick them so they're at their peak.

Beets: Start pulling when they reach golf ball size. Small beets are the most tender, but larger beets are sweeter.

Broccoli: Wait until the head has stopped growing, but cut it before the individual flower buds begin to open. Secondary side shoots often form after the main head has been harvested (they'll be smaller when they reach maximum size). Cut while buds are still tight.

Brussels sprouts: Sprouts are at their best when bright green, firm and compact and no more than an inch in diameter. A light frost will improve the flavor. Start picking at the bottom of the stalk and work your way up.

Cabbage: You can start harvesting as soon as heads begin to form. The heads will keep getting larger until they split. When the leaves become extremely tight, grasp the head and twist it from a quarter to a half of a turn. This will slow growth and delay splitting by as much as 10 days.

Cantaloupe: When a melon is nearly ripe, the stem will start to crack. When it's ready to be picked, the stem will be cracked all the way around, a condition known as full slip. The fruit should separate easily from the stem.

Carrots: Begin pulling as soon as they're big enough to cut up for salads. If you planted them thickly, you can eat the thinnings. Don't let carrots get more than an inch or so in diameter, or they will become woody. John Seymour, author of *The Self-Sufficient Gardener* (Doubleday & Co., 1979), offers this advice: "If you pull carrots out of the rows at random, you will attract carrot flies. When you pick early carrots for eating fresh in summer, start at one end of the row."

Cauliflower: Pick the heads while the curd is firm, smooth and tight. Whether you've tied the leaves up or grow a self-blanching variety, check the heads every few days because they quickly pass their peak.

Corn: Pick late in the day; the sugar content will be highest. Corn will be at its prime for only 2 to 3 days, so as soon as silk appears, mark your calendar to begin harvesting in about 17 to 20 days. When the corn is ripe, the silk is dry and dark brown. (On supersweet types, it may be golden brown.) To check an ear before picking it, carefully peel back the husk to expose about two inches of kernels. Press on a kernel with your fingernail until it "bleeds." If the fluid that comes out is milky, the corn is just right. If it's watery, replace the husk and wait a few more days. If the fluid is pasty, the corn is becoming starchy.

Cucumbers: Start picking cucumbers as soon as they're about three inches long. Pick while the skin is bright green and slightly glossy. The skin of overripe cucumbers is yellow and thick, and the seeds are large and tough.

Eggplant: Although fruit size varies, the skin of prime fruit will have a sheen to it and the flesh will be firm. If the seeds inside are brown and the skin develops hints of green or yellow, your eggplant is past maturity.

Green beans: Pick beans before seeds begin to swell, about 2½ weeks after flowering.

Green leafy vegetables: Harvest these vegetables in early morning, when water content is highest. The younger the vegetables when you harvest, the sweeter and more tender they will be. Pick the outer leaves first, before any yellowing or browning begins. Don't delay picking spinach, lettuce or Chinese cabbage. After a few days of hot weather, the plants will begin to bolt, or flower, and the leaves will become tough and bitter tasting.

Chinese cabbage: harvest as soon as head begins to form.

Head lettuce: cut when head feels firm.

Loose leaf and semiheading lettuces: cut as soon as heads develop a full appearance.

Spinach: leaf blade should be less than 6 inches.

Swiss chard: pick when the leaf blade is 6 to 10 inches long.

Onions: Pick onions when young, as scallions, or when they are mature — after the tops dry and fall over.

Peas: Harvest peas starting at the bottoms of the vines. Taste some to gauge how big the pods should be when picked. Pick snow peas when they're no more than $1\frac{1}{2}$ to $2\frac{1}{2}$ inches long. Sugar snap peas should not be touching inside, and the skin should be smooth and evenly green, not white and lumpy.

Peppers: You can pick peppers at almost any stage. The larger they get, the thicker the skin will become. Let a few remain on the plant to turn red; they'll become incredibly juicy and sweet. Always *cut* peppers from the plant, and leave about one inch of stem on the fruit.

Potatoes: For fresh eating, begin digging potatoes any time after the plants have flowered (new potatoes). If you plan to store the crop, wait until the vines have died back. Handle carefully, because potatoes tend to rot where bruised.

Radishes: You can start picking your radishes when they reach the size of a small acorn, but after they grow to about one inch in diameter, they get pithy and strong-flavored and begin to split.

Squash: Harvest squash by cutting, not twisting. Summer squash, including zucchini, is most tender when about 3 to 5 inches in diameter (scallop types), 3 to 10 inches long (zucchini) or 4 to 6 inches long (crookneck). Larger fruits are not quite as flavorful, and if allowed to stay on the vine, will slow down production. Winter squash is best harvested for storage when the skin is hard and resists thumb pressure. The stem will turn gray and begin to shrivel. Leave a few inches of stem attached.

Tomatoes: For maximum sweetness, flavor and juiciness, pick tomatoes when they have reached full color, about five days after the first pink shows. Overripe tomatoes lose their firmness and begin to soften.

Watermelon: This is one of the trickiest vegetables to pick at the peak of perfection. Veteran gardener and author Gene Logsdon suggests growing one variety for several years, until you become familiar with its appearance when ripe. Another approach is to pick when the stem and the two tendrils on the vine closest to the melon die. The melon should also be ripe when it loses some of its shine and the underside turns from white to yellow.

Ornamentals

Nothing perks up a yard or garden more than some lovely ornamentals. From annuals to perennials, they bring a riot of color to any landscape. Here are some tips for growing these beauties.

PREPARING QUICK-START ANNUALS

Most annual flowers are easy to start from seed, but some, such as those listed below, will sprout faster and more completely if you give them a little special treatment. (These lists are adapted from *Park's Success with Seeds,* by Ann Reilly, George W. Park Seed Co., 1978.)

Seeds that Need Light to Germinate

After sowing seeds, press them gently into the soil, but don't bury them. Place flats under a fluorescent light or in a sunny window.

Begonia (*Begonia* species)
Blanketflower (*Gaillardia* ×*grandiflora*)
Browallia (*Browallia speciosa*)
Creeping zinnia (*Sanvitalia procumbens*)
Flossflower (*Ageratum houstonianum*)
Flowering cabbage (*Brassica oleracea* var. *acephala*)
Flowering tobacco (*Nicotiana alata*)
Impatiens (*Impatiens wallerana*)
Mexican sunflower (*Tithonia rotundifolia*)
Ornamental pepper (*Capsicum annuum*)
Petunia (*Petunia* ×*hybrida*)
Pocketbook plant (*Calceolaria crenatiflora*)

Red salvia (*Salvia* species)
Shasta daisy (*Leucanthemum maximum*)
Snapdragon (*Antirrhinum majus*)
Strawflower (*Helichrysum bracteatum*)
Sweet alyssum (*Lobularia maritima*)
Tickseed (*Coreopsis grandiflora*)

Seeds that Need Darkness to Germinate

Cover seeds with a thin layer of finely milled peat and cover the flat with a board or put in a dark closet until seedlings appear.

African daisy (*Gazania rigens*)
Bachelor's-button (*Centaurea cyanus*)
Blue lace flower (*Trachymene coerulea*)
Borage (*Borago officinalis*)
Bugloss (*Echium* species)
Butterfly flower (*Schizanthus* ×*wisetonensis*)
Larkspur (*Consolida ambigua*)
Nasturtium (*Tropaeolum majus*)
Painted-tongue (*Salpiglossis sinuata*)
Phlox (*Phlox* species)
Pot marigold (*Calendula officinalis*)
Pouch nemesia (*Nemesia strumosa*)
Sweet pea (*Lathyrus odoratus*)

Seeds that Require Soaking and Scarifying before Sowing

Immerse seeds in hot water for up to 24 hours, then nick each seed with a razor blade before planting.

Butterfly pea (*Clitoria ternatea*)
Morning-glory (*Ipomoea* species)

Seeds that Need a Cold Treatment before Sowing

Sow seeds in a flat, then slip the flat into a plastic bag and refrigerate for three days.

Flowering cabbage (*Brassica oleracea* var. *acephala*)
Pansy, Viola, Violet (*Viola* species)

Seeds that Need a Cool Temperature to Germinate

Most seeds germinate best between 65° and 75°F, but these like it cooler, about 55°F.

Annual phlox (*Phlox drummondii*)
Big quaking grass (*Briza maxima*)
Blue daisy (*Felicia amelloides*)
Blue globe daisy (*Globularia cordifolia*)
California poppy (*Eschscholzia californica*)
Sweet pea (*Lathyrus odoratus*)

Seeds that Should Not Be Stored

These seeds are short-lived and should be sown as soon as possible.

Burning bush (*Kochia scoparia*)
Delphinium, Larkspur (*Delphinium* species)
Scarlet sage (*Salvia splendens*)
Transvaal daisy (*Gerbera Jamesonii* hybrids)

Seeds that Should Be Sown Outdoors

Some seedlings don't transplant well, and these seeds are best sown where you want them to grow or in individual pots.

Annual phlox (*Phlox drummondii*)
Blue lace flower (*Trachymene coerulea*)
California poppy (*Eschscholzia californica*)
Creeping zinnia (*Sanvitalia procumbens*)
Flax (*Linum* species)
Love-in-a-mist (*Nigella damascena*)
Lupine (*Lupinus* species)
Mignonette (*Reseda odorata*)
Morning-glory (*Ipomoea* species)
Nasturtium (*Tropaeolum majus*)

GARDENING WITH BULBS

Besides true bulbs such as tulips and lilies, gardeners often lump other fleshy-rooted plants into the bulb category, including those with corms, tubers, rhizomes and tuberous roots. To ensure beautiful blooms:

→ In general, plant spring- and summer-blooming bulbs in the fall and fall-blooming bulbs in the spring. Plant all tender bulbs (those not hardy in cold climates) in the spring.

→ Work several inches of compost or rotted manure into the bed before planting. If the soil is poorly drained, make a raised bed.

→ The sooner you can plant bulbs after they become available, the better. As a general rule, set bulbs at a depth approximately three times their greatest diameter.

→ Add a teaspoon each of bonemeal and blood meal to each planting hole.

→ If natural rainfall is low, water bulbs deeply after planting and any time they are actively growing.

→ After bulbs bloom, don't cut off the foliage. The plants need it in order to store energy for next year.

→ Plant a low-growing ground cover such as periwinkle (*Vinca*) in between the bulbs to mask the dying foliage.

STORING TENDER SUMMER BULBS

These colorful, summer-blooming bulbs are hardy only in the warmest regions of the country. Elsewhere, they can be dug up, stored over the winter, and replanted in spring. Here's how.

Begonia, Tuberous

1. Dig the tubers before frost and trim the stems to about four inches. Dry the tubers outdoors for two to three days, then gently pull off the stems.

2. Place the tubers in a cardboard box and cover them with dry sawdust, vermiculite, sand or peat. Store in a cool basement or unheated room at about 45°F.

Caladium

1. Dig the tubers in early fall, before frost. Gently brush off soil, and put the tubers in a warm, dry location to dry for about a week.

2. Pack the tubers in a box as you would begonias. Store in a cool room at about 50°F. Check the tubers every four to six weeks. If they begin to shrivel, sprinkle the packing material lightly with water.

Canna

1. After the first frost, cut off the stalks and leaves and dig the canna rhizomes. Allow them to dry.

2. Pack the rhizomes on their sides in a box as you would begonias. Keep them in a cool (24° to 35°F), dry place. Before planting in spring, cut into two- to three-inch pieces.

Dahlia

1. After the first light frost, trim the foliage back to four to six inches above the soil. Dig the tubers, handling them gently to avoid bruising. Rinse with a garden hose, then allow to dry slightly.

2. Store as you would begonias, but the temperature must be between 35° and 45°F. Divide the tubers in the spring, leaving at least one bud per tuber.

Gladiolus

1. Dig the corms any time after the foliage yellows, up until the first frost. Trim the leaves back to about one inch, then place in a warm (75° to 80°F), well-ventilated room for about three weeks.

2. Pull off the remaining stub of foliage, then store the corms in old nylon stockings or onion bags hung from a wall or ceiling. The ideal storage temperature range is between 35° and 45°F.

PLANTING PERENNIALS

Follow these steps to planting perennials for optimum growth.

1. Plant perennials as soon as possible after you receive them. Unwrap bare-rooted plants from the packing material and sprinkle roots with water if they appear dry. Rewrap and store in a cool place if you can't plant them right away, then soak the roots in water for a half hour to an hour before they are planted in the ground.

2. Dig holes for all but the smallest perennials with a spade or shovel, rather than a trowel, so you'll be sure to make them deep and wide enough for the roots to spread out.

3. Mound the soil in the center of the hole, then set the plant into the hole, fanning the roots out on the mound.

4. Using a trowel, fill the hole with soil, pressing it gently around the roots. Be sure all the roots are well-covered, but don't cover the crown of the plant (the point just above the roots where the leaf and flower buds emerge).

5. Water gently but thoroughly.

PREPARING FOR A PERENNIAL GARDEN

Because a perennial garden will be in the same spot for many years, it's especially important to carefully prepare and plan for your garden before you plant it.

Preparing the Soil

1. Double- or single-dig the ground, mixing in plenty of compost or well-rotted manure.
2. Adjust the pH with lime or sulfur, if necessary.
3. Smooth out the surface of the soil, using a metal rake.

Planning

Draw up a garden plan on paper to help you visualize plant placement and color schemes. Place tall-growing perennials at the back of a one-sided (traditional) border, and toward the center of an island bed or a border that will be viewed from both sides. Put low-growing plants near the front or along the outer edges of a border or bed. Medium-height (12- to 18-inch) flowers go in the middle. (In general, most spring-blooming plants are short and most summer-blooming plants are tall.)

Start your plan with larger, reliable backbone plants such as daylilies, irises and peonies, then fill in around them. Don't forget to include bulbs and a few clumps of long-blooming annuals.

Plant a variety of perennials for season-long bloom, but for the best effect, place plants of the same species in groups of at least three, unless you're transplanting a large clump.

DIVIDING PERENNIALS

A few perennial flowers can remain in one place and bloom reliably year after year, but the majority need to be dug up periodically and separated into several smaller, more vigorous parts. Most plants are divided either in early spring or after the first fall frost. Perennials need dividing when:

the center of the clump dies
the clumps are large and tangled

the plants grow less vigorously and bloom sparsely
weeds are growing through the clumps

To divide perennials, lift the clump out of the ground using a garden spade, if it's a small plant; use a spading fork to lift large, vigorous clumps. If the foliage gets in the way, cut it back to about three inches in height. Then separate the clump into smaller parts, each one having at least five growing points, or "eyes." Use one of the four methods below for dividing the plants, and replant each section at the appropriate spacing and water well (discard the center of the clump if it's dead, weak or weedy).

→ Gently pull apart shallow-rooted plants such as primroses by hand. Each segment should have several leaves.

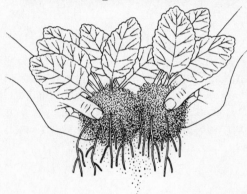

→ Use an old knife to separate intertwined roots of small plants such as hens-and-chickens.

➜ Pry apart the roots of larger plants such as phlox with a hand fork.

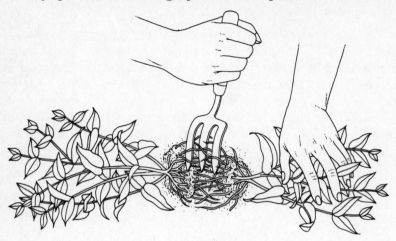

➜ Divide big plants with tightly growing roots, such as daylilies, with two spading forks. Plunge one fork into the center of the clump. Then insert the second one so that they are back to back and the tines are interlaced. Pry the clump apart by pushing the forks inward, then outward until the clump breaks in two.

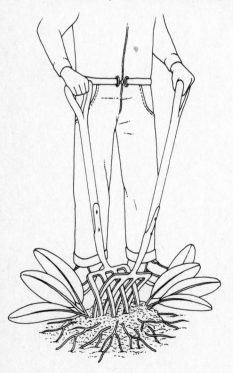

WHEN TO DIVIDE PERENNIALS

Most perennials need dividing after three to five years, but some need it more frequently or not at all.

Every One to Two Years

Bee balm (*Monarda didyma*)
Golden marguerite (*Anthemis tinctoria*)
Hardy aster, Michaelmas daisy (*Aster* species)
Mugwort (*Artemisia vulgaris*)
Shasta daisy (*Leucanthemum maximum*)
Snow-in-summer (*Cerastium tomentosum*)
Yarrow (*Achillea millefolium*)

Rarely or Never

Anemone (*Anemone* species)
Baby's-breath (*Gypsophila elegans*)
Balloon flower (*Platycodon* species)
Bleeding-heart (*Dicentra spectabilis*)
Butterfly weed (*Asclepias tuberosa*)
Candytuft (*Iberis* species)
False indigo (*Baptisia* species)
Flax (*Linum usitatissimum*)
Gas plant (*Dictamnus albus*)
Monkshood (*Aconitum* species)
Oriental poppy (*Papaver orientale*)
Peony (*Paeonia* species)
Sea lavender (*Limonium* species)
Stonecrop, Sedum (*Sedum* species)
Tritoma, Red-hot-poker (*Kniphofia* species)

GROWING BEAUTIFUL ROSES

With sensible soil preparation and the help of a few organic sprays, it's possible to have beautiful, healthy roses.

Choose resistant varieties. Shrub roses such as Simplicity, Carefree Beauty, Bonica, Father Hugo and rugosa rose are especially resistant, as are some antique varieties. In a trial at the University of Nebraska in

Lincoln, hybrid tea and floribunda varieties Sunsprite, Spanish Sun, Goldilocks, Forty-Niner and The Fairy had a low incidence of black spot. (However, resistance may differ in other geographical locations.)

Plant roses in an area where air flows freely, rather than next to a wall or dense shrubbery. Roses do best in a soil enriched with compost or well-rotted manure. Apply four inches around the base of the plants each spring.

Broadcast an organic fertilizer such as Fertrell or Erth-Rite over the bed in the spring, but avoid heavy feedings later in the season.

Mulch roses deeply—with shredded leaves and compost if they are available. Mulch deeply in early spring to cover fallen rose leaves before they give rise to disease spores.

Prune to let in the sun, removing no more than one-fourth of the total wood.

Prevent the spread of disease. At the first sign of black spot, apply sulfur dust or spray, covering the plant thoroughly (including undersides of leaves). Keep insects away, too. The worst pests throughout most of the United States are aphids, thrips, spider mites and Japanese beetles. Spray thoroughly with Safer's Insecticidal Soap at the first signs of their presence. Japanese beetles can also be lured away from roses with pheromone traps, available at most garden centers.

MAKING CUT FLOWERS LAST

Some cut flowers will stay fresh-looking for up to two weeks after cutting if they're given the proper care. Follow these steps to longer-lasting blooms.

1. Take a two-gallon bucket of water with you into the garden.

2. Using sharp pruning shears, cut the flower stems, allowing extra length so you can trim them later. Strip off the leaves from the lower two-thirds of the stem.

3. Place the cut flowers into the bucket so the water covers most of the stem. Put the bucket in a cool place for several hours or overnight.

4. Arrange the flowers in a vase filled with water, trimming off too-long stems and any leaves that would be under water. Change the water daily.

In an informal experiment, Joan Jackson, garden editor for the *San Jose Mercury News* found that adding any of the following ingredients to the water helped flowers hang on longer: ice, a teaspoon of sugar or sugar-free lemon-lime soda (mixed half-and-half with the water).

Pest Control

No matter how carefully you tend to your garden, the day will come when you will find yourself face-to-face with pests. They may range from the merely troublesome to the downright destructive, and they may seem to be taking over, but there *are* safe, organic ways to deal with them and keep your garden intact.

CONTROLLING PESTS SAFELY

Rather than resorting to pesticides (whether natural or synthetic), an organic gardener will attempt to understand and augment the natural forces that work to keep potential pests in check. Follow these steps before you take action to control a pest.

Observe and identify. What does the plant injury look like? Look closely for other signs of insects, such as frass (debris or excrement). Try to locate the pests, checking under leaves, at tender growing points, on the surrounding soil surface or even inside stems. Many pests, such as slugs, are nocturnal, and you may see them only at dusk or sunrise. Use a visual guide, such as *Rodale's Color Handbook of Garden Insects,* by Anna Carr (Rodale Press, 1979), to help you identify them.

Learn its life cycle. Which stage is most damaging, how many generations are there each season and when are the peaks? It's also useful to know when eggs are laid and what they look like.

Evaluate the damage. A few holes in the leaves may be unsightly, but is the injury affecting the health and vigor of the plant? If it's minor, control may not be necessary. Spraying an insecticide at the first sign of damage can sometimes kill beneficial species before they have a chance to work at preying upon the harmful insects.

Choose a course of action. If damage becomes severe, try one of the techniques outlined below in "Fighting Garden Pests."

FIGHTING GARDEN PESTS

If you determine that pest control measures are necessary, the following methods and products can be used to target and reduce garden pests without threatening beneficial creatures, the environment or yourself.

Indirect Action

Choose resistant varieties. Some plant varieties have been selected and bred with varying degrees of pest and disease resistance. Experiment with different varieties to see which ones seem to be the least preferred by the pests in your garden.

Maintain good garden sanitation. Some pests and diseases overwinter in crop debris. By removing dead plants and rotted fruits and vegetables, you can often lessen the number of pests the following season. Cultivation can also destroy overwintering pests and expose them to predators. A straw or grass mulch encourages certain ground-dwelling predators.

Rotate your crops. The life cycles of certain insects can be interrupted by not always planting the same crop in the same location each year. A summer or winter cover crop can also prevent pest buildups.

Manage your soil properly. A weak plant is more susceptible to pest attack, so give careful attention to soil building and irrigation, which result in vigorous, healthy plant growth. Too much nitrogen, a pH that's too low or too high or poor drainage may encourage certain pests, stunt plant growth and/or reduce yields. Water deeply and early in the day, so foliage has time to dry before evening, when conditions are ideal for disease infection. When cultivating weeds, try not to damage delicate plant roots. This not only weakens plants but may invite root-rot pathogens.

Be aware of your plants' needs. Follow plants' preferences for light. Most vegetables require at least six hours of full sun, and will become weak and spindly with less. Also, don't plant so intensively that plants are excessively crowded—they won't receive enough light, and diseases may develop without enough air circulation.

Time your plantings and harvests. Many crops can be planted earlier or later than usual to miss heavy pest infestations. Learn the peak emergence times and life cycles of major pests in your area. (Send a self-addressed, stamped envelope to Rodale's Organic Gardening, Research and Reader Service Dept., 33 East Minor Street, Emmaus, PA 18098, and ask for the reprint, "Insect Emergence Times.")

Try interplanting. Some pests can be confused and dispersed by interplanting a crop they find undesirable with the host crop (the one they prefer). Mixed plantings may also provide shelter and food sources for beneficial insects.

Direct Action

Population explosions of pests can often be prevented by taking early action on egg-laying adults, egg masses and young larvae.

Use physical and mechanical controls. If you know the pest's life cycle, you can trap the adults, use barriers and handpick the eggs, larvae and/or adults.

Use biological controls. These are living organisms that are released, sprayed or attracted to your garden to control pests. To lure these organisms to your garden, grow plants that provide them with food and shelter. Some organisms are available commercially, and others occur naturally. Biological controls include:

Botanical poisons: for example, pyrethrum, rotenone, ryania, sabadilla. Even though these insecticides are plant-derived and break down quickly in the environment, they are still poisonous and should be handled very carefully (see "Spraying Safely" below). They also kill a broad range of insects, including beneficials. For these reasons, botanical insecticides are not the best solution, but sometimes they are the only solution.

Parasites: usually insects that lay eggs inside pests. The larvae feed from the inside. These often specifically attack only one kind of insect.

Pathogens: usually a fungal, viral or bacterial disease that infects and kills a certain group of insects. (For example, *Bacillus thuringiensis* for cabbage loopers and other caterpillars.)

Predators: usually insects that feed on pests. Often one species of predator, such as the praying mantis, will consume many types of insects, including beneficials.

Other sprays and dusts: soap sprays, diatomaceous earth, horticultural and dormant oils, pheromones, sulfur and boric acid are also alternative pest controls; they are less toxic than the botanicals.

SPRAYING SAFELY

Even botanical insecticides (those that are derived from plants) are poisonous and should be handled with care. Follow these do's and don'ts when using botanical products.

DO read label instructions completely before using a dust or spray.

DO store all sprays in a locked cabinet out of the reach of children and pets. Keep all dusts in a cool, dry, dark place. All liquid pesticides should be stored away from heat or open flame.

DO wear gloves and a face mask whenever handling or applying dusts or sprays. Many of them can irritate skin, nasal passages and lungs.

PEST-CONTROL MATERIALS
YOU CAN GROW OR MAKE

General All-Purpose Insect Spray

1 garlic bulb
1 small onion
1 tablespoon cayenne pepper
1 quart water
1 tablespoon liquid,
  nondetergent soap

In a blender, mix garlic, onion, pepper and water. Let steep, then stir in liquid soap. Use immediately, or store in a tightly covered container in the refrigerator for up to one week.

Pyrethrum

This poison is made from the flower heads of *Chrysanthemum cinerariifolium*. (CAUTION: Some people are allergic to the flowers and extracts.)

To make pyrethrum dust: Pick the flowers while the petals are still fresh and the pollen in the center is beginning to be released. Dry the flowers out of direct sunlight and then grind up the flower heads.

To make pyrethrum spray: Soak the ground flower heads overnight in methyl alcohol. Dilute this solution with approximately 100 times as much water before spraying. Store both the dust and the spray in dark, airtight containers because they will quickly break down if exposed to light and air.

NOTE: Because commercial preparations of pyrethrum usually contain a chemical synergist called piperonyl butoxide, which can increase the potency of the pyrethrum fourfold, they will work more effectively than the homemade preparation, which will stun, or knock down, insects, but may not actually kill them.

(continued)

Chrysanthemum cinerariifolium seeds are available from:

Casa Yerba Gardens
Star Route 2, Box 21
Days Creek, OR 97429

Redwood City Seed Co.
P.O. Box 361
Redwood City, CA 94064

J. L. Hudson, Seedsman
P.O. Box 1058
Redwood City, CA 94064

Richters
P.O. Box 26
Goodwood, Ontario
Canada L0C 1A0

Peaceful Valley Farm Supply
11173 Peaceful Valley Road
Nevada City, CA 95959

DO change your clothes and wash your hands as soon as spraying is completed. Bathe, and wash your clothes as soon as possible.

DO contact your local poison-control center immediately if a pesticide poisoning is suspected.

DO go through the motions of loading and pumping a duster or sprayer before you step up to the counter to pay for it. Make sure the lid fits tightly and that the reservoir can be emptied completely of its contents. Check to see how easy it is to disassemble the applicator in case it clogs.

DON'T spray on a windy day. Apply pesticides only to those plants you wish to treat.

DON'T mix wettable powders in the sprayer itself. Instead, use a separate, disposable jar or can to make the solution before adding it to the sprayer.

DON'T reuse pesticide containers.

DON'T add a new pesticide to the sprayer or duster until making sure the applicator is empty, clean and dry.

Seeds and Seedlings

Every bountiful garden began as a plot full of seeds or seedlings. In this section we'll show you how to start and store seeds successfully and how to choose seedlings wisely to get your garden off to the best possible start.

STARTING SEEDS INDOORS

If you choose to start your own seeds, you'll find a much wider choice of varieties as well as a huge cost savings over store-bought plants. But there *is* more work involved. Here's the best way to go about it.

1. Choose uniformly sized containers that are deep enough for unrestricted root growth and have holes in the bottom for drainage. Arrange them in plastic or wooden flats so they'll be easier to move around.

2. Fill the containers with a soil mix that holds in moisture, but is light in texture.

3. Water the soil thoroughly and plant the seeds:

→ When planting in individual pots, sow two seeds per pot for insurance. If they both germinate, pull one out.

→ If you plant seeds in flats, sow them in "minirows," 1½ to 2 inches apart. When the seedlings germinate and develop true leaves, transplant to individual containers.

→ To sow large quantities of small seeds with accuracy, pour them onto a plate, pick up a seed with a moistened toothpick and drop it onto the soil surface. Larger seeds can be precisely placed with tweezers.

4. Cover the seeds:

→ Cover seeds to a depth of three times their size with a layer of vermiculite, screened soil or compost.

→ Very small seeds such as begonia and petunia don't need to be covered; you can just press them into the soil.

5. Label the flats or containers and cover them with one of the following to retain moisture:

aluminum foil
another flat or a board
a sheet of glass
plastic wrap or a plastic bag
wet newspaper or burlap

6. Provide heat. Optimal germination temperature varies for different kinds of seeds, but most germinate well between 65° and 75°F. (Cold soil is a common reason for slow or spotty germination.) Place seed flats:

on top of the refrigerator
near a wood stove or fireplace
on a soil-heating cable

TRIED-AND-TRUE SOIL MIX RECIPES

→ Equal parts of sphagnum peat moss, perlite and vermiculite plus small amounts of composted cow manure, lime, bonemeal, wood ashes and alfalfa meal.

→ Four parts composted grass clippings and leaves, four parts composted cow or sheep manure, one part coarse builder's sand and one part vermiculite, sterilized at 250°F for 1½ to 2 hours. (You can sterilize the mix by putting it in a large pan and heating it on an outdoor grill.)

→ Equal parts of commercial potting soil or leaf mold, perlite or sharp sand and sphagnum peat moss.

7. Provide light. If you're fortunate enough to have a greenhouse, or you have south-facing windows with wide sills, sunshine may be all that's necessary. (Move seedlings away from windows at night if it's very cold.) But most gardeners will need to purchase a fluorescent light or two. Here are some tips for lighting:

→ A four-foot-long shop light fixture works well and is usually more economical than a commercial grow light.

→ Hang the fixture as close as possible over the seedlings without letting the foliage touch the glass.

→ Leave the light on for 16 hours a day (a timer makes this easy.)

→ As seedlings grow, raise the fixture or lower the flats.

→ Rotate the flats each week because the light is weaker at the ends of the fluorescent tubes.

8. Water regularly:

→ Water the seedlings from the bottom or with a plant mister.

→ Never let the soil dry out completely.

GETTING VEGETABLES OFF TO A QUICK START

By following the instructions in "Starting Seeds Indoors" earlier in this chapter, you'll get good germination from almost all vegetable seeds. But here are some tips to keep in mind when starting the following vegetables from seed:

> **Asparagus, okra, and parsnip:** presoak seeds for 24 hours
> **Corn, cucumbers, melons and squash:** sow seeds outdoors where you want them to grow or indoors in individual pots
> **Lettuce:** sow seeds on the surface and press in gently

STORING SEEDS

If you have leftover seeds at the end of the season, don't throw them away! Most vegetable and flower seeds remain viable (able to germinate) for at least two to three years if you keep them in a cool, dry place.

1. Cover the bottom of a one-gallon mason jar with a one-inch layer of silica gel (available from camera shops).

2. Put the seeds, in their packets, inside the jar and seal tightly with a canning lid.

3. Keep the jar in the refrigerator.

DETERMINING WHEN TO START SEEDS

How early should you start vegetables and flowers from seed? It depends on how many weeks the plants need to grow before they are big enough to be transplanted to the garden and on how hardy they are.

1. Start by calling your local Cooperative Extension Service to find out the average last frost date for your area.

2. With the help of a calendar and the listing in the box "Earliest Safe Time to Plant in Spring" on the facing page, you can pinpoint the safe setting-out date for a particular crop.

3. From that date, count backward the maximum number of weeks indicated in the box "Seed-Starting Timetable" on page 312 for your particular crop. (For example, in the case of tomatoes it is seven weeks.) This will bring you to the correct seed-sowing date.

4. Repeat the process for the other vegetables and flowers you plan to start indoors.

GROWING ASPARAGUS FROM SEEDS TO SPEARS

It takes three years for asparagus to reach maturity, but those tender spears are well worth the wait! Here's everything you need to know to grow this delicious vegetable.

EARLIEST SAFE TIME TO PLANT IN SPRING

These are the weeks before the *average last frost date* when it's *usually* safe to sow seeds or set out plants. Plantings made earlier than the recommended dates run more risk of being killed or stunted by cold temperatures. (S = seeds, T = transplants)

Seven Weeks
Cabbages (T), onions (S or sets)

Six Weeks
Asparagus (T), peas (S), potatoes ("seed" pieces), radishes (S), spinach (S or T), turnips (S)

Four Weeks
Beets (S), broccoli (T), brussels sprouts (T), collards (T), head lettuce (T), kale (S), leaf lettuce (S or T), onions (T)

Two Weeks
Carrots (S), cauliflower (T), celery (T), Chinese cabbage (T)

One Week *After* Average Last Frost
All flowers (S), asparagus (S), corn (S), okra (S), snap beans (S), squash (S), tomatoes (T)

Two Weeks *After* Average Last Frost
Cucumbers (S), eggplant (T), lima beans (S), muskmelons (S), peppers (T), sweet potatoes (T), watermelons (S)

Planting
1. Prepare the soil the same way you would for any vegetable crop, adding as much organic matter to the soil as possible, and adjusting the pH to about 6.5. (See "Creating Healthy Soil" and "Translating a Soil Test" later in this chapter.) If the soil is poorly drained, make a raised bed. (See "Making a Raised-Bed Garden" earlier in this chapter.)

2. Dig a furrow 6 inches deep, 12 inches wide and as long as you need it to be. Figure on 5 to 10 feet per person. Over a six- to nine-week period,

SEED-STARTING TIMETABLE

These are the average number of weeks needed to grow plants to a transplantable size.

3 to 4 Weeks
Vegetables: Cucumbers, muskmelons, summer squash, sweet corn, watermelons

5 to 7 Weeks
Vegetables: Broccoli, brussels sprouts, cabbage, cauliflower, kale, lettuce, tomatoes
Flowers: Cockscomb, gaillardia, zinnia

6 to 8 Weeks
Vegetables: Eggplant, peppers
Flowers: Aster, coleus, cosmos, nasturtium

8 to 10 Weeks
Flowers: Ageratum, alyssum, marigold, salvia, statice, strawflower, verbena

10 to 12 Weeks
Vegetables: Asparagus, celery, onions
Flowers: Dahlia, dusty miller, gloriosa daisy, impatiens, petunia, phlox

12 to 14 Weeks
Flowers: Bachelor's-button, begonia, dianthus, snapdragon

you'll be able to harvest about a pound of spears per foot of row. If you make two rows, allow 4 feet between them—3 feet for the eventual spread of the asparagus crowns and 1 foot for a path.

3. Plant either seeds or 1-year-old crowns. (Older crowns take just as long to yield the first harvest.) Seeds are about one-tenth the price of crowns, and some experiments have shown that the resulting spears are more tender and are higher-yielding—as much as 40 percent higher. To sow seeds, broadcast them into the trench in the spring, spacing them about

3 to 4 inches apart. Cover them with about ½ inch of soil, and reshape the furrow with small trenches on the sides to prevent erosion when it rains.

Crowns can be planted in spring or fall. To plant crowns, untangle the roots and spread them out in the trench, spacing the crowns 12 to 18 inches apart. Cover with 1 to 2 inches of soil.

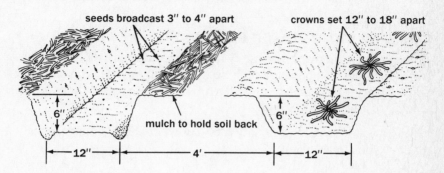

4. After the spears emerge, mulch the bed. (See "Choosing a Mulch" earlier in this chapter.)

5. When the first spears grow about eight inches tall, add another inch or so of soil to the trench. Repeat the process gradually until, by the end of the season, the trench has become a slight mound.

Growing

1. Apply ½ inch of manure to the bed each spring.

2. Water during dry spells, especially during the last half of the season, when the roots are storing food for next year's crop.

3. In the fall, before the berries drop, cut the browning stems near the ground and compost. If the berries are allowed to drop to the ground, they will self-sow, but the resulting plants will be inferior.

Picking

1. Don't pick any asparagus the first or second season, or you'll hurt later yields.

2. The third season, harvest for two weeks, then stop because the crown will still be small.

3. Add another two weeks of harvest each year until you're picking asparagus for six to nine weeks.

4. Pick spears when they're six to nine inches tall. Hold a spear near the base and bend. It will snap just above the tough, fibrous base. You can also cut spears near the ground with a knife and trim off the tough section.

5. When you end the harvest, each crown should send up about a dozen spears. If there are only three or four, you harvested too long.

CHOOSING STORE-BOUGHT PLANTS

Growing your own plants from seed takes work and almost daily attention. Instead, you may choose to purchase some or all of your vegetable and flower plants from a nursery or garden center. Before you buy, here's what to look for and what to avoid.

➝ A short, stocky plant will adjust to garden conditions more quickly than an older, taller plant.

TOUGH TRANSPLANTS

By subjecting your seedlings to a series of minor stresses, a process called hardening off, they'll be able to withstand transplanting with less shock.

➝ Grow the plants at temperatures 5° to 10°F below their optimum. That's about 50° to 60°F for cabbage, broccoli and brussels sprouts, and 60° to 70°F for eggplant, peppers and tomatoes.
➝ Let plants wilt slightly between waterings.
➝ Fertilize sparingly. It's okay for the seedlings to look a little pale. If your soil mix includes compost or rich garden soil, your plants may not need any fertilizer.
➝ Keep light levels as high as possible to prepare seedlings for the more intense sunlight outside.
➝ A week or so before transplanting to the garden, take the plants outdoors for a few hours at a time for the first few days, then leave them out all day for three more days, bringing them in each night.
➝ If no frost is predicted, leave them out overnight for a few more days. Now seedlings should be fully hardened off and ready to plant.

➔ Forgo the tomato plants with flowers, unless early tomatoes are really important to you. Young plants without blossoms will fruit later but bear more.

➔ Foliage should be somewhat pale. If it's rich, green and lush-looking, it's a sign that the plants have been overfertilized. The toughest transplants have been grown slowly with a minimum of fertilizer.

➔ Ask the greenhouse operator if the plants have been hardened off. If not, you'll need to put them through the process for a week to 10 days before they're planted. (See the box "Tough Transplants" on the facing page.)

➔ Plant roots should be bright white. If they're brown, or not even visible, the plant may have root rot. Ask the operator to pull a plant from its pot so you can see the roots.

➔ Check plant size. Plants in market six-packs should be no more than about two to four inches high. A two-inch pot will provide plenty of room for a six- to eight-inch plant.

CREATING HEALTHY SOIL

It takes healthy soil to make a hardy garden. You can do everything right, but if your soil is deficient, your vegetables and ornamentals are not going to grow well, if at all. Take these steps toward improving your soil before you garden, and you won't be disappointed.

Test the soil. Using a soil testing service or a home testing kit, find out what nutrients are at low levels in your soil, and whether it's acid or alkaline. (You can get a mailing container from your Cooperative Extension Service.) Take a trowel full of soil from several different locations and mix them together in a bucket. Make sure the soil is completely dry before testing it. After the first test, retest once every two or three years.

Follow test results. If you receive chemical recommendations from the soil testing service, translate them to organic materials and use the appropriate amount. (See "Translating a Soil Test" later in this chapter.) Apply the recommended amount of lime or sulfur to adjust the pH.

Apply organic materials. You can compost them first and spread them into a two- to three-inch layer over the surface of the garden beds. Or you can dig the organic materials into the soil with a garden fork. If the supply is limited, use them only in furrows and transplant holes. You can also apply them as mulch. A one-inch-thick application each year is usually sufficient.

Vary materials. If you use animal manure, combine it with a vegetable product, such as straw, sawdust, grass clippings or leaves. Try to use different manure and vegetable matter blends each year to lessen the possibility of any one nutrient building up to an unbalanced level.

Plant green manure. To prevent wind and water erosion, and to keep nutrients from leaching out of the soil over the winter, plant a cover crop of winter or annual rye in the garden after the first killing frost.

Avoid compaction. Before you work the soil, check its moisture content by squeezing a ball of soil in the palm of your hand. It should fall apart easily. If it sticks together like modeling clay, it's too wet—wait until it is drier. Once you've tilled and/or hand-dug your garden for the first time, designate paths, and never walk on the planting areas.

TRANSLATING A SOIL TEST

Some soil testing services will include recommendations for organic fertilizers if you request it. But if chemical fertilizers are recommended and you want to substitute organic materials, here's how to do it:

→ If your test indicates, for example, that your garden needs 50 pounds of 5-10-10 fertilizer per 1,000 square feet of garden, the numbers indicate you need a fertilizer that contains 5 percent nitrogen (N), 10 percent phosphorus (P) and 10 percent potassium (K).

→ Your 50-pound bag of 5-10-10 is equal to 2.5 actual pounds of N (5 percent of 50 pounds, or 0.05 × 50), 5 pounds of P (10 percent of 50 pounds, or 0.1 × 50) and 5 pounds of K (10 percent of 50, or 0.1 × 50). The other 37.5 pounds in the bag are fillers.

→ If you'd rather use organic fertilizers instead of a commercial 5-10-10 mix, refer to the table, "N-P-K Content of Common Organic Fertilizers" on the facing page to find the N-P-K rating for the organic materials you'll be using. Horse manure is rated at 0.4 percent N, 0.2 percent P and 0.4 percent K. So to find the amount of horse manure needed to give you 2.5 pounds of nitrogen, divide 2.5 pounds by 0.4 percent (2.5 / 0.004) to get 625 pounds of manure.

→ How much phosphorus and potassium are in 625 pounds of horse manure? One-and-a-quarter pounds of P (625 × .002) and 2.5 pounds of K (625 × .004).

→ So you still need 3.75 pounds of phosphorus (the original 5 pounds minus the 1.25 in horse manure) and 2.5 pounds of potassium (the original 5 pounds minus the 2.5 in horse manure).

N-P-K Content of Common Organic Fertilizers

	%N	%P	%K
Blood meal	15	1.3	0.7
Bonemeal	4	21	0.2
Cottonseed meal	3.2	1.3	1.2
Greensand	0	1-2	5
Hay, alfalfa	2.5	0.5	2.1
Hay, red clover	2.1	0.5	2
Hay, timothy	1.3	0.6	1
Kitchen scraps	3.5	0.1-1.5	2.3-4.3
Leaves, oak	0.8	0.4	0.2
Manure, horse	0.4	0.2	0.4
Manure, pig	0.6	0.4	0.1
Manure, poultry (includes chicken, duck, goose and turkey)	1.6	1.5	0.9
Manure, sheep	0.6	0.3	0.2
Pine needles	0.5	0.1	trace
Rock phosphate	0	20	0
Seaweed	1.7	0.8	5
Straw, wheat	0.5	0.2	0.6
Wood ashes	0	1-2	4-10

You can obtain the potassium from wood ashes, which contain an average of 7 percent K. It will take 36 pounds of wood ashes (2.5 / 0.07). Ashes are also about 1.5 percent phosphorus, so you get an added bonus of ½ pound of P. (CAUTION: Wood ashes are a very alkaline material. Never apply more than you need.)

→ Now you only need 3.25 pounds of phosphorus (3.75 minus the ½ pound you got from the wood ashes.) Rock phosphate is rated at 20 percent P. You'll find that you need about 16 pounds of rock phosphate (3.25 / 0.20) to round out your fertilizer requirement.

The soil test is merely a guide, and so are the figures arrived at through these calculations. And keep in mind that the ratings for various organic materials will vary from batch to batch, too. The true test will be your garden's performance.

TAMING SANDY SOILS AND TOUGH CLAY

Nearly everyone is plagued with not-so-perfect soil. If your soil is particularly sandy or contains a lot of clay, there are some simple techniques you can use to improve it.

Sand

Water and nutrients tend to run right through sandy soils because sand particles are big and have large air spaces between them. These soils contain a high level of oxygen, and aerobic soil organisms burn up organic matter quickly. To make sandy soil more manageable:

→ Add a fairly slow-decomposing form of organic matter such as partially rotted sawdust. By improving the soil texture, it will keep later additions of organic materials from burning up so quickly.

→ Plant a cover crop—winter rye is a good choice in many parts of the country because it pulls up minerals from deep in the subsoil. Till it under in the spring when it reaches 9 to 12 inches in height.

→ Use a tiller as little as possible, since every pass churns additional oxygen into the sandy soil.

→ When watering, don't use an overhead sprinkler. (Water hitting the surface will evaporate quickly.) Instead, water with canvas soaker hoses or plastic hoses that have holes, and face the holes toward the ground.

→ Cut weeds at the surface with a sharp hoe after soil is watered, then mulch heavily to help retain the soil moisture as long as possible. You can use compost and lawn clippings as mulch to add much-needed nutrients.

→ Shovel manure and compost two to three inches thick over planting beds or directly on rows. Turn the material into the soil surface only.

→ After seeding, tread on rows or roll with a lawn roller to ensure good contact between germinating seed and soil.

Clay

Because the individual clay particles are so fine, they stick tightly together, trapping water and preventing optimal root growth. When dry, some clay soils are so hard they are unworkable. To make clay more manageable:

→ Add copious amounts of organic matter every spring or fall, using compost, mulch and cover crops.

→ Grow in raised beds rather than rows, so valuable organic matter isn't wasted on pathways.

→ Add precomposted material in a four- to six-inch layer for quickest results. You can also layer ingredients such as manure and leaves about eight inches deep.

→ Add sand, combined with organic matter, to help improve the texture of clay.

→ Incorporate organic materials when the clay is midway between wet and dry. It should crumble easily in your hands.

→ Always keep the soil covered, either with mulch or cover crops. The mulch keeps soil and compost moist so plants can make the most of it. Cover crops trap the nutrients you have added and their roots break up the heavy soil.

BRINGING THE SOIL INTO BALANCE

Most crops grow well at a soil pH between 6.2 and 6.5. It takes more lime to raise the pH of a loamy soil, which is rich in organic matter, than that of a sandy soil. The more organic matter a soil contains, the more buffered—resistant to change—it is.

How to Raise pH One Point

→ In very sandy soil, add 3 to 3½ pounds of finely ground calcitic limestone per 100 square feet. (See the box "Liming Materials" below.)

→ In sandy loam, add 5 to 7 pounds per 100 square feet.

LIMING MATERIALS

Limestones take six months to a year to neutralize soil acidity; wood ashes take a few weeks. For best results, thoroughly mix the material into the soil in the fall, then repeat the application every three or four years, if a soil test shows it's warranted.

Calcitic limestone: contains primarily calcium, an alkaline element. Apply at the rates shown above.

Dolomitic limestone: contains calcium and magnesium. A good choice if your soil tests low in magnesium. Substitute 0.86 pound of dolomite for every pound of calcitic lime.

Ground marble dust: use at the same rate as calcitic limestone.

Crushed oyster shell: use at the same rate as calcitic limestone.

Bonemeal: use 1.25 pounds for each pound of limestone recommended.

Wood ashes: use 1.25 pounds for each pound of limestone recommended.

→ In loam, add 7 to 10 pounds per 100 square feet.

→ In heavy clay, add 7 to 8 pounds per 100 square feet.

NOTE: You'll notice on your soil test results that if a two-point increase in pH is needed, *more than* twice the above amounts will be recommended. That's because a soil pH of 4.2 is 10 times as acidic as one of 5.2, and 100 times more acidic than a pH of 6.2.

How to Lower pH One Point

→ For all soils, add one to two pounds of ground sulfur per 100 square feet, or one pound of Dispersul (a granular, water-soluble source of sulfur that contains 10 percent bentonite clay) per 100 square feet. You'll need five pounds of sulfur to lower the pH one point.

MAKING THE BEST OF ALKALINE SOIL

If you live in the inland West or in an area where the soil is derived from limestone or marble, chances are your soil is alkaline, or basic. A high pH (over 7) is often accompanied by high sodium and high salinity, also detrimental to plant growth. But gardening in alkaline soil doesn't have to be a struggle. Here's how to make the best of your situation.

Have the soil tested. The test should determine pH, percentage of soluble salts (salinity) and exchangeable sodium percentage (ESP). If the ESP is over 20, the test results should show the cation exchange capacity of the soil and the quantity of sodium.

Test your irrigation water. Have it tested for sodium content, salinity and pH. If it's high in any of these, use collected rainwater to supplement it.

Treat high sodium and high salinity problems together. Then take care of the high pH.

Reduce the ESP. If the soil test shows a high ESP (20 percent or greater), reduce it by applying powdered gypsum at the rate recommended in the soil test results. To apply gypsum, broadcast and scratch it into the soil, then irrigate heavily two or three times shortly after application. It's important to leach the soil thoroughly because the sodium sulfate that forms after applying gypsum is harmful to plants.

Reduce the salinity. If the soil test shows high salinity (0.5 percent or greater), water deeply to drive the salts below a one-foot-deep root zone, where the majority of plant roots are concentrated. Six inches of water will reduce salts by half, 12 inches will reduce them by 80 percent and 24 inches will reduce them by 90 percent.

Flood the garden six to eight weeks before planting. After planting, don't let the soil dry out, or the leached salts will be drawn up to the surface.

Lower the pH. If the pH is over 7.5, add finely ground sulfur (for rates, see "Bringing the Soil into Balance" earlier in this chapter). Dig sulfur in thoroughly before planting. CAUTION: Sulfur is harmful to soil organisms until neutralized, which takes up to three months. Leach the soil after two to three months by watering thoroughly.

Add organic matter. Organic matter lowers and stabilizes pH, and in the long run is better for the soil than sulfur. The humus also helps hold soil moisture. Apply at least 200 to 250 pounds per 100 square feet (up to half the soil volume). You can use almost any organic material except manure, which tends to be very high in salts and sodium in many parts of the West.

9

Shortcuts to

Landscaping and Beautiful Lawns

A healthy, attractive lawn can be a real asset to any homeowner. Although it takes time and effort, the results are well worth the labor—not only do you surround yourself with a beautiful landscape, but you may increase the value of your property in the process. In this chapter we'll take you step-by-step through planning a landscape, selecting ground covers, seeding a lawn, planting a tree and much more.

Landscaping

There's more to landscaping than just planting a few trees and shrubs. You should start by analyzing your site and drawing up a plan. From there, it's a matter of choosing the best plantings for your climate. But did you know that you can also plant to reduce noise and pollution? We'll show you how.

PLANNING TO LANDSCAPE

Don't rush right out and buy every tree and shrub you can find in order to create an instant landscape. Whether you're landscaping a bare yard or adding to mature plantings, there are four steps you should take before you begin.

Analyze your site by considering the following factors:

    condition of the soil
    existing vegetation

seasonal path of the sun
seasonal rainfall and drainage patterns
seasonal wind patterns
topography of the land

Prepare a rough plan of your site, showing the various factors listed above, including the location of your house. Make several copies of your plan for the next step.

Add to your plan by drawing in trees, shrubs, flowers, vegetables and any other types of vegetation you'd like to add. Don't forget to include gardens, if any. This is also the time to think about walls, berms and fences. Experiment with several different designs until you find the one most pleasing to you.

Choose your vegetation by visiting nurseries and parks, touring house gardens and looking through catalogs. Refrain from buying plants that are too unusual or exotic—it's best to stick to native vegetation that you know will do well in your climate. And keep in mind that some kinds of vegetation are better than others at blocking out summer sun or letting in winter sun, at diminishing winds and at decreasing noise. Here are a few basics to get you started:

> **Flowering plants:** for color and fragrance
> **Ground cover:** for texture and soil protection
> **Shrubs:** for screening and bank cover
> **Trees:** evergreens for year-round screening of noise and eyesores; deciduous for summer shade and winter sunlight

AVOIDING POTENTIAL LANDSCAPING PROBLEMS

As you go about planning your landscape, keep in mind that some problems may arise due to improper selection or placement of vegetation. By understanding what may go wrong, you can avoid these potential problems.

Roots of trees such as elm, willow, poplar and maple can clog sewer lines. This problem occurs where there is already a break in the line that allows water to escape into the surrounding soil. The roots develop quickly in wet soil and can grow into the line break, making it larger.

Shallow-rooted shrubs and trees can interfere with pavement. If they are planted too close to a sidewalk or paved area, their growing roots can crack the pavement and lift it out of the ground.

Tree branches can cause problems with overhead utility lines. Be sure to use plants and trees with a maximum height or branching pattern that won't interfere with the lines.

Trees planted too close to the house will fill up the gutters with leaves every fall. If you're not keen on climbing the ladder regularly to clean it all out, make sure the trees you plant near the house have branches that won't hang over the roof. Be aware that wet, fallen leaves can be a real hazard on steps and walkways.

Fruits and flowers from trees can be a nuisance. Some fruits, such as those from the horse chestnut, are toxic if eaten in quantity. Others, such as ginko fruits, produce an unpleasant odor as they decompose. And sometimes just the sheer quantity of fruit can be annoying to clean up, as with crab apples.

Flowers present their own set of problems. The male flowers of the ailanthus, for example, have a strong, unpleasant odor. And pollen, from any species, can be a real irritant to susceptible people. Another point to keep in mind is that petals dropped from rose bushes or flowering trees can make walkways dangerously slick.

PLANTING TO REDUCE NOISE

If you live near a highway or in any type of noisy locale, you can utilize plants as noise filters. Here are some points to keep in mind:

→ Plantings of a single species are not as effective for noise control as mixed plantings, which will muffle a greater variety of noises.

→ Plants not only muffle sounds, they also make their own noise, such as the wind rustling through the leaves. Plants also attract animals, such as birds and squirrels, which contribute their own sounds. All of this helps mask offensive noises.

→ Studies have shown that plant barriers are very effective for buffering and deflecting highway sounds. Such a barrier should be 25 to 35 feet wide and should include both trees and shrubs. Hedges and other narrow plantings are relatively ineffective in controlling noise.

→ Barriers should be planted in conjunction with landforms that either depress or elevate the noise source. If there is no change in grade, the plantings should be arranged to channel the noise up and away—ground-hugging plants should be closest to the noise source, with taller ones a bit farther away and towering trees at the perimeter (see the accompanying illustrations).

level grade

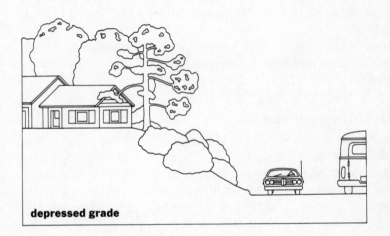

depressed grade

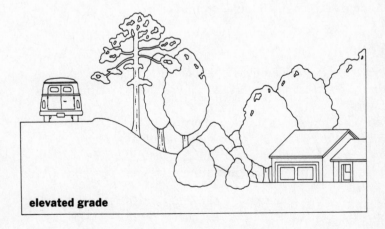

elevated grade

PLANTING FOR POLLUTION CONTROL

The plants in your landscape can do their part to fight pollution—you can plant vegetation that will act as natural air filters. These plants can remove some pollutants from the air on contact, through sedimentation or through absorption.

→ Leaf surfaces, especially hairy ones, can trap dust and soot. If you live near a dusty road or a rock quarry, plant a dense buffer of hairy-leaved vegetation between yourself and the dust source.

→ Plants control air-polluting gases by introducing oxygen into the atmosphere and diluting the polluted air. But certain gaseous pollutants—sulfur dioxide from fuel combustion, fluorides from phosphate fertilizers and ozone from the atmosphere—can kill vegetation. (See the box "Pollution-Tolerant Trees" on the facing page.)

→ In addition to absorbing and metabolizing offensive odors, plants provide their own pleasant fragrances that deodorize unpleasant smells.

SELECTING GROUND COVERS

Ground covers are popular landscape plantings because they grow quickly and require a minimum of fuss. Use them to prevent erosion, cover bare spots, fill in under trees or around shrubs, fill in crevices in walks and paths and cover banks and slopes where nothing else will grow. Ground covers aren't all alike—you can't plant pachysandra in the open sun and expect it to grow like crazy. Some ground covers do thrive in full sun, but others, such as pachysandra, do best in shade. There are evergreen ground covers as well as deciduous ones, and many even sport flowers. Below are some of the more popular ground covers.

Good in Sun

African daisy (*Gazania rigens*): yellow and orange flowers

Bearberry (*Arctostaphylos uva-ursi*): red berries; white or pink flowers

Broom (*Cytisus* species): yellow flowers

Creeping thyme (*Thymus serpyllum*): purple flowers

Crown vetch (*Coronilla varia*): pink and white flowers

Junipers (*Juniperus* low-grading varieties): green, purple or blue shrubs

Moss pink, Mountain phlox (*Phlox subulata*): pink, purple or white flowers

Snow-in-summer (*Cerastium tomentosum*): white flowers

POLLUTION-TOLERANT TREES

The following list of trees, adapted from *Nature's Design* by Carol A. Smyser (Rodale Press, 1982), includes trees that are tolerant of, or resistant to, certain pollutants. Generally speaking, they will survive higher-than-normal concentrations of the pollutants mentioned. For information on pollutants that are not mentioned here, check with your county Extension agent or the United States Department of Agriculture.

Tree	Pollutant
American plane, buttonwood, sycamore	Resistant to fluoride
Balsam fir	Tolerant of ozone and hydrogen chloride; moderately resistant to sulfur dioxide
Black gum, pepperidge, sour gum	Tolerant of ozone and sulfure dioxide; moderately resistant to chlorine
Colorado blue spruce, Colorado spruce	Tolerant of ozone and peroxyacetyl nitrate (PAN); moderately resistant to 2, 4-D
Digger pine	Tolerant of ozone
Douglas fir	Tolerant of ozone and PAN; moderately resistant to sulfur dioxide
Drummond red maple	Tolerant of sulfur dioxide, ozone and hydrogen chloride
Eastern cottonwood	Resistant to sulfur dioxide
Flowering dogwood	Tolerant of ozone, PAN and sulfur dioxide
Junipers	Tolerant of hydrogen chloride and sulfur dioxide
Live oak	Tolerant of sulfur dioxide
Piñon nut pine	Tolerant of ozone
Slash pine	Moderately resistant to ozone
Southern magnolia	Tolerant of chlorine
Sugar maple	Tolerant of ozone and sulfur dioxide
Sweet gum	Tolerant of PAN; moderately resistant to 2, 4-D and sulfur dioxide
Western red cedar	Tolerant of sulfur dioxide, ozone and hydrogen chloride

PRUNING GROUND COVERS

Believe it or not, some ground covers could do with a little pruning every now and then. It's actually helpful to prune when you are first setting out the plants, especially if they're the trailing or branching type of ground cover. Pruning will help the plant send out buds along the remaining stem that will later develop into a multistemmed plant. The result is that the pruned plant will spread out and grow faster than the original plant would have. Periwinkle, Baltic ivy, British ivy and wintercreeper all benefit from being pruned at planting time. An added advantage is that the cuttings can be rooted and planted elsewhere.

You can also prune established ground covers. When they begin to look a bit ragged, remove all the dead plants, then step back for an overall view of the beds before you begin the serious pruning. Simply cut out the straggly plants with a pair of hand shears.

Spring heath (*Erica carnea*): red flowers
Thrift, Sea pink (*Armeria maritima*): pink or white flowers
Two-row stonecrop (*Sedum spurium*): pink to purple flowers

Good in Shade

Baltic ivy (*Hedera helix* 'Baltica'): no flowers
Bugleweed, Carpet bugle (*Ajuga reptans*): purple or blue flowers
European wild ginger (*Asarum europaeum*): greenish purple or brown flowers
Japanese spurge (*Pachysandra terminalis*): white flowers
Lily-of-the-valley (*Convallaria majalis*): white to pink flowers
Periwinkle (*Vinca minor*): lilac-blue flowers
Plantain lily (*Hosta* varieties): white, blue, lilac or violet flowers

Good in Sun or Shade

Cotoneaster (*Cotoneaster* varieties): red berries; white or pink flowers
Daylily (*Hemerocallis* varieties): yellow, orange, red or purple flowers
Hay-scented fern (*Dennstaedtia punctilobula*): no flowers
Mondo grass (*Ophiopogon japonicus*): light lilac to white flowers
Wintercreeper (*Euonymus fortunei* var. *radicans*): pink flowers

ATTRACTING BIRDS TO YOUR YARD

You can have a yard full of singing, chattering birds by providing these four requirements: food, water, shelter from predators, and nesting sites.

Food

By choosing natural plantings that offer food for various species of birds, you can eliminate the bother of maintaining bird feeders. You may, however, wish to supply bird seed in the winter when natural foods are scarce. If you do so, you must be vigilant in keeping the feeder well-stocked because birds will rely on your feeder for winter food. Here are some plantings that are good sources of bird food:

→ Corn, grain sorghum, millet and sunflowers attract seed-eaters such as cardinals, goldfinches, juncos and sparrows.

→ Blackberry, dogwood, flowering quince, highbush cranberry, honeysuckle, mock orange, privet, raspberry, rugosa roses, viburnum and yew attract fruit-eaters such as bluebirds, brown thrashers, cardinals, catbirds, grouse, mockingbirds and scarlet tanagers.

→ Flowering crab, hackberry, hawthorn, horse chestnut, mountain ash, mulberry, redbud and sweet gum attract a variety of fruit-, seed- and nut-eaters such as cedar waxwings, fox sparrows, grosbeaks, grouse, mockingbirds, purple finches, robins and yellow-bellied sapsuckers.

→ Annual and perennial flowers such as aster, cosmos, daisy, marigold, poppy and zinnia provide summer-through-fall feeding for many bird species. And don't forget pine trees—they provide food, shelter and nesting sites for a variety of birds and wildlife.

Water

Provide water for drinking and bathing in an area that is somewhat open but still protected by trees and shrubs. If you're lucky enough to have a stream, pond or creek on your property, you've probably already discovered how attractive these bodies of water are to many birds and wildlife. If you aren't blessed with one of these natural watering holes, a birdbath or small ground-level pool will do just as well. Don't set them out in the middle of nowhere—birds need some type of nearby cover in which to hide and feel protected.

Shelter

Provide shelter from predators by planting hedges and shrubs. Some birds also nest in these sites.

BIRDS AND THEIR CHOICE OF MAN-MADE SHELTER

Most birds prefer to nest in some type of cavity—in other words, a closed box with an entrance hole suitable for their size. Others like shelves or open-sided boxes.

Bird	Type of Shelter	Entrance Hole Size (in inches)
American kestrel	Cavity	3
Barn owl	Cavity	6
Barn swallow	Shelf	
Bluebird	Cavity	1½
Brown thrasher	Shelf or open-sided box	
Carolina wren	Cavity	1⅛–1¼
Chickadee	Cavity	1⅛–1¼
Downy woodpecker	Cavity	1⅛–1¼
Flicker	Cavity	2½
Great crested flycatcher	Cavity	2
Hairy woodpecker	Cavity	1½
House finch	Cavity or shelf	
House sparrow	Cavity or shelf	
Mourning dove	Shelf	
Nuthatch	Cavity	1⅛–1¼
Phoebe	Shelf or open-sided box	
Purple martin	Cavity	2½
Red-headed woodpecker	Cavity	2
Robin	Shelf or open-sided box	
Saw-whet owl	Cavity	2½
Screech owl	Cavity	3
Starling	Cavity	2
Swallow	Cavity	1½
Titmouse	Cavity	1⅛–1¼
Wood duck	Cavity	4
Wrens (Bewick's and house)	Cavity	1

SOURCE: Adapted from *Wildlife in Your Garden* by Gene Logsdon (Rodale Press, 1983).

Housing

Provide housing for birds in the form of birdhouses. Bluebirds, chicka-
dees, flickers, purple martins, woodpeckers and wrens are particularly
attracted to birdhouses. Be sure you build or buy a house designed for the
kind of bird you want to attract and be sure it's located where the bird
will feel safe. (See the box "Birds and Their Choice of Man-Made
Shelter" on the facing page.)

The Lawn

Whether you're seeding a new lawn or trying to figure out how to keep
the neighborhood pets off your grass, here are tips to help you tackle the
job of lawn care and maintenance.

PREPARING FOR A NEW LAWN

Before you start a new lawn, whether from seed or sod, follow these five
steps to help create grass that is both healthy and beautiful.

Have your soil tested. A loamy soil is best, and most likely your soil will
need organic additions (such as compost, manure, peat moss, sawdust or
shredded bark) to make it suitable for good grass growth. (See "Creating
Healthy Soil" and "Translating a Soil Test" in chapter 8.)

Clear away all debris—mainly rocks, twigs and branches. If your house has
been recently built or renovated, be on the lookout for construction
debris such as nails, scrap wood and pieces of concrete.

Establish a rough grade by filling in low spots and leveling hills. You want
to create a gentle slope away from your house to assist drainage away
from the foundation. If you have soil that does not drain well, you may
want to install drain tile a few feet below the surface. Consult a contractor or landscaper for advice.

Fertilize the soil. Work organic amendments (such as those listed earlier)
and high-phosphorus fertilizer into the top five to seven inches of soil.

Level and grade the finished seed bed just prior to planting. Rake and
smooth the entire area to make it as level as possible and to eliminate any
rocks. You're now ready to sow seed or lay sod.

When to Sow Lawn Seed

Fall or Early Spring	Spring or Early Summer
Bent grass	Bahia grass
Bluegrass	Bermuda grass
Fescues	Buffalo grass
Ryegrasses	Carpet grass
	Centipede grass

CHOOSING SOD

If you're thinking about buying sod for your new lawn, carefully inspect it before putting your money down:

→ Check the edges to see if the soil has dried out.

→ Look for a uniform green color—don't buy sod with poor coloring or any yellow.

→ The sod should be clipped close to stimulate root spread after it is planted in your lawn.

→ Sod thicknesses will vary with grass variety, but generally, the sod should be from ¾ to 1 inch thick. If it is thicker, it will root slowly, and if it is too thin, it will dry out quickly.

→ Don't buy sod that falls apart easily when handled.

WATERING ESTABLISHED LAWNS

When it comes to watering the lawn, most of us kill our grass with kindness—we water it too often. There are no hard-and-fast rules about how often to water. The best bet is to let the grass be your guide.

The time to water is just as the grass begins to wilt. You'll be able to tell when it's at this point because the grass color changes from bright green to a dull blue-green. Another clue is its loss of resiliency. Walk across the lawn; if your footprint remains visible for more than a few seconds, your grass needs watering.

How you water is just as important as how often. Shallow watering keeps the upper layers of soil near saturation most of the time, which encourages shallow rooting and promotes weak turf that is susceptible to disease, insect attack and damage from traffic. So forgo the periodic light sprinklings. Instead, when grass shows the first signs of wilt, water thoroughly to wet the soil to a minimum depth of six inches. Don't water during the brightest part of the day because the water evaporates rapidly —early morning or late afternoon is preferable. And try not to water late at night—a late-night watering leaves the grass wet throughout the evening, and wet turf is susceptible to fungus disease.

Water deeply, but not often. Frequent heavy watering is just as bad for your lawn as frequent shallow watering. Waterlogging the soil not only encourages shallow rooting, but it also encourages the establishment of water-loving weeds and accelerates the growth of crabgrass. It could even drown trees, if practiced for a long enough time.

Never water your lawn at a rate faster than the soil can absorb the water. Whether you water with sprinklers or a hose, water should be distributed finely and evenly. If you don't have an underground sprinkling system, you must constantly move your sprinklers to ensure even watering of the entire lawn.

MOWING YOUR LAWN THE RIGHT WAY

Mowing your lawn isn't just a matter of getting up early on Saturday morning and cranking up the old machine. The trick is to mow based on your lawn's schedule, not yours.

Mow at the correct height. The type of grass that you have will determine the height you should be mowing at. (See the box "Mowing Heights for Common Grasses" on the next page.)

Mow lightly and frequently. Light, frequent mowing causes less stress to the grass than heavy, infrequent cuttings.

Mow higher and less often in the summer. Your lawn will have more staying power during drought, and tall grass helps shade the soil and reduce soil drying.

Use the right mower. Reel mowers are best for close cutting, but they can't handle grass taller than four inches or grasses such as Bahia and saint augustine, which send up tall seed heads. They also have a hard time cutting tough grasses such as rye. Rotary mowers will handle high grass and weeds, but won't cut evenly at heights of one inch or lower. Rotary blades also need frequent sharpening—about once a month—to perform well.

MOWING HEIGHTS FOR COMMON GRASSES

A general rule of thumb is to mow when the grass grows from one-quarter to one-third taller than its mowing height. Then mow down to the proper height, as shown in the table below.

Grass	Mowing Height (in inches)
Bahia grass	2-3
Bent grass	¼-1
Bermuda grass	½-1½
Bluegrass, common	2½
Bluegrass, improved	¾-1½
Buffalo grass	1½-3
Carpet grass	1-2
Centipede grass	1½-2
Dichondra	½-1½
Fescue, red and tall	2-3
Ryegrass, annual and perennial	1½-2½
Saint augustine grass	1-2½
Zoysia	½-1½

ACHIEVING AND MAINTAINING A HEALTHY LAWN

A healthy lawn should have a minimum of pests, weeds and diseases, with maximum grass growth. Follow these steps to achieve and maintain a healthy lawn.

Take care of the nutritional needs of your soil. Have your soil tested by your local Cooperative Extension Service or a reputable soil testing firm. The test results will dictate what steps you should take to get your soil up to par. (For more information about soil tests, see "Creating Healthy Soil" and "Translating a Soil Test" in chapter 8.)

Make sure your soil is well-drained and aerated. This allows water and oxygen to move down into the root zone to help produce strong, healthy grass roots. Organic fertilizers will help prevent compacted soil and the leaching of nutrients while increasing the soil's ability to retain water.

Plant a variety of grass species. When a multispecies lawn is attacked by pests or diseases, only some of the grasses will die off, while the resistant varieties will survive and continue to provide healthy cover. Check with

---

SHOULD LAWN CLIPPINGS BE REMOVED?

What's the best way to handle grass clippings? Bag, mulch or leave them on the lawn? Horticulturists at the University of Illinois decided to find out by testing a mulching mower against a conventional rotary mower and a bagging mower. Mowing at intervals from twice a week to once every other week, researchers found that turf quality was best when the grass was mowed with the conventional mower and the clippings were left on the lawn. The problem with the mulching mower was that the chopped-up clippings tended to clump together, especially when the grass was high. (This clumped grass will not sift down and decompose—instead, it may mat on top and suffocate the grass underneath.) The researchers also found that weeds were worse when the clippings were removed and no nitrogen was added to the lawn.

SOURCE: *Rodale's Organic Gardening* magazine, August 1985.

---

your local Cooperative Extension Service to find out which varieties do best in your locale.

Even lawns that have the best start can be damaged by improper watering. Frequent light applications simply saturate the upper soil, resulting in weak, shallow roots. Water should be applied slowly and at infrequent intervals. (See "Watering Established Lawns" earlier in this chapter.)

Frequent light mowings cause less stress to grass roots than infrequent heavy mowings. Never remove more than one-third of the leaf area at a time. (See "Mowing Your Lawn the Right Way" earlier in this chapter.)

FERTILIZING YOUR LAWN

In order to keep your lawn looking its best, adequate turf grass nutrition is essential. If your soil isn't in the best of shape, you may find it necessary to apply a complete fertilizer—one that contains nitrogen, phosphorus and potassium. Here's why:

Nitrogen: required in the largest amount, it's responsible for the overall growth and color of grass

Phosphorus: encourages root growth and development

Potassium: enhances the turf's tolerance to extremes in temperature, moisture and wear

---

HOW TO APPLY FERTILIZERS

Follow these tips for proper fertilizer application.

Apply fertilizers evenly. Heavy concentrations result in burn spots on the lawn. To get the most even distribution, use a mechanical spreader rather than spreading by hand.

Use a mechanical spreader. Dry fertilizers can be applied with either a drop-type spreader or a rotary (centrifugal) spreader. A drop-type spreader is good for applying ground limestone.

Rotary spreaders usually cover a larger area with each pass than do drop-type spreaders. However, the fertilizer is more likely to be blown by the wind as it comes out of the rotary spreader, so it becomes more difficult to make a uniform application. Rotary spreaders are good for applying granular lime and sulfur materials.

Make at least two passes over your lawn. Apply half the fertilizer in one direction, then apply the remainder at a right angle to the first application. This helps eliminate the streaks that result from uneven fertilizer application.

But how do you find out which nutrients your soil needs? Start by having your soil tested, then continue to have soil tests every two to three years. (For more information on soil tests, see "Creating Healthy Soil" and "Translating a Soil Test" in chapter 8.) The frequency and rate of fertilization will be determined by the results of your soil test.

Once you've had your test and have chosen your fertilizer, follow the guidelines above for proper application techinques.

FIGHTING LAWN DISEASE

Most lawn diseases are caused by fungi that are spread by wind, water and equipment. Fortunately, not many fungi can actually damage a lawn, although they can be unsightly. Follow these steps to fighting lawn disease.

Avoid overwatering your lawn. Fungi thrive in wet soils. Aerate the lawn periodically to encourage good drainage.

Dispose of grass clippings if you have a fungus problem. Most fungi live on clippings as well as on living grass.

Mow the infected area of the lawn last, then clean the mower blades. Fungi can be spread by equipment.

Plant mixed lawn grasses. Mixed grasses are less susceptible to any one fungus or disease. (See "Achieving and Maintaining a Healthy Lawn" earlier in this chapter.)

REPAIRING SMALL AREAS OF LAWN

It's easy to repair those weedy or bare spots that are keeping your lawn from looking picture perfect. Follow this simple technique recommended by Eliot C. Roberts, as outlined in the March 1986 issue of *Rodale's Organic Gardening* magazine:

1. Dig out any weeds, including their root systems.
2. Loosen the soil with a long-tined fork, spread a one-inch layer of compost on the surface with a metal rake and broadcast grass seed.
3. Rake lightly and cover with a thin layer of straw or salt-marsh hay.
4. Water lightly and frequently to keep newly seeded areas moist.

The grass seedlings may not germinate for 10 or more days, and it can take up to a year for the grass to become fully mature. An alternative to seeding is to lay sod on areas that need repair. Sod is more expensive, but you get immediate results, and it may be the only way to get a thick lawn on a steep slope. To lay sod:

1. Prepare the soil as described above for seeding.
2. Water the soil lightly, then place the sod strips tightly together without stretching them, staggering the ends. If you're sodding a slope, lay the strips lengthwise across the slope. Cut pieces to fit with a hatchet or spade.
3. After all the sod has been laid, fill in any cracks with screened topsoil.
4. Soak thoroughly and water every two or three days for two weeks or until the grass has rooted securely. If the sod shrinks at the ends, top-dress with screened soil and seed with the same grass variety.

Both seeding and sodding have the best chances for succeeding in early spring and fall in the North and in mid-spring to late spring in the South.

DETERMINING WHETHER TO START A NEW LAWN

Although patching an existing lawn is no problem, sometimes the lawn is in such bad shape overall that it's best to start a new one from scratch. You should probably start all over again if:

→ Weeds make up close to 50 percent of your lawn and show no signs of abating.

→ Your lawn browns easily because it was seeded on fill or gravel and thus has poor water-holding capacity.

→ The bare spots are far too numerous to patch individually.

IMPROVING GRASS GROWTH UNDER SHADE TREES

One of the hardest places to keep grass growing strong is under shade trees. Usually you end up with unsightly dirt patches with bits of grass growing through. If this is a familiar problem, start by raking out the area, then follow these steps to improve grass growth.

1. Before sowing grass seed, fertilize well or add five to seven inches of topsoil over shallow tree roots to prevent them from robbing nutrients from the grass.

2. Prune low tree branches to 10 to 15 feet above the ground and trim some limbs from the top of the tree to allow more sunlight to reach the grass below.

3. Be on the lookout for grass that begins to thin out, and plan on reseeding spots each year to maintain good cover under trees.

KEEPING PETS OFF YOUR LAWN

After all the hard work you've done to get your lawn and landscaping looking good, the last thing you want is the neighborhood pets running rampant through your shrubbery. Here's what you can do to deter animal marauders.

Don't leave pet food out all day or overnight. If you feed your own pet outside, take in the dishes and any leftover food. Leftovers are an invitation to area pets and wildlife to come and dine at your place.

Keep trash containers tightly covered. If dogs or raccoons are tipping over your cans and knocking off the lids, you may want to keep the cans inside your house, garage or shed.

Keep trash containers clean when not in use. The odor of uncleaned containers will attract dogs and other animals.

NEW GRASSES FOR WEED, INSECT AND DISEASE RESISTANCE

The new generations of improved lawn grasses can provide a beautiful lawn with a minimum of maintenance. Here's a rundown of what's available.

New proprietary-named grasses have been bred for dense growth. They are the first line of defense against weeds because weeds can't start in turf that has formed a good, dense stand and maintains that stand throughout the growing season.

Insect-resistant cultivars have been developed. Some of these grasses contain endophytes, fungi that make the turf undesirable for insect infestation. The endophytes protect grasses against insects such as the billbug, chinch bug, sod webworm and southern armyworm by producing, or causing the grass plant to produce, repellent or insecticidal compounds. The endophytes do not harm lawn grass in any way and are not harmful to humans or pets. This type of biological control is permanent with the establishment of the sod.

Disease-resistant grasses have been developed. Grass diseases come and go, making control a time-consuming effort. New grasses have been developed for disease resistance and they are far superior to common grass types. Using blends and mixes of lawn grasses with improved resistance will build hardiness and add beauty to your lawn.

For information describing new grasses for weed-, insect- and disease-resistant lawns in your region, send a self-addressed, stamped, legal-size envelope to the Lawn Institute, P.O. Box 108, Pleasant Hill, TN 38578.

Don't feed the neighborhood animals. This includes both wild and domestic animals. Once you start feeding them, they'll never go away.

If a neighbor's pet is giving you problems, talk to your neighbor before you do anything else. Simply request that they restrain their pet from entering your yard—that's usually all that's necessary to stop the animal's wanderings. If the animal has done serious damage to your lawn or landscape and your neighbor is being uncooperative, then it's time to call the police to enforce any pet ordinances.

Consider buying insurance. If you've spent a great deal of money on shrubbery, have it insured, then fence off areas or plants that you want to safeguard.

Trees and Shrubs

You can spend a great deal of money buying trees and shrubbery for your yard, so it's wise to protect that investment. It all starts with careful planning. Once you've chosen your trees and shrubs, you should know how to care for them, from planting to pruning. In this section we'll show you how to plan, choose, plant, prune and more.

PLANNING FOR TREES IN YOUR YARD

Before you buy and plant trees in your yard, there are several factors to consider, beyond those discussed in "Planning to Landscape" earlier in this chapter.

Know where your home's utility systems are located. It's important to know where your water and sewer pipes, septic system and underground utility lines are. Tree roots that grow into or around one of these systems can wreak havoc.

Locate overhead utility lines. If you avoid planting too close to overhead lines, you save yourself the headache of pruning as the tree grows.

Know the contours of your property, especially where the low spots are. A tree that sits in a constant puddle of water will not thrive.

Think about the future. Do you plan to have a swimming pool, patio or addition to the house someday? If so, plant your trees accordingly—don't put them in places they'll have to be moved from later.

Keep clear of construction areas. If you're planting trees on a lot that doesn't have a house on it yet, or if your house is still under construction, make sure you keep trees out of the path of construction equipment.

CHOOSING TREES FOR YOUR YARD

Although looks and price contribute to the appeal of certain trees for the yard, there are other considerations to be weighed before you make your final decision. Ask yourself these questions:

Purpose: Is the tree for shade or beauty? Will it be part of a screen of trees for privacy or will it be used for wind or noise control?

Hardiness: Will it survive dry spells, poor soil and/or rough winter winds?

Pest and disease resistance: Will it stand up to insects and resist most diseases?

Neatness: Will the tree stay relatively neat or will it litter your yard with blossoms, fruit, nuts, cones, seeds or bark, as well as leaves?

Root habits: Will its roots compete with grass growth?

Mature size: Will the tree eventually be too big or too small for your yard?

Shape: Do you want a tree that's rounded, pyramidal, upright, spreading or weeping?

Colors: Do you want colorful leaves in autumn and/or colorful blossoms in spring?

Budding: Do you want all the trees on your property to bud at the same time in spring?

BUYING AND PLANTING BALLED-AND-BURLAPPED TREES AND SHRUBS

Here are some things to keep in mind when choosing and working with balled-and-burlapped plantings.

Look for a firm, well-tied ball. Don't buy a tree or shrub whose root ball is cracked, crumbly, loose or dried out.

When picking up the plant, never use the trunk as a handle. Instead, cradle the root ball with one hand supporting the bottom, or get someone to help you carry it in a sling of canvas or burlap.

When planting, dig a hole six inches wider and six inches deeper than the root ball. For trees with trunk diameters of four inches or more, and for large shrubs with a root ball of three feet or more, the hole should be up to two feet wider than the root ball, but still just six inches deeper.

The root ball should be planted so that its top is level with the surrounding ground. At the same time, the root ball must be at the same depth as it was when growing in the nursery. Never plant it at a depth lower than it grew before. Fill the bottom of the hole with enough soil to bring the root ball to the proper depth.

Place the tree or shrub in the hole with the burlap intact. The fabric will eventually decompose.

Support large trees. Only trees taller than eight feet or with trunk diameters of more than six inches need to be supported (with wire, stakes or guys).

TRANSPLANTING TREES

If you want to move a tree, be forewarned that the transplant may not be successful. It's best to move only very young trees—they have a better chance of surviving and thriving.

Evergreen trees should be transplanted between growth blushes. In the North, this means after the new spring growth has hardened in late summer or fall. In the South, it is any time when the evergreen is not putting out new growth.

Deciduous trees should be transplanted only when they are dormant. The best times for planting are in the fall after the first frost but before the ground freezes and in spring after the ground thaws but before the leaves appear.

Prune the roots several months to a year before the actual move. This helps prepare the tree for transplanting. To prune the roots, drive a spade into the ground in a circle around the tree about 6 to 12 inches from the trunk, cutting through any roots that extend beyond what would be the root ball.

When digging up the tree, leave as much earth on the roots as you can to protect them. Soaking the ground around the tree several days before the move will help the soil cling to the roots.

When moving the tree, try not to handle the root mass too roughly. Any roots larger than ¼ inch thick that have been broken should be trimmed with pruning shears—jagged and damaged ends encourage disease.

Nurserymen use a special balling spade for digging up trees. The spade is longer and narrower than the usual garden spade and helps keep the soil around the roots. If you plan to do a lot of transplanting, you should buy a balling spade and learn how to use it correctly.

Transplanting Evergreens

Follow these steps for transplanting evergreens to produce the least amount of stress on the trees.

1. Tie the branches by attaching rope to the trunk of the tree and winding it over the branches, pulling them in close to the trunk.

2. Dig a deep, spacious trench all around the tree. The object is to retain an unbroken ball of soil with as many undamaged roots as possible. (See the table "Evergreen Root Ball Dimensions" below.)

Evergreen Root Ball Dimensions

Plant Height or Spread (whichever is greater, in inches)	Ball Diameter (in inches)
18-24	12
24-30	14
30-36	16
36-42	18
42-48	20
48-60	22

Source: Reprinted with permission from *Nature's Design* (Rodale Press, 1982).

3. After you've dug below the depth of most roots (which is equal to about three-quarters of the root ball's diameter), undercut the soil to create a ball. Round off the surface close to the trunk and remove any loose soil.

4. Wrap a strip of burlap around the root ball and sew it in place. Gently rock the ball from side to side to break it free and slide another piece of burlap under it. Then sew or tie the burlap to hold the root ball firmly.

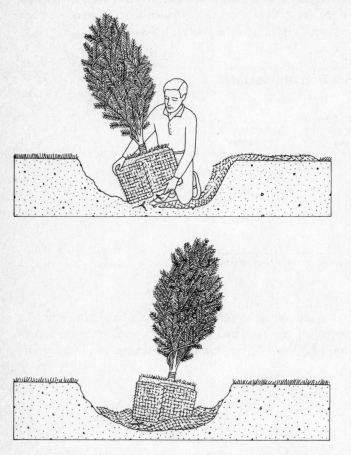

5. Plant your balled-and-burlapped evergreen as outlined in "Transplanting Trees" earlier in this chapter.

Transplanting Deciduous Trees

Follow these steps for transplanting deciduous trees to produce the least amount of stress on them.

1. Tie the branches as described above for evergreens. However, if you dig up the tree while it's dormant, you don't have to tie the branches.

2. Dig a trench around the tree outside of the spread of roots you think you can move. (Because deciduous tree roots spread far, you won't be able to save nearly as many as compared to evergreens.)

3. After you've dug the trench down several spade depths, undercut the roots and remove the soil.

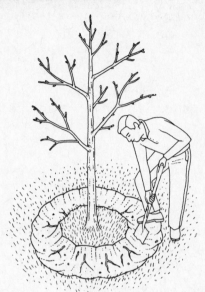

4. With a stick or hand trowel, carefully comb out soil from between the roots. Break the roots free, if they aren't already loose, and lift the tree out of the hole. Wrap the root ball in wet burlap. Keep the roots moist until the tree is replanted—preferably the same day.

PRUNING TREES CORRECTLY

Although it's not necessary to prune your landscape trees, pruning will promote the trees' health and encourage a pleasing shape. But before you rush out there and start chopping away, heed some advice from Jim Ritchie, a contributor to *Trees for the Yard, Orchard, and Woodlot* (Rodale Press, 1976).

Research the tree you plan to prune. Determine its natural form, habit of growth, rate of growth and height at time of flowering. The object here is to familiarize yourself with what the tree should look like naturally so you can prune to help it look its best.

Don't leave short stubs. If you're taking a twig or branch off completely, trim it flush with the main stem instead of leaving stubs. Short stubs don't heal quickly.

Don't prune flowering trees before they flower. Since the buds form the season before, you'll be cutting them off before they have the chance to open.

Cut carefully. When you prune back a branch, cut on an angle and leave a small portion of twig above a bud.

PRUNING TREES IN THE FALL

Fall is the perfect time to prune trees, especially those that "bleed" profusely in spring, such as beech, birch, maple and walnut trees. Other trees commonly pruned in the fall include ash, elm, honey locust and poplar. To prune correctly, you'll need:

> a crescent-shaped pruning saw
> a hooked pruning knife
> hand pruning shears
> long-handled lopping shears
> tree-wound paint

The hand shears are good for cutting branches up to ¾ inch in diameter. The long-handled shears are good for limbs between ¾ and 1¼ inches in diameter and for those limbs beyond the reach of hand shears. For larger limbs, you'll need the crescent saw. After the branch or limb is removed, use the hooked pruning knife to smooth the rough edges around the resulting wound, then protect the area with tree-wound paint.

Saplings

To correctly prune a sapling, remove any upright suckers that appear at the trunk base or along the lower branches. Cut off any branches that grow at narrow angles to the trunk, while retaining those that grow more horizontally.

Single-Leader Trees

To correctly prune a tree with a single leader, first prune away any competitors. Then cut back any out-of-proportion limbs to keep the tree's natural shape.

Older Trees

From time to time, it will be necessary for you to prune away deadwood and overgrowth from older trees. Remove any inward-growing branches. Also be on the lookout for two branches that rub together, inviting injury. Eliminate the less attractive branch.

FEEDING YOUR TREES

To grow healthy and strong, trees need four elements: food, air, water and sunlight. The lack of any one of these could spell disaster for your trees. But how do you know if your trees need help? Check below for a list of some common symptoms of a malnourished tree:

→ The tree loses leaves at the very top (it's dying back).
→ The leaves are off-color when they shouldn't be.
→ Dead limbs are plentiful or readily noticeable.
→ The leaves are smaller than usual.
→ Twig growth is less than normal.
→ The tree has been physically damaged.
→ The tree is overcome by insects or disease.

Once you've determined that your tree needs help, here's what to do.

Feed the tree. Work a mulch of well-rotted manure into the ground over the root zone of small trees in the fall to build up the soil for the winter. For large trees, punch holes at least a foot deep in a circle around the tree at the drip line (the outer edge of the widest branches). Fill the holes approximately two-thirds full with fertilizer, then top off with dirt.

The best time to feed trees is in late fall or in March. Fruit and flowering trees can be fertilized again just after blossoms or fruit appear.

Fertilize when the ground is damp so the nutrients can work their way into the soil and to the roots.

Provide air for the tree. Punch feeding holes in the soil to open pathways for air to flow freely in the root zone. Because trees need air below ground as well as above ground in order to breathe, a good, porous soil is important. Don't trample the ground near the roots with vehicles or heavy foot traffic. When planting a tree, remember not to locate it in a low spot where water will collect and create waterlogged soil.

Water the tree. Give a good soaking to the root system of young trees at least once a week. Very small trees may only need a few pailsful of water each week. Depending on the condition of your soil, you may not have to water older trees between rainfalls. If your soil holds moisture for long periods of time, rainfall will probably be sufficient. Mulch worked into the topsoil will help keep it from drying out. If you do have to water your trees, just remember that a quick sprinkling with the hose won't do any good at all—the soil must be *thoroughly* watered. You may want to turn on the lawn sprinkler to really saturate the root zone.

Provide sunlight for the tree. Keep it away from other trees that could eventually grow to block the light. If you put up a fence or add on to your house, be sure your trees don't end up being shaded for most of the day.

CHOOSING SHRUBBERY
When choosing shrubbery, think about the role it will play in your landscape. Shrubbery can:

> block unsightly views
> divide property into areas for playing, entertaining and gardening
> protect soil from erosion
> provide barriers to noise and wind
> provide privacy
> shelter areas from the sun

Don't forget that while shrubbery performs all these functions, it also adds color and fragrance to your yard.

The easiest way to have virtually maintenance-free shrubbery is to buy shrubs that will grow to fit the space you need to fill. Although it is possible to train a shrub that naturally grows wide and bushy to grow lean and tall, why bother? Buy a shrub that grows lean and tall in the first place, and your maintenance will be minimal. By the same token, don't waste your time making multiple plantings of tall, skinny shrubs to fill a

LOW-MAINTENANCE SHRUBS

The United States Department of Agriculture (USDA) has compiled this list of 40 shrubs that will flourish in their respective zones (see the zone map on page 351). These shrubs were chosen by the USDA because they require little maintenance, are hardy and have few pest problems.

Shrub	Zone	Flower Colors	Flower Season
Alabama fothergilla (*Fothergilla monticola*)	5	White	Mid-May
Aralia (*Acanthopanax sieboldianus*)	4	——	——
Beautybush (*Kolkwitzia amabilis*)	4	Pink	Early June
Bumalda spiraea (*Spiraea ×bumalda*)	5	Crimson	Late June to July
Burning bush (*Euonymus atropurpurea*)	3	——	——
Bush or Shrubby cinquefoil (*Potentilla fruticosa*)	2	Yellow to white	Mid-May to September
Camellia (*Camellia japonica* varieties)	7	White to red	October to April
Chinese hibiscus (*Hibiscus rosa-sinensis*)	9	White, pink, red	Summer
Chinese witch hazel (*Hamamelis mollis*)	5	Yellow	March
Crape myrtle (*Lagerstroemia indica*)	7	Pink to red	August
Forsythia (*Forsythia ×intermedia*)	5	Yellow	Mid-April
Fragrant snowball (*Viburnum ×carlcephalum*)	5	White	Late May
Fringe tree (*Chionanthus virginicus*)	4	White	Early June
Glossy abelia (*Abelia ×grandiflora*)	5	Pink	August
Henry St.-John's-wort (*Hypericum patulum* var. Henryi)	6	Yellow	July
Indian hawthorn (*Raphiolepis indica*)	8	Pinkish	May
Japanese andromeda (*Pieris japonica*)	5	Creamy white	Mid-April
Japanese barberry (*Berberis thunbergii*)	4	Yellow to reddish yellow	Mid-May

(continued)

LOW-MAINTENANCE SHRUBS—*Continued*

Shrub	Zone	Flower Colors	Flower Season
Japanese boxwood (*Buxus microphylla* var. *japonica*)	5	——	——
Japanese holly (*Ilex crenata*)	6	Inconspicuous	Late June
Japanese pittosporum (*Pittosporum tobira*)	8	Creamy white	May
Japanese yew (*Taxus cuspidata*)	4	——	——
Jetbead (*Rhodotypos scandens*)	5	White	Mid-May
Maries double file viburnum (*Viburnum plicatum* var. *tomentosum* 'Mariesii')	4	White	Late May
Mock orange (*Philadelphus coronarius*)	4	White	Early June
Mountain laurel (*Kalmia latifolia*)	4	Pink and white	Mid-June
Oleander (*Nerium oleander*)	7–8	White, yellow to red and purple	April through summer
Pfitzer juniper (*Juniperus chinensis* 'Pfitzerana')	4	——	——
Red chokeberry (*Aronia arbutifolia*)	4	White to red	Late May
Rhododendron and Azalea (*Rhododendron* varieties)	2	Various	April to July
Rose-of-Sharon (*Hibiscus syriacus*)	5	White to blue	August
Rugosa rose (*Rosa rugosa*)	2	Pink to white	Early June
Russian olive (*Elaeagnus angustifolia*)	2	Silver and yellow	Early June
Shining sumac (*Rhus copallina*)	4	Greenish	Early August
Slender deutzia (*Deutzia gracilis*)	4	White	Late May
Strawberry tree (*Arbutus unedo*)	8	White	Winter
Summer-sweet (*Clethra alnifolia*)	3	White	Late July
Tatarian honeysuckle (*Lonicera tatarica*)	3	Pink to white	Late May
Vanhoutte spiraea (*Spiraea* ×*vanhouttei*)	4	White	Late May
Yellow-root (*Xanthorhiza simplicissima*)	4	Brownish purple	Early May

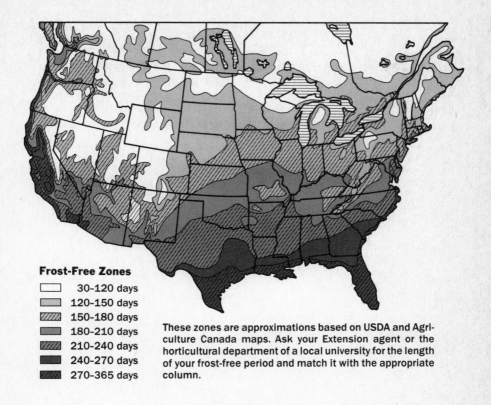

Frost-Free Zones

- 30–120 days
- 120–150 days
- 150–180 days
- 180–210 days
- 210–240 days
- 240–270 days
- 270–365 days

These zones are approximations based on USDA and Agriculture Canada maps. Ask your Extension agent or the horticultural department of a local university for the length of your frost-free period and match it with the appropriate column.

large area when fewer bushy types would fill in even faster. A word of caution: don't place plantings too close to your house if you have wood siding. A bush growing against a wood-sided house can rot the wood.

SHOPPING FOR SHRUBS

As with any other major purchase, shrubbery should be bought after you've done your homework and looked around. Here are some tips for smart shrub shopping.

Comparison shop. Even though most of us wouldn't dream of buying a television or car without comparing prices in our area, many people go to the nearest garden center and pay the asking price for shrubbery. But a bit of comparison shopping may well prove to be a money-saver. Go to several garden centers before you make your choice.

Check the tags. If they're so faded that they're almost illegible, that probably means the shrub has been in its pot for quite a while and may be root-bound. Look for a healthier specimen. If the tags are legible, be sure that, at the very least, they state the common and Latin names of the shrub. It's even better if they also include some cultural information (such as planting information and water and sunlight requirements).

Look for well-branched, symmetrical plants with strong shoots. Don't be fooled by large but weak plants — go for the smaller but more vigorous ones.

Look for leaves with good color. Stay away from plants with yellow, withered or brown-edged leaves, or those with any signs of pests or disease.

Check the roots. You should see a few small roots at the base, but the rest should be covered by soil. Be sure the plant is firmly anchored. Give a gentle tug at the base of the stem to check.

10

Shortcuts to

Planning for Your Later Years

If you're at or reaching retirement age, you should know how important it is to plan for financial, physical and emotional well-being in your later years. In this chapter we'll show you how to make the most of this time in your life, including how to understand your pension plan, check out insurance options, stay healthy and fit, adjust to your retirement and more.

Finances

As you get older you may find that you have several sources of income — perhaps from your employer's pension plan, Social Security and investments. This is also a time in your life to reconsider your insurance needs, as well as plan your estate. Here's how to control your finances wisely.

UNDERSTANDING RETIREMENT INCOME

Plan, understand and keep track of your sources of retirement income. The earlier in your career you begin planning, the more financially secure your retirement will be. Most experts feel that, single or married, planning should begin no later than age 40.

Write to the Social Security Administration. Request Form SSA-7004 (Request for Social Security Statement of Earnings). This is a preaddressed postcard that you fill out and send back in to obtain information on your record of contributions to Social Security. Check the statement for errors.

If errors are not caught and corrected, your benefits may be adversely affected. Errors over three years old may be difficult, if not impossible, to correct.

Consult your company's pension officer. Get periodic updates of your projected monthly retirement income. This will provide you with an accounting of your status in company plans. Keep up-to-date on your projected benefits because company pension plans can alter, affecting your benefits. Be sure to get annual updates starting at least five years before your expected retirement date.

Talk with a financial planner. Every four to six years, meet with a financial planner, perhaps your banker, to review your plans and projections for retirement security. The review can help you decide how to take the best advantage of your growing financial assets and of changing tax laws and benefits.

Create a retirement budget. Each time you meet with your financial planner, work out your total projected monthly income, and estimate your monthly retirement expenditures. Balance the expenses against the projected income. If the income won't be sufficient, the financial planner can give advice on added sources of income.

EVALUATING YOUR COMPANY'S PENSION PLAN

Unlike vacation and sick leave benefits or life insurance programs, a company pension plan is a promise—one that is not always kept. Employees know all about their company's vacation benefits or the amount of life insurance the company carries on them, but too few know much about their pension plans. So that you know what to expect, evaluate your plan periodically—if it falls short of your expectations, you'll want to have time to make plans to supplement it.

Understand the vesting process for the plan. Vesting roughly translates as ownership. If you are partially vested in a plan, you have partial ownership and will be eligible for a portion of the retirement plan's value when you retire. If you are fully vested, you are entitled to full benefits when you retire. Generally, after a certain number of years of service, usually 4, you'll become partially vested in the plan; after 10 years, you become fully vested. But these criteria might be hampered if you had a break-in-service such as a sabbatical or leave of absence. The years before the break might not count in figuring your benefits.

Find out how the pension benefits are figured. Are they based on the past five years' salary level? On all years of full-time employment? Are benefits calculated from a specific date? Again, don't assume. And, because this information can change, keep up-to-date.

Find out what happens to the pension benefits if you die. Not all plans provide for spouses to get the money. In some instances, when filling out forms for retirement, the employee has choices about how to receive the benefits: lump sum, monthly payments to the worker only or benefits with a contingency plan to ensure funds for the spouse, should the retiree die. Many workers assume that pension benefits will continue to be paid out over the lifetime of the remaining spouse, but this is often not the case.

Find out if your plan is portable. Social Security, of course, is portable, but not all private pensions are. Portable pensions are particularly important to workers in manual labor occupations who work for one company, but may switch jobs and unions. For example, a worker might move from a loading dock to the paint department or assembly line and may have a vested interest in the former union's pension plan that she or he doesn't want to lose. Portability may also be a consideration when a transfer, within the same firm, requires moving to another state.

Ask for a copy of the pension plan's tax return, called Form 5500. Your pension plan's Summary Annual Report, required by law, usually doesn't have much information on the fund's assets and liabilities, but Form 5500 does. It should be available for the asking, but it will probably be difficult to understand, so ask your tax advisor or financial planner to help you interpret the figures. Form 5500 can tell you if the cash reserves are low (a bad sign) and if the funds are diversified or not.

Find out what firm is responsible for handling the plan's investments and how those investments have been doing. Check the reputation of the firm charged with the actual fund management. If you can't get accurate information from your pension officer, that's another sign of trouble. From the Summary Annual Report, possibly aided by Form 5500, you should be able to learn how the investments are doing.

Find out if there is a Cost-of-Living Adjustment (COLA) clause. Social Security and military and government pensions include built-in cost-of-living adjustments tied to certain factors in the economy. If your pension plan has no such clause, your pension benefits will remain static while inflation eats away at them.

If you want to retire early, find out what it will do to your benefits. Can you elect to start receiving your pension at a later date when you would receive full benefits? Can you make voluntary contributions to your plan to increase its value?

Talk to a recent retiree. Ask how long it took before the benefits began to arrive and how cooperative the pension officer was in expediting the paperwork and procedure.

CREATING YOUR OWN PENSION PLAN

Pension plans are promises that don't always come true. Too many workers, who contentedly took for granted that their company pension benefits, plus Social Security, would equal financial independence, have found themselves back at work through necessity. Although you can't protect yourself from all of these problems, you can take steps, no matter what your age, to provide for a secure retirement income. If you decide to put together your own pension package, get an expert's advice. Tax laws, state regulations and personal circumstances make every case unique.

Individual Retirement Accounts (IRAs): A prime appeal of IRAs is their tax advantages. Employees can put up to $2,000 a year into an IRA. The amount of your annual contribution that is tax deductible, however, depends on your level of income and your participation in another retirement plan. Nevertheless, earnings on your contributions accumulate tax-free until withdrawn. A third of all workers have taken advantage of IRAs. But even without the tax incentive, IRAs are good investments for retirement security.

Keogh Plans: If you're self-employed or own a small, income-producing business on the side, you can qualify for Keogh Plans. The basic Keogh lets you put away up to 20 percent of your net, self-employed income or $30,000 a year, whichever is smaller. Keogh contributions are tax deductible, providing a tax shelter. Regulations are complicated, and the types of Keoghs and investment possibilities are numerous, so get financial advice before launching one.

401(k): Some employers offer company-sponsored savings plans, the 401(k), which is designed as a source of retirement savings. These plans let you save a portion of your salary and defer it from taxation. Some employers will match your contributions. Check about the limitations and considerations of employer-sponsored programs.

Annuities: Often described as reverse life insurance, annuities are plans you purchase that pay you while you're alive. Purchased as a source of retirement income, annuities can be tailored to your retirement needs, paying you monthly benefits. Insurance companies are the most common providers of annuities, making fixed monthly payments to you and providing some insurance coverage. When you purchase an annuity, you contract to receive a certain monthly payment timed to begin when you retire. The cost of the annuity, which is generally purchased over several years, depends on your age when you begin purchasing it, the age at which you will begin to collect on it and the dollar size of the monthly income you want. Annuities differ from insurance in that you can't borrow against them and there are usually no survivor benefits.

PLANNING FOR YOUR ESTATE

You may be reluctant to think about a time when you won't be around any more, but it's important to put your financial house in order now, while you still have say over who gets what. Here are some tips to help you plan your estate.

Make a will and keep it current. This advice sounds very basic, yet less than half of American adults draw up wills, and many of those who do, don't keep the documents current. If you fail to leave a will, the state in which you die will disperse your estate according to its own formula, which may not be what you want at all. If you don't keep it current, the consequences can be just as dire. And don't settle for a handwritten (holographic) will, it may not be valid.

Some states recognize wills drawn up on a preprinted form—you just fill in the blanks and do not need the services of a lawyer. However, if you use a preprinted form, be sure to fill it out *exactly* using the correct legal language, and have it witnessed properly. For most people, though, creating a will requires the assistance and advice of a lawyer.

Mention everybody in your will, particularly if you have a relative who will inherit nothing from you, but who might make a claim on your estate. For example, if you will not be leaving your nephew anything (for any reason), you might include a line that specifically states you are leaving him nothing, except, perhaps, your affection. This tells your executor and your heirs what your wishes are concerning your nephew. If you fail to mention him, particularly if the estate is large, he might well make a claim against the estate for having been overlooked when you wrote the will, which can tie up settling the finances while his claim is examined.

Name your spouse as beneficiary on at least one life insurance policy. If probate court ties up an estate's assets, the survivor will need money to live on until the estate is settled. The life insurance proceeds will provide the needed funds.

Give money to your children while you're still around. This is one way to reduce the size of an estate. However, check with your tax or financial advisor first. Under some circumstances, the gifts can be considered attempts to decrease an estate's size "in contemplation of death," and might be counted in with the total estate.

Register stock under your and your spouse's names. Label the registration as "joint tenants with rights of survivorship and not as tenants in common." This is one way for modest estates to pass assets outside a will, and thus avoid probate court. Assets such as property and stock that are held under joint tenancy automatically and immediately pass to the surviving spouse. States differ in their probate practices, so get legal advice before settling on this method of ownership.

Periodically reevaluate your will's executor. Naming a family member might work in some families, but it can cause family stress. Family relationships change—the person you picked 10 years ago might be the wrong person today. Naming a friend might be good, but if the friend moves away, becomes ill or isn't interested, change executors. A financial advisor, lawyer or other trusted professional might be adequate, but might retire or change companies.

UNDERSTANDING YOUR INSURANCE OPTIONS

As you get older and your family circumstances shift, your need for life insurance changes, too. Many people tend to keep the protection they've always had and look at insurance as an investment for their survivors. However, life insurance can take on many forms to suit changing needs, particularly for retirees.

Add up your life insurance policies. Do you really need all that protection? People buy life insurance for the ability to borrow against it and to provide for their dependents. As you near retirement, you may not need one or both of these benefits. Talk to your insurance agent about what you do need.

Check your policies' conversion clauses. Some policies are ideally suited for converting to cash (which you can invest) or to an annuity (which pays you cash in periodic installments). Also ask about policies for which you pay premiums until you retire, but not afterward.

If you plan ahead for retirement, look at universal life insurance. With universal life, part of your premium pays for life insurance protection while the other part goes into an interest-bearing savings account.

PLANNING FOR YOUR RETIREMENT

If you are presently thinking about retirement, or in the early planning stages, here are some ways to gather good information about retirement.

Interview former coworkers and friends who have retired. Ask them how they planned for their retirement and if their plans are working out. If they had it to do again, what would they do differently?

Attend your company's preretirement planning seminars. If your company doesn't offer such a program, encourage the company officers to provide it. These sessions are valuable not only for what you learn during the meetings, but for the lists of additional resources they generally provide. Your pension officer should be able to supply you with the names and phone numbers of groups offering local seminars. Adult education classes and community-college courses may also offer this information.

Start your own retirement research at your local library. There are plenty of books covering every aspect of retirement planning, from how to rate locations across the country and abroad, to complex estate planning guides and investor's handbooks. Notices of senior citizens' meetings are also posted on most library bulletin boards, so check there as well.

Contact local chapters of retirement organizations. Local groups keep lists of useful information that they are usually happy to pass on. The American Association of Retired Persons (AARP) has a very large membership of men and women over age 50, has a network of state and local groups and provides magazines, newsletters, seminars and services to its members. For more information, write to AARP, 1909 K Street NW, Washington, DC 20006.

Health and Happiness

As you enter your later years, you have a lot to look forward to—travel, more time with your spouse, the chance to pick up on old hobbies or learn new skills—the list is almost endless. But in order to take advantage of the leisurely pace, you should be in the best possible physical shape. In this section we'll show you how to stay healthy and fit, adjust to your retirement, rekindle your marriage and more.

STAYING HEALTHY AND FIT

You're not getting older—you're getting better. But to make the most of your later years, you should be sure to stay in shape. Here's how.

Manage stress. Retirement has its stressful side. Adjusting causes stress, aging causes stress, worrying about finances causes stress and changing family relationships causes stress, too. A new phenomenon for today's retiring generation is aged parents. This catches many newly retired men and women in the middle—aging parents to care for on one side and adult children who also have demands on the other. Methods of managing stress include taking time to put the demands on your life in perspective so you can better understand your feelings; doing something physical such as a brisk walk, a swim or a game of golf and talking with your spouse and other family members about the pressures you face.

Be active and watch your diet. As the body ages, it seems to get harder each year to exercise properly, turn down an extra piece of chocolate cake or keep a normal routine. However, most experts agree that even though it's harder, it's important to a healthy future to keep active and eat moderately.

Relax. Take it easy, but don't make relaxing your full-time occupation. Schedule your time so that you leave daily periods for relaxation, but schedule action time, too. The schedule doesn't need to be rigid, just an outline that can be helpful. For example, in the summer, midday may be uncomfortably hot, so schedule a quiet period for reading and catching up on your correspondence from noon until 2:00 P.M. If you're a real morning person, take a brisk daily walk before breakfast. If you love the calming effect dusk has on you, spend that time listening to music.

Conduct a home safety check. Home accidents are a particular problem for senior citizens, so be sure your home is as safe as possible. A common home accident is a fall caused by a loose rug or slippery bathroom floor. Other injuries occur while getting in and out of the bathtub. If you live alone and worry about a home accident or about becoming ill, check with your local senior citizens' groups for information on telephone check-in programs. With such programs, if you don't check in daily by a certain time, someone will visit you immediately.

Preserve your health. In order to have a more enjoyable retirement, take steps to keep your body in top form. Be particularly concerned with these three aspects of your health: vision, hearing and hypertension.

According to the American Optometric Association, you should have your eyes examined no less than once every two years. Wear sunglasses when outdoors on bright or sunny days. Exposure to small amounts of one type of radiation, over many years, can cause cataracts, and another type of radiation can cause serious damage to the retina—the delicate seeing mechanism inside the eye. The lenses of your sunglasses should be dark enough to screen out 75 to 90 percent of the available light. Medium-gray or dark-gray are good lens colors because they do not modify the colors of the objects you see.

Oftentimes, poor hearing is misdiagnosed as senility. Have your hearing checked more frequently as you get older, and guard against prolonged exposure to loud noise.

According to the latest figures, nearly 60 million Americans have hypertension, with perhaps 40 percent of them over the age of 64. Unfortunately, many people on medication for high blood pressure do not have their disease under control because they fail to take their medicine properly or they stop taking it altogether. If you're taking medication for hypertension, be sure you're taking it correctly. If you've never been tested for hypertension, ask your doctor to do so during your next physical examination.

Reevaluate your eating habits. Some researchers are convinced that many elderly persons are malnourished because their food no longer tastes or smells as enticing as it did when they were younger. Our senses of taste and smell tend to diminish as we grow older. The typical 20-year-old, for example, has at least twice as many taste buds as the average 75-year-old. Without the sense of smell working in conjunction with the sense of taste, food loses its flavor. Some people don't get the nutrients they need because their appetites are impaired by certain types of medication. Often, antirheumatic and antimicrobial drugs, as well as diuretics, tend to dull the appetite.

Try to eat a balanced diet, even if your food no longer tastes as appealing as it once did. If you think some medications you are taking may be suppressing your appetite, speak with your doctor about it.

UNDERSTANDING SENILITY

For many middle-aged and older people the fear of losing their mental faculties is probably greater than their fear of cancer. In Robin Henig's book, *The Myth of Senility* (Farrar, Straus & Giroux, 1986), she contends that so-called senile behavior can be created when physicians, families and old people themselves expect senility to be inevitable with age. The majority of people do not "go senile" no matter how long they live. Only two mental functions tend to show a gradual decline with age — speed of response and memory.

Many symptoms that mimic senile dementia are caused by ailments that are reversible. These include anemia, high blood pressure, excessive medication, depression, vitamin deficiency or a heart attack. As many as 100 physical disorders can cause symptoms that would respond to treatment if properly diagnosed; unfortunately these are often just diagnosed as senile dementia, with tragic consequences.

One must recognize, of course, that some forms of senile dementia are not myths but cruel facts of life. Progress has been slow in finding a cure for senility, including Alzheimer's disease, but, in the meantime, the most valuable thing that can be done for victims of senility is to find those functions that remain intact and to encourage the use of those functions for as long as possible.

ADJUSTING TO YOUR RETIREMENT

Married or single, retirement brings with it a host of changes, the most important being a major alteration in your status, not only among your peers, but at home, too. Adjusting to retirement doesn't happen overnight—it takes time and planning. To make the transition easier, here are some things to consider.

Decide who's retiring. When one spouse retires from a job, what about the other spouse? Traditionally, the husband retires, but the wife continues as before. This one-sided approach is giving way to joint retirement planning so both spouses can benefit from the change in life patterns created by retirement.

Consider new "rules" for the home front. An old adage declares: She married him, for better or worse, but not for lunch. If it's the husband who retires, he may feel—and she may feel—that he's an intruder in his own house, someone who interrupts her routines, makes new demands and isn't as helpful around the house as she had hoped. The key is to talk about the changes in life around the house beforehand—it will make adjusting to retirement smoother for both of you.

Face the fact that the transition to retirement can be a period of depression. Work is a major source of status; without a job to go to, that status no longer exists. Even if you think it won't happen to you, the chances are high that you'll discover the ups and downs quickly. Easing into retirement can help. For example, if you're nearing retirement and have amassed a large pool of vacation time, ask your personnel officer if you can begin to work part-time, or three weeks per month. Once you get used to having more time for yourself (and your spouse), you'll begin to learn how to refocus your energies—an important part of a successful retirement.

If you're planning a "single" retirement, your need for a support group will be important. The group can center around any activity or cause that's of interest to you. Join before you retire so when you leave work you're "connected" to others. Remember, you don't retire "from" something, as much as you retire "to" a new phase of your life.

Set aside a special time each day to share with your spouse how you're feeling about your retirement. Pick the same time for your daily talks, unplug the phone, turn off the television and talk (listen, too). When you both share your feelings, it will help each of you to better understand the emotional changes the other is experiencing. It also helps bring couples closer—it may have been many years since you talked so openly about your feelings.

Don't say "yes" to everything. Be discriminating about how you spend your new-found time. One retirement trap is saying yes to all those groups and organizations you always said you'd help once you retire. Be picky.

CONSIDERING A RETIREMENT ALTERNATIVE: WORK

Retirement is the beginning of a new career for many. As the lure of early retirement appeals to more workers, and because people are living longer and healthier lives, retirement can be the time to finally try out those dreams of doing something special. Do a little investigating in your community to learn what's available. And don't forget the numerous programs for older persons managed by the federal government, which range from foster grandparent programs to the Peace Corps. For locally run, federally funded programs, or locally organized projects, contact your community's social or human services office, or senior citizen and volunteer hotlines. For information on the Peace Corps, VISTA (Volunteers In Service To America) and RSVP (Retired Senior Volunteer Program), write to Action, Washington, DC 20525.

Consider working at something new. This can help supplement your Social Security and pension benefits. You don't have to remain in the same career, so look around. Local senior citizens' agencies and organizations can provide helpful information including "Over 60 Counseling" offices. Just keep in mind that if you work in retirement, you can lose some of your Social Security benefits. Under the 1983 law, for every $2 you earn, you will lose $1 in benefits if you earn over a certain amount. In 1989, you will lose $1 in benefits for every $3 you earn over the limit. Check with your local Social Security office to see how this will affect your benefits.

Work around your neighborhood. Local schools need tutors, substitute teachers and aides. This is a great way to share your knowledge with children who would love having regular contact with a member of an older generation. Make a list of local businesses a short distance from your home—your skills might fit in perfectly. Ask your local library about part-time help. Check with your church. Consider politics—retired men and women have the time to devote to local elections and community service.

Work for free—volunteer. The skills and knowledge you have gained over a lifetime can be shared with scouting and youth organizations. Or give your time to a cause you have always felt strongly about. Some communities operate volunteer programs that try to match the volunteer to the right activity.

Work overseas. The federal government's ACTION program operates the Peace Corps, which welcomes older Americans to work in developing countries. Business and religious groups also operate offices overseas.

REKINDLING YOUR MARRIAGE

Retirement can be a surprise for both spouses, even if it's well-planned. Why? Because the husband and wife usually have aimed their lives in separate directions—his was his work, hers was her work. In retirement, couples often find they share little in common, and coping with a partner's demands can be traumatic. Dr. Jan Jones Sarpa, a private psychologist in Washington, D.C., who specializes in counseling women and couples, offers four good ways to put the spark back into marriage.

Find a physical activity that you both like. If it's golf, take lessons. If you've always wanted to ride bikes, get a pair of sturdy bikes and invest in safety helmets. If it's walking, get comfortable shoes. Studies show that men and women who exercise for 30 minutes three times a week can increase their energy levels and flexibility, and improve their mental and physical health. Exercising is good fun and a nice way to do something together.

Rediscover the "good old days." Talk about the things that attracted the two of you when you first started dating. What were some of the special things you did? Chances are you have long forgotten that you used to go dancing every Friday night, or went to the movies, or for walks or to the ice-cream parlor. Retirement is the time to do these special things again.

Touch each other. "Couples entering retirement have often grown apart sexually," says Dr. Sarpa. "One easy, nonthreatening exercise to help marriage partners become reacquainted is touching from the shoulders up, for 10 minutes. We often don't really look at our spouse. With this simple exercise you rub, touch and pat your partner's shoulders, neck and face and really look into your partner's eyes. You can continue the exercise on the limbs; it's not meant to be intimate, just a pleasant way to make contact."

Join a group. Local YMCAs, church and community organizations and hospitals sponsor discussion groups. If you've never been interested in belonging to groups, retirement is the time to widen your circle of activities, and a discussion group about marriage or retirement's demands would be a good place to start. You'll meet new people who are facing similar challenges in their lives, people with whom you can share experiences and feelings.

DECIDING WHETHER TO MOVE OR STAY PUT

The majority of Americans who retire stay put. They keep their familiar home and routines, surrounded by friendly faces and a comforting, long-established service network. But whether you choose to stay in your community or move away, there are options to explore before making any long-term commitments.

If you decide to stay in your home, there may be ways to cash in on this dormant investment. A variety of programs, some specially designed for older homeowners, can provide cash or tax advantages. For example, under a typical sale-leaseback arrangement, you sell the house and get the right to rent it for the rest of your life. Plus, you might qualify for the one-time $125,000 tax exclusion on the capital gain from the sale of the house. The buyer, often one or more of your children, usually becomes responsible for insurance, taxes and upkeep. There are other inventive programs that may help you tap into your house's capital; check with a financial advisor to find out what options you have.

If you like your community but are tired of maintaining a larger house than you need, you'll probably have several options—a smaller home or an apartment, a condominium or a cooperative. But don't sign a contract until you have experienced living in a more confined space first. You may discover that living in an apartment building with tenants above you reminds you of having children trampling around upstairs. Or you may miss your own backyard and private garage. Check into all the present and future costs of condominiums and cooperatives—extra expenses such as monthly "tenants" or "homeowners" association fees can rise with inflation.

If you want to move within your community, take a hard look at your present neighborhood. Ask yourself this question: Are home values relatively stagnant? If they are, look in healthier housing markets where your property value will appreciate. With the profits from your home's sale, you can probably purchase a smaller home or condominium that will appreciate in value, plus leave you money left over to invest.

If you want to move away, don't do it on a whim; make your move based on careful research. If you've always dreamed of living in some exotic spot, retirement gives you the chance to experience it. Rent an apartment for a few months at the best *and* worst times of the year. Renting at different times of the year will give you the opportunity to check out the weather as well as the local services, medical care, organizations, neighborhoods and the cost of living, plus you can begin to make new friends.

If you think life in a retirement community might be for you, ask about a short-term rental in the community that appeals to you, before you buy. Many communities will be happy to rent if you're a prospective resident. The same things that attract new retirees to these communities also quickly drive some away—rules and regulations, planned activities every day and the absence of children and young adults in the neighborhood.

If you want to retire to a foreign country, keep in mind that it can be tricky, but rewarding. Social Security checks can be mailed abroad, but Medicare benefits don't apply. What you might save in lower housing or living expenses can be eaten up in transportation to visit the grandchildren in the United States and in high telephone bills. Taxes, residency status and your legal rights abroad depend on where you're planning to live. Check it out thoroughly with both governments before you move. Contact the Social Security Administration for information on receiving your check abroad and the Internal Revenue Service about your tax status in the United States while living abroad. Contact the other country's United States-based embassy or consulate for information on foreign taxes, property ownership, residency requirements and the amount of money you can bring with you or earn there.

11

Shortcuts to

Hassle-Free Traveling

Travel should be a joy, not a headache. Whether you're going just an hour or two away from home or visiting another country, going away on business or taking the family along, we'll show you how to best arrange for your trip. In this chapter you'll find useful travel advice—from dealing with travel agents to packing tips—plus we'll show you how to make the most of group travel, cruises and country vacations.

Arrangements

Sometimes the most trying part of traveling is all the arrangements that must be made. In this section we'll show you how to get your trip off to a good start with careful arrangements.

DEALING WITH A TRAVEL AGENT

Travel agents can save you planning and travel time, often find the best bargains and lowest airfares and, best of all, often have firsthand knowledge of your destination. Usually their fees are paid by the hotels, airlines and tour companies, not by you. Here are tips to help you get the most from an agent.

Look for an agent with knowledge of your destination. Travel agents frequently specialize—some are experts in cruises, European trips or exotic adventures. Find someone who is familiar with where you want to go.

Find out what extra charges an agent can bill you for. Services such as writing a letter to request an overseas hotel room, altering reservations and canceling tickets are generally not free.

Don't take your checkbook along for the first meeting with the agent. The first meeting should be a get-acquainted session. You should think over any plans you make. Don't decide on the spot to do what the agent suggests—sleep on it.

Don't let an agent push you toward a particular tour package or cruise if it's not exactly what you want. Tour operators, airlines and cruise ship companies often stage promotions for travel agents—if an agent sells a certain number of trips, she or he gets a free vacation.

HUNTING DOWN THE LOWEST AIRFARE

Even travel agents have a hard time keeping track of the endless number of airfares and changing discounts, so you can't assume they will get you the lowest-priced ticket available. Although it takes some legwork, if you want to locate the lowest fare, here's what you can do.

Do the research yourself. Travel agents, who receive payments from airlines based on the number and amount of tickets sold, will usually try to be helpful but might not always be able (or willing) to get you the lowest price. Take time to do the phone work yourself.

Call twice to each airline that flies to your destination. Don't settle for what one representative quotes; call a second agent. You're likely to discover that each quotes you a different fare for the same trip—even if you ask them both for the lowest price possible.

Avoid changing airlines in midtrip. Fly as directly as possible, or at least try to use the same carrier for connecting flights.

Avoid high traffic times. These are early mornings, late afternoons and Fridays. Ask the reservation agent if the airline offers lower fares for off-peak travel.

Make your reservations as far ahead as possible. Lower fares are often available if reservations are made 14, 21 and 30 days ahead of the trip. But make sure your plans are firm before you reserve your ticket—there is usually a penalty for canceling or changing your flight for these discount, book-ahead fares.

Travel off-season. Prices for accommodations and airfares usually drop for off-season travel.

Join a discount-travel club. Several travel clubs offer very low prices for airfares, charters and cruises, but they charge an annual fee that can be as high as $50 per family. Travelers need to be flexible because these groups often purchase tickets only 21 days before a trip is to depart—when the carrier or operator sells the remaining seats to a discount club for a low price in order to fill seats—leaving little time for you to prepare for your trip. Look in your newspaper's travel section for ads and information about discount clubs.

PREPARING FOR SMOOTH FLIGHTS WITH CHILDREN

Flying with children doesn't have to be an ordeal. Follow these suggestions to smooth flying.

Request a front-row seat. When making flight reservations, tell the agent you are traveling with children and want seats with the most room in front of them. This is usually the first row of seats in each travel class.

Request an empty seat next to yours. If you're traveling with an infant, let the ticket agent know, and ask if the seat next to yours can be left unoccupied. If the flight isn't filled, you may be able to use the empty seat for your baby.

Order special meals. Most airlines offer meals for children. With a few days' notice, at no extra charge, your children can enjoy dishes such as hot dogs, fried chicken or spaghetti.

Ask for some diversions for the kids. Ask the flight attendant if she or he has special coloring books, airline wings or other flight items for children. Ask at the beginning of the flight because the crew is busy and may forget to pass out these items until the end of the trip. (Decks of cards are sometimes available, too.)

Pack a small surprise for each child, such as a small notebook. Once under way, surprise each child and ask her or him to keep a "Captain's Log" of the flight.

CHOOSING THE RIGHT LUGGAGE

No one wants to lug around more suitcases than are necessary, and no one wants to have her or his luggage fall apart at the airport baggage terminal or out on the sidewalk! You can avoid these travelers' pitfalls by heeding this advice.

Travel light. Select only what you can manage by yourself. The piece or pieces you take shouldn't be too heavy for you to carry or so bulky that you can't get on a bus or train with them. Walk around the store with the pieces you want to buy. If it's hard to pull the suitcase on wheels while holding your purse and a garment bag, look for alternative luggage. Remember: at most customs locations it is almost impossible to get help with baggage. Train and bus travel are also difficult with bulky luggage.

Look for built-in wheels on midsize and larger suitcases. Be sure the wheels are sturdy and securely fastened to the body of the suitcase. The pull-strap (leash) should be detachable so it can be removed when you check the baggage. The strap should also be made of a strong material; straps that aren't strong can break during use. (To prevent problems from broken pull-straps, carry an old leather belt that you can use as a substitute in an emergency.) Look at the size of the wheels—small, rubber-covered wheels will wear out quickly. Look for large, sturdy ones. As nice as they are, wheels can sometimes be a problem. They can be hard to roll, particularly over rough sidewalks where they can get stuck, and suitcases with wheels can be hard to steer.

Consider purchasing a fold-up luggage cart. This is particularly useful if you travel alone or need your hands free to tend to children. Carts are easy to store, even on an airplane, and are especially helpful when going through customs, where you're usually completely on your own.

Check on size and weight requirements. If you do a lot of international flying, make sure the baggage you're buying meets the carrier's size and weight requirements, otherwise you could be charged for excess luggage.

Look for handles that are padded, comfortable to grip and sturdily attached. To see how a suitcase will feel when it's full, put a smaller one inside the case you're considering buying; this will give it bulk and weight. Carry it around the store for a few minutes, then put it down. If it was comfortable to carry around, it's probably right for you.

Look for garment bags made of sturdy, tear-resistant fabric. Stay away from lightweight plastics that rip easily. Even if you carry your garment bag with you in the trunk of your car or carry it onto a train or plane, it still takes a beating. Look for these features when buying a bag:

> easy-to-clean fabric
> a front zipper that can be locked
> outside pockets that have lockable closings
> a padded carrying handle that protects your hand from the hangers
> wide and sturdily attached shoulder straps

Consider buying hard-sided luggage. Soft-sided suitcases are lightweight, easy to carry and pull and a little easier to wedge into a car's trunk than hard-sided ones. The drawback, however, is that rough handling can damage them more readily than it will harder-sided suitcases.

If you like to shop on trips, buy an extra, lightweight bag that folds up into a small square. Some actually come in a handy little pouch. Pack this along with your clothes so you'll have an extra suitcase for all those souvenirs you pick up along the way.

Purchase a luggage strap for each suitcase you plan to ship in the baggage compartment. These wide, heavy-duty straps wrap completely around a suitcase. The strap will cover the locks to help discourage theft, hold the suitcase closed should a lock break due to rough handling and make your case easy to identify.

Once you've purchased your luggage, mark it. Think up a unique identifying mark—a brightly colored piece of yarn tied securely to each handle or a six-inch length of metallic tape affixed to one corner of each bag. The same mark should be on all pieces. When your bags appear on an airline's conveyor belt, the mark will save you time in identifying them.

PACKING EFFICIENTLY

Many of us dread packing. Trying to figure out what, and how much, clothing to bring; what to do with all the heavy shoes and how to protect delicate items—all in all, it's a real chore. But here are some tips that will make you an efficient packer in no time.

Coordinate your wardrobe. Mix-and-match separates in which several items have multiple uses can save suitcase space and weight.

Limit the number of shoes you take along. Shoes are heavy to carry, so take only what you will need, including your most comfortable walking shoes and only one pair of dress shoes. You may not even need your slippers, and *never* pack a new pair of shoes—you don't need the agony of breaking them in on a trip.

Start packing with the heaviest items (shoes) on the bottom at the back of the suitcase. Pack shoes in plastic bags (so any dirt or shoe polish won't rub off on clothes), then pack heavier items such as jeans and slacks. Add the other items on top.

Alternately, you can pack in layers, making it easier to find things. Purchase a box of medium-sized, white plastic trash can liners. Put a bag in the suitcase before you start packing, and then add the shoes and other heavy items. Cover this bottom layer with another bag. Cover that with the slacks, shorts and shirts. Add another bag and pack the underwear.

To find your favorite shorts, lift out the top few layers, using the white "layer markers," and you won't mess up the entire suitcase for just one item. The bags double as laundry and storage bags.

Tuck small, fragile items, such as your travel alarm clock or small flashlight, into your shoes. The shoes, wrapped in bags, act as cushions.

Avoid packing hard-to-care-for clothes, such as items made from linen and other dry-clean-only fabrics. Although silk may be hand-washed, you may not be happy with the resulting crinkly look. Hand-wash a silk item at home first to see whether you really want to take it along.

Pack an aerosol can of antistatic spray. Wash-and-wear clothing often contains synthetic fibers that can cling to the body.

Don't pack jewelry in baggage you will check. You should never carry valuable jewelry on vacation, but pack what jewelry you do take into a small jewelry bag. Put it on the bottom of your purse or carry-on bag so that you have it with you, and not in your checked baggage.

Allow kids to pack for themselves, but first give them guidelines. Explain to your children what they can each take (for example, three pairs of slacks, six pairs of socks, and so on), and let them get it ready. Have them put the clothing on their beds for you to inspect, and then let them pack it in their own suitcases. This is a good way to let children know they're part of the "getting ready" process, too.

Check out the climate of your destination beforehand. Your travel agent or the hotel manager at your vacation site can tell you what the climate of your vacation spot will be like—don't assume you know. Ask about the temperature during the day and night, the humidity and the amount of sunshine and rainfall. This will be a great help in determining what clothing to bring.

Carry a small piece of hand luggage if the trip will last more than a few days. An old-fashioned, square train case is fine; a flight bag is not as sturdy, but good, too. In addition to your toiletries and other small and frequently needed items, put in a small container with enough detergent for one load of laundry. Wrap the container in a sealable, plastic bag. Before closing the luggage, put an old, folded-up towel on top of the contents. Should any bottle open, the towel will absorb most of the liquid; if a hairdryer is in the case, the towel will also act as a cushion to protect against rough handling.

Pack things to help you pass the time if there's a delay. Some good items to have on hand are a book, deck of cards, crossword puzzle collection and some food.

PROTECTING YOUR VALUABLES

Whenever you travel, you carry along things of value—your clothing, accessories, photo and movie equipment, even your baggage. Separately, each item may not seem valuable, but if lost or stolen, their combined cost would add up. You can protect yourself against losses, but you must plan ahead and be careful while traveling.

Never carry much cash. Bring internationally accepted traveler's checks instead. Make two lists of the check numbers—leave one copy of the list with a friend and pack the other copy in the back of a suitcase.

Purchase a combination of $50 and $100 traveler's checks if your trip is overseas. If you pick smaller amounts, you may wind up spending a lot of time trying to locate places to convert them into currency, and you pay a premium each time you change currency.

Carry one credit card that is accepted in the area of your travels. Be sure the card can be used for a line of credit should you run short of funds. Before leaving on your trip, sort through all the other cards in your wallet. Take only what you might need—don't take credit cards good for local department stores or several gas credit cards. Stash the cards you don't take in a safe place, such as your safe-deposit box.

Carry anything of value (money, traveler's checks, passports) in money belts. Those that you wear around your waist are the most common, but there are other kinds, too, such as those that buckle around your shin, hidden by a pants leg. Pickpockets often find distracted tourists easy prey. And several European cities have developed reputations for problems with Gypsy children who, in groups of twos and threes, set upon travelers. These ragamuffin kids shove pieces of cardboard into your waist and as you try to push them away, they pick your pockets and your purse.

Check your insurance policy before you leave. See how much personal property protection you have for your clothes, baggage and camera equipment, should they be lost or stolen. Your homeowner's insurance policy usually provides some coverage while you're away from home. But if your trip includes staying in a hotel overseas, added insurance might be a good idea.

Check the airline's policy on lost baggage reimbursement. If, between the airlines and your private insurance, you feel underinsured, you can purchase additional personal property insurance protection from your insurance or travel agent. Some insurance companies have representatives selling travel insurance right at the airport.

If you carry a shoulder purse, use one that has a strap long enough to go around your neck and your shoulder. Straps hung from just the shoulder can be quickly snatched away.

Leave home any photography and video equipment that isn't essential. Cameras and video equipment are heavy and bulky to carry, not to mention attractive to thieves.

PLANNING TRIPS FOR SENIORS

Travel at any age is rewarding. To help you get the most from your vacation if you're a senior citizen, the U.S. Department of State offers several tips in its booklet *Travel Tips for Senior Citizens* (U.S. Department of State, Bureau of Consular Affairs, Publication 8970, Washington, DC 20520).

Learn about the countries you plan to visit. You'll get more out of the trip if you have some knowledge about the culture, history and scenic beauty you'll encounter.

Purchase trip insurance. Trip insurance, sold through travel and insurance agencies, protects you from losing your money should you change your vacation plans before, or during, your vacation. For example, if you have prepaid your hotel and transportation fees and then must change your plans due to an emergency, the tour operator might not refund your money. Trip insurance can cover all or most of these costs. Some policies also cover transportation home should you change your plans due to an emergency in the middle of the trip. Since coverage can vary, read the policy carefully before purchasing this insurance.

Be aware that Medicare does not provide payment for hospital and medical services outside the United States. Some health plans, such as those run by certain health maintenance organizations, may not provide any coverage outside your geographic area. Contact your insurance agent about medical and hospital coverage overseas.

Check a charter flight tour operator's reputation before signing up. You can get information from a consumer protection group such as the Better Business Bureau. Some charter businesses work on a shoestring, and the chance of bankruptcy and stranding travelers overseas is not uncommon.

Leave a detailed itinerary with a friend or relative. Include names, addresses, phone numbers and dates. If applicable, add the numbers of your passport, traveler's checks, airline tickets and credit cards. Keep another copy at the back of your suitcase.

Don't overprogram. Sudden changes in diet, climate and activities can take some adjusting. Leave time for relaxing.

Don't take along a lot of cash. Instead, use a well-known brand of traveler's checks and carry at least one internationally recognized credit card.

Contact seniors' groups for more travel information. The American Association of Retired Persons (AARP) offers its members travel discounts and useful travel information. For information or discount programs and memberships, write to AARP, 1909 K Street NW, Washington, DC 20006.

Elderhostel sponsors programs and study vacations for senior citizens at American colleges. For a catalog of their programs, contact Elderhostel, 100 Boylston Street, Suite 200, Boston, MA 02116.

PLANNING TRIPS FOR HANDICAPPED TRAVELERS

Frommer's Guide for the Disabled Traveler by Frances Barish (Frommer/ Pasmantier Publishers, 1984), is packed with useful, firsthand tips for travelers with impaired mobility, those who need special equipment (such as a cane, crutches or a wheelchair) or those who have a pacemaker. The book also provides lists of helpful organizations and sources and includes vital door measurements for wheelchair travelers.

Plan ahead. The key to successful business or pleasure travel for the disabled is careful planning, based on reliable information. To make sure, for example, that the doors are wide enough and the ramp is not too steep for a wheelchair or that you can rent a car with hand controls, call and make your arrangements beforehand. The recognizable symbol of a wheelchair in a hotel guidebook may mean that the handicapped are welcome, but it does not necessarily mean the hotel's rooms are easily accessible to them.

Consider using a travel agent experienced in assisting handicapped travelers. The Society for the Advancement of Travel for the Handicapped, 26 Court Street, Brooklyn, NY 11242, may be able to suggest just such an agent in your area.

Check your insurance. Make sure your policy will cover you for medical and hospital costs at your destination.

When traveling by plane, tell the travel or airline reservation agent everything about your needs. Airlines try to provide ample assistance, so be honest about how much help you will or won't need. Try to book direct flights whenever possible so you don't have to change planes, and try to fly at off-peak hours so your plane isn't too crowded. Most airlines do not have lavatories easily accessible to wheelchair travelers, but some do. For your comfort, be sure to ask.

When traveling by train, make your reservations as early as possible. Although Amtrak stations and trains are becoming increasingly accessible to handicapped travelers, most trains have only one wheelchair space, so the earlier you make reservations, the greater your chances of being accommodated. *Access Amtrak, A Guide to Amtrak Services for Elderly and Handicapped Travelers* is available through Amtrak's Office of Customer Relations, P.O. Box 2709, Washington, DC 20013.

When traveling by bus, inquire about special fares. Greyhound and Trailways offer programs under which a disabled traveler and a companion can travel for a single fare. Look in your telephone directory for local numbers to call for more information.

When traveling by car, be aware of the locations of accessible restrooms. Because looking for accessible restrooms along America's highways can be tricky, send for the booklet *Highway Rest Areas for Handicapped Travelers*. It is published by the President's Committee on the Employment of the Handicapped, Washington, DC 20210. The booklet lists over 800 rest areas in the United States (except Hawaii and Oregon).

MAKING CAR TRIPS WITH CHILDREN ENJOYABLE

Family road trips can be great fun, but sometimes getting there can seem endless. Here's how to make the most of car trips with kids.

Limit each child to the toys and books that can fit into a school backpack. (Backpacks are soft-sided and can be wedged into small places.) Help preschoolers pick what to take, but let school-age children select the items for the backpack—this allows them to feel that they are helping prepare for the trip, too.

Position the children (or anyone in the back seat) so they can see the horizon. Many children get car sickness because they can't see the horizon.

Carry milk and fruit juices in small, ready-to-drink containers. These containers are hard to spill, come with the straws already attached and don't need a bottle opener. They are less cumbersome than a thermos bottle and don't require paper cups. If you're traveling in summer, you can freeze individual juice containers before you leave home. They'll thaw during the trip and be cold and ready to drink later in the day.

Bring along healthy snacks that don't mess up the car. They'll be cheaper than buying something along the way and probably better for you, too.

And food can keep fidgety or bored kids occupied for a while as you travel. (See the box "Healthy Finger Foods and Snacks for Toddlers" in chapter 5.)

Pack a Frisbee or plastic ball. Traveling with children requires frequent stops. Playing with a Frisbee or ball for a few minutes at each stop will help the children—as well as the parents—work off their energy.

Purchase a small tablet and box of colored pencils for each child. Wrap them in bright paper before the trip. When the children become restless, hand each of them a "present" and suggest that each child draw a picture, play a word game or "collect" license-plate states.

Pack a pillow and deck of cards. The pillow can serve as a "table" for a game of cards and, of course, as a headrest.

Make the children responsible for the car's litterbag. Children are often careless about littering the car during a trip, and this will make them more aware of keeping the interior neat. This responsibility also helps them feel important. Switch the responsibility between the children each time there is a rest stop.

SELECTING ACCOMMODATIONS

There are innumerable hotels, motels, inns, bed-and-breakfasts and other places in which to spend the night or stay the entire length of your trip. Here's how to select accommodations suited to your needs.

Decide what recreational facilities are important to you and choose to stay in a place that has them. In addition to pools found at many hotels and motels, a number of hotels have fitness rooms, or spas, and some even have running trails. Ask if there is an additional fee for their use. Also check to be sure they'll be open when you're there.

Ask for a room away from elevators, ice and soda machines and stairwells. These noisy locations can keep you up at night.

Ask for a room with a small refrigerator if you're traveling with children. A cold glass of milk or juice in the morning should help curb their hunger until you can get them to breakfast.

If you're a nonsmoker or particularly sensitive to smoke, ask if no-smoking rooms are available. The rooms won't have any ashtrays and the curtains won't smell of stale smoke.

Find out how convenient your accommodations will be. Is your hotel, motel or campsite really near town as the ads say, so you won't have an expensive taxi ride each time you leave? What, if anything, is within easy walking distance? Is the neighborhood safe for walking or jogging?

If you're driving to a hotel or motel in the heart of a city, find out what the parking charges will be. Many places charge flat day-rates, provided you don't use the car. Each time the car is retrieved from the garage, there may be a sizable fee (plus tip).

If you plan to stay at a bed-and-breakfast or inn, check to see if you'll have a private bath. Because many of these places are based on the European style of accommodation, few rooms have private baths. If the prospect of a trip down the hall in the middle of the night doesn't appeal to you or your kids, make sure you reserve a room with a bath.

If you find yourself going back to the same place year after year, consider a time-share arrangement. For a specified amount of money, $10,000, for example, you get the right to a two-week vacation in a fully equipped apartment, for 20 or 25 years. Check with real estate agents and developers for leads to time-share properties. Don't leap into any time-share agreement—read the contracts, check the reputation of the time-share management or development firms and talk to others who use the development.

Foreign Travel

Traveling abroad is quite different from seeing the sights in your own country. From getting your passport to knowing what to tip, there are lots of "secrets" to learn about foreign travel. Here are some tips to help you make a trip abroad run smoothly.

OBTAINING A PASSPORT

You should apply to either the Passport Division or a Passport Agency of the U.S. Department of State if you live in Chicago, Honolulu, Houston, Los Angeles, Miami, New Orleans, New York, Philadelphia, San Francisco, Seattle or Stamford. Otherwise, apply to the clerk of the federal court or at designated post offices. If you're applying for your first passport you need to submit:

> two identical current passport photos (full face from a front view, 2 × 2 inches)
> a piece of identification with a physical description on it (most state driver's licenses will qualify)
> certified birth certificate (if you were born in the United States), not a photocopy, with a *raised seal*, which must be from the state,

not from the hospital; or a naturalization certificate (if you are a naturalized U.S. citizen)

$42 if you are 18 or older, payable by a $35 check for the federal fee and $7 in any form for the execution fee; the passport is good for 10 years

$27 if you are under 18, payable by a $20 check for the federal fee and $7 in any form for the execution fee; the passport is good for 5 years

If you have an expired passport and want to renew it, then submit:

two new, but identical, passport photos (see above)

your most recent passport

$42 if you are 16 or older, payable by a $35 check for the federal fee and $7 in any form for the execution fee; you can renew by mail with special forms you can obtain from your courthouse

$27 if you are under 16, payable by a $20 check for the federal fee and $7 in any form for the execution fee; you must renew in person

PREPARING FOR YOUR TRIP ABROAD

To get your trip abroad off to a good start, here are the five most important things you can do—no matter where you travel.

Carry enough foreign currency to get you through at least your first few hours in the country. Make sure some of it is in small bills and change. A large number of travelers hurry through customs only to stand in long lines at airport currency exchange locations—where a premium is usually charged—to get the proper money to purchase rides to town, buy a snack and tip hotel bellhops. To avoid the line and the extra charge for changing money at airports, bring it with you. Most U.S. banks—at least the larger branches—exchange international currency.

Know the currency. Practice making change and memorizing the different coins and bills before your trip. When shopping in local stores and using local restaurants, you'll feel more confident if you understand the currency, even if you don't know many words of the language.

Learn a little of the language. You don't have to take a language course to learn a few words to help you get along easier in a foreign country. Many books and audiocassettes are available at stores and libraries. Numerous pocket guides, which tuck neatly into pockets and purses, include a few pages of common phrases and numbers.

Carry the address and phone number of the local American diplomatic office. If you need assistance overseas, the first and best place to contact

---

DISCOUNTS FOR STUDENTS

With an International Student Identity Card, full-time students, 12 years and older, will be able to save on a number of tours, travel packages and admission fees in the United States and overseas. (This is not to say, though, that students without this card but with other proper identification will be denied all such discounts; the card just makes things easier and will be recognized in some places where a college or high school ID card won't.) To obtain your identity card, write to:

Council on International Educational Exchange (IEE)
205 East 42nd Street
New York, NY 10017
(212) 661-1414
or
312 Sutter Street
San Francisco, CA 94108
(415) 421-3473

About 350 college campuses can also issue these cards.

---

is the U.S. Embassy or Consular Office. The information is available from the U.S. Department of State, but it's also printed in most guidebooks.

Take a half-day trip around the city the first day you're there. Ask at your hotel (or tour group guide) about a brief morning tour of the city you're visiting. This is a good, and usually inexpensive, way to get oriented to the city and its neighborhoods.

KNOWING HOW MUCH TO TIP
Americans traveling overseas have a reputation for tipping heavily, probably because we don't take time to learn the rate of exchange and local currency. However, undertipping is common, too. The first rule of tipping is to learn the coins—you can't judge value by size. Here are some other tipping guidelines.

Get a practical pocket guide for the city or country you're visiting. Tipping practices vary widely. A comprehensive guide will cover local tipping practices. In *Baedeker's Paris: The Complete Illustrated City Guide* (published by The Automobile Association for the United Kingdom, reprint 1984, and available in U.S. bookstores) there is practical general information on tipping in restaurants, hotels, theaters and taxis that holds true for most of Europe.

Never tip an owner. If your lodging is in a bed-and-breakfast home, don't tip the family members. And never tip for professional services (such as medical or dental).

Always tip for "services rendered." This means tipping waiters, maids and so forth—usually between 10 and 15 percent of the total bill. In restaurants, however, the bill or menu may say *servis compris,* which means that service is included. Then no extra tip, or just a small additional tip, need be left. Remember that the men and women who provide services for you may earn little salary and depend on tips for their livelihood.

In hotels, leave the maid a tip at the end of your stay. The amount can be figured on the number of nights plus the amount of service you required. (There aren't clear guides in this area; rely on your common sense.) The tipping rule of thumb for bellhops is $1 per bag.

When in doubt about tipping during your trip, ask the concierge or tour guide. The hotel's concierge, who can arrange reservations, theater tickets, plan day-trips and get your letters mailed, should be tipped at the end of your stay, depending on how much of this service you required. Again, there are no clear guidelines.

If you're on a guided tour, tip the guide at the end of the trip. If you're on a day's outing, tip when you've returned to your hotel. If you're spending a week with a guide, tip before returning to the airport. Estimate 10 to 12 percent of the tour's land price, per person.

TRAVELING IN TROUBLED TIMES
Terrorism and political unrest in countries you want to travel to or through are reasons for exercising caution when you're globe-trotting.

Contact the U.S. Department of State before your trip. The State Department operates the Citizens Emergency Center (202-632-5225) and issues advisories about countries where Americans should be extremely cautious. The department also issues warnings about countries that should be absolutely avoided.

Fly direct routes to avoid layovers. Immediately report any suspicious activities in the airport to the authorities.

Consider flying to an alternate airport rather than one that's known to be unsafe. If your destination includes stopping at an airport where terrorism has already occurred or where security is considered lax, land at a safer airport and take the train to your destination. For example, instead of flying into Rome, fly to another Italian city and take the train into Rome.

Don't dress in any manner that could call attention to yourself. If you're in the military, travel in civilian clothes with a civilian passport. Many terrorist groups seek out Americans as their first targets of violence.

Don't dawdle in airports. Arrive early, check in immediately and head straight for your gate or other secured area. When you reach your destination, leave the airport as quickly as possible once you're through customs. Airport lobbies are the usual site of terrorist actions.

TAKING CARE OF YOUR HEALTH WHILE ABROAD

Health standards in other countries vary greatly. The most common problems are intestinal and stomach discomforts, often referred to as traveler's diarrhea or Montezuma's revenge, that are caused by changes in diet and drinking water, even in Europe.

To prevent the all-too-common symptoms, cramps, stomachaches, nausea, headaches and vomiting, take these precautions:

→ Don't drink the water. No tap water, no ice cubes—don't even brush your teeth with it. Buy some mineral water and use that instead. It's usually okay, though, to drink boiled water as in coffee and tea, as well as fruit juice, milk and soda.

→ Don't eat anything that you suspect has been sitting out for a while, any fruit you don't peel or anything such as salad greens that might have been rinsed in local tap water.

If you do succumb to intestinal or stomach illness, take these measures:

→ Don't eat any solid foods until the symptoms decrease.

→ Drink plenty of fluids. Fruit juices are good because they will help to replenish the nutrients that your body has lost.

→ Take the medication that you had the foresight to get from your doctor before you left home. Most travelers don't think about getting such medication, and in most instances it's probably not necessary. But if you're planning to do extensive traveling, and/or will be spending a lot of time in less-developed areas of the world, such medication may come in very handy. Of course, you should not assume that every case of stomach cramps, diarrhea and/or vomiting is traveler's diarrhea. If the problem persists, it is wise to seek professional medical help wherever you are.

Before visiting some countries, a vaccination for infectious diseases that are prevalent there is a good idea. If you think you'll be traveling to such a place, you can contact the Centers for Disease Control, Department of Health and Human Services, 1600 Clifton Road NE, Atlanta, GA 30333. This agency publishes a list of required and recommended vaccinations for every nation. They also publish *Health Information for International Travel,* available for $4.25 from the Government Printing Office, North Capitol and H Streets NW, Washington, DC 20401. Foreign embassies and consular offices here in the United States also have health information available, as do travel agents and some health-care providers.

If you're planning to be overseas for some time, or have a health problem such as diabetes, arthritis or a heart condition, have a checkup before you board the plane. Your doctor can give you the peace of mind of knowing that you're in good shape to take a trip, and she or he can write a simple medical report that you can carry with you in case you need medical assistance. This report may list blood type, allergies and medications you're taking.

   If you do have a medical condition, and especially if you'll be traveling alone, get a medical necklace or bracelet that has a description of your medical condition embossed on it.

Write for more information from two groups that provide reliable medical treatment in many countries throughout the world. Both have English-speaking doctors who charge set fees and are on call 24 hours a day. They also have some very valuable information on health hints and immunizations that they'd recommend, depending upon where you're going. One group is International Association for Medical Assistance to Travelers (IAMAT), 350 Fifth Avenue, Suite 5620, New York, NY 10001. There is no charge for their service, but donations are encouraged. The other association is Intermedic, Inc., 777 Third Avenue, New York, NY 10017. They charge a small membership fee.

Vacations

Vacations should be times of fun and relaxation—not stress and worry. You've waited all year to take your vacation, and you don't want anything to go wrong. To help take the worry out of vacations, we'll show you how best to plan for one, the pros and cons of group travel, all about country vacations, and how to pick a cruise. From a weekend getaway to a month-long fling, we'll show you how to make the most of your vacation time.

PLANNING A CAREFREE VACATION

All good vacations have one thing in common—careful planning. Just because you're going away on pleasure, and not business, doesn't mean that you shouldn't do a bit of homework first. Start with these suggestions, and you'll be sure to enjoy the rest of your vacation.

Involve every member of the family in the planning stage, including children. Adults often think they know what their children want to see, but rarely bother to ask them. To ensure that children feel part of the vacation, let them help plan, and don't be surprised if what they want to see and do is different from what you expected.

Research before making reservations. When you pick your destination, read up. Find out what there is to do and see, where to stay, how to get around and how best to get there. Libraries, travel agents and tourism organizations can provide abundant information.

If money is a concern, make a budget and stick to it. Decide how much you want to spend. Divide that amount by the number of days you plan to be away; this gives you the average amount you can spend per day. With this amount in mind, you can better figure out how much to allocate toward each category on your budget—transportation, lodging, food, expenses and so on. Be sure to plan for the unexpected, such as car repairs, extending the trip, extra shopping or an unbudgeted night-on-the-town.

Know what your rights and responsibilities are as a travel consumer. Read and understand the fine print in any travel agreements you sign. (Know if your tour operator can change the departure times or destinations, or if you'll have added service charges and entry or port fees.)

Plan a few specific activities for your vacation. Curb any impulses to plan for every hour of your trip, but also don't leave the time completely unstructured. Make reservations for popular attractions, such as riding a donkey in the Grand Canyon, staying overnight in a national park or eating in a historic tavern in Colonial Williamsburg. Leave much of the rest of the time flexible for last-minute plans that will be affected by the weather, your energy level and mood as well as the unexpected.

VACATIONING IN SOMEONE ELSE'S HOME

Swapping houses and renting private cottages, apartments and villas, both in the United States and overseas, is increasingly popular. You can rent a London flat, swap houses with a family near Paris, rent a beach

FOR MORE TRAVEL INFORMATION

Here are some good sources of travel information:

→ Travel videos are increasingly available. If you own a VCR, check with a videotape rental shop or chain bookstore. Some of the videos show a country's scenic beauty and others take a practical look at shopping, walking tours and nightlife. Some travel agencies also have videos, but these are usually provided to them by hotel chains, airlines and cruise ship lines, so they may be biased in favor of the provider.

→ Bookstores specializing in travel books are also on the increase, often staffed by travel-lovers who can dispense firsthand information as well as books, guides and maps.

→ Before purchasing a travel guide, borrow it from the local library and study it to make sure it has the practical information you want, such as what days and hours museums are open, how to get from the center of town to a castle in the country or how to use the local subway. If it meets your needs, then buy your own copy. You can also ask friends who have already visited your destination about what guides and maps they found most helpful. Maybe they'll have some to lend you.

→ If your trip is within the United States, contact that state's department of tourism or the city's chamber of commerce for more information. Many will provide you with a lot of useful material for no charge.

→ For vacations that take you to a national park or forest, write ahead for information about sights, lodging, hours, facilities, reservations and fees. (National Park Service, Department of the Interior, Washington, DC 20240; U.S. Forest Service, U.S. Department of Agriculture, Room 3008 South Building, Washington, DC 20250.)

→ If your trip is outside the United States, contact that country's United States-based embassy or tourist office. Overseas-based airlines usually have general tourist information that you can get by contacting their United States information/reservation number.

house anywhere from Maine to Florida or idle in the sun at a villa on a Caribbean island. Living in someone's home, cottage or apartment can be a pleasant experience and can be cheaper than staying in a hotel, but it can have its pitfalls. To avoid disappointments, here are steps to locating the right property.

Be realistic. The brochures printed by rental and swapping organizations show every property as picturesque and desirable. This just isn't the case. If possible, contact the owner or renter by phone and ask very specific questions about the condition of the property, the neighborhood and the terms of the rental or swap.

Be practical. Check for hidden costs. If the ad says maid service is available, do you pay extra?

Circle all the "distance" words in the ad. Find out how near you would be to public transportation or how close to the beach, before you swap or rent.

If renting or swapping abroad, inquire about the bathroom facilities. Is the bathroom private or shared? Is it on the same level as the bedrooms? Will there be enough hot water available for your group?

Check the neighborhood of the property you're thinking about. Detailed maps should help. Do some detective work and find out what the area is like, because this will have an impact on your visit.

Get a list of the things you will be responsible for. These may include phone bills, utilities, a car, caring for a garden or pets or stocking the cupboard. Get a list of the things you're not supposed to touch, too.

Remember that living standards differ between nations and even between regions of our country. A historic cottage in Wales may sound delightful, but if you don't ask, you might arrive to find the toilet is an outhouse and there is no heat or hot water. A cabin in the Rockies may be described as a "warm and cozy hideaway," but it's a two-mile trek off a country road— over which you must tote your groceries.

For a closer look at swapping homes, read *Home Exchanging, a Complete Sourcebook for Travelers at Home or Abroad* by James Dearing (East Woods Press, 1986). Several agencies have been created in the United States and Europe to facilitate exchanges. For a fee, usually between $20 and $40, you can have your property listed, plus get the list of available homes. The Vacation Exchange Club (12006 111th Avenue, Youngstown, AZ 85363) offers a personal search service.

PLANNING A COUNTRY VACATION

You can take a wagon train across the prairie, live on a working farm or ranch or reside in a cottage on a British estate. Some country vacations can be educational, some physically exhilarating, others can give city dwellers a chance to experience a different way of life and some offer a resort atmosphere. But country vacations aren't for everyone, so before you commit your family to the country, here are a few tips to remember.

Ask about the sleeping arrangements. Will you get your own cabin, sleep in a guest house, or share the family's house? Is it air conditioned? How much privacy will you get? And what about a private bathroom?

INFORMATION SOURCES FOR BICYCLISTS

Libraries and bookstores have some good books on bicycle touring and on bicycle tours in this country and overseas. And magazines such as *Bicycling* and *Bike Report* run feature stories and advertisements that can provide some of this information, too. There are organizations that specialize in setting up tours and/or developing tours and maps for those who want to go it alone. Here are two of them:

Bicycle USA
Suite 209
6707 Whitestone Road
Baltimore, MD 21207
(301) 944-3399

Send $3 for a copy of the *Bicycle USA TourFinder*, which includes the names of more than 150 bicycle tour operators, tour costs, mileage, accommodations and other information.

Bikecentennial
P.O. Box 8308
Missoula, MT 59807
(406) 721-1776

Send for their free catalog, which lists tours, maps, accessories and books.

Find out about the temperatures (and mosquitoes!) during the day and night. In the country, the evenings are often clear and cool, so you'll need warmer clothes for sitting beside a campfire.

Ask about what "work" you and the children can do. Maybe you'll be able to learn to milk cows, work with horses, ride a tractor or collect fresh eggs. Most children love country vacations, and if they know what to expect, it makes the vacation even more exciting. At some country vacation spots, though, you're *expected* to work, and if this isn't what you had in mind, choose something else.

Ask about the extras. Riding lessons, trail rides and overnight camp-outs may involve additional charges.

Do some research. Most states, through their tourism departments, can put you in touch with farm, country and ranch vacations. A little research at your public library can turn up the addresses, or check with a travel agency.

If you want to enjoy a country vacation abroad, you can do that, too. Contact the country's United States-based tourist office or a travel agency. If you want to stay, for example, at a cottage on Althorp, the childhood home of Princess Diana, you'll find it available for rent, although it's somewhat expensive. Contact Villas International, Ltd., 71 West 23rd Street, New York, NY 10010 (800-221-2260).

VACATIONING FOR A WEEKEND

No one says a trip has to be a long one to be a vacation. Here are some ideas for nice, relaxing weekend vacations.

Map your route. Get a map and a marking pen. With your hometown as the center, draw a circle about 150 miles out (or a three hours' drive); this is about as much as you'll want to drive each way in one weekend. If you can choose almost any weekend, time it to a local festival or country fair.

"Get away" at a nearby hotel. Many major hotel chains offer getaway packages at special low rates. Get a baby-sitter if you have children, make reservations at a quiet restaurant or call up room service and relax.

Leave the country. Airlines offer weekend packages to romantic spots only a short flight from most East Coast cities. If you've only got one day, check with your travel agent for the airlines that offer one-day getaways to island beaches.

Take a cruise. Some cruise lines offer weekend getaway trips "to nowhere." Check with your travel agent.

INFORMATION SOURCES FOR HIKERS

Two organizations in particular are noted for their hiking clubs—groups of people who enjoy hiking and are experienced in trails, equipment and techniques. On the East Coast, there is the:

Appalachian Trail Conference
Information Department
P.O. Box 807
Harpers Ferry, WV 25425
(304) 535-6331

They can provide you with a list of all their chapters or those in the state or states you're interested in.

On the West Coast, and elsewhere, there is the:

Sierra Club
730 Polk Street
San Francisco, CA 94109
(415) 776-2211

Ask for a list of their chapters in 40 states.

Be hometown tourists. Every city, no matter how small, has its history. Start at your local library to learn about your city's "roots," then spend a weekend walking through the streets and lanes, tracing your city's origins.

Go to school. Many colleges and universities offer weekend educational experiences. You can live in the dorm and attend classes, and you might not even need a prior degree, just an interest in the topic. Contact the schools in your area.

TRAVELING WITH A GROUP

If you're traveling alone or visiting a foreign country for the first time, traveling with a group—usually on a package tour—can be a good idea. However, due to foul-ups and schedule changes, the tour can fall short of your expectations. To get the most out of group travel, here are things you should know.

Consider traveling with a group to which you belong. Many organizations, such as alumni, fraternal, religious and professional groups, sponsor trips. Sometimes referred to as affinity groups, this type of group has a built-in common bond.

Know the tour operator. Find out as much as you can about her or him from the travel agent booking the group trip.

Be sure the tour operator is bonded or has an escrow account. The bonding firm or financial institution and its address should be listed on the travel contract. Federal regulations require a tour operator to hold a percent of the travel fees in escrow until a few days after the trip. Any check you write should be made out to the account, not to the tour operator. (This should be clearly defined in your contract.)

Know the particulars before you sign the contract. Is your group operator providing baggage handling and transportation to hotels, airports and train stations, or will you be on your own?

Know what changes can and can't be made by the tour operator. Know if dates, times and airports can be altered by the operator at her or his discretion. If your trip includes stops in several cities, be sure you know if the tour operator must make all the stops, or if some may be skipped or changed.

Check out the hotels, particularly if the trip is overseas. Hotel ratings are not based on the kinds of standards Americans take for granted. Ask a travel agent to look up the hotel in a worldwide directory, then ask the agent to help you pinpoint its location on a map. Be sure to check whether or not you'll have a private bath.

Find out if group transportation is included between cities. If your trip includes more than one city, check the transportation between destinations, and ask how long the trip should take. Often, each city-to-city trip means an entire day on a tour bus, with extra time in the destination city as the bus goes from hotel to hotel, leaving off guests who stay at different classes of hotels.

Don't feel compelled to sign up for the group's meal plan. As a general rule of thumb, you'll eat better and spend less if you eat on your own.

Check out any side trips before you sign up. Although it might seem an easy way to visit a special place, a group side trip may not be satisfying. Tour operators usually plan side trips to include participants from several hotels and plan stopovers during the day. This means you often get far less time at the place you want to visit than you had hoped. It also means you will probably spend a great deal longer in transit (going from hotel to hotel) than planned.

PICKING THE RIGHT CRUISE

You can cruise down the Mississippi, discover Norway's fjords or sail through the Panama Canal. Dollar for dollar, cruises may be the best way to get the most mileage from your vacation fund. Cruise packages can include airfare from your hometown to the port of departure, special fares and recreation programs for children and a variety of accommodations. Here's how to pick the right one for you.

Work with a travel agent who is an expert in cruises. Ask your travel agency which agent there has the most experience.

Tell the travel agent where you want to cruise and how much you want to spend. Because you've got many choices, this will help the agent focus quickly on the options best suited to you.

Plan early. If you want a specific deck, location or cabin, book early— months ahead, if possible. As a general rule, the higher the deck, the higher the price. But each deck has its trade-offs. Generally, cabins on top decks, where lounges and other activity centers are located, get more traffic and thus, more noise, particularly at night. Cabins on lower levels also have drawbacks. You're nearer the noise and throbbing of the engines, and the cabins are usually smaller and can give travelers a feeling of claustrophobia. Plans for each ship are available at your travel agency. Study the plans and pick the cabin that best suits your needs. For the consumer, the rise in cruising's popularity means the addition of more cruise ships and some lowering of prices, but it also means more demand for space.

Know the different cruise accommodation terms. Accommodations with beds are usually more expensive than those with berths. Cabins on the outside (with a porthole) are more expensive than inside cabins.

Decide if you want to sail at night or during the day. Pick a cruise that sails primarily at night if you're interested in getting the most time in each port of call, otherwise, stops will probably be brief. If your main interest is spending time on the open seas, pick a cruise that sails mostly during the day.

Ask about a cruise to meet your special needs. For instance, if you're taking children, several cruise lines will welcome you, and your travel agent can tell you which ones.

Find out about the different events occurring during your cruise. There might be a formal night, a costume party or a special dance for which you'll need special clothes, so pack accordingly.

Try to to lose a few pounds before the cruise. Food is available almost around the clock. If you want to eat those rich, gourmet confections for which cruises are justifiably famous, you can try to lose a few pounds before you set sail. While on the cruise, you can jog, swim (although pools are usually small) and maybe play tennis. Some ships feature exercise centers and even aerobic dance classes.

Ask your agent what you pay for during the cruise. Bar bills, tips, beauty salon and barbershop services are all extra. Excursions into port are usually sold through the cruise ship and not included in the price of the cruise.

MIXING BUSINESS WITH PLEASURE

There may be times when your business takes you to an interesting place and you'd like to mix in some vacation time, too, or take along your spouse and/or family. There's no reson why you can't, though you may not be able to write it all off on your taxes, and you'll have to try extra hard to fit in time with the family. Here are some suggestions for mixing business with pleasure.

Check with your tax advisor before you travel. If you want to hold a business meeting on a seven-day cruise to Hawaii, there are special requirements your advisor can explain, such as the percentage of time that must be devoted to the meeting on the cruise to qualify for a legitimate tax break.

Keep all the necessary receipts, letters and other records that pertain to your trip. Writing off a vacation for tax purposes might be the red flag the Internal Revenue Service needs to audit your tax returns.

Keep in shape while you're traveling by staying at hotels with fitness facilities. *Executive Fitness Newsletter,* published by Rodale Press (33 East Minor Street, Emmaus, PA 18098), often selects a city and prints a list of hotels with such facilities in each of its issues. Hints to help make business travel less stressful are also included.

Conferences can be exhausting, so try to stay a few extra days to see the city. Ask the hotel manager if the hotel will allow the extra days at the conference rate, which is generally lower than the normal daily rate. Sometimes this conference rate will also apply to your family.

Check all the airlines that serve your destination city to see if the family can tag along for a reasonable additional cost. Several airlines sporadically offer business travelers cut-rate flights for their spouses and children.

FILING A COMPLAINT

Even on the best planned vacation, something can go wrong. Try to resolve your problem at the time it occurs. For example, if your baggage is lost, work with the airline immediately. However, not all problems—including lost suitcases—can be resolved quickly, and some problems need extra help from the law and regulating agencies and associations. If that is the case, follow these guidelines for getting the help you need.

Get all the paperwork before you go home. If your overseas hotel room is ransacked, get copies of police reports and statements before leaving. Getting the necessary paperwork for insurance purposes once you're back home may be impossible.

Find out if there's a legal time limit under which you must file your complaint. If you wait too long, your complaint may not be answerable.

Complain to a federal agency. If your problem is with a transportation firm (airline, bus, train), complain to one of the federal agencies listed below, as well as to the firm:

> **Airlines:** Civil Aeronautics Board, Consumer Affairs, 1825 Connecticut Avenue NW, Washington, DC 20428.
>
> **Interstate buses:** Interstate Commerce Commission, Office of Compliance and Consumer Assistance Programs, 12th Street and Constitution Avenue NW, Washington, DC 20423.
>
> **Trains:** AMTRAK, Office of Consumer Relations, P.O. Box 2709, Washington, DC 20013.

Complain to everyone. This doesn't mean just your travel agent and neighbors—complain to local consumer and business groups, congressmen and consumer protection agencies. Letters should be factual and to the point and should describe as clearly as possible what the problem is. List all the steps taken to date to solve the problem and who you have contacted. Local consumer groups probably cannot assist in solving your problem, but they usually keep the complaint on file to warn others about the problems you've experienced with a specific company. If your complaint requires assistance from a federal agency, your congressional representative can help.

Index

Page references in italic indicate illustrations; page references in boldface indicate charts and tables.

Rodale Press, Inc., publishes PREVENTION®, the better health magazine.
For information on how to order your subscription,
write to PREVENTION®, Emmaus, PA 18098.

Rodale's Book of Shortcuts

Edited by Cheryl Winters Tetreau and Carol Hupping

Looking for better breakfast ideas? How about the best ways to deal with stress? Still searching for the perfect compost recipe? Interested in learning a faster way to clean the bath? How about checking out cheaper in the super-market, or combating a wet base-ment? It's all here, and more. There's no need to wonder where to turn next when one problem turns into another around the house or in the yard. *Rodale's Book of Shortcuts* can help you deal with problems and everyday tasks quickly and efficiently, so you can make the most of your day. You'll find hundreds of tips and techniques, plus good, old-fashioned advice on all kinds of topics. You'll learn:

- the best questions to ask your doctor about the drugs prescribed for you

- nine ways to beat the "blues"

[continued on back flap]